Half THE WORLD AWAY

Ian Lacey is from Gorey, County Wexford, Ireland. He studied environmental conservation at University College Dublin, worked for The Wilderness Society in Denver, USA and also the World Wide Fund for Nature in Laos, Southeast Asia. He has been published in Ireland and internationally on topics including travel, nature conservation and mental health. This is his first book.

Visit www.ianlacey.com to see what's coming next.

Half THE WORLD AWAY

A 27,000 km bicycle journey
from Alaska to Argentina

IAN LACEY

CORCOVADO

First published in 2016 by
Corcovado Publishing

Dublin, Ireland

www.ianlacey.com

All rights © 2016 Ian Lacey

Paperback	ISBN: 978-0-9955442-0-8
Ebook – Mobi format	ISBN: 978-0-9955442-1-5
Ebook – epub format	ISBN: 978-0-9955442-2-2
CreateSpace	ISBN: 978-0-9955442-3-9

All rights reserved. No part of this book may be reproduced or utilised in any form or by any means electronic or mechanical, including photocopying, filming, recording, video recording, photography, or by any information storage and retrieval system, nor shall by way of trade or otherwise be lent, resold or otherwise circulated in any form of binding or cover other than that in which it is published without prior permission in writing from the publisher.

The right of the author of his work has been asserted by his in accordance with the Copyright, Designs and Patents Act 1988.

Produced by Kazoo Independent Publishing Services

222 Beech Park, Lucan, Co. Dublin

www.kazoopublishing.com

Kazoo Independent Publishing Services is not the publisher of this work. All rights and responsibilities pertaining to this work remain with Corcovado Publishing.

Kazoo offers independent authors a full range of publishing services. For further details visit www.kazoopublishing.com

Cover photos by Ian Lacey

Front cover photo: Cycling at sunrise past Lago Cardiel, Argentina

Back cover photo: Taking one last look into Colombia, near Ipiales

Cover design by Red Rattle Design

Printed in the EU

For Mam and Dad

Contents

Prologue   xiii

Chapter 1   *The Dalton*   19

Chapter 2   *Wild Open Spaces*   39

Chapter 3   *Amongst Giants*   63

Chapter 4   *West Coast*   85

Chapter 5   *New Beginnings*   117

Chapter 6   *South by Southeast*   147

Chapter 7   *The Small Places*   170

Chapter 8   *Crossing Continents*   195

Chapter 9   *Valleys and Mountaintops*   221

Chapter 10   *To the Lost City*   247

Chapter 11   *Salt and Sand*   272

Chapter 12   *Crossing the Spine*   290

Chapter 13   *Carretera Austral*   309

Chapter 14   *To the End of the World*   335

Epilogue   357

Acknowledgements   360

Bicycle Specifications and Equipment List   365

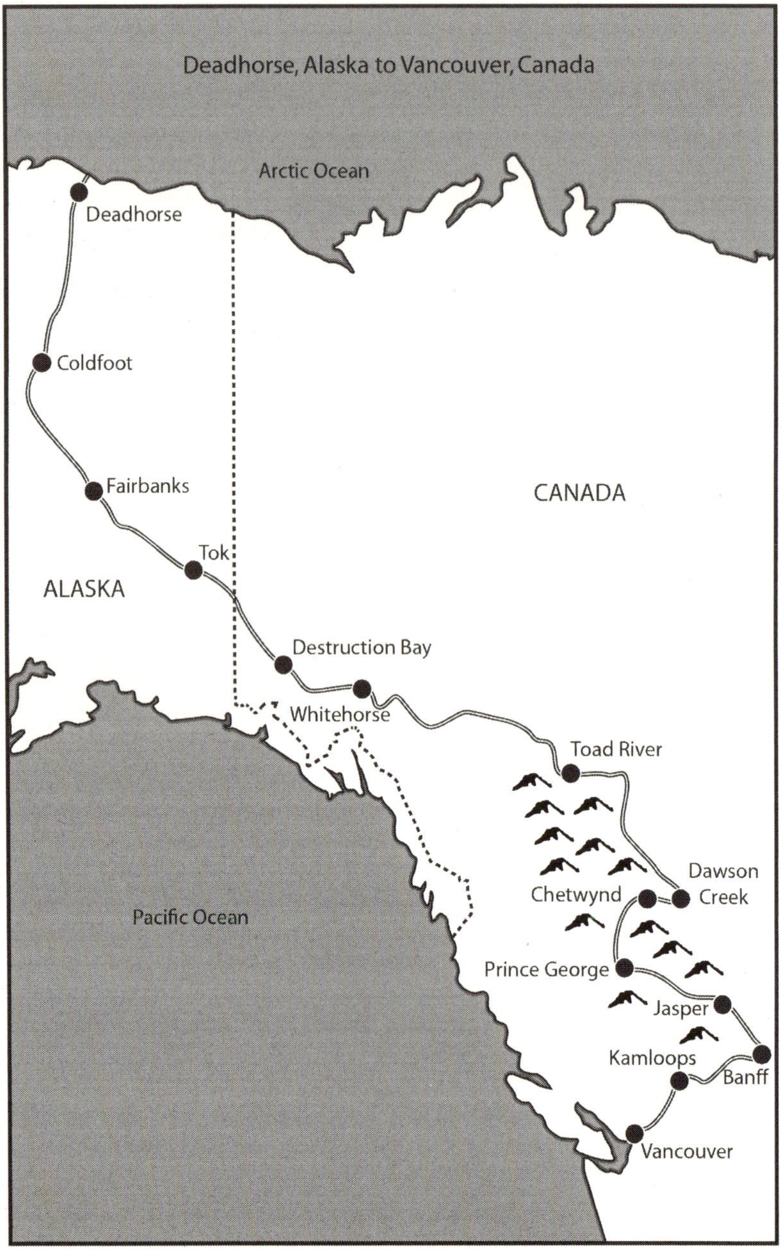
Deadhorse, Alaska to Vancouver, Canada
Arctic Ocean
Deadhorse
Coldfoot
Fairbanks
Tok
ALASKA
CANADA
Destruction Bay
Whitehorse
Toad River
Dawson
Creek
Chetwynd
Pacific Ocean
Prince George
Jasper
Kamloops
Banff
Vancouver

Vancouver, Canada to San José, Costa Rica

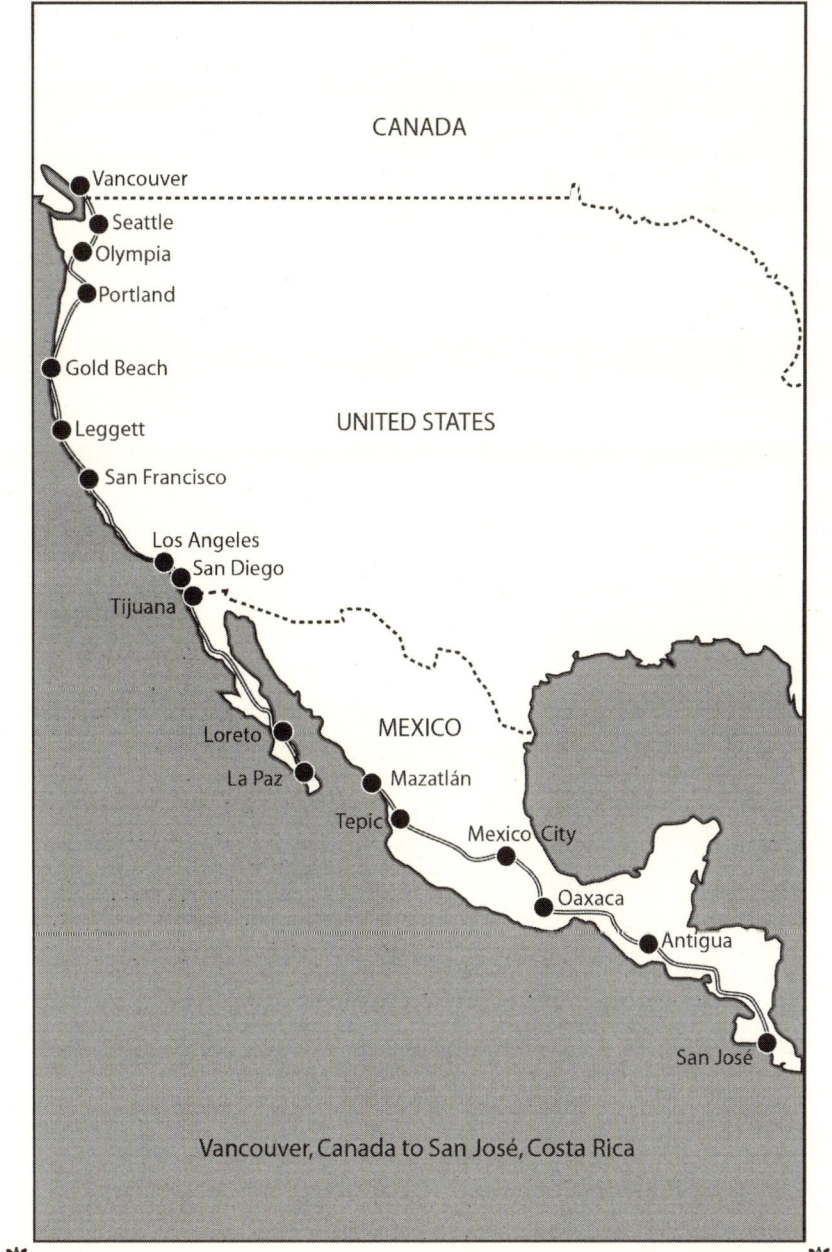

San José, Costa Rica to La Quiaca, Argentina

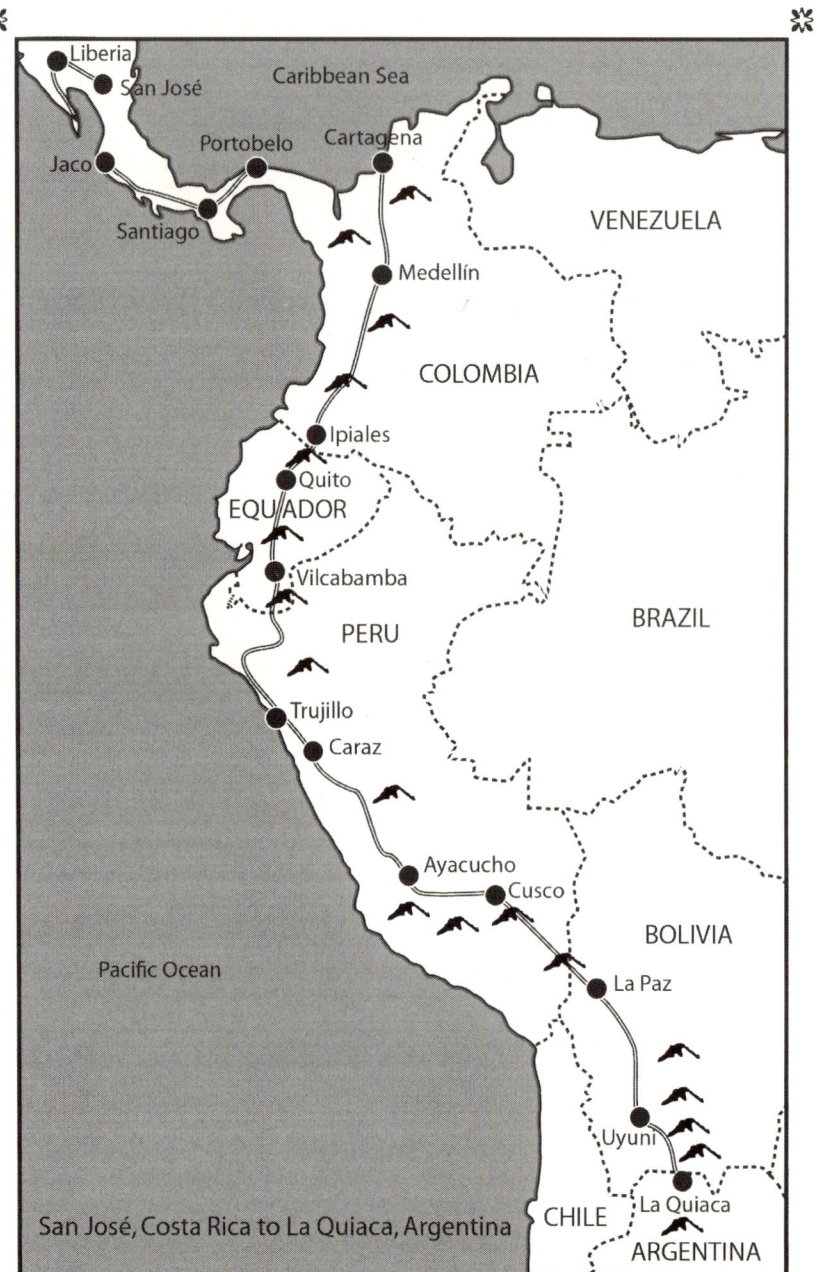

La Quiaca, Argentina to Ushuaia, Argentina

Prologue

THE IMMENSITY OF WHAT WAS passing beneath the wing hardly registered. The solitary thought in my head was that Alaska was big and seemingly very empty – from 25,000 feet, anyway. Thousands of circular ponds dotted the brown, lifeless landscape and I knew that somewhere within it ran a ribbon of road for hundreds of miles, its endpoint the historical pioneer town of Fairbanks, at the head of the ALCAN Highway and the waiting Americas. Whether it was because of the many conflicting emotions I had so recently been feeling or because these all now seemed redundant, I felt somehow deadened to the fear I had expected to feel at this point of the journey. After all, we were soon to be cycling out into the Arctic tundra on a gravel road for 800 km, carrying over 40 kg of gear, at any one time, up to two weeks away from the nearest town; and I had never ridden a bicycle continuously for more than three hours before. Yet now somehow such statistics meant nothing to me, and neither did the dull expanse below.

It was back again: all I could think about was Áine – my girlfriend, and that most recent act of leave-taking, one which I had rehearsed countless times in my head during the previous months, somehow thinking that if it played out flawlessly and exactly to plan, I could make a comfortable transition to this new life and, perhaps, be absolved a little of my guilt. Was she ok; did she secretly hate me for doing this; how would her feelings change in the coming months? How would *my* feelings change?

I tried not to think about it anymore, and just kept peering down. The same non-descript expanse was below me: no obvious signs of life, just a vast emptiness as far as the eye could see – a landscape reflective of my own desensitised, numb emotional state. It wasn't even that I felt particularly sad; in truth, I felt very little at all, except an acute detachment from the present. I was becoming an observer of the beginnings of my own journey, silently waiting to deal with the psychological initiation of cycling from Alaska to Argentina. Not for the first time leading up this point, I wondered if I was being naïve and unrealistic, possibly from reading too many travel and adventure books, which are sometimes over-dramatised to make the story more exciting. The actual shock associated with this moment had occurred in Dublin Airport three days previously, when I left my girlfriend and a life I had just found a perfectly happy rhythm to. Cycling 27,000 km, away from it all, for no sensible reason seemed then like the dumbest thing in the world.

Taking my eyes away from the window, I looked back at the shuddering, unventilated cabin. Our plane was headed to Deadhorse, Alaska – the northernmost point accessible by road in the Americas, and a town rooted in a decades-old structural semi-permanence on the frigid shores of the Arctic Ocean. Oil is the reason and burly men are overwhelmingly the stock, a reality recreated in the microcosm of the cabin where there was not a single female passenger. Man played to his primal side without shame in this space, and every time the tall, blonde, and strikingly pretty stewardess passed along the single aisle, heads tilted cautiously and without fail to catch a glance at her form. I imagined what David Attenborough would make of this animalistic behaviour and imitated his voice while narrating the scene to Lee – my friend and cycling partner – all the while hoping the 250 lb man in front didn't hear.

When the plane touched down in late afternoon, a chill air diffused inside the cabin as its doors opened to the first of the many unknowns that would fill the next 15 months. I felt better that we were here, after one year of planning and almost two of dreaming – but in truth, it was an anti-climax, devoid of any kind of uncontained excitement or whatever form mid-twenties exuberance should take. Practicality took over from the allure of the situation. It was perhaps the only way of guarding against the self-doubt and insecurity that bubbled silently under our individual facades and the common feelings we may have been too scared to admit or talk about. After all, we couldn't know if we were physically or mentally prepared for this undertaking; neither could we be sure if we'd be happy to spend so much time in each other's company. Personally, this latter worry was far more daunting for me than the fact that I could count on one hand the number of times I'd been on a bicycle in the past year.

I first met Lee Saville in Denver, Colorado in February 2010 at a friend's birthday party. It was there, in a festively lit taco shop on Colfax Avenue, over US$1 tacos and cans of Pabst beer, that we came to the conclusion that life and all it incorporated was meaningless. To the observer, this conversation may have seemed like a couple of pseudo-intellectuals babbling about nothing in any great detail, fuelled by too much cheap alcohol. However, I think we both unreservedly believed this in an ingenuous, untested way and this sweeping, shared supposition about the nature of life probably built an instant foundation for the continuation of our friendship, even though we rarely discussed it again.

From the beginning, Lee and I were obviously very different characters, but I suppose that's what kept our friendship interesting, because of a mutual desire to understand the tenets underlying each other's nature. On the surface, I'm pretty sure I was seen as a rambler, a gift-of-the-gab sort of Irishman who could talk nonsense and fact in equal measure. Lee was quieter and certainly more thoughtful in disposition, but had a sense of humour that could bring a room to tears. On two occasions during the first weeks of our trip, for example, I laughed so long and hard at his five-minute orations on American food culture and a raven he was convinced was tracking us, that I was physically unable to pedal my bicycle.

That period in Denver in 2010 also saw the genesis of my idea to cycle from Alaska to Argentina and, like everything in life, it was a matter of sliding doors – right place, right time, and right circumstances. Whilst attending a bi-annual gathering of regional environmental organisations including The Wilderness Society, for which I was working at the time, an icebreaker session was suggested to begin the conference. Each delegate was asked to introduce a person from the present or from history with whom they would like to have dinner if the chance arose. The usual suspects made their appearance, including presidents from Lincoln to Kennedy and environmentalists from Muir to Thoreau – these last two being prerequisites for the conservationist crowd. Then, a representative from Wyoming made his case for Göran Kropp, a Swedish mountaineer, perhaps little-known outside his field. Usually a person so frightened by the prospect of public speaking that zoning out until my turn comes is my preferred coping mechanism, I nevertheless tuned in for this account of the Swede and his exploits. It was one of Kropp's epic journeys that caught my attention – having cycled from Stockholm to Mt Everest, he then ascended the world's highest mountain without the aid of bottled oxygen, climbed back down again, and cycled home to Sweden. With my turn to speak looming and as I scrambled to compose a few sentences about the ill-fated Chris McCandless, I all but forgot about Göran Kropp and his great adventure.

However, several weeks later, while browsing for travel literature in the Denver Library, I stumbled across the tiny, single-shelved 'Human Adventure' section, and saw the pale blue spine of Kropp's *Ultimate High: My Everest Odyssey* staring back at me. It took me just three nights to march from cover to cover of the book and on its completion, there was a stirring. My childhood had thickly-bound atlases and time spent imagining the colour of landscapes where unusual place names were inked; as an adolescent, I had been captivated by the images of *National Geographic*; in my early 20s, it was Bill Bryson, Stanley Stewart, and stories of Shackleton's voyages which held me in their grip. All these had left an enduring mark at each stage of my life, slowly incubating a wanderlust that for a long time had very little outlet due to my age, stage of education, and financial circumstances. Now however, Kropp's harrowingly raw account of a seemingly impossible human-powered journey convinced me once and for all that life would perhaps be very little without a challenge.

I was buzzing and could physically feel it, very much aware that it was critical to capture the energy of the moment before time inevitably washed it away. It took me just minutes to figure out what the challenge would be. Drawing inspiration from the giant world map mounted on my living room's wall, I fixed upon an imaginary and unbroken line running down through the Americas, and decided that I should travel it by bicycle – for no other reason than the fact that I could. In that moment, for the first time in my adult life, I sensed that I had tapped into some sort of authenticity of spirit, and a great clarity enveloped the idea. Straight ahead, without any obstacles in my way, I could now see a clear path laid down for the next two-and-a-half years of my life.

1
The Dalton

Deadhorse, Alaska to Fairbanks, Alaska – 812 km

DEADHORSE, ALASKA IS A PURPOSE-BUILT, weather-beaten town at the very top of the world. It's a place where galvanised doors swing from their hinges and clatter with ghostly regularity, while monotonous rain falls, collecting in shallow puddles in the middle of rutted dirt roads. It has a permanent population of 47 and a transient one of 3,000 – all dedicated to draining Prudhoe Bay, the largest oil field in North America, situated just a few miles to the restricted north. For two months of the year Deadhorse is shrouded in complete darkness, and for another two, it is illuminated by 24-hour sunlight. Consisting almost entirely of warehouses and machinery dens that serve the industry, the town is also the starting point for the Alaska (Alyeska) Oil Pipeline, which runs 1,287 km through Arctic and Subarctic Alaska to the town of Valdez on the state's southern shores, where its 'black gold' is emptied onto container ships that sail to the 'lower 48', and an energy-hungry nation. Standing still anywhere in town, you will hear the dull hum of pump houses emanating from the active fields, while an enduring polar wind sweeps frigidly southwards, casting the artificial noise into an endless distance. It seems odd to think that such a bleak and utilitarian speck in this otherwise wild land should be one of the most meaningful places I've ever visited, such was the road and experience that led out of it.

Lee and I checked into the $120-per-night Prudhoe Bay Hotel, a sturdy, prefabricated building adjacent to the town's small airport. It was a place which evoked memories of temporary school classrooms from my childhood, with blemished grey walls and white chippings from shedding doorframes littering the entrance corridor. Further inside, the raised wooden floor depressed and echoed hollow each time a heavy resident walked over it, while picture frames holding prints such as 'Oil Platforms in 1988' and 'Prudhoe from the Air' also quivered with passing footsteps. Throughout the structure, guests roamed in obligatory blue plastic shoe covers, whose purpose was to protect the remaining mud-free patches of carpet, preserving with that a thin line of distinction between workhouse and hotel.

Late in the evening, seated at what is perhaps the world's most northerly buffet bar, Lee and I ate largely in silence. Fox News provided enough garish background noise to compel us to glance at the screen between short spoken utterances, as we briefly discussed the vital tasks that would make the next day's cycle a little easier. We needed to finish reassembling our bicycles, organise food bags, pack panniers, pump tyres, grease chains, shower, and call home one last time.

In the weeks and months preceding our passage to Alaska, we never talked about the fact we would soon be spending at least one year in very close company with each other – it had somehow always seemed a trivial point for discussion compared to seemingly more important issues, such as reaching a consensus on the most durable gear and bicycle componentry. The practicalities of living together, of seeing each other every day, and of potentially having different individual preferences for where and when we travelled: these issues were rarely broached in the planning of the journey. It was only really on my transatlantic flight from Dublin to Denver that I first gave the matter any serious thought, as my diary entry indicates:

> **Diary: 11 July 2011, Flight EI105, Dublin to New York**
>
> *The fact of the matter is that I don't know Lee all that well. How much can you ever get to know someone from seven months living abroad and then via Skype for half a year? Well enough to spend perhaps a year together on bicycles? I hope so, otherwise all sorts of questions will soon be raised.*

Pondering this now in the hotel canteen, I began to wonder how it was going to pan out. Would we be happy, being in such close proximity all of the time? Every day while cycling, we'd each be looking at the back of the other for long stretches of it. We'd be eating together, sleeping with our tents side-by-side, doing our laundry, brushing our teeth and using the Internet at the same time. If one of us was ill or tired, would the other have to stop? Who would cook dinner in the evenings, and who would clean up? When I'd stop to pee, maybe Lee would have to as well. And vice versa. All these seemingly pedantic questions had no easy or immediately reassuring answers – we would only discover the upshot with the passage of time.

After dinner, I retired to our cramped bedroom and felt the usual worrying symptoms of an illness that had plagued my physical and mental health for the previous two months, causing serious self-doubt over my ability to even begin the cycle.

In December 2003, during my final year at secondary school, I had been diagnosed with ulcerative colitis, a chronic autoimmune disease of the colon, which, when left untreated or during a flare-up, causes severe fatigue and anaemia. Its most frustrating symptom is the need to use the bathroom regularly, and in some cases, without appropriate warning. Although since diagnosis, I had generally been able to manage the condition well, I had fallen out of remission just eight weeks before our departure to Alaska, and now I felt brittle and exhausted. A strong course of steroids hadn't helped to rid my body from the sense of weakness. The subsequent recommendation from my consultant was an unwelcome one: I was told to stay in Ireland, recuperate, and try again next year. Friends, family, and strangers could all observe my physically poor, increasingly gaunt state and a body weight that dropped steadily over the weeks prior to departure: I had lost 12 kg in two months. The increasingly uneasy tone with which people began to express their concern worried me. I couldn't comprehend what was causing the flare-up, nor could I come to terms with the fact that something out of my control could be the ruination of a journey I had lived on paper for far too long.

I chose to ignore the signals from my body, which felt weak and ineffectual before a single revolution of the pedals had been turned. I knew that the faith and support of my family, friends, and community wouldn't wane if I decided to abandon travel and unaccustomed exertion because of ill health, but I didn't want that goodwill to go wasted either. Considerable funds had been raised locally to support the ride, and our chosen charity, and national radio stations and newspapers had all offered words of support and anticipation. Most importantly, my family and Áine had accepted the fact of my pending absence and the potential consequences of it. I hoped that this collective, positive energy would serve to fuel a recovery that seemed altogether unlikely to the doctors – at least, not without stronger drugs and bed rest.

> *Diary: 14 July 2011, Flight AS147, Denver to Anchorage, Alaska*
>
> *I'm hungry again, but not sure if it's the steroids kicking in or not. I feel ok but haven't been keeping up with the supplements Mam gave me, because they're all packed away. I'm hoping that won't impact on our first few days. I know it'll be a mind-over-matter job for a while, and the only way I'll battle through is by convincing myself there's nothing wrong. That may be stupid, but I'm here now and need something to hold on to.*

Now, on the eve of our first cycling day, I reasoned with myself that Fairbanks, which was anywhere from 10 to 14 pedalling days away, would be not only an opportunity for food and shelter, but for also hospital, medical attention or reassessment, should I need it. As I stared at the partially darkened ceiling of my hotel room, with daylight persisting through an unfamiliar night, my mind kept conjuring up a disturbing image: that of a pitiful cyclist hunched by the roadside, breathless and pale, who has no choice but to recognise that the journey is over before it has even begun.

Night turned to dawn and then to morning over Prudhoe Bay, without any observable difference in sunlight. We'd soon be on the Dalton Highway, a compact gravel road built for the lumbering trucks that serve the slowly diminishing oil industry of the north. Although I was used to manoeuvring along rough, pot-holed country roads in Ireland, they had always been sealed, and provided a reasonable, if not always perfect, consistency. The Dalton's gravel however, shaped as it was by itinerant winds and rain, would be a fresh and unpredictable challenge to christen the maiden days of our journey.

Our single remaining task before departure that morning was to collect pre-ordered white gas and bear spray at Prudhoe Bay General Store, which wasn't nearly as charming as the rural, white-painted clapboard versions seen in American period films. Instead, it was located inside a giant, two-storey blue warehouse close to the highway. Orderly and clean, the space was filled with the faint odour of trampled carpet and gasoline. Heavy-duty local necessities, such as padded gloves, welding helmets and boots, lay alongside key rings, flags and novelty mugs for the few tourists that might venture up the Dalton. I bought a sticker for my bicycle that read, 'Deadhorse, Alaska', the text stamped under an upturned orange cartoon horse that appeared to be unusually jovial about its demise.

Outside the store, Lee and I took pictures in front of an enlarged, rusting metal version of the cartoon horse sticker. Bright smiles complemented our new North Face and Patagonia branded hats, jackets, and shoes, which, destined for months of admirable service on the road, would very soon lose their pristine newness.

As we were prepared to leave, a jeep approached and a white-haired man wearing a black armless fleece stood out, gently closed the door, and walked towards us. He introduced himself as Rick Olsen, a 65-year-old automation engineer from Oregon, who worked two weeks on and two weeks off in Prudhoe Bay. Rick's affable nature belied the fact he'd been working at the fields since 1980: he hadn't that air of toughness I imagined such an environment would ultimately fashion in a person over time. Then again, it wasn't just buff oilers that worked well pads and drilling platforms. Rick's job was 'to put computers on hardware', as he described it, installing control systems to regulate the movement of oil, gas, and water during production. Although his schedule demanded half a year in Alaska away from his wife, the pay made it worth his while.

'Working this schedule gives us a chance to travel,' said Rick. 'We've lived in Seattle, Santa Cruz and Phoenix before changing to Oregon, and now we'll be able to retire there on a little tree farm we're developing.'

This echoed the sentiments of a technician from California we had met roaming the hotel the previous evening. 'Grafting ten years in the bay gets me all I need to send my girl to school, half the house mortgage, and the kitchen extension. Small sacrifice for a comfortable future,' he had told us.

We spoke to Rick for a few minutes and answered all the soon-to-be inevitable questions about our trip: 'Why are you doing this?'; 'When are you going to finish?'; 'How will you handle the bears?'; 'Will Mexico be safe?' We responded as if we'd been asked a thousand times, but internally, each of us was aware that our replies would probably evolve through experience and encounter. Rick said his house and tree farm were in Florence, Oregon, and invited us to visit him if we passed that way. 'It'd be nice to make acquaintance again, after all that distance,' he said.

Over four months and 5,600 km later, I would indeed share lunch with Rick and his wife Becca, and get the chance to recount to them all that lay beneath Rick's regular five-hour plane commute. Perceptions of time and distance were about to change significantly for me.

Navigating our way to the Dalton Highway, we passed enormous signposts advertising urethane application and asbestos surveys; one of these bore the strapline: 'Quality, Experience and Integrity – from Anchorage to Deadhorse'. To the north, well pads planted with drilling towers and silos lined a dim horizon fronted by turbulent water. In the opposite direction, the only distinct man-made feature to be seen was a thick gravel line that disappeared somewhere into the middle ground and would soon carry us away. We were both glad to be leaving industry for isolation; these were our first steps into a new world.

Just after 2.30 p.m. we made our first revolutions along the Dalton. This was the very beginning of the Pan-American Highway, the longest motorable road in the world and over 25,000 km from its terminus in Tierra del Fuego, Argentina – our ultimate destination. It didn't feel as daunting as I imagined it would, and a childlike excitement bubbled up, dispelling the anxiety I felt earlier in the morning.

Diary: 16 July 2011, Day 1: Camp by Sagavanirktok River, Alaska

I had a nervy, shaky feeling in the morning and wasn't sure exactly how to place it. I couldn't pinpoint if it was to do with the ride, or . . . the fact that isolation and potential loneliness were only minutes away, or if indeed it was something else. It's funny how, when a moment such as this arrives, it feels as if you've made a crazy choice and perhaps you haven't thought it through enough.

It was cold and lightly overcast as Deadhorse slowly became a pale grey dot in the distance behind us. There was a sufficient glow from above the clouds to encourage hopes of some Alaskan sunshine, which might warm our extremities, chilled from facing the elements. As Lee quickly adopted a sound confidence in handling his heavily loaded bicycle, I repeatedly fell to the hard surface, having surrendered control on loose gravel or by veering too close to the steep banks on either side of the road.

'You ok?' Lee would stop and ask. 'You'll get it soon enough, don't worry.'

We were carrying two weeks' worth of food, 12 litres of water each, and almost 40 kg of gear on each bicycle: all the necessities for living comfortably on the road. Winter clothes, cycling shorts, shoes, thermals, pots and pans, stoves, fuel, a water filter, bike tools, medication, tents, and sleeping bags – all these were stuffed into our bulging pannier bags, alongside luxury items such as our laptops and iPods. Our initial wish was to travel frugally, but that was an aspiration that would take an extensive period of time and experience to be able to get the essence of. Many items we initially deemed essential would eventually become unnecessary, and with this reassessment, the weight we carried would become lighter, and the cycling easier and more enjoyable.

Once out of Deadhorse, the Dalton Highway runs resolutely straight and flat towards the Brooks Mountain Range, which separates North Central Alaska into what is known as the North and South Slope. The North Slope, where we now cycled, comprised a barren, treeless landscape decorated only by lonely mosses and grasses prepared to brave the seasonal extremes in temperature that range from 28 °C in the summer, to – 52 °C in the depths of winter. Dotted ubiquitously upon this terrain are thousands of gently rippling lakes, the size of football fields to several times larger. These lakes, as we learned later from the staff at Fairbanks Geophysical Institute, were 'kettle holes': the sediment-filled residual bodies of water which punctuate the Arctic, left behind after the retreat of the glaciers. When the sun shone, as it did for the greater part of our ride to the Dalton's end, these iridescent bodies reflected the sky, hills and flora, casting upwards, mirror-like, the most unusual and resplendent greens and blues you could ever wish to see.

Native fauna didn't veil its presence either, and just 20 km from Prudhoe Bay, a herd of over 100 caribou crossed the road with such relaxed authority that we had no choice but to respect nature's unhurried pace. Proud females, protective bulls, and their off-spring: all looked upon us, unafraid and as neighbours, as they trotted slowly westwards to better grasses. Stretches of countryside, which appeared vacant and solitary at first glance, opened up as we passed through them, revealing a palette layered rich with colour and life.

Conversation-wise, Lee and I exchanged only brief, general remarks throughout the day. We spoke about where we might camp; what we would prepare for lunch and dinner; the niggling knee pain we both felt – the consequence of previous injuries now ominously resurfacing. It was unnatural not to talk more, the Dalton being a road to encourage rather than hinder exchange. Our surroundings had none of the regular distractions, save for the rapidly swelling swarms of insatiable Arctic mosquitoes around our heads, and the odd black cloud in the distance. We were all alone out there, without a sound except for the crunch of gravel underneath our tyres and a sharp buzzing, when one of the more daring mosquitos would get a little too close.

My way of handling departure from Ireland, and the profound unhappiness of leaving Áine, was to talk. Lee too had forgone friends and family and a secure routine of life; at Denver International Airport, an hour before the flight to Alaska, he and his girlfriend had even officially parted ways, with both accepting that it would be too hard to maintain the relationship while he was on the road. That couldn't have been undemanding on his emotional wellbeing, and I was aware of it. His way of coping with this was to figure it out alone, and without the need to verbalise: a kind of self-containment which he would readily attest to as a facet of his character. Yet as we rode ever so slightly southwards, and with thousands of kilometres in front of us, my immediate understanding was that we both faced a similar sense of loss and insecurity, and that surely even the tiniest parallels in our situations should bind us closer. It was only with the passing days and weeks that I would realise that Lee and I were quite different people in this regard.

At 9.30 p.m. that night, after covering 65 km, we stopped riding and set up camp by the wide and braided Sagavanirktok River, just a few metres from the highway. The river's raging watercourse crashed over boulders in its path, pitching spray wildly above its free-flowing advance to the Arctic Ocean. I watched it for a while and mulled over the realisation that this was the longest distance I had ever cycled in one day. It was raining hard and cold, as a low cloud affirmed its temporary residence over the gentle valley we were located in; the sun, which still hung over the grey horizon, struggled to break through the bleakness above. My clothes were already damp, verging on wet, from a storm that had swept in at speed a couple of hours earlier, forcing a scramble for us to robe up in waterproofs. Water had also found its way into my pannier bags and a large dry sack stuffed with a sleeping bag, Thermarest sleeping mat, and some clothes. It may not have been pleasant for our first day, but it was to be a common experience from now on.

Lee was in charge of food, and had prepared a week's worth of dinners in advance. After managing to keep the stove alight despite side winds and pelting rain, we devoured a pasta-based meal with some dried corn, peas and carrots to the din of raindrops falling on the bare pan surface. It felt like the camp dinners from old family holidays, the food almost imperceptibly laced with the odour of white gas. Just past midnight, we stumbled into our tents, tired and wet, to listen to the unruly wash of the Sagavanirktok nearby. Although we felt a little miserable, we also finally felt *here*, out and into what had existed only in imagination and day-dreamed image since the idea of the trip had first been formed in Denver over 18 months previously. To be taking these first steps then, despite the elements that rattled the tent and the doubts that circled our minds, seemed a positive and heartening thing.

The Dalton Highway, often referred to as the Haul Road, was named after James W. Dalton, an Alaskan expert in Arctic engineering, who had consulted for the state's northern oil surveys. Built in just five months of 1974, it stretches 666 km from Deadhorse to the junction with the Elliott Highway. From there, another 115 km of paved road connects to Fairbanks, a frontier town of 31,000 people, which is over 580 km from the next biggest settlement – Anchorage – in the far south of the state. Along the Dalton, place names such as Prospect Creek and Coldfoot allude to stories of exploration and the austere environment it transpired within, while topographic features have also inspired truckers to coin designations such as Oil Spill Hill, Beaver Slide and Oh Shit Corner. History speckles the landscape: now redundant gold mining camps lie hidden behind distant bluffs, and seasonal hunting settlements sit on the shores of unnamed lakes. Permanent human habitation along the highway is limited to just two refuelling camps, one at Coldfoot in the far north, and the other along the Yukon River in the south. In between, the Arctic Circle makes its crossing and US records are set – such as the longest stretch of road without services (386 km), and the lowest temperature in the country in recorded history (− 62 °C).

As the highway's construction was an immediate necessity for supporting the Alaska Pipeline and the oil fields it sprung from, it was built with a speed and efficiency only such a big industry could afford or facilitate. Nowhere is that more keenly reflected than in the total disregard for the nature of the physical geography and for any obstacles it might be seen to present – and much to the chagrin of any cyclist endeavouring to navigate it. The east-west topography is bisected by the highway's obstinate north-south bearing, resulting in some truly exhausting and mentally debilitating climbs for the cyclist. None embody this phenomenon more than the Atigun Pass, which bridges the north and south slopes of the Brooks Range.

Diary: 17 July 2011, Day 2: Camp at Happy Valley, Alaska

The ride was quite hilly and my legs felt the pain a lot more than Lee's today. I'm tending to stay in a low gear and travel slowly, while Lee can take on a hill and move about 2 km/h faster than me. The first rise today was at mile 59, right where the pipeline came back into view (it must have been underground for a while). This also marked the start of sealed surface, which was so very sweet to feel underwheel. It added another 4 km/h to our speed, which may not seem very much, but which tossed some energy into the equation and allowed us to outrun those mosquitoes when it was flat. Lee smacked a group of them on my head today and stained blood on his hands and my new hat!

My hands are pockmarked from the bites. My hat is also quite useless as they can pierce the head cover. I'm slowly getting used to their presence, but they're bloody aggravating. Even dinners in the evening are half whatever we're eating, half mossie.

I had been aware of the 1,444-metre Atigun Pass before I left Ireland. From my research, I knew the climb to the summit would be incomparable in distance to mountain passes in the South American Andes, but that it would still represent a brutal challenge we had never before faced. As a person whose standard cycle was an 8 km round-trip commute to work in Dublin, I didn't know what it took to climb a mountain or what it could potentially take out of us, and therefore the Atigun Pass was truly intimidating. All we understood was that it would be an average 12 per cent grade for its final 3–4 km: an incline so steep that a car in first gear would moan laboriously up it. It was also a grade 4 per cent superior to the infamous Alpe d'Huez climb in the Tour de France. Even though the Atigun Pass was much shorter, the *maillot jaune* (yellow-jerseyed race leader) had never had four loaded pannier bags, spare tyres, a water bladder, and a ruptured 4 kg plastic bag full of beans and noodles sagging from his side!

It was late afternoon when Lee and I approached the Pass, and gathered fresh drinking water from a roadside stream. The water gushing through the valleys of the North Slope is so incredibly pristine to drink, since the absence of agriculture and of large populations of animals removes the threat of dangerous bacteria and viruses in it. Youthful brooks bound from this central rise of mountains to feed elder rivers, as they continue on a path towards the Arctic Ocean in the north and the Bering Sea to the west. The supply stream we chose was clear enough to expose the light grey, gracefully rounded pebbles underneath, and so cold as to freeze my fingers numb. It was the first time I had ever drunk from a stream without dissolving iodine or having it passed through a ceramic filter. After the Dalton Highway, it would be over 14 months before this pleasure could be re-enacted, in Chilean Patagonia, where human settlement is also at a sufficient distance to avoid the pollution of flowing water.

Diary: 19 July 2011, Base of Atigun Pass, Alaska

Our day took us into the Brooks Range, where we snaked our way in through a gap in the hills and down into U-shaped valleys that were daubed in a hundred colours of green. It was mesmerising, gazing at the wonders of these million-years-old hills. They rise so abruptly in the distance, casting shadows and a presence one can't help but respect. Rivers and the pipeline regularly crossed our path for company, never straying too far from us.

Just after 3 p.m., with a pleasant afternoon sun in attendance, we stood to evaluate the Pass, just a few kilometres away, cut thinly into the green mountainside. The three preceding days' cycling had seen us climb gently from the coast at an unnoticeable grade. However, ahead of us, we could clearly appreciate the embodiment of our first real physical test on the journey – one protracted ascent stretching left to right across our field of vision, from where the valley closed to its end, through a 90° dog-leg turn to the south, up another gravel rise, and over the top of a narrow 'V', sliced between two curved peaks.

Grinding out the climb was an exercise in the tolerance of unfamiliar pain. An acute pressure bit my lungs, as the road rose suddenly for several metres before dropping back to the standard grade again. It felt as if my front wheel would lift off the ground, each turn and shift of body weight depriving it of contact with the surface. The sound of heavy panting became the soundtrack to our ascent. 'One revolution at a time,' I said to myself between breaths. I wondered how the chain hadn't snapped from the force exerted on the cranks turning the wheels, dragging them round and round at a speed that was slow enough to allow me to count the chain links rolling underneath. Small fluorescent road markers spread at 10-metre intervals were a constant reminder of how new and arduous this was, given the agonising length of time it took to pass each one.

Lee was out of sight by the time I reached the midpoint on the first long drag – I supposed he was at the top, eating energy bars with his feet up, such was his fitness and endurance greater than mine. At one point, a couple of booming 18-wheeler trucks descended past me in low gear, their engine brakes clanging fiercely and echoing throughout the tight valley. The climb was a challenge for both man and machine, no matter which direction we were travelling. Embarrassingly, my cleats twice became stuck in the pedals as I attempted to dismount; one time, as a battered minivan rounded the corner to catch the collapse. My shoes were still locked in as I hit the ground, sweat dripping from chin to shirt. I gave a half-hearted wave and a broken smile that did anything but reflect what I really felt.

It took just under two hours to complete 4 km climb to the summit, where a wide pull-out waited for tiresome trucks. Lee's bike was propped against a mound of stones and he was searching for something in his rear pannier bags and eating some cookies – almost as predicted.

'How did you like it?' he said.

'Yeah, different alright,' I answered, wiping sweat from my brow. 'Better now I'm at the top.'

Lee had been there for 45 minutes and was dressed in fresh clothes for the descent to the South Slope. I was a little dazed and tried to utter some words between gasped breaths. I could tell we were both excited about what lay ahead. The climb had been painful and as overwhelming mentally as physically, much unlike anything I'd ever been through before. But the sensation upon reaching the summit was more than just relief: it was absolute satisfaction, in knowing we had got there by our own power alone. I could see it in Lee's eyes too: an expression of keen anticipation, of wanting more of the climbing, the exasperation, and the triumphant release of having done it all unsupported, and together.

The South Slope presented far grander aquatic, topographical and floral diversity than its northern neighbour. Where flat, grassy plains were in constant view on our opening days, now we had the quiet pleasure of pedalling through a tree-tunnelled road bordered by lilac-coloured meadows of fireweed, which blossomed in the charred spaces left behind after forest fires. On our ride towards the tiny refuelling camp of Coldfoot – where we devoured a hot meal from its only diner – we passed the most northerly spruce tree along the pipeline, a welcome return to more a familiar terrain of trees and mixed vegetation.

Upon reaching the top of many short and steep climbs, we could see the immense expanse of this secluded section of Alaska, and indeed the world, run enticingly into the distance. It was fitting to wonder what was out there alive and roaming, what hadn't seen human interference or development on its homeland. On this part of our cycle, we had already watched a wolf follow us along a slender ridgetop, its deep black eyes fixed on ours. So too, we had come upon a powerful moose peering out from the forest, cracking wood underfoot and inspecting our close passage with curiosity. These wild places really are the last strongholds of original nature, and out there in Alaska, in the breeze that moves the spruce and aspen, and on the land that nurtures the caribou and Arctic fox, lies a source of enrichment for our human spirit and a humbling we should seek more often.

Our camping arrangements were determined entirely by our exhaustion, as the constant sunlight effectively meant we could ride all night if we wished to. Normally our search for a secluded space out of sight of trucks and rare passing cars began in late evening, around 9 or 10 p.m., when our bodies reminded us it was unnatural to carry on at such an hour. Although we could rather easily conceal our presence from people – behind small hills or down gullies at the roadside – it was impossible to cloak ourselves from bears, our biggest concern upon stopping for rest at night.

Black and brown (grizzly) bears together inhabit almost all of mainland Alaska, with the former more concentrated in forested areas with an abundance of food. We thought it unlikely that we'd cross the path of either on the North Slope, where tall vegetation is non-existent, but the South Slope brought with it different considerations. We were aware that cooking at night and the food stores we carried would be the primary enticements for any bear, so before sleeping we would store our most important rations in a 'bear bin' – a large plastic container with a locked lid we had bought in Anchorage – and walked it 200–300 metres downwind of where we slept. According to the bear safety manuals we scanned before leaving, hanging food from a tree is a much safer approach, but a combination of laziness and a false sense of security got the better of us by the time we got to the South Slope, where trees high enough to hang it from finally appeared. Whatever made more sense or not, we hadn't a single encounter with a living bear on the Dalton, just a deceased one – or rather, part-thereof. A day after Atigun Pass, we had found the torn-off limb of black bear lying in middle of the highway; most likely the casualty of a truck strike, the rest of the body already scavenged.

At the end of our first week on the Dalton, a series of prominences – most notably Finger Mountain and Beaver Slide – forced us to drag the last remnants of energy to the surface. Without a day off in a week's riding, we were beginning to look and feel tired and dirty. Salt-stained T-shirts from persistent sweating, muddy jackets, and scraggly, knotted hair reflected the elements we had braved and the roads we had travelled. The incessant sun from Atigun Pass to Bonanza Creek camp – over 210 km in total – had burnt our skin and scoured a sunglasses' shape around my eyes. As always, the mosquitoes, which appeared to grow bigger and more desperate as the days passed, continued to bite, riddling our backs and arms with hundreds of sores.

Our sluggish pace on the ever-increasing number of winding ascents through the northern boreal tree line also caused some unexpected problems. Halfway up Finger Mountain – so named for a diminutive pointed rock at its summit – I drank the last of my water, which tasted like warm plastic from having been exposed to the afternoon sun. Streams were either drying up or becoming progressively sparser. The hills of the rolling Jack White Range, which we had cycled through 24 hours previously and, from Gobblers Knob vantage point, now witnessed shrouded in mist, had thwarted our progress in finding a flowing water source. Around us now, all that remained were stagnant pools of water in the ditch that divided us from the pipeline.

At the crest of Finger Mountain, we watched as a labouring minivan of tourists pulled into a clearing, and three generations of one family piled out. One by one, they placed hands on hips, stretched backwards, and shook out pains and stiffness from muscles that had likely been cooped agonisingly inside for hours. In that sense, I thought, I was glad to be travelling out in the open. I approached, hoping to spot a genial-looking passenger, one likely to show some charity to us. An elderly man interpreted my intention from the empty water bladder dangling out of my hand, and summoned the driver to fill our containers from the large tank stored in their boot.

'Big, big drags ahead boys,' the driver said. 'That road just shoots right through the hills without much care for incline.'

While it was surely an advantage to know what type of road conditions and terrain lay ahead, I found it was often more comforting to ride unaware. That way, we could always imagine the most recent climb to have been the last, and pedal on in ignorance and hope.

Apart from the family at Finger Mountain, we had had limited chances for social interaction since leaving Deadhorse seven days before, and so relied solely on each other for entertainment and company. We had fallen into a timed schedule of eating, cycling, eating, sleeping and this seemed to satisfy a mutual preference for routine. There was a growing synchronization of our needs, to the extent that we were usually awake, hungry, and tired at the same time. Conversation was at a minimum while cycling, partially as a result of our differing physical abilities at that stage, which allowed Lee to cycle faster and further ahead of me. I was always last to reach the top of a hill and maintained a position anywhere from 100 metres to 1 km behind him. He was naturally stronger and although I could accept this as the reality, it didn't sit well with me. I didn't like being slower and less fit, having him wait for me each and every time we settled into a climb, watching his outline disappear around a corner as I puffed and struggled for breath. Yet, as the days merged into each other, I aimed to put this out of my mind, accept our individual abilities, and try to build up a companionship we had so far been struggling to form.

The final two days on the Dalton were agonising on our legs, with the burn of lactic acid a constant accompaniment to each climb. The surface quickly devolved from hardened mud and gravel to compacted rocks. The bikes rattled under the strain from shunting between and over these, dislodging water bladders, tyres, and, in my case, the plastic food bag attached insecurely by elastic rope to my rear rack. The strutted, shiny grey pipeline shadowed us, abiding by every curve and bend in the thickly forested landscape, now made up of quaking aspen, black spruce and poplar. Although overall we were making no real gain or loss in elevation, we expended an incredible amount of energy on the uphill sections, which accounted for over 80 per cent of our daily riding time. There was no wind and no rain, nothing to cool the brow, dry out our dripping woollen shirts or settle the dust thrown up in clouds by passing trucks. The reward at the end of the Dalton was exactly that: the fact that it was the end. We made a stop 85 km before that, at the Hotspot Café, a clearing of several wooden buildings occupied by just one crusty, chain-smoking lady selling hamburgers to the passing trucker fraternity.

At the Hotspot, we devoured a couple of heavy set half-pounders, along with an unhealthy dose of Coca-Cola and Danish pastries to follow. After setting up our tents in the car park tight against the forest edge, Lee and I read quietly at a picnic table and shared a hipflask of whisky given to us several nights previously by two red-haired, leather-skinned men from Maine we met at the base of Atigun Pass. Navy blue light broke softly between the swaying branches of nearby trees: the evenings were growing darker as we moved further south and away from the all-night sunlight of the north.

I felt warm and content as my body absorbed the alcohol. I realised it had been eight days since I had used the Internet, the same period since sleeping indoors, and 10 full days since I had turned on a mobile phone. It had been hard work during the day, but gratification always followed in the form of dinner and crawling into the sleeping bag to write in my diary. We were rarely agitated from cycling through the beautiful yet unforgiving northern frontier. We just accepted it as the job at hand; there was too much more to come to waste any valuable mental energy thinking on it. In the evenings, I wore my one set of clean clothes, and they were all I would need to stay comfortable. The chill air became less noticeable every night and I woke infrequently, as my body became accustomed to the rigid contours of a sleeping mat and the tiny dome of the tent that was my room. The colitis that plagued my preparation for the journey appeared to be calming and I questioned that fact no further. Such thoughts, on the first night we didn't go to sleep straight after eating, were reassuring and uplifting. The fear that we might not adapt to living on the road had been partly exorcised, I thought, as I turned another page of my book and tipped the last of the whisky into my steel camp mug.

We reached the end of the Dalton Highway at 11.30 p.m. on 23 July, eight days after leaving Deadhorse. Our altitude had jumped sharply in the final section, as we forged our way through the mountains and the sweet-scented forest that clung to their slopes, alongside the hardy Yukon River.

Diary: 23 July 2011, Camp at junction of Dalton and Elliott highways, Alaska

Today was rough riding: the worst so far. We had a 19-mile unpaved section that was the most horrific road I have ever seen. Someone joked earlier that the engineers left it like that to deter people from coming up the Dalton, and I can see why. We chanced it, as it had turned 9 p.m., and we could either camp out or go the last piece and end the highway. We both agreed that ending would be best and it took two massive climbs to get there. We're sleeping in a pull-out at the junction with the Elliott Highway. It rained at dinner, served at midnight, and there were some animals moving unseen in the woods nearby, but we decided to sleep at 1 a.m., with faint light brushing over the tent top. We met a Spanish cyclist named Juan, who was coming from Ushuaia and is now just 650 km short of Prudhoe according to his GPS. He looked ragged and his bike told a story all by itself. I'd like us to look that way at the finish.

A new day arrived as dew on the inside of my flysheet and rain lightly patting the tent. We were potentially on our last day of cycling for a short while, as the city of Fairbanks was just 120 km away, down a slick asphalt road. The first hour was conquered in poor form, both of us labouring slowly up and down a series of soft inclines. The rain had made it inside our clothes, so we rode in a warm dampness that could be felt with every flex of the legs and movement of the upper body. The Elliott Highway was clearly engineered to provide gentler grades than the Dalton, whose difficulties we hoped were now left behind us. At the end of narrow private lanes channelled out of the forest, we saw houses appear, albeit infrequently, and this was an unmistakable sign we were nearing people and services.

After a couple of hours the rain clouds parted, with light grey sheets of fast-moving moisture replacing darker ones until bands of blue could peer through. We passed a few cars and little else in the run-up to lunchtime. Too lazy to make the tuna and bagel sandwiches we had been eating at lunch for over a week now, we tore open our emergency ration packs of pasta and meatballs. These were intended for a crisis only, but as we weren't going to be trekking in the wilderness or rafting alone on inaccessible rivers, this situation was unlikely. I ate two foil packs and fell asleep in a gravel pull-out, with the sun hardening the dirt on my face. Lee followed suit soon after, head cushioned on his big yellow foam mattress. We were fatigued and listless, unable to battle the post-lunch heaviness of eyelids that seemed to become more leaden with each day.

When afternoon rolled in and our lethargy was temporarily shaken off, we passed a scribbled sign which said, 'Arctic Circle Trading Post – 1 km'. Given the dearth of any kind of human activity in this part of Alaska, it would be fair to describe the timber building we found there as nothing short of a fantasy for the exhausted and eternally hungry cyclist. We opened the door to shelves overflowing with chocolate and crisps, and a glass counter displaying hard-boiled sweets and candy canes, on top of which were muffins and pastries cascading from fat wicker baskets. Other neat rooms were partitioned off for novelty Alaskan T-shirts with images of wolves and bears, Native American woodcarvings, and books concerned with Alaskan hunting traditions. Thick, knotted wooden beams supported a triangular roof, from which shiny pendants hung. On a shaky wire stand in the corner, magnets and comical stickers were for sale, one of them reading: 'Welcome to Alaska – where the Mosquito is our State Bird'.

'Where you boys coming from? Deadhorse?' a stocky, white-haired man in denim dungarees yelled enthusiastically as he exited from a storage room.

'Yep. And pretty wrecked after that road,' we responded.

'I take it your last stop will be Ushuaia, Tierra del Fuego then? 'End of the World', they call it,' he said. We nodded in agreement.

Joe Carlson and his wife Nancy are the proud proprietors of the Arctic Circle Trading Post, and have raised 23 children, 18 of them adopted, in the five buildings that comprise their quirky Alaskan estate. Their boundless energy when we met them hinted at anything other than a lifetime bringing up children. They've seen cyclists come and go at the Trading Post, and a dozen or so times a year, Pan-American travellers visit their store on their way to or from Deadhorse or Ushuaia.

Joe ushered us outside and pointed to the business cards and postcards of cyclists and motorcyclists who had pulled in to the Post on the beginning, middle or end of their journeys. He has acted as curator to the memories and adventures of these cyclists since 1991, when a Japanese man turned up, on his way around the world. On closer inspection, names that meant nothing to many, meant everything to me. I recognised solo travellers, couples, and groups – some supported and some not – whose websites and journeys had been a resource and inspiration in preparation for our own adventure. Lee and I stapled our cards to the window frame and took a photo, promising to send a postcard when we reached Ushuaia.

We left Joe with a wave, and on a caffeine and sugar high that was bound to cause problems later. I couldn't help but think of Ushuaia and the emotions arrival there would bring, but I knew the most important parts were in between, and the smallest of steps were the key to reaching that farthest of goals. It was about the journey and not the end-point, but as I had been mentally framing it all within the first and final kilometres, I took a moment to imagine our ultimate destination once more as we rolled out of the Carlson's driveway and back onto the Elliott Highway. Daylight was fading and yet there were some hours left to go, so I began the process of stretching out my beat-up legs into a steady cadence for the remaining 70 km. Fairbanks, a shower, and a bed, were just around the corner.

2
Wild Open Spaces
Fairbanks, Alaska to Dawson Creek, Canada – 2,731 km

FOR THE PAST 300 YEARS, the Irish have been recognised as a people of perpetual flight, committing themselves to a time-honoured exodus from a land often stifled by the individual or collective turmoil of social inequality, food shortages, and persistent unemployment. The years immediate to the Great Irish Famine of the mid-1840s witnessed the greatest human passage, and born from this was an emigration trend that has continued into the annals of Ireland's most recent history. The United Kingdom, Australia, and the Americas were the cradles in which these immigrants nurtured a new existence. In the case of the Americas, they spread to the four corners, frequently reaching latitudes and geographies unfamiliar, tracing the footsteps of their revolutionary forefathers to the nations of Argentina, Chile, and Mexico. Indeed, one is as likely to see the surnames of O'Higgins and Brown as those of San Martín and Belgrano if one were to seek to interpret the history of such places through street signage alone. Further north, in the United States and Canada, more intrepid Irish immigrants continued the tradition of labouring in rural mill towns, on the expanding railroad network, and in the construction projects of these two developing nations, while urban arrivals frequently ended up in the public service as police officers and firefighters. This custom – the grand, ongoing act of departure, implantation, and assimilation – impacted on burgeoning Pan-American societies, unfailingly weaving a native Irish thread into the cultural heritage of these territories.

With such fascinating elements of Irish history daubed neatly along the spine of the Americas, I decided that the bicycle journey should also seek to explore them. The advantages of travelling overland and by bicycle necessarily favoured the search for the newest immigrants and the ancestral Irish, whose relations had broken fresh ground in the overseas chapters of Irish history. The slow pace of bicycle travel would enable us to experience at first-hand what sense of place meant in the context of such history, given that we would be consistently immersed in the terrain. The little nuances that make up weather conditions, geography, sensory impressions and frequent contact with local inhabitants – native and non-native – are often neglected when journeying by car or tour bus, because of speed of travel and pre-determined schedules; travelling by bicycle allows interaction with it all, at one's own pace.

In May 2011, a few months before our trip, I was therefore delighted to receive an email from a Cork woman named Elaine O'Riordan, right after I appeared on national radio, asking for people with relatives living in our areas of proposed travel to come forward and connect us with them on our road south. Elaine – writing with an invigorating tone – forwarded me a message she had sent to her uncle, Eddie Brosnan, and his wife Catherine, who had settled in Fairbanks, Alaska three decades previously, and had built their lives on the Alaskan curve of the Arctic Circle:

20 May 2011: Email from Elaine O'Riordan to Eddie and Catherine Brosnan

Eddie and Catherine, I don't actually know these lads, but Ian was on the radio today, talking about the craziest thing ever. He and his friend Lee are going to cycle from Prudhoe Bay (know that place??!) to the southernmost town in Argentina – starting on 15 July. It's inevitable they'll visit Fairbanks, and so I really wanted you to know they were passing through. Catch them and take them to Mass! That's where they'll meet the Irish community.

In her email, Elaine also included a few paragraphs of background on Eddie and Catherine:

HALF THE WORLD AWAY

My favourite Uncle (also known as 'the Godfather'!) – Eddie – has lived in Fairbanks, AK for about 30-odd years now with his beautiful wife, Catherine and their three gorgeous daughters, Fiona, Trina, and Gráinne. I would love you to meet up. If you get a puncture, just ring Eddie – he can fix anything! See that pipeline thingy that runs the length of the state? Well he built it! (Practically!)

We first caught sight of Eddie Brosnan as he cranked slowly along the pedestrian flank of the busy Johansen Expressway, and in the opposite direction to our travel. We had just endured nine days' cycling without a rest, as well as that morning's ride from the township of Fox on the northern limits of Fairbanks, where we had slept within a copse of trees that grew in the shadow of the Fox Hilltop Diner. We had now covered 854 km, according to my odometer.

Eddie's plain, light-blue polo shirt was the same hazy colour as the sky above and its short sleeves were having one of the few outings the short Alaskan summer would allow it. Tall and trim, he was a solidly built man, bald on top but with a big welcoming smile; he spoke with an accent that melded Alaskan character with his slower Limerick drawl.

'You boys made it. We were wondering where you were! Figured it'd be eight or nine days down the Dalton,' Eddie said, shaking our hands. 'Come on. Follow me. We'll get you back to the house for some food and rest. You've gotta be tired.'

While trailing Eddie's thin, steel-frame bicycle towards the house, we passed by Walmart, Home Depot, and an assembly of other chain stores that lined the far side of the expressway, in the same patterned manner as any other mid- to large-sized American town. McDonald's was in lively effect on our closer periphery, and the smell of traffic fumes contaminated the air around us. The scene felt as far away as imaginable from the image of Alaska one usually dreams up, and contrary to the one we had just experienced. We had met just one lonely crossroad in the last ten days, no traffic lights, and had been free to pedal on whichever side of the road we wanted, such was the infrequency of passing cars and trucks. Through Fairbanks' confusing, semi-urban maze, Eddie guided us to his home just after 12 noon, where we were greeted by warm, motherly hugs from his wife, Catherine.

After showering and beginning one of several laundry cycles for our now offensively-smelling clothes, we sat down to a lazy afternoon with Eddie and Catherine in their earthy brown coloured living room, which, although a little dark, had a hypnotic ambience and sense of comfort to it.

Eddie, slumped back into the dark leather recliner, meandered through stories about summers fishing on the Chitina River, and winters that can cause 'lock in' at − 25 °C, while Catherine shuttled back and forth from the kitchen with ice-cold bottles of Heineken, salmon sandwiches, and biscuits, which we demolished without care for the most basic table manners. Jasper, their miniature Yorkshire Terrier, chewed on our shoelaces, tying them in knots as we spoke. Later, Catherine pulled out dusty maps of Alaska, Yukon, and British Columbia in Canada, to spark remembrance of road conditions and sights along the highways they had often travelled and which we'd soon be on too.

Eddie Brosnan came to Fairbanks in late August 1975 at 20 years of age. Having served four years as an apprentice mechanic in Kilmallock, County Limerick, he had departed Ireland on the advice of his brother, Denis, who had himself just shipped up to Alaska from New York to find work on the Alaska Pipeline, which was in its early days of construction. Work on the project brought with it plentiful jobs and, according to Eddie, 'good money' to labour in the freezing northern territory of the state. Before reaching Fairbanks, Eddie was based in New York for six weeks while he waited for his Social Security number to be issued. In the two months that lapsed between his arrival and the receipt of his papers, he had traversed many of the lower 48 states with another brother, Tim, who was in the furniture moving business.

'A week after arriving in New York, I was offloading furniture in LA,' Eddie recalled over a glass of Yukon Jack whiskey with us. 'I was only 20 but I was living the dream. Still, life in Fairbanks wasn't without its difficulties in the 1970s. Finding a bed to sleep in was almost as tough as finding a job unconnected to the pipeline.'

Once this difficulty was overcome, Eddie worked his time as a security guard in a hotel and drove a cab for several weeks, whilst trying to edge himself out of the Labourer's Hall and towards employment in one of the remote camps that took charge of construction and maintenance of the evolving pipeline. With another brutal winter setting in, the hope of working construction further north became slimmer. However, good fortune struck when Denis visited and loaned him just enough money to purchase a set of the mechanic's tools essential for this type of work in the Arctic.

'The next day I took a dispatch and went to work as a heavy-duty mechanic. Even though I had been just an apprentice in Ireland, and I knew nothing about the equipment I was supposed to repair, I had a lot of company on the job, and as they say, you earn while you learn.'

During the previous days, while Lee and I had been skirting the silent and sun-struck pipeline over and underground, we had found ourselves frequently reflecting on the magnitude of the human effort which must have been required to construct the 1,300 km serpent. Passing lonesome, murmuring pump houses and the empty camp sites, which had once been occupied by hundreds of crews, had conjured up images of what life must have been like in what was then an untouched wilderness.

'We were pipeline widows,' Catherine told us over a moose stew dinner. 'There was a great deal of us in Fairbanks in the late '70s and early '80s, because all the husbands were up north for months at a time. It hit me straight away when I got here.'

Catherine's emigration to Alaska from Cork was one bound up inextricably with the twinned endeavour of falling in love and then getting married. Meeting Eddie on one of his trips back to Ireland, and quickly agreeing to marry him, by the spring of 1979, she was 14 degrees of latitude to the north and 6,000 km from home. To cushion the acute change in pace and lifestyle, Catherine embedded herself in the shrinking Fairbanks–Irish community, which was already dispersing as work on the pipeline wrapped up.

'The "little church" in downtown Fairbanks was the communal sanctuary for Irish immigrants then, and where new folk would meet others,' Catherine said. 'After Mass on Sundays, coffee and doughnuts were served and the church became the place to maintain our Irish culture. Friendships were formed there and these friends became my new family. When you are so far away from your own, you depend on each other. We were always there for each other, in good times and bad. But each time some of those Irish left, you wondered if we should too. But we stayed, and so did others.'

That circumstance may have applied to the local Alaskans also. On a walk around downtown Fairbanks, which bows its form to the curving banks of the Chena River, we noted how inactivity governed streets that fronted single-storey steakhouses and antiquated bars with names such as 'Mecca' and 'The Big I', representing a century-old pioneer past.

'When I arrived, downtown 2nd Avenue was the Times Square of Fairbanks,' Eddie remembered. 'There were lots of bars in that area and the streets were always crowded. Workers came in from the slope loaded, and they would ring the bell on the bar and buy drinks for the house. Many was the time you would have drinks backed up and you wouldn't have a chance to buy one. These days a lot of those bars are gone.'

It seemed that isolation was no defence against the sway of consumer culture and the modern march of the young out of Alaska. The strip malls we had cycled by on our way into Fairbanks and the cooling coals of throbbing industry have only contributed to the emptying of the downtown area and the loss of its former rough-and-ready charm, leaving instead only the crumbling relics of recent history.

Yet, 34 years later – despite a move to Anchorage – the Brosnans still call Alaska home. They openly say that they're still not sure why they live here, but intimate that the combination of freedom, the pace to life, and the people, are just about enough to keep them where they are.

'You can be driving through Fairbanks and get a flat tyre and, 50 years later, you're still here,' Catherine joked.

The fact that they have raised three daughters who still live and work in the state – despite Catherine's assumption that the continental US would have greater appeal once they graduated school – is another testament to many Alaskans' attachment to home and pride in their state.

'The lifestyle is pretty good here. We can go fishing down south during the salmon run and relax for a week. We get some moose meat and caribou from neighbours, and when the girls were young, we used to go camping and had all the space in the world for it,' Eddie explained. It was plain to see that Catherine and Eddie were Irish by name, but very much Alaskan by nature.

Lee and I pedalled out of Fairbanks with a creaking in our bones and a stinging in our prematurely relaxed muscles. Eddie cycled with us to the junction of the Johansen Expressway and Steese Highway, where these two double-lane carriageways merge into an organised stream of two-, four-, and 18-wheeled traffic.

'You boys take care, now. That's a long old road south you've got but as long as the weather holds, you'll see some pretty great scenery. Alaska is big and wild, and Canada's got more of the same, whichever way you go.'

We parted the same way we had met – with handshakes and smiles; on this occasion, forever grateful for the Alaskan hospitality.

As the kilometres swept by, the ground remained flat. This was the alluvial plain of the Tanana River, a swathe of land between the Brooks Mountains of the north and the Alaska Range to the south. Our general direction was south-eastwards; only a handful of rural settlements would present themselves before the Canadian border, roughly 500 km away.

We soon skirted the low-fenced exterior of the US Army base of Fort Wainwright and not long after, we crossed paths with North Pole, a small town basking in perpetual Christmas spirit due to the advantage of its close latitudinal ties. Lee played on a gigantic red sleigh while I sent postcards from Santa Claus to Áine's nephews in Ireland. Equipped with a reindeer enclosure, the world's largest fibreglass Santa statue, and a store full of candy canes, chocolates, and Christmas ornaments, it was one of the more extreme festive breaks from reality. In the sky above were booming military aircraft that rattled the atmosphere on their descent to, or flight from, Eielson Air Force Base, 5 km away. Never have two such entrenched facets of modern American culture – military zeal and rampant consumerism – existed in such peculiar proximity.

It took two days to reach the town of Delta Junction, and these were saturated by a lethargy induced by the road's only memorable characteristic – its unwavering flatness. On one side was the calm Tanana River, which snuck carefully around sandbanks in its path, leaving a wide, plaited pattern scoured on the landscape. Its direction was contrary to ours as it flowed as a worthy tributary towards its supreme mother river – the Yukon, and in search of the Bering Sea. On the other side, patches of spruce forest grew peacefully in the space between shallow lakes and the occasional bulbous hill.

Diary: 30 July 2011, Berry Creek, Alaska

Today was definitely the most boring day of cycling thus far. We started out from the campsite at Delta Junction earlier than usual at 8.50 a.m., and made our way to a steakhouse which we heard had great breakfasts. The road was straight for 55 km and that's all there is to say about that. There were some distant mountains, probably the Alaska Range; we evaded their undulations but the high trees on either side of the road did little to give us a commanding view of anything. I fell into tiredness again on the bike, grasping for energy to cycle on a road that required almost none to pedal. The actual highlight of the day was Lee loaning me his iPod, my first access to music for a long while. I listened to U2, Bon Iver, Katy Perry, Radiohead, Iron and Wine, Damien Rice, and Mumford and Sons on a playlist, singing along for nine miles. Music adds a real soundtrack out here. Camped in the drizzle at Berry Creek now, and we spilled our dinner on the tarmac but ate what was left. Hope the bears don't smell it.

With infinite time to think, I found that the loneliness of being away from Áine was growing. I missed her dearly. Since leaving Ireland 20 days previously, only a handful of opportunities for communication had arisen, and while the brief Skype calls made in Fairbanks did little to quell the pain of absence, they did just enough to stop me from becoming visibly down. It was increasingly tough to fall asleep at night, though. I often found myself staring blankly and restlessly at the light green arch of my tent, wondering how she was and what she was thinking about.

I met Áine almost two years before, in a pub in my hometown. I had just completed my Master's degree at University College Dublin and Áine was at liberty, having just finished a BA of her own on the same campus. I knew her from secondary school, but at that stage by name only, as she was in the year below me. She was always active in some artsy project or ethnic endeavour, or at least I believed as much from the colour and bohemian style of her clothes. We had never spoken but my indirect and unendorsed assumptions about her character were that she was smart, lively, extroverted, and a definite hippy. After finding common ground in our enthusiasm for travel and pending insecurity of career, we began seeing each other, and that was that. Within the space of a few weeks we had found a connection and rhythm in the relationship that brought unconfined happiness to me.

Soon after, I moved to Denver for a seven-month internship that I hoped would put my recently certified environmental education to practical use. Upon my return, Áine was readying herself for a five-month, study-abroad term in Bilbao, Spain. This lent us six months of broken time together, and just four consecutive weeks in each other's company by the eve of my departure to Alaska. Despite these circumstances, we stayed as close as two people could during separation, but the decision to then leave on a one-year bike trip seemed to us, and to others, a senseless action to take. Yet it was happening. I hadn't foreseen the pain detaching from our life together would bring, and now I was yet again wondering about rationality and choice, and trying to uncover why the pull of cycling the Americas apparently deserved my commitment more than being with the person I loved.

Diary: 1 August 2011, Sourdough Campground, Tok, Alaska

I spoke to Áine on the phone today, and it was great. Again, broken record here . . . But I miss her a lot. Today was pretty bad. I get these waves of sadness, thinking about all the forthcoming time apart. She tells me she loves me more for the time away, and I hope that doesn't change. I don't want to let her down, nor have this distance between us, but I've made the selfish choice. As I said to her, we're not supposed to be apart this long – and that must sound ridiculous coming from me. There's nobody to talk to about it; I can't think of one single person who'd understand. Maybe Mam, but other than that, Áine is the one I'd want to say this to. It makes it harder, expressing all this to her because long-term, it will be so difficult.

After a four-day ride of 340 km from Fairbanks, we arrived in the pleasant town of Tok, Alaska. Tok is the self-proclaimed 'Main Street of Alaska' and it's easy to see why it believes itself to be so. As it's the only small zone of buildings and commerce necessary to pass through when travelling between Alaska and its south-eastern neighbour-state in Canada – Yukon – it has been an important trade centre throughout history.

Embracing a laid-back community of 1,600, Tok began life as an Alaska Road Commission Camp during the construction of the Alaska–Canadian Highway, known locally as the 'ALCAN'. The highway – which officially winds 2,232 km from Dawson Creek, British Colombia to Delta Junction, Alaska – was built in response to the Japanese attack on Pearl Harbour in 1941, because of concerns over national security in the north-western United States. With the cooperation of the Canadian government, the US Army built the road over boggy, mosquito-infested territory as a supply route to Alaska, in just 234 days. Tok, at its far northern end, is just one of the many camps-turned-settlements that have matured since the road's completion, and is the last raft of aspiring urbanism before leaving the state.

We decided upon a rest day in Tok, considering that 620 km of road lay between us and Whitehorse, Canada – the next big town. For safety and self-sufficiency's sake, the most important aspect of touring on two wheels is in the planning of reaching services, which almost exclusively consist of gas stations for stove fuel, and, if one is fortunate, a village and its supermarket. Gas stations are an obvious necessity for vehicles; marking the way every few hundred kilometres, they are frequently managed by local Native American families. Tok and its Three Bears General Store gave us the option to stock up on food for another seven to ten days, which was more than we needed, but which we took as a precaution, since we now knew that in reality towns would not always appear where they were marked on the map.

We were still eating the pre-packed dinner bags that Lee had prepared in Denver, which, when combined with hot water and through limited culinary effort, would provide us with Mexican pasta soup, macaroni and cheese, and mixed vegetable couscous. However, we were now longing for the taste of fresh vegetables and fruit, and so made the decision to diversify mealtimes with whatever could be found in Tok's surprisingly well-stocked supermarket. Carrots, cucumbers, aubergines, tomatoes, plums, pears, spaghetti and spices were bought, alongside cheeses, sweets, a six pack of beer, and a couple of litres of chocolate milk. The weight was incredible, but it was weight we knew we could eat.

Since leaving Fairbanks, our camp-and-cook routine each night had become quicker and more efficient. We'd usually find a shaded area on the smoother ground by a roadside bank and out of sight of traffic. When possible, we'd prefer to pull into one of the free Alaska state campsites before the late darkness fell. Tents were pitched, mattresses inflated, and sleeping bags rolled out. Water was then filtered from a stream and stoves lit for dinner. We argued nightly over the merits of using my thunderously loud camp stove with a simmer function, or Lee's calmer and more traditional machine.

'That thing sounds like a jet engine. How can we talk over that?' Lee would jibe, while I'd try to point out how his stove consistently burnt the bottom out of the pan and pasta.

Although we had casual conversations over these dinners, we seldom broke new ground in getting to *really* know one another. There was a growing disparity between what I wanted to talk about and the subjects Lee was prepared to discuss, and this made it increasingly difficult for us to build any kind of deeper connection. I wanted to understand Lee's past and what he did before we met; the interests, traits, and habits that coalesce to form a person's character. However, Lee appeared to be simply concerned with the present and future. In his thinking, being on this journey meant breaking certain links with his previous life and surrendering to the road and its experience, waiting to discover how it could influence him. Although I set out with a very similar, if perhaps less idealistic attitude, I didn't want to be drawn away from my ties to home, for fear of what I might lose if I abandoned them. Most importantly, I had a relationship with Áine to maintain, and that required substantial time and effort now that I was *in absentia*. I would often want to delay camp departure in the mornings if I stumbled upon a phone box; in the evenings too, if such services existed, I would take an hour to call her after dinner, although this would occur perhaps just twice per week. Evolving from this, there would for Lee and I, be a pattern of temporary separation when we pitched up at night, and I felt Lee's frustration about it. As I understood it two weeks in, he believed I wasn't truly 'there', invested in all we set out to do and see, willing to devote a clear mind and my full attention to the journey.

Once we approached the Canadian border and thereafter, the ALCAN's surroundings displayed a genteel beauty. The spruce-planted plains of the Tanana River were eventually swept up into the wrinkles of the land, setting us weaving in and out of countless valleys with unbounded streams at their centres. The 4,000-metre snow-crested Wrangell Mountains pierced the distant horizon and stole away from us at an angle, until their contours met the horizon and sank back into the earth. The lakes were deep and dark-watered, and seemed possessed of ancient qualities on a grand and mythical scale.

Ten kilometres from Destruction Bay – a 40-strong community named after the carnage of a devastating storm in the 1970s – our first moment of true fear occurred, entirely without warning. Pedalling through a lingering rain that was growing heavier as the afternoon dragged on, I suddenly jammed the brakes in panic, as three bears appeared, 20 metres ahead and across the road in a low grassy ditch. I could feel my heart pounding under the sodden woollen base layers stuck to my skin, when Lee jolted to a stop behind me. He walked his bike alongside mine, sitting on the top tube as he moved.

'You see that?' I said in a shaky voice.

'Yeah, I do. Mother and two cubs, right?' he said, his whispers almost pinched away in the breeze. 'She's gonna be protecting those cubs for sure. Let's think this out,' he added, wiping away the rainwater tricking down his face.

Basic bear safety procedures should have come rushing back to my head with some kind of familiarity, as I had spent a few hours one evening at home memorising the recommended rules of engagement in this exact situation. In this moment, however, I felt at a bit of a loss. From the shaggy, light brown coat, and cumbersome, flabby profile, we identified the mother as a grizzly. 'Play dead' was the protocol if attacked or under serious threat of attack, I remembered.

Thirty seconds must have passed before the mother grizzly noticed our presence, her head slowly rising to lock probing eyes with ours. Motionless, she watched us, patiently analysing the form and shape and intention of these two humans, soaking wet and frightened, on the far side of the road. Then, she rose up in slow motion to balance on her hind legs. Her back drew upwards like a stretched steel coil and her huge padded paws hung tightly in front of her chest, rain dripping from them to the ground.

'We can't be submissive,' Lee mumbled beside me. I could feel my legs trembling.

'Yeah. Ok, let's move on and keep our eyes trained in their general direction,' I said, nodding towards the bears. 'Let's take it slow, though.'

We peered across the asphalt being pounded by rain and towards the grizzly and her cubs; the younger bears were rummaging in the longer grass. The mother's demeanour, if one could actually ascertain it, appeared to lean more on the side of curiosity than anger. She hadn't made any defensive moves while we were stalled, but perhaps our movement could spark her into action.

As we extended our legs into slow revolutions, the grizzly recoiled from her two-legged stance back to four, her blackened eyes sustaining our primal fear. A steady pace carried us past the family and 100 metres to the other side of them. The rain and rasping cold were imperceptible to us now, as adrenaline kept only our critical senses heightened for any sign of hostility. Within a couple of minutes, we had moved far enough away to feel safe again. Ahead there was only a smothering grey mist, but upon throwing one last glance behind, we were able to see that the three brown dots had already forgotten us and resumed their foraging in the grass.

Diary: 6 August 2011, Haines Junction, Yukon, Canada

What a horrific night's sleep! We reached Destruction Bay after crossing the 1,000-mile mark yesterday, but I was too wet and tired to write an entry here. We slept inside a laundromat on the advice of some maintenance workers – never again. It was pelting rain outside but stiflingly hot within, and some lady kept walking over our sleeping bags throughout the night to fiddle with the electrics in a room behind. For dinner, we feasted on the 'famous Talbot Burger' inside a small diner by the roadside, while a drunk local spouted 'expert' thoughts on American football and bear control. For a place consisting of little more than a few ramshackle buildings on the shores of Kluane Lake, I get this sense of entrenched identity from the inhabitants, but am at a loss to understand it. I'm always left wondering, how did people come to be here? What keeps someone attached to a place as separated from others as this is? The lovely girl we ordered dinner from last night told us she had answered an ad on Craigslist and moved here from Ontario for 'a change'.

Yukon is a land which time has generously spared from trammel. Roughly the size of Spain, it has a population of just 38,000, of which two-thirds reside in its largest town, Whitehorse. As we traversed its southwestern corner on the ALCAN, history and nature emerged in plentiful supply. The long and slender Kluane Lake became our companion, as we were thrust inland, having rounded the curve of its southern tip. Kluane National Park and Reserve protects the nearby mountains and the precious habitat of Dall sheep, caribou, and bald and golden eagles. Vast swathes of boreal forest, growing denser as we pressed ever southwards, stood unbroken in every direction we looked. From the top of lofty Beaver Hill, we could see ice and snow packed in narrow rock gullies descending from the upcoming valley's mountaintops, as the sky seemed to extend ever wider over northern Canada. We momentarily caught sight of the settlements of Burwash Landing and Takhini River, which maintained diminutive communities of the Kluane, Champagne, and Aishihik First Nations.

The crossroads town of Haines Junction provided services to restock our food cache, and we dined in a hotel restaurant under a television showing a college basketball game. While in this area, we would frequently cycle by old, dilapidated cafés and roadhouses rusting quietly in the company of tall yellow weeds; each property was boarded up and indistinguishable from the last. The air carried a heavy smell of spruce and wet moss, while the subtlest pleasure was to be had in hearing the afternoon jingle of aspen leaves.

On one of the many short climbs before Whitehorse, three guys in a small car stopped and flagged us down. They were waiting for us at the side of the road, and had brand new orange bicycles strapped tightly to the roof.

'Are you guys *350South*?' the blonder-haired of the three said. He had a hopeful expression on his face.

'Erm, I guess we are. How do you know that?' we answered in surprise.

'Oh, well, we recognised *that* hairy face from your website,' he responded, pointing at Lee, before we all broke into laughter.

Isaiah, Nathan and David Berg were three brothers in their 20s driving from their family farm in Starkweather, North Dakota to Anchorage, before embarking on their own bicycle ride to Tierra del Fuego, with a 10-month time frame to complete the trip. They were the biggest group in just a handful of cyclists we had met between Deadhorse and Whitehorse, but the first with comparable Pan-American ambitions. Thereafter in fact, the road began to offer up greater numbers of touring cyclists along our route, and within just 72 hours, we had encountered a small number more, some of whom would eventually become good friends.

The first of these characters was a 30-year-old Welshman named Robert Aubrey-Fletcher. Lee and I bumped into Rob on the corner of 4th and Steele Street in Whitehorse after a murky, mid-afternoon arrival to the historical gold-rush city. Pale and thin with black tufted hair, Rob pedalled quickly towards us upon catching a glance of our loaded bicycles. The first thing we noticed about him were the four bright orange panniers hanging from his bike, which clashed spectacularly with the dark, wooden lacquered buildings behind him. Rob spoke with a peculiar Oxfordian-Welsh accent and in a frenzied manner, launching straight into a story about problems he'd been having in Whitehorse.

'I was sleeping just over there with some protesters last night when the tent was shaken and someone shouted, "Get the hell off my property!",' he started. 'I was eating at a shelter earlier in the day because there was free food. It's really expensive here, you know. Anyway these protesters told me I could camp with them for the night. Bloody tired now though, and I think some of my gear was stolen.'

Lee and I noticed the handlebar bag was missing from his bike and assumed it had been taken in the alleged pilfering.

'No, I'm just selling all this stuff. Sold the bag to a motorcyclist a few days ago. Too heavy, carrying all this crap. I can't even cycle over a small hill with the weight, let alone get to Argentina,' he said in a rueful tone. 'Anyway, gotta get rid of more now. Gonna go find some people around here to buy it. Ok spot though, Whitehorse, if you're staying. Nice pubs,' he said, before taking off and disappearing around the corner.

Moments later, one block away from where we encountered Rob, a touring cyclist who was wearing a puffy insulated jacket and hunched over a blue bicycle, rode from a side street and came to a stop beside us.

'Hi, I'm Markus,' the soft-spoken man presumably in his mid-thirties said, as he shook our hands.

We introduced ourselves and asked where he was from and where he was headed to.

'I'm Austrian,' said Markus. 'I'm coming from Fairbanks and going to Ushuaia. If you guys are this far north and in Whitehorse, I would say you might have the same route, yes?'

'Same as. We're going all the way south too but started out a few weeks back in Prudhoe and came down the Dalton. Looking for some food here now, because we just got in. Why don't you join us?' we asked.

Markus Höfle had departed Fairbanks three weeks previously, on this, his third attempt to ride from Alaska to Argentina. It would be some time before I discovered why he had stopped short of his target of Ushuaia twice before, but he seemed relatively resolute about making it to 'El Fin del Mundo' (The End of the World) this time around. Something significant had to be driving Markus, if he was prepared to challenge himself to another 27,000 km over 18 months, but I never asked at the time. Instead, we listened as he spoke adoringly of his love for Latin American culture – the dance, the music, the language, and the uninhibited spirit of life. He talked of the thrill of reaching high mountain passes in the Andes and the alien expanse of the salt plains of Bolivia, effervescent salsa in Colombia, and the charm of Mexico's colonial cities. Fluent in Spanish, he encouraged us to start learning before we travelled over the United States–Mexico border.

'Your life will be made so much easier through connections with the people and that's the most important thing, if you are to understand a country and its ways,' he told us.

We chatted for an hour about the usual things bike tourers tend to discuss – the value and benefits of travelling by bicycle, equipment preferences, and the route ahead. I immediately warmed to Markus and his outlook on travel and life. He was gentle and kind-hearted and out here to see the world through others' eyes. There was no pretence to his stories. Intuitively, he just seemed like a good person.

We stayed in Whitehorse for three days and did little more than soothe our appetite for leg rest and the local beer. Rest days were becoming a jumble of laundry, eating, grocery shopping, and phone calls to home, but little else. Northern Canada and south-eastern Alaska had plenty to offer in terms of wild outdoor pursuits, but as they aren't recognised as urban centres of bounteous entertainment, our days off were primarily concerned with respite from touring and equipping ourselves for the next leg of the journey.

As we ascended the road which eventually led out of Whitehorse, we noticed a very familiar orange-panniered bicycle and its rider about 300 metres behind us. Rob Fletcher was pedalling frantically in his lowest gear on a level section of the ALCAN, coming to a stop behind us a couple of minutes later, completely out of breath.

'Hey, you guys again!' he exclaimed as he pulled a cigarette out of his pocket and lit it. 'Thought you lot would have been long gone by now.'

'Nah, we stayed an extra day and did nothing. Just drank a lot of coffee,' Lee said.

'We're actually headed to a place called Tagish Lake, just two miles down the road. After seeing where we were on our website, some other cyclists invited us to stay in a cabin by the water. Want to join?' I asked, as he took another long drag on his cigarette.

'Sure! I'm knackered already and I've only been cycling an hour!'

Diary: 13 August 2011, Timber Point Campground, Yukon

Last night we stayed at Tagish Lake with Eric and Amaya, two cyclists who have been travelling around the world for the past five years. Rob came too after we met him again on the road just 20 miles from Whitehorse. Rob is definitely eccentric but I like him a lot. He's originally from Swansea, I think, but now lives near Oxford, and I've a feeling 'events' follow him around. He started this trip from Anchorage with a friend from home but after two days his friend bailed back to England as he had a nine-month-old baby and a wife. Rob had let him plan this whole trip and all he had to do was fly to Alaska to begin – it was never his dream journey, but his mate's instead. Rob even says he knows nothing about bikes and doesn't particularly like cycling, but just went on a whim – at least he's honest. We all had to laugh when he told us he just set up a website for himself called 'Twat on a Bike'! He had us in stitches, telling a story about a bear that faced him on the road and all Rob did was shout and throw rocks at it – not exactly in the bear safety handbook. We lost him today at Jake's Corner, a junction with a road leading to Skagway on the coast, which has a ferry terminal with boats running to Prince Rupert, further south. He told us to head on and that he'd catch up with us but his insistence on us pushing ahead makes me wonder if he continued at all.

Lee and I wouldn't see Rob again for quite some time but were left wondering whether it was his sluggish riding pace or an underlying aversion to bicycle touring that had separated us that time. Rob, as far as I could understand, was out here in Yukon, alone on a bicycle, with no real idea how it came to be. I could empathise with his situation, as there was a shade of similarity between him and myself, given my own internal questioning on leaving Áine. The big difference of course was that I planned this methodically for over eight months and now felt lost because of a decision to gamble on a relationship, whereas Rob didn't organise a thing and was just now experiencing the first symptoms of the realisation that he had just gone along with someone else's ideas without any input of his own. This partial fellowship of circumstance provided some strange comfort to me, and I felt better, knowing he was out there, attempting to cycle from Alaska to Argentina without a clue about how to do it.

As we progressed through Yukon, we were nearing a fork in the road that would determine our path through the remainder of Canada; the decision concerning which route to take had been an unresolved issue in recent campsite conversations. At this, our second major junction in over 2,300 km and 32 days of riding, the intersection offered two choices of path into the heart of British Columbia. Option one was to continue as normal along the ALCAN Highway, which would escort us down into the Northern Rocky Mountains and then eastwards onto the drier Canadian plains, before beginning its second winding southern descent to Dawson Creek. There we could connect with the John Hart Highway to Prince George, where semi-wilderness would all but end and human habitation would take over. The alternative was to follow the Cassiar Highway threading through wild glacial valleys closer to the coast, passing very few settlements but with higher concentrations of bears and a more direct line south into Canada.

After a morning loitering around Watson Lake and visiting its bizarre Signpost Forest – an immense collection of over 92,000 place name signs planted by tourists from around the world – we elected to ride the ALCAN, on the grounds that we had already ridden half of the historic road's length and were disinclined to pedal 25 km back to the junction with the Cassiar.

While I was comfortable with riding either to its limit, I had a preference for the ALCAN in other respects too. Since Fairbanks, I had been growing a little wearier each night, especially at dinner when my eyes would grow heavy and exhaustion would creep in. It was easy to sleep, but it was never long enough. We had been clocking up 90–110 km days and cycling for over seven hours on each of them. Riding was becoming harder, when it should have been easier. The ulcerative colitis I had been battling internally for over three months was beginning to flare up more intensely each day, after that initial period of calm on the Dalton. My medication wasn't working, and the constant gurgle in my stomach was food passing through me, partially digested, and its nutrients largely unabsorbed. Once more, I felt feeble and worn. The afternoons provided some relief from the cold morning shivers, but I was always ready for a return by nightfall to feverish shaking and a limp physical state. Assembling the tent pole, clipping the flysheet, and staking the tent into the ground were still manageable chores, but they were chores nonetheless.

Although Lee was aware of the situation, we rarely spoke about it. I didn't want to worry him, but he could no doubt sense the severity of it from my camp behaviour – walking slowly around, a disinterest in talking, and groaning to myself under my breath. The only solace was the absence of a visible anaemic pallor – this lay hidden under a face reddened by daily exposure to a beating sun.

Diary: 20 August 2011, McDonald Campground, Muncho Lake, British Columbia

It won't be easy to recount the last six days. Tiredness and apathy have led to my diary remaining empty. I've felt very weak, pedalling has been a grind, and the partial remission I felt out of Fairbanks has disappeared. I always feel that I need to use the toilet even when I don't. If it gets any worse than this, I'll need treatment – a course of steroids and other drugs, and complete bed rest – and I don't want it to come to that. I think of Dad and Mam and others at home following us, all the excitement they get from seeing our progress. Ending here would be truly unfulfilling, as we've just cracked the surface of this thing.

We entered the Northern Rockies around Liard Hot Springs, where an early finish allowed us time to soak outside in 40 °C, sulphur-infused water surrounded by boreal forest. In winter it must be majestic, the trees blanketed in snow with only a couple of still, steaming pools interrupting the white. The next day, muscles relaxed, we made it to Muncho Lake, a water-filled crevasse in the mountains where, we were told, wild strawberries grew. This was a dream for Lee, his existing passion for wild fruit heightened by the location. On the many occasions when I'd lose him on a climb, I'd arrive later to find him scouring the roadside bushes for any edible berry he could find. Sometimes, he'd arrive back to his overturned bicycle with a Tupperware container full of blueberries or Saskatoon berries, and I knew then we'd never go hungry.

At Muncho Lake we were pummelled by severe headwinds that accompanied the advance of a stirring storm. One hour before we first noticed the escalating wind, we passed directly through a rapidly evolving weather front moving south to north, and contrary to our direction. Instantaneously, we hit a wall of air, the conditions changing from cool and calm to warm and breezy. It was the most incredible sensation, a real-life science and geography lesson amidst the towering Rockies. Up ahead a volatile sky was forming, with smooth, fulgent clouds swallowed up into turbulent swathes of thick and choppy greys, getting ready to shed their anger on the land below.

This, our first real battle with the elements, when wind and rain combined forces so fiercely, lasted five or six hours and conspired to delay our progress rounding the cloistered lake. The wind was strong enough to shift us back and forth across the road, scouring dust from the unpaved surface into our faces. At the top of the pass overlooking the lake, we wheeled downhill to Toad River, a glacier-blue watercourse that thrashed its way over boulders and riffles at the base of some exquisitely folded, bare rock mountain faces. We followed the torrent with a tailwind for 30 km towards Toad River Lodge after the ALCAN turned east, and caught favourable whipping winds from the moving storm. On several occasions, we spotted bears ahead or were warned in advance of their presence by motorists. As we approached, we would wait for cars or campervans to pass by, so that they could shield us as we slunk along their opposite side.

In the poplar-shaded campground attached to the lodge, we pitched the tents and I went inside the attached restaurant to call Áine, who I hoped wasn't asleep as the eight-hour time difference made it 1 a.m. at home. When I made it back to the tents after a brief chat with her, Lee was writing in his diary.

'How's everyone?' he asked, without looking up from the paper.

'Good, they're not too bad. I spoke to Áine and got my parents as well before they went to bed.'

'No more phone calls for you, now,' he said, still writing in his diary.

'What do you mean?' I knew somehow he meant it, despite a hint of a playful tone within the message.

'No more phone calls in the morning. We have to leave early and we can't do that with you talking every time we stop. It's impossible to get out early.'

'Well, I want to talk to my family and Áine. How am I supposed to do that if I don't call when we stop? You know it's important to me.'

'We need to figure something out then, 'cos we're always narky in the mornings when we get out too late, and that's not good to continue with,' Lee said with finality.

I didn't answer. A sense of irritation was forming into resentment uncommon to me. Instead of expressing it however, as usual in such circumstances, I just simmered for a while, buried it, and attempted to make normal conversation for rest of the evening. Of course, what I later realised was that our inability to turn our brief tête-à-tête into an argument was our biggest failing, as it would have undoubtedly allowed us to address properly the issue of my phone calls home and anything else that was restricting us from getting on well together.

Diary: 22 August 2011, Tetsa River Campground, British Columbia

Started out at 5.20 a.m., when I got up to call Áine and actually found her on Skype as there was a Wi-Fi signal in the building. She looked beautiful compared to a haggard me! We caught up and talked about travelling and the fact that we'd be happy just doing anything together – she even joked about us becoming organic grocers or just farmers, if that would do. After yesterday's annoyance at the lodge with Lee, today was better and we talked for the first 30 minutes of cycling, which never happens. We spoke about personal relationship stuff and from it I gathered (we both did) that we're very different people. I rely on others more for happiness, which perhaps leaves me more vulnerable, whereas Lee admits that he is solely responsible for making himself happy. I got a real boost just from us talking for a while, and I think he did too.

After the disagreement at Toad River, I decided to better organise the time I spent talking or emailing home, by rising earlier in the mornings or calling a little later at night. It was a compromise I believed might alleviate some of the tension that existed between Lee and myself, and I knew it was imperative to stamp this out sooner rather than later. However, even by changing my habits, I was growing unable to shift my annoyance around the situation, and because of this, conflict between us began to manifest in other ways.

Since Deadhorse, I had not made a mountain pass or topped a hill climb ahead of Lee, and rarely spent time cycling in front, although this was now more to do with habit rather than capability. So, when Lee stopped to write a note in his diary as we crawled up the first curve of Indian Head Pass after leaving Tetsa River, I took stock of the fact that I was about 200 metres in front him. There and then, I decided I wanted to reach the top first. Staring resolutely at the ground that passed underneath my wheels, I accelerated and was away. I couldn't see the top but I assumed it would be at least 3 km ahead – the road scurried off to the left behind a rocky bluff and reappeared in the distance, running perpendicular to us under green vegetation which clung to the overhanging rocks.

I could hear my bike creak with pressure as I rode with an unnatural fervour. Across the gaping valley to my side, I saw cars creeping around the restrictive contours of the mountain, a couple of kilometres away. Adrenaline was coursing through my body and the recent fatigue and sickness of mornings had evaporated in an instant. I realised the idiocy of pushing myself unnecessarily through a brainless exercise in physical competence, but put the awareness of this at the back of my mind.

One kilometre from the top, I heard Lee coughing behind me. Then I heard it again, ringing faintly in my ears. Cycling at 8 km/h – which was particularly fast on a pass of such a steep grade – I sensed he was racing after me. If anything, hearing Lee supplied that final drive of energy I needed, and two minutes later I rolled over some loose gravel and met the tarmacadam surface one last time, as the rising road eased off into a gentler open section. I came to rest in front of some interpretation signs for the Muskwa-Kechika Management Area, which lay in a giant green basin below. For the next hour we didn't exchange a single word, except for me to ask Lee to take a photo on top of the pass.

While I felt the act had been completely foolish and juvenile, I also couldn't help but welcome the satisfaction of getting there first, particularly as Lee had finished 100 metres behind and despite what I believed to be his best efforts to catch me. But then again, he had a right to. If I was prepared to race to the summit, then he was indirectly being asked to compete. I could have stayed with him all the way up and just pushed that little bit harder than usual on the final section to move ahead. However, I didn't. The issue of phone calls to Ireland still drew ire and played some part in what incentivised the rushed ascent. What was worse, I could feel myself harbouring some unhealthy resentment against Lee, and perhaps he was doing likewise.

After its brief interlude in the Rocky Mountains, the ALCAN Highway drifted east and out onto the Taiga Plains of Western Canada. We were regularly cycling 110–120 km per day, and with the flat expanse around the industry towns of Fort Nelson and Fort St John, we ended these in daylight and at a canter. It felt like a long time since we slept with the sun still circling the treeless horizon in Alaska's north. Now at least, the stars and broad brushstroke of the Milky Way brought added character to the night.

With sizeable towns down to one every two days, we migrated away from our staple dinner of Vienna sausage, tuna, and cheesy pasta. The curiosity and generosity of locals often led to snack and food donations, with our greatest coup being a freshly caught salmon. Hospitality didn't end at food either, and on several occasions we were invited to stay with families as far away as Vancouver.

Our arrival at the Mile '0' RV Park in Dawson Creek heralded the end of the 2,232 km ALCAN Highway and a full 45 days in the saddle for us since Deadhorse. While this first chunk of our route was insignificant in relation to the total distance we needed to travel, it was crucial in terms of the fundamentals of living and reading the road, which we had now established for ourselves. We knew how to interpret the landscape and what its visual clues were telling us. A river on the map meant a descent to its channel and an ascent back out again. The bigger the river, the higher the climb. We would find water where ice-capped mountains rose nearby, with meltwater surging from them into the valleys we passed through. Living on the road had fallen into a routine, and duties were completed with a habitual ease. Stove on, stove off, eat food, wash pots, read our books, and sleep. Lee needed his coffee in the morning and I needed my tea. Camping under a forest canopy kept us dry, but setting up by a river would provide us with a constant supply of water. When the sun came out, so did our wet clothes, and we'd hang them from the panniers to dry as we rode. Time had brought experience, and experience had brought confidence. We had conquered the early fear of failure and to now cycle the length of the Americas, along this unknown and ever-changing road, appeared within the realm of possibility.

3
Amongst Giants
Dawson Creek, Canada to Vancouver, Canada – 2,290 km

ON FIRST IMPRESSION, DAWSON CREEK lacked any kind of aesthetic or cultural charm, and failed to convince us that taking a rest day there was a good idea. While it was the regional hub for agriculture and industry, it was similar to the other patchy settlements we had cycled through in the preceding week: Fort Nelson, Fort St John, and Taylor – all sprawling northern working towns suffering under the dense waft of smog from the manufacturing and gas processing plants located on their peripheries. Their human catchment areas were huge and as a result, they appeared to develop and function as service centres only, with little of interest to offer the traveller, except for an unembellished monument or two commemorating their esteemed founders. We had cycled through each of these towns on cloudy, disconsolate days, and I wondered what they would look like when the sun shone, and whether the more favourable light would do any more to endear one to them.

Dawson Creek did have one minor attraction, though – a three-legged signpost marking Mile 0 of the ALCAN Highway, and to that we paid some fleeting attention. It stood high and authoritative at the exact point where the Spirit River Highway, the John Hart Highway, and the ALCAN met – a white wooden banner with a Canadian flag at the centre and the stars and stripes of the United States at each end: an acknowledgment of its neighbour and the territory in which the road ends. Lee took the requisite pictures of me standing under this sign, and afterwards we shot some video footage about the personal significance of riding 2,232 km from the start to finish.

Although this type of forced filming and narration seemed rather unnatural to us both, we had an obligation to do it because of our agreement with an Irish television production company, who had undertaken to produce a television series and perhaps also a full-length documentary film based on our travels.

Several months before leaving Ireland, I had contacted a handful of national production companies, in the hope one would put some money, equipment, and faith behind us by filming the entire trip, and in the process, act as a platform to raise considerable funds for The Carers Association of Ireland, the charity we chose to support. As exciting as the deal initially felt, the filming obligations began to agitate us both as we progressed through Canada. Every evening, we were each required to record individual three-minute video diaries, talking about the highs and lows of the day, how we felt overall, and how our relationship was developing, including anything which irritated one about the other. We were also to gather each day at least five to 10 minutes of action footage, from a camera mounted on our bicycles, with a view to capturing the most interesting people we met, and noteworthy places, such as the Mile '0' landmark in Dawson Creek.

Since it was I who had initially pursued and developed the documentary concept, I knew that the responsibility to film and return the footage to Ireland was also mine to fulfil. Given that Lee too would be tired and sometimes burnt out in the evenings, I could understand he wasn't always interested in pouring his thoughts and feelings out to a camera, for people he didn't know or particularly care about. In truth, I was finding the filming a slight hindrance too, not only because we were consistently expected to talk about each other on camera – which was not always easy – but also because this commitment necessarily brought with it severe time constraints within which to complete the trip. When initially approaching the film company, I had pitched the idea as: '350South – a 350-day bicycle ride from Alaska to Argentina'. The '350' element to the trip came about from an early desire to support 350.org, an international organisation aiming to build a grassroots movement to tackle the climate crisis. Later, we decided instead to support The Carers Association – a national charity close to my heart, since my mother had been a carer for her own mother in our home for 20 years. Despite the change, we kept the original name and timeframe for the project. Weeks before we arrived in Dawson Creek, however, Lee and I were already cognisant of the great difficulty we would have in completing the trip within this time, and we were even more aware of just how limiting the 12-month timeframe would be, if we wanted to experience in any kind of meaningful way the people, places, and the wealth of chance encounters that might cross our path.

Given my own internal conflict, between having to fulfil my self-inflicted filming responsibilities and recognising the increasing difficulty in doing so, along with Lee's general apathy towards the project, the whole issue became a point of conversation we chose to avoid. We both believed that pulling the camera out when we encountered new people was inappropriate, and only served to heighten the inhibitions of others who engaged with us. We also were aware of an artificial, contrived feel to our behaviour on camera, as we sought to tread an uneasy middle ground between 'being ourselves', and providing scenes and insights which we thought would make interesting television.

Edging away from Dawson Creek on Highway 97 and towards the Rocky Mountains, we were aware of just how time-constrained we were in the short term too. We had eight days to cycle 790 km to the ski-town of Jasper in order to meet with Anna Rodgers and Ros Bartley, our director and cameraman, who were flying from Ireland to capture some professional footage of us cycling through the procession of glaciers, waterfalls, and mountains that form the Icefields Parkway within Banff and Jasper National Parks. If we arrived on time, we would have covered roughly 1,800 km in 20 days, and without a single day off. Statistics like these and the unforgiving realities that accompanied them didn't help to quell the joint sense of frustration that our trip was somewhat out of our immediate control.

A couple of hours west of Dawson Creek, we were battered by a mid-afternoon squall and a subsequent thunderstorm. There was palpable fury in the storm's reckless careening across the heavens, tormenting barley and canola fields, and, far away where the sky touched the ground, stirring wooden windmills into violent spinning. At dusk we arrived in the community of Chetwynd. Damp and weary, we found a place to camp behind the home plate of the local high school's baseball field.

Huddled upon a slender terrace overlooking a floodplain, Chetwynd is just one of many tiny Canadian communities that market their unique identities with an unshakable pride. Downtown, the clean streets are tree-lined and well-kept, and have that agreeable atmosphere effortlessly created through the simple presence of abundant, leafy vegetation in public places. There is a monument declaring Chetwynd the 'Chainsaw Sculpture Capital of the World' and running east and west away on either side of this sit dozens of two-metre high wooden sculptures: wolves howling at the moon; bald eagles; flailing octopi; roaring bears; sleeping cowboys – there's even an oversized, chestnut-coloured Yoda. The spotless demeanour of each of these artefacts, and the perfectly trimmed grass around them, are indicative of a community dedicated to their conservation. Indeed, each year, thousands of visitors from all over the world gather here to attend the annual Chetwynd Chainsaw Carving Championship and see the next batch of elegant and quirky creations of that year's competitors. Doubtless the event serves as a unique opportunity to broadcast the town's matchless personality to the rest of Canada.

On leaving the next day, I thought again about the unique character of this small community. For a place such as Chetwynd, in a country as big as Canada, creating an inimitable identity, and fostering a community pride in it, seemed all the more important as we departed back into the anonymity of British Columbia's wide open spaces. With vast distances between villages and towns and as much from towns to cities, the only physical fibre of connection between these and the wider nation lies as a thin, nine-metre wide strip of asphalt running for hundreds and thousands of kilometres through some of the most remote and uninhabited landscape in the Americas. Canada never felt as big, and us as insignificant within it.

As Chetwynd disappeared, we cycled alongside the winding Sukhana River. On the John Hart Highway, the traffic was beginning to pile up; road construction crews were drilling, earth-moving, and steamrolling every 20–30 km, forcing us to load our bicycles into the back of pilot cars that escorted lines of patient traffic safely around heavy machinery perched dangerously by the cliffs, emptying loads of boulders and soil down the steep banks of the river valley.

'You guys should get off those bikes and put your hands to some use up here! Plenty of jobs,' a plump, greasy-haired lady in a safety jacket told us, as she drove us around a section of road that had collapsed into the river. 'Hell, I'm getting CA$400 per day just for driving this damn car 2 km up and down the road!'

The patchy scars industry and construction had inflicted upon the landscape in these pockets of northern Canada announced the end of partial wilderness. The sound of distant tree-felling and the sight of giant revolving pump jacks and restricted dirt roads leading to mining camps: all were daily reminders that Canada's wealth of natural resources above and below ground were being rampantly plundered. And as much as we imagined this to be a remote part of the world, people were still here, furtively working beyond the poplar and pines. How far must one travel in this open country, I wondered, before finding a truly untouched natural space, living and breathing, still intact, despite the advancing fronts of human activity? What value did wildness have, alongside oil, lumber, and ore? Surely the emotional well-being of a nation would be enhanced by knowing of the existence of – yet perhaps never even touching – a protected sanctuary, the original domain where bears, beavers, and elk existed, and continue to exist, unpressured and free? It would however become increasingly hard to ignore the unfortunate reality of the present, and the depressing omens for the future, the further south we moved into a populous North America.

As we turned in 120–130 km days in order to reach Jasper on time, camping was always left until the latest possible hour, when our shadows would begin their stretch along the road in the coolness of the golden evening sun. Since leaving Alaska over six weeks previously, we had lost over 10 hours of daylight time, and were now operating with just 14, each passing day shaving more minutes off as we cycled into mid-Autumn. We heard from a shopkeeper in Dawson Creek that snow had arrived in Prudhoe Bay and northern Yukon; now the early stages of the long winter were chasing us south.

Even with our habit of only searching for camp close to sunset, it was never difficult to find some flat ground or shaded space near the roadside. Knowing when and where to find it became an art swiftly mastered, and at this point, 48 days in, we both could intuitively recognise a good spot when we saw one. Aside from safety, a nearby water source was the most crucial factor determining the location of a home for the night. Although we could effectively carry about 25 litres of water between us, this added an extra 25 kg to the bikes and so we rarely filled our water bladders and two-litre plastic bottles to the brim, otherwise they would have to be simply emptied over the asphalt, should we be failing on a steep climb. As dinner and breakfast alone required at least seven litres of water for cooking and washing up, finding a brook or stream was always on our minds at nightfall, and fortunately it was rarely a problem to do so.

 I had first enjoyed the simple pleasures of camping as a child, on family holidays in Western Europe. My parents would load my sister, Alice, and me into the back of our dented red Volkswagen camper van, and drive from Ireland through France and over the Alps, to end up in Italy or Switzerland before turning around for home again. Natural spaces to pitch our tent were either non-existent or privately owned, so our sleeping arrangements were generally limited to designated campsites with shower blocks, kitchens, and boisterous games rooms for the children.

 Now however, as we cycled through Alaska and Canada, the innate satisfaction of wild camping became a major factor in developing our own sense of 'journey'. Being able to choose our own space to sleep at night was a victory for a freedom and liberty, the like of which I had never experienced before. I'd drift off to sleep wondering if anyone else had ever slept in the exact spot where I found myself. Had they heard the nearby, probably nameless, gurgling stream in their ears as they lay down for the night? Had they drunk from it? Eventually our bodies and minds became accustomed to the rising and fading temperatures and the changing weather, as we learned to adapt to the cold and heat or wind and rain, slowly choosing to forget what home comforts were like so that we could embrace this new way of life and rein in any wishes we had to return to the old. Although we had expensive mountaineering tents, multi-fuel stoves, and dependable water filters, we were living in accordance with the road, independent of as many services as we could afford to do without. It felt right to be outside from dawn until dusk and equally so at night, when we were just tenuously separated from our immediate environment by the threadlike flysheet of a tent. And it all presented a great opportunity to cook, eat, and rest in some startlingly beautiful places.

 Two days out from Prince George, we camped in the grounds facing

Bijoux Falls, a beguiling waterfall deserving of such an enchanting name. It was tucked quietly off the highway at the brow of a hill and surrounded by a dense grove of tall spruce trees. While we sat reading at a picnic table after dinner, an indigo-toned blue jay watched us for over an hour, dancing from branch to branch in the bushes, inspecting our camp intently for any scraps of food. His slick movements behind the front-line of leaves were spellbinding – the sharp twist of his head, the curling of his feet around the damp twigs of the bush, his eagerness and his patience. Settling into the sleeping bag later that night, I could hear the jay rummaging around our camp. The beauty of the falls, the glorious setting and the bird were gratification enough after a day's work on the bicycle.

Prince George, which identifies itself as 'British Columbia's Northern Capital' – despite its geographical location in the southern half of the province – came upon us after a series of draining days of eight to nine hours in the saddle through agricultural countryside occasionally breached by a bare, brown canyon. The only time to rest while awake was between 7 and 9 a.m., when we would dismantle the tents, boil water for the oatmeal and coffee, pack up the pannier bags, and eat breakfast. We had fallen into a pattern of long cycling days, which were broken only for lunch, a snack, or to take a time-out on any mountain pass that was beginning to overcome us. At times, this section of the road felt more like a job than a tour, now that rushing for the camera crew in Jasper meant our daily destination was predetermined and bereft of any opportunity for spontaneity.

The post office in Prince George was holding a letter from Áine – or at least I hoped it was. I was afraid we might have got there too early or even too late, so I was more than grateful when the postmistress returned with a brown package bearing familiar writing. I chose not to open it or read the letter inside until I had some time alone, which wouldn't materialise until the following night at Goat River Rest Area, a shaded lay-by in the depths of a beautiful, deeply-hewn granite gorge 60 km from Prince George. The trees bowed in irregular form and through them shone the yellow light of evening, painting all manner of shapes on the tarmac. Seating myself against a picnic table with scorch marks on its legs, I opened the letter and pored over Áine's words.

She wrote in an ebullient manner, and page after page contained news from home and details of her plans for the year, which I already knew about from our Skype conversations – after all, the letter was now nearly one month old. This didn't lessen the excitement of it, and I read and re-read the pages, as if it were the first time I had heard the news. Áine had an interview for a European Union Aid Volunteer programme coming up and if she got through, she would be based abroad, possibly in the Caribbean or Africa. She was still in Dublin now and in a new house, close to where we had lived together before I left; she was minding children for a family across the city. The letter was full of our jokes and half-written in that weird, nonsensical language most couples have when playfully communicating with each other. Reading it, and seeing her handwriting, brought an interlaced sadness and joy to the surface for me – joy, because her words, the lilting letters and the drawings she had scribbled in the corners drew her personality out from the paper; and sadness, because I desperately wanted her close to me.

> **Diary: 4 September 2011, Goat River Rest Area, British Columbia**
>
> *Have just opened Áine's letter and spent nearly half an hour reading through it. It's amazing what a handwritten letter can do to someone; you end up reading it and hearing the writer's voice in your head, and this was the best voice to hear. It was bouncy and, in typical Áine fashion, went randomly from one subject to the other without a care for continuity – just like in real life. It also helped that the package was crammed with Chocolate Oranges, a Walnut Whip, Haribo, Meanies, Pink Wafers, and Lyon's teabags. I've just shown them off on the video diary and am trying not to ravage them while I write.*
>
> *Goat River is gorgeous. It's just across the road, and so deep and beautiful and clear, right to the bottom. Must go explore!*

According to our calculations at Goat River, we were 220 km from Jasper. We felt strong too, healthy and fit, despite this being our 18th consecutive cycling day. Even the pain of my colitis had abated as it had succeeding the Dalton, and I was hopeful that this time it would remain that way. Our muscles took some time to unwind in the mornings but after an hour or so, they were warm and into full motion, flexing with mechanical regularity.

I tried to maintain a strict schedule of stretching and rolling out the knots in my thighs, but my attempts were generally botched by laziness. Lee was better at this, much more regimented. After erecting his tent in the evenings, he would take the bear bin out, place it on the ground on its side and roll his legs over it while balanced in a push-up position. To alleviate the transitory guilt I felt from witnessing the greater respect he seemed to have for his body, I would sometimes run my mini-thermos along my legs for a minute or so in my sleeping bag at night, and tell myself what a good workout that really was.

Our accelerated pace propelled us to the town of McBride on the outskirts of Jasper National Park on 5 September, which also happened to be Labour Day. Everything was closed, except for a well-stocked supermarket close to the train station. McBride is located on the Yellowhead Highway, in a big open valley between two vast ridges of mountains. Where the road stretches off into the distance, the valley tightens until it engulfs the lower lying landscape that runs directly into it.

Lee was incredibly excited to be cycling into this, the heart of the Canadian Rockies. This was understandable, as he grew up in Conifer, Colorado on the foothills of their southern cousins, and the mountains were his natural home.

'Jesus Christ man, how do they do it? How do they do it? Look at those badass folds over there,' he shouted one day, riding past some skyward-pointing rock formations.

When Lee was in this kind of form, passing good-humoured comments on everything we saw, it was impossible to stop me from laughing. He was quite often this way, talking breathlessly about biology or physical science: both subjects he found eternally fascinating. He could spend an hour over explanations of why certain tree species thrive in a particular place, and how their systems and anatomy had evolved to manage dramatic temperature ranges. He was well-informed and astute, and knew much more about various aspects of our environment than he ever let on. These were among my best memories of Canada – the free-flowing travel and conversation as we moved through a country that commanded wonder.

I too was excited to reach the Rockies. I had been here 10 years before, and remembered quite vividly staring up at the sheer, razor-sharp south face of

Mt Robson, the highest mountain in the Canadian Rockies, after it emerged into view around a corner in all its eminent splendour. It was a mountain with a blazing presence, I remember thinking. There is just something about those highest mountains, those enormous presences incising the uppermost sky. They almost seem to demand unconditional respect, such is their raw ambition to become the tallest entities on our planet; they command further admiration for the millions of years of work, of endurance and resistance, required to achieve that feat.

From McBride, the Yellowhead Highway sneaks past open farmland freckled by hay bales and herds of cattle, before rising steadily and into the Rainbow Range of the Rockies, where the road swings in and out of the gently cambered spurs of nearby mountains. The landscape had altered from dry and parched earlier in the morning to a fertile green, now in early afternoon; the lofty peaks granted the sun only limited time to heat the land wedged between them. At the crossroad settlement of Tête Jaune Cache, we turned north and cycled alongside the Fraser River and then over the countless bridges that spanned its tributaries. Just 60 km further along, the Fraser shies away from the Yellowhead and backtracks due south into roadless territories, where one can find the source of the mighty Vancouver-bound waterway.

Before pressing on to arrive at Robson River campground, we stopped at the Mt Terry Fox lookout and memorial, which I remembered from before as a poignant place. Terry Fox was a Canadian athlete who attempted to run across Canada for cancer research, after his right leg was amputated due to osteosarcoma, a bone cancer that originated near his knee. After this treatment, he went into a period of remission and a return to health, and he set himself the goal of raising CA$1 for each of Canada's 24 million citizens, in the name of cancer research, which he felt was in need of greater funding and support. Beginning on 12 April 1980, Terry ran over 5,000 km in 143 days, before ending his attempt in Thunder Bay, Ontario after the cancer returned and spread to his lungs. Terry died nine months later but left a lasting legacy in Canada and further afield, one aspect of which is the annual Terry Fox Run, the world's largest one-day fundraising event for cancer research. The memorial, which faces Mt Terry Fox — a smooth 2,650-metre peak named in his honour — tells his story and continues to inspire passers-by and those who make the trip specially to visit it.

Leaving the memorial, we rode off and enjoyed the respite of one long downhill section of road. I glanced at my map and checked the names of nearby peaks that seemed to be inspecting us from on high, their broad faces gazing down at two miniature figures entering their territory. Overlander Mountain, Resplendent Mountain, Cinnamon Peak, Emerald Ridge: to have coined such names, I found myself thinking, whichever white explorer had thus distinguished them from their native designations must have been as taken aback by their arresting beauty as we were. Now the peaks were readying themselves for sleep, their top layers of snow-covered rock glowing blood-red as an already invisible sun approached the horizon.

Jasper rests at the very bottom of Yellowhead Pass and reaching it involves a long and twisting descent into 'Wild Rose Country', a very fitting moniker for the province of Alberta. As towns go, Jasper is a fairly unique place, in that its environmental charter prohibits any further urban expansion. Constrained therefore within its own borders, it is a progressive town in governance and ambience, and partially occupies a substantial area of flat, semi-forested land at the base of four mountain ranges, within the Athabasca River Valley. It has the same kind of qualities native to countless other environmentally aware and developmentally responsible municipalities, such as Boulder, Colorado or Asheville, North Carolina. I've always felt that in such towns, these qualities explicitly reveal themselves through the nature of the human activity in evidence, and the spirit in which this is undertaken. For example, Jasper had tidy and sculpted green spaces where teenagers slacklined between the trees. Micro-breweries and vegan restaurants that touted the use of local organic produce stood side-by-side on the streets. Shop windows had advertisements for yoga classes, Pilates, and newer eastern teachings I had never heard of. This was clearly a vibrant mountain community with a strong environmental ethic, a common coupling of traits for towns that are built on an appreciation of the lifestyle options on offer in such surroundings.

We retired to a pub and had two tankards of beer each. After an hour, the familiar figures of Anna Rodgers, our director, and Ros Bartley, our cameraman, appeared. The four of us were to spend the next six days together and the plan was to make significant progress in terms of filming, if relatively little in terms of kilometres travelled. Anna and Ros's goal was to gather enough quality video footage to be able to prepare a trailer for a documentary film, which could be used to attract sufficient financial support from the Irish Film Board to enable the completion of a full-length version.

Anna began by prepping us on what she wanted from the week, while Ros explained we'd need to ride past the camera several times over, several times a day to achieve the 'action' shots (never did a term feel so misplaced as that one!). We would also be required to give longer, more in-depth interviews about the trip so far, and would be filmed performing our normal day-to-day activities, such as cooking, setting up tents, and maintaining the bicycles. The pair joked about the dramatic advantages and commercial potential of a possible bear attack or seeing us getting lost in the wilderness; however, they had at heart a genuine grasp of what trailing us would be like. Our basic activities would be the same at each step of the journey, with only the backdrop and our place within it changing.

We cycled just 15 km the next day, and this was as close to a rest day as we had experienced in three weeks. The entire afternoon was spent filming on The Whistlers – a popular mountain reached by tramway overlooking Jasper, and then with Helen and Gerry Kelleher, a local couple who had offered to let us camp in their backyard. Helen is originally from Cork but moved to Canada in the 1980s, initially working with the regional tourism board. Our meeting with the couple would contribute to the Irish diaspora element to the documentary, which had now been identified as a 'hook' to encourage financial backing of the project. Although this idea was mine at the outset, Lee and I had discussed and refined it as we travelled, and we had now decided not to pursue it too forcefully in any research or preparation, preferring instead to take it up only if obvious opportunities arose. We both favoured chance encounters with locals over organised ones; we decidedly disliked the idea of a contrived meeting just for the purposes of filming someone and their story. In the 54 days before Jasper, we had taken the camera out numerous times to record the people we came across by chance – people that would only be around us for a few minutes or less, such as other cyclists, small-town storekeepers or passers-by on the highways. Even then, our experience in many instances was that, as soon as we pressed the record button, the natural response of those we interviewed was to tighten up and speak uncomfortably once they faced the camera. Consequently, we often ended up taking our leave from them with the regret that we hadn't simply used the opportunity to get to know them in a more real way with what little time we had.

Although until this point Lee had been generally disinterested when it came to filming, he was in high spirits for the entire time Anna and Ros were with us. In fact, having new company had the effect of totally changing the atmosphere, dynamic, and our routine interactions. With a fresh focus for our direct attention, different faces to tell our stories to, and new topics of conversation, Lee was in his element, and he had all of us in tears of laughter every day. I hadn't seen him so outgoing and talkative in a long time, as he vied to come up with the most slapstick comment on whatever subject was under discussion. And while we didn't have a physical break from cycling for very long at this juncture, the mental breather from the intense and oftentimes strained company we had been keeping with each other paved the way for relations between us to become friendlier once again.

We visited all the principal sights along the Icefields Parkway, the scenic thoroughfare linking Jasper in the north to Lake Louise in the south. We passed by the wide and thunderous Athabasca Falls and the silent Bridal Veil Falls, named for its slender, mist-like cascade from a precipitous cliff edge. We fought painstakingly up the 2,035-metre Sunwapta Pass, where a black bear was visible as a faraway dot in our peripheral vision. We camped close to the 6-km long Athabasca Glacier, which protrudes as a giant toe of the greater Columbia Icefield and lumbers down the valley, terminating close to the road. The Parkway was wide and hosted minimal traffic, yet its sizeable shoulder was in a dreadful condition.

Even though we were enveloped by some of Canada's highest mountains and most extensive ranges, the cycling was easy-going compared to northern reaches of British Columbia and Yukon. We always preferred one or two lengthy climbs as opposed to a day on rolling terrain, as that way, we could focus our minds on the top and put our heads down to grind the mountain out.

Since Deadhorse, we had suffered just one broken chain and one flat tyre, both on Lee's bicycle. We weren't sure if this was particularly good luck, or simply a consequence of the higher-grade componentry we had fitted before leaving. Our fortune ran out impeccably, however, at Saskatchewan River Crossing – a most awkward place to experience technical troubles. It began when Lee noticed a faint protrusion on the rim of his rear wheel.

'Hey, come here. Can you see that there, on the rim?' he asked. He was running his finger over a bump that made noise each time it spun around and connected with the brake pads. 'I think the rim has snapped,' he groaned.

I kneeled down and looked closer. There was a two-inch crack parallel to the braking surface. I didn't know much about bicycles, but I understood that 30–40 kg of pressure was only going to enlarge the crack until the entire thing came apart.

'We haven't been riding over any gravel. Did you hit anything, a pothole maybe?' I asked.

He shook his head. Throughout the trip, we had been careful to keep a safe tyre pressure so as not to exert any undue strain on the rim. The only conclusion was that the weight of food, gear, and water upon a brittle rim had been reason enough for it to fail. It was impossible to repair, and Lee would need a new wheel built in a bicycle shop that could source better quality parts.

'I'll call around and see if there's a shop close by,' I said and walked into the souvenir store to find a phonebook.

Of course, there wasn't a bike shop in the middle of the Rocky Mountains, and we both knew it. I got hold of mechanics in Calgary and Revelstoke, but they were 260 km and 300 km away. Lee, who took over calling duties after inspecting his bicycle some more, found a store in Banff, 135 km further ahead, that could source a rim within four or five days. We decided against riding that distance for fear the crack would widen, eventually making cycling impossible. Needless to say, when Anna and Ros arrived back from an afternoon filming scenery, they were most likely silently pleased with the fact they had some misfortune to document.

Lee's wheel problem forced us into taking motorised transport for the first time on the trip. Earlier, and further north, we had ridden in a couple of pilot cars around road works, but we had had zero choice in that matter. This was officially the first time on our journey that we would miss cycling a section of road. Both Lee and I adamantly believed that every inch of road from Deadhorse to Ushuaia should be cycled, unless it was absolutely unavoidable to do otherwise. We felt that doing so would bring us a sense of achievement which would far outweigh any toil experienced over endless Andean passes, washed out roads, and any struggle against mental debilitation. Also, the idea of an unbroken cycle ride from the northernmost point accessible by road in the Americas to the southernmost city in the world just had a nice sound to it.

Some would argue that the notion of cycling every inch of the route was absurd and that laying this down so rigidly as a rule rather than simply a preference might end up hindering the actual enjoyment of the ride. Now however, halfway through Canada, we were to already to fall short in the effort, and yet, although I could have easily pedalled to Banff in a day and a half, I decided instead to stick with Lee in solidarity.

Banff, however, did break the pattern of successive days in each other's company and as such our time there was imbued with a sense of self-determination. On the first day, after the departure of Ros and Anna, who were heading back to Ireland, we met a couple of the seasonal blow-ins who had come to work on ski slopes and stock supermarket shelves to enable them to pay for weekends snowboarding and skiing. They offered us couches for a few days, and so we spent a couple of nights in their house off the main tourist drag and away from the clamour of late-night partygoers and fluorescent 24-hour pizza houses. On the second night, unable to settle inside where it was too hot and the air stale, I camped in the garden amongst sun-stained plastic tables and some flowerbeds.

Sixty-three days had passed and in that period, Lee and I had spent no longer than a few hours apart from each other. We got on well, but it wasn't as natural and fun as we had had it in Denver, as sedentary guys drinking beer together and talking nonsense into the night. While we had never really fought, unease surfaced in the form of extended periods of silence, grumpiness, and brief, heated exchanges on issues such as the video diaries and the appropriate time to call halt to a day's cycling. At times greater tension crept into our companionship and this, I am convinced, was exacerbated by our refusal to engage with it, and just argue it out. As a consequence, the opportunity for some mental space afforded by our time apart in Banff gave rise to some alternative thoughts on the trip which hadn't previously occurred to me.

Diary: 16 September 2011, Tunnel Mountain campground, Banff, Alberta

Recently, I've been thinking about what it would be like to travel solo for a while. It's been really nice spending some time apart in Banff and just hanging around in coffee shops, emailing, writing blogs, Skyping Áine, Mam, Dad and Alice, and reading. I wonder if it would be possible to experience even more if it were just me? I think having the freedom to make all your own decisions would be amazing. It's easy to get lazy making them when it's two people.

Once Lee's bicycle was repaired, we departed Banff and rode back along the Icefields Parkway to Lake Louise, where Route 1, otherwise known as the Trans-Canada Highway, splinters to the west and wanders through Yoho National Park and on towards Revelstoke, British Columbia. Lee was happy and I was experiencing an uncomplicated *joie de vivre* too, spurred on by the tunes on my iPod that Áine had sent to Prince George, and which I now listened to for the majority of the day. It had been a massive addition to the journey in that sense. Jorge, a Spanish friend, with whom I would travel with in southern Mexico many months later, would repeatedly tell me that, 'Cycling is about cycling – no music, nothing external: just the road ahead.' I'd like to agree with such a purist approach, but many find that the allure a trip holds at the outset does not always persist to the same degree for its entirety. Truth be told, on very many days the surroundings are just dull, and the goal is simply to get from one place to another, hoping that the monotony can be relieved by a warm meal, starry sky, or a good book. And even when one rides through a landscape which the most romantic words may fail to describe, music can complement it more than any other thing, adding a soundtrack to what will eventually be multi-layered memory.

Rain showers were skirting the green, alluvial plain below Kicking Horse Pass as we descended 1,600 metres towards it, our bicycle frames flexing with the bumps from an uneven surface. A light haze lingered in the air and the sun's rays broke weakly through to lighten the dripping, black rock that surged upwards from the roadside. In late afternoon, we passed the Spiral Tunnels, a section of railway track which had been blasted out of the mountainside in 1909 to provide an easier gradient to enable the Canadian-Pacific Railway to scale the Rocky Mountains. If one is lucky, it's possible to see a train enter the first tunnel and appear out from the second, doubled back on itself and steaming up the 2.2 per cent grade before the final carriage has even entered the mountain's warren.

Even more dynamic, epoch-defining mountains of Canada rose around Rogers Pass within the Selkirk Range. Our elevation plateaued while our path stayed in proximity to the Columbia River, but as soon as our bearing changed westwards once again, we began a slow ascent into the clouds. The rain, which started as light drizzle, now escalated to a persistent deluge. As water streamed down gullies at the roadside, I watched from inside the hood of my rain jacket, which framed my vision. Raindrops pounded the jacket and it crackled around my ears. The tape on my handlebars was sodden, and so were my waterproof gloves. My shoes were saturated with water, and I scrunched my toes within them. It grew unnaturally dark at an early hour, and we could see nothing on the map that indicated a town, a service station, or a roadhouse with shelter.

Lee was drenched, and his hair stuck to his head in wet clumps. He asked what we should do.

'I don't know. Maybe keep going a little while and see what's ahead,' I responded. 'There are some red triangles on this tourist map, here. Might be something to check out.'

We kept moving and I prayed we would find a house or empty building to camp in – anything with a roof. The road entered a new grade, with the olive-green pine trees appearing to lean backwards at an angle from the slope. My speedometer dropped from 6 km/h to 4 km/h.

After another kilometre, we passed a small lay-by with some grass and a picnic table. Lee didn't want to camp there, as it was illegal to do so within a national park and a ranger could move us out in the middle of the night.

'Come on, we have to. Nobody with even an ounce of compassion could shift us in this horror,' I said.

We set up as rapidly as our frigid hands would permit, but not in enough time to prevent water forming in shallow pools inside my tent. I stored the pannier bags in one of the vestibules and crawled in through the other side to find a cloth to wipe down the lining. I opened the two front pannier bags, where I kept my clothes, some scotch tape, a few tools and a small stainless steel pot. All was wet, everything inside a darker shade of its original colour – T-shirts, pants, cycling shorts, socks, and underwear.

Frustrated and soaked through, we boiled some pasta, threw in some tuna and cheese and ate this on the picnic table, which was partially covered by overhanging trees. It was the first significant, lengthy downpour of the trip and didn't appear to be letting up. I woke twice in the middle of the night and could still hear the rain beating down on the dome of my tent, sending streams of water to the ground outside, its level rising hour by hour until the blades of grass disappeared from view.

The next morning, we awoke to that familiar sound once again. The warmth of the sleeping bag was almost too difficult to rise from. I could see drops of rain fall from the end of the flysheet onto the ground and collect in a small puddle where my panniers rested against each other. But then, by what felt like the grace of some benevolent force, the skies began to lighten and a tinge of blue became visible on the far side of the wispy, quickly parting clouds. Within an hour, the mist had lifted to reveal mountain ridges blanketed in snow from the migrating storm. Huge, crudely-shaped pinnacles of rock rose in three directions around us, turning our previously bleak surroundings into an amphitheatre of natural grandeur. By the time we reached Rogers Pass, our clothes were still wet, but the air was fresh and had a biting chill to it. On the grounds of the Glacier National Park visitor centre, which sits in a rock bowl at the top of the pass, I laid all of my spare clothes on the grass to dry. I bought a coke in the nearby hotel but was later given a free meal of potatoes and bacon by a Costa Rican chef named Rodolfo after I finished warming my socks under the bathroom hand-driers. A sorry-looking cyclist could generate any amount of pity, I thought.

It is 275 km from Rodgers Pass to Kamloops, and within those kilometres British Columbia – which we once more found ourselves in – undergoes a strange climatic shift. The land of mountain ranges, protected areas, alpine grasses, and ubiquitous rivers is left behind for the dry, uniform, and browner plains of a Canadian 'Wild West'. Thirty kilometres from Revelstoke, the real change confronted us with full force. We spent our morning's ride rounding Three Valley Lake and Griffin Lake, in what I felt was one of the best days riding so far. A gentle, sloping gradient, where pedalling was necessary but required negligible effort, pleasantly cool air like that of bright, spring mornings in Ireland, and a basalt-coloured valley, half-lit in the morning sun all conspired to make a striking vista.

Around midday the temperature began to rise and the hills grew scorched. Vegetation was subtly yellower, but some stands of pine could be seen on the fringes of hills. Farther along, in the more open plains, sagebrush was dominant and the semi-aridity was fully in evidence. We were in an area where cold weather and precipitation was blocked from entering, sandwiched as it was between the Rocky Mountains to the east, and the Coast Range to the west. The crass presence of industry always seems somehow stronger and more potent in such climates, and the Canadian-Pacific Railway rattled passed us every hour, carrying, westwards towards Vancouver, grain, coal, fertilisers, sulphurs and chemicals, forest products and spare automobile parts.

After Kamloops, Lee and I entered the most fractious period together since we had begun. Disagreements over issues such as seeking an Internet connection at campsites rather than looking for areas to wild camp, and the fact that the production company was suggesting changes to our route plans and public interactions, became incendiary points of conversation.

'Sometimes it feels like you're not even here,' Lee told me in Cache Creek. 'Wanting to use the Internet every time we stop. It's like you're not even on the trip.'

In no way did I feel disconnected from the cycle, but he felt that I was, and maybe I needed to examine what that meant for him. Yet I didn't want to apologise for needing to contact Áine, so I didn't. It was too crucial to my happiness and our relationship at this stage. The real issue, I felt, had more to do with our incompatible personalities and how this affected our shared space. Silence pervaded too much of our time together, and eventually we both allowed it to remain that way. We were both at fault, both equally unable to reconcile it. I felt Lee was a little too solemn, and when he broke out of this and into a more jovial state, I couldn't just adapt and quickly embrace the change. I felt that I was toning down my own personality to match his, but some of his reserve was likely created from that discordancy as well. Yet Lee never complained or insinuated that he wasn't happy with me as his cycling partner. My own concurrent inability or unwillingness to express my feelings and thoughts about our friendship perhaps frustrated him, as I'm sure he would have preferred me to be honest and open and more assertive in daily decision-making – which I was happily passive about. However, I should've taken more responsibility for my own approach to the situation and confronted it, but I didn't, and this probably made it more difficult for us to be candid about the rooted negativities in the situation.

In advance of an enormous 14 per cent climb onto the Coast Range Plateau, we stopped to view the final stages of a salmon run on the Seton River, peering into the water from a wooden bridge built two metres above the flow. Hundreds of salmon lay stationary in the water, too weak to travel any further in this, one of nature's greatest migrations. Others, white in colour – a sign their lives were coming to an end – laboured against the stream by the grassy riverbanks. The stronger salmon had already travelled to their birthplace weeks earlier to spawn, and these were the ones left behind, the lost party of a wild journey.

In Pemberton, a bucolic town skulking in the valley at the other end of the Plateau, I challenged my fear of confrontation, and finally spoke with Lee about our deteriorating friendship. For once, we talked calmly, although with evident strain. Our grievances with one another were debated in a constipated manner. We each agreed to become more aware of our unconstructive behaviours – the crankiness, daily sense of frustration, anger, and general mood. To my mind, these weren't necessarily negative – they were pretty normal, but it was perhaps important to guard against the damaging ways we expressed them.

As we moved out of Pemberton in the rain, Lee asked me how Áine was doing and I asked him how his family were. This was a rare foray into personal territory and the lives we lived behind just cycling, and I had a renewed hope that we could manage our friendship a little better. But 'manage' sounded pessimistic, and I was already convinced that splitting from each other was the only way to purge our joint discontent.

We first caught sight of the Pacific Ocean at Howe Sound, an island-dotted inlet located south of Squamish, the rock-climbing capital of Canada. It wasn't the ocean proper, but would be the closest we'd come to it until reaching Oregon on the US coast a month later, and it marked 73 days since we had left the Arctic Ocean at Deadhorse. As we were firmly within population centres once again, our camping spots had to become more imaginative. In Squamish, we befriended a girl working in Starbucks and she advised us to search for a camping site in the woods that grew near the centre of town, which were accessed by a muddy path behind a small humpback bridge. As we pitched in the midst of nettles and thistles, it was uncomfortable and wet, but it didn't cost a penny. Not once on the trip thus far had we considered paying for indoor accommodation, conscious of the need to keep our costs down. Whenever we slept inside, it was through the hospitality of others.

From Squamish, we calculated it was 80 km to Vancouver, and achievable within the day. The sun shone periodically through bright, fluffy clouds and the air was warm with a gentle salted breeze whisking in from the Pacific. Along Howe Sound, tiny villages hung discreetly from the cliff sides. The road rose and fell with tiny increments, as it obeyed the contours of the land. Near Britannia Beach, we met Paul Everitt, a British traveller touring across Canada from Halifax to Victoria on his quadra-cycle, or as he preferred to call it, 'bikecar'. Human power has no limits, even in terms of eccentricity, I thought.

As the traffic began to heave in rush hour around the city, my legs grew stronger and felt charged as we advanced towards our destination. Around 5 p.m. and just after Horseshoe Bay, the Sea-to-Sky Highway turned east and followed the smaller, craggy Burrard Inlet. With deep crimson light cast from the sun, we caught our first glance of the soaring skyscrapers which are neatly packed into downtown Vancouver, their windows glinting in the light. We could see cars driving along the waterside roads, cyclists speeding past them, and enormous tankers breaking waves in the ocean.

'We've just cycled from Prudhoe Bay, Alaska, to here. From tundra to metropolis,' I said to Lee. We both smiled, noting this smaller accomplishment within the greater one.

I thought about the previous two-and-a-half months – how incredible it was to see all of this by bicycle. In the overwhelming sentiment of the moment, I savoured a sense of the freedom, the most pure and honest joy from the simplest of machines. Of the 74 days, we had spent just seven sleeping with a roof over our heads. We hadn't missed a thing on the bikes. We had heard every sound and interpreted every smell, our eyes constantly exploring the newness around us.

We descended towards Lions Gate Bridge and joined the enclosed bike path. The land- and seascape was golden now. Off to the west, somewhere distant over Stanley Park, the sun radiated its remaining intensity across the city, calling a close to the day and the northern leg of our Pan-American ride.

4
West Coast

Vancouver, Canada to San Diego, United States – 2,900 km

OUR ARRIVAL IN VANCOUVER WAS made even more pleasant because of Dave Wodchis, a landscape gardener with a colourful bicycle touring history, who offered us a place to stay. Dave knew about us through a friend who had been contacted by our production team, in a bid for us to meet other cyclists, and he was more than happy to trade two beds for some road stories.

> **22 September 2011: Email from Dave Wodchis:**
>
> *Do you have a place to stay in Vancouver? I can offer you hospitality and connect you with lots of cyclists in the city for a meet-and-greet. I've cycled a lot, including South America to Ushuaia, Lhasa to Everest, blah blah, blogged too. I'm part-Irish but typically Canadian. Anyway – offer's open – not much advance warning needed. In fact, none really.*

'Ok, so the house is yours for a few days. I come and go, but here are keys for you to get in and out. Bread, cheese, other food – all yours. Fridge has plenty in it and most importantly, the Kilkenny beer is on the bottom shelf. I figured you might go for that first,' Dave said, with a grin on his face.

The shelves and walls in the living room were decorated with all sorts of trinkets and handicrafts from Dave's travels. He lived in a way that was conducive to getting away and exploring the world. Working hard for a couple of years, he'd take trips that were the most out-of-the-ordinary, and he would come back, replete with anecdotes and tales of misadventure in some remote corner of the globe. His cycling stories resonated with us, and as we had only taken in a tiny segment of the Americas, stirred us a little more for the path ahead.

'I remember Ushuaia so well, arriving there, muddied up from the wind and rain in Patagonia,' he recalled. 'But for me it was Peru that made South America. Big, big climbs, friendly people, back roads and trails either side of incredible mountains.'

I was interested to know what were the biggest challenges ahead, things we might not expect or hadn't comprehended from research.

'Well, here you've got sealed roads for one. You're not gonna find that, once you hit the real South America. The big transport arteries are paved but the fun stuff is away from that. Plus, dirt roads that just go on and on forever are only forgiven for the downhills that do the very same!' he said, laughing for a moment as if he knew something we didn't. 'You'll love it, though. That's where the adventure kicks in. This is just an appetiser.'

Dave intoned his words as he spoke about the roads, the mountains, and the people, his voice and hands rising and falling along with the imaginary contours of the landscape. His eyes were bright and awash with nostalgia.

'One night, I had pitched tent in southern Argentina. It was one of those weary days, where all I ached for was some bed rest. Of course, the people are so sociable there that you're never guaranteed a full night's sleep. So around midnight, I heard someone call out to me from the other side of the flysheet. "Hello, are you in there?" said a man.'

Dave lowered his voice to a whisper. 'I popped out my drowsy head, only to see some bearded *gaucho* with a fork in his hand asking me, "Do you want to share some meat?"'

Dave was smiling as he leaned forward in the seat. 'This is what you can expect. Maybe not just like that, but you'll get some cheery local with a can't-be-beat offer and it's a shame not to take it. Share time with locals. It will change your entire perceptions of the continent.'

I had been looking forward to the first day in Vancouver for quite some time. Both Lee and I had agreed to spend time apart and gain much-needed space, so I planned to walk around the city, doing little more than drinking coffee and watching the haste of city life go by.

Vancouver is throbbing with arts and culture, which lives side-by-side with green spaces, super-fit residents, and hundreds of miles of bike and running lanes. It's also a perfectly placed metropolis, if there ever was one. With the picturesque Victoria Island to the northwest, the ocean just minutes away, mountains on the doorstep, and west coast sunshine a few hours to the south, it has 'liveable' attributes in abundance. However, the previous two-and-a-half months looking at forests, hills, rivers, and the land around us had been exploration enough for me, and although I'd usually stretch to a museum or landmark, I opted out this time. Instead, I had organised to meet Marcus Dietmann, an 18-year-old German we had crossed paths with a week before. We had been looking for information about a campsite and flagged down a passing car, in which Marcus was one of three passengers, all solo backpackers hitchhiking to Vancouver.

Marcus wanted to know *everything* about bicycle touring. From the moment he met us, he was captivated, and even more enthused about continuing his trip south on two wheels, so I said I'd help him plan it out.

'I went up to that bus in Alaska. You know, that one from *Into the Wild* — the book?' Marcus told me over a coffee.

'Yeah, I do. I remember seeing photos of Chris McCandless outside of it.'

I had read *Into the Wild* by Jon Krakauer a few years before, and was fascinated by the life of US-born McCandless, who after university had just upped and left his normal life to travel the United States, often just living off the land. In September 1992, his body had been found inside an abandoned bus in Alaska: he had apparently died of poisoning after eating seeds containing toxic chemicals.

'He never should have died out there. Wasn't actually that far from safety — just a few kilometres away, there was a bridge over the river he couldn't cross. I mean, we got to see it in summertime, so I can't imagine what a freezing winter there would put you through.'

Although aware that McCandless was now something of an icon, and that a visit to his bus was an increasingly popular 'pilgrimage' experience, I was intrigued as to why Marcus had sought it out?

'I'm not sure. Why does anyone go to a place like that, whether it's a famous monument or a holy site? I guess there's just some draw to it and instead of wondering why you are interested, it's best just to go and find out from there.'

His outlook on travel belied the fact he was just out of high school. He felt that he should have an experience before committing to four years at university, and travelling by any means, whether it was bus, car, foot or bicycle, he was determined to get it. So I explained to the best of my ability what he should expect from cycling the west coast of the US, despite the fact I had yet to do it myself. It all seemed such a light endeavour to him, and before we finished our drinks, he had pledged to make it happen. It was some weeks later that he cycled out of Vancouver on a tourer he earned by working in a bike shop, and a short spell after that, we would meet again in San Francisco.

Lee and I spent seven days in Vancouver, and as a result I came to the conclusion that there can be no underestimating the power of time alone. In fact, it became so enjoyable that by the time we were ready to leave the city, I had made the decision to travel solo, for the time being at least. Truthfully, I knew I craved a permanent split, but I felt a responsibility to Lee because I had compelled him to come on this trip, even when he had initial doubts during the planning. Now, with over a year of travelling left, I was deciding to go it unaccompanied, forcing him once more into a decision about his own future. But I had yet to figure out exactly how to tell him I wanted the remaining 24,000 km to myself.

I felt thoroughly miserable about my decision, as an interminable rainstorm followed us out of Vancouver and towards the Canada-United States border. Then again, this was the Pacific Northwest, where sombre skies and rainfall are regular features of everyday life. Mid-afternoon, we rolled into the US and eventually arrived in Bellingham, Washington State, where the warm and cosy confines of our Vancouver host, Dave's house, were replaced by a sodden back garden hosting an overturned wheelbarrow and the relics of a once functioning barbeque: a man we bumped into at a local supermarket had offered us space to camp in, seeing as we couldn't find another free option and the hour was late.

As we prepared dinner, the air was motionless and the only noise was that of rain clanking onto sheet metal at the rear of the garden. After tinkering with the stoves until they lit, I made an attempt to tell Lee about my decision. Considering we weren't saying much anyway, it seemed like the appropriate time.

'Hey, I've been thinking,' I said almost apologetically.

'Yeah?'

'Well, um . . . do you . . . ever feel that we don't get along as well as we should?' He didn't answer, but palpable unease swept through the garden. 'In Vancouver, I decided that I should continue on my own for a while. I don't know exactly what to put my finger on, but we've not really been enjoying time together as much as we should. I think I'd like more space for a bit, because we've spent so long with each other and I think we've both suffered from it.'

'Ok,' Lee said. I knew he was listening intently but he didn't hint at agreement.

'I feel . . . I think I've been far too quiet on the trip and it's not your fault, but I'm not being entirely myself. We've even said this before. About how I am naturally a talker but have found myself being too quiet, and how you don't like speaking about personal stuff too much. Because right now, we're not really getting on so well in that regard,' I said, to conclude.

'I've thought about cycling on my own too, but don't think I would ever have acted upon it,' Lee said. 'We're alike in so many ways, but dissimilar in many too.'

It felt awkward and strained, standing there in the pouring rain, dressed head-to-toe in waterproofs, with only one muted slant of light from the house illuminating the garden. There was no true clarity in this response, but I sensed he accepted my decision.

'So, what you're saying is that you want to split for good?' Lee continued.

'Not entirely, I just want to see how it goes for a while and then maybe we could work something out,' I said.

'Basically, you're saying you want to split for good. You can be honest, you know,' he responded sharply.

'I am being honest, and I don't know what'll happen down the line, but this is all I know for now.'

He was right: I had a strong inclination towards separating from each other permanently, but hadn't the courage to say it. He had identified my own weakness before I could do anything to address it internally, and perhaps bring it up later when I had worked out a way to vocalise things.

We ate dinner without engaging any further with each other, though we were physically just a metre apart. I went to bed with a stifling feeling of pressure over me as I shuffled into my sleeping bag. The issue was out in the open but by no means resolved. I didn't want to make a noise he could hear, as I was embarrassed by my very presence, and was weighed down with an irrepressible sense of guilt for having done something as simple as expressing the truth.

Diary: 4 October 2011, Bellingham, Washington

After leaving Áine at the airport, this was the hardest thing I've had to do. I could be blowing this out of proportion, but the feeling is rotten. Lee didn't seem angry or annoyed but was definitely frustrated about my beating around the bush. But how do you tell someone you can't see the original deal through to the end?

In the morning we rode to Everett, a mid-sized town about 35 km north of Seattle. We were in a surprisingly good mood, considering the tense discussion the night before, and took in 105 km of unremarkable urban scenery. During the day, a decision was made to go our separate ways in Seattle and reconvene in San Diego about six weeks later. Not only would entering Mexico together be prudent for safety reasons – if we were to believe what we'd been told – but this would also give us the chance to start afresh, although we both knew deep down that if almost three months wasn't time enough to form a bond, then what was? But agreeing to reunite did allow us headspace for a time and say farewell instead of goodbye.

In just over 1,700 km of coastal cycling ahead of us lay Mt St Helens and the Cascade Range of Washington State, Redwood forests, Big Sur, San Francisco and the sun-soaked beaches in southern California, along with a distinct change in climate. Where before there was always an element of surprise in travelling through the partial wilderness of our route, I now had a firm idea of what was ahead. The cities were a major draw – Seattle, Portland and San Francisco being centres of liberal political leaning, with environmentally conscious citizens, and of course, incalculable microbreweries. I'd likely meet a greater number of touring cyclists and camp within state parks, which, if I were fortunate, would host a shower block and bathroom. These luxuries, along with regular shops and gas stations, had appeared only every couple of hundred kilometres in Canada, and would now be in plentiful supply along my projected route in the United States.

I didn't wish to stay long in Seattle, as the prospect of my newfound touring independence held too much excitement to linger in the city. So I decided I would stay to watch Ireland play Wales in the Rugby World Cup, and leave the next day. Lee was booked into the same city-centre hostel as I was, but had decided to go rock climbing for a couple of days with some people he met. As it was dark, I took the bicycle to a bar that was showing the Ireland–Wales game, riding on the footpath for safety. But with the lighting out on a section of the path, I didn't notice a raised concrete slab right in front of me, and I hit it with such force that I was thrown over the handlebars. I landed headfirst into the traffic lane, and pounded the surface: fortunately, my helmet absorbed enough of the impact for me to remain conscious. Further down the road, I could see the blurred lights of cars approaching at speed. Dazed and hurting, I had enough sense to wrap my bloodied hand around the bike frame and drag it to the kerb. I looked down at the rest of my body, but saw nothing – it was too dark to even make out the condition of my clothes. I then sat resting against a steel fence, feeling the cold steel pressing into my back.

Ahead, in the direction I was travelling, the faint signage of a gas station was visible, but when I started to get up a sharp pain ripped through my midriff, cutting into me with every minor turn and action. It was almost unbearable, but subsided if I took shallow breaths and stayed upright as I made my way along the road. At the station, I went to the restroom to take a look in the mirror. My pants and top were torn, my right knee was bleeding, and there were scrapes in long lines along my hands and right shoulder. All cosmetic, I hoped.

I didn't sleep much that night. Every time I moved from a sitting to standing position, the pain was excruciating. Getting into bed was the hardest: I needed to lie down on my chest first before turning slowly onto my back. Undressing myself, taking a shower, and climbing stairs all brought on acute bursts of pain that would force my whole body to recoil towards my abdomen. Foolishly, I didn't see a doctor – I knew it was my ribs and that nothing but rest would repair the damage. They may have just been bruised, but the pain was so severe and so deep that at least one rib was surely broken. Unexpectedly, I found that a hunched cycling posture didn't produce any ill effects at all, or none that I could feel, at any rate. So instead of staying put, I opted to leave Seattle a few days after the accident, to forge through whatever pain came and move south, in as protracted a manner as necessary.

I left Seattle on an overcast mid-October morning, saying goodbye to Lee outside our hostel. 'I guess I'll see you down the track somewhere.'

'Yep. We'll stay in touch as we go, and see what happens. There aren't too many miles between here and southern California anyway. It'll pass quickly,' he answered.

'True,' I said. 'It feels like yesterday since we left Deadhorse, eh?'

I secured my dry bag to the rear rack and locked my panniers. We gave each other a hug and that was that. We'd already discussed the pertinent facts of our situation in the week before, even if some elements were still unresolved. And for once, I accepted that just as it was.

I boarded the Bremerton ferry in Seattle and sailed west across Puget Sound, with scores of boisterous seagulls circling and swooping overhead. The short crossing meant avoiding Interstate 5, which runs through sprawling suburbs and out of Seattle before reaching Olympia, the state capital. I'd make it there within two days on an alternative route, but on near-unoccupied roads channelling through areas of Douglas fir and alder.

It felt a little strange without company once I left Bremerton behind. When a line of cars would pass and then disappear around a bend, the natural silence would creep in. Where before I could hear Lee whistling or the distant creak of his pedalling, there was now a complete absence of sound, save for my tyres skimming shallow puddles.

I camped in Belfair State Park, getting in remarkably late despite covering just 30 km. As far as I could tell, I was the sole resident of the campground, and so I chose a large site in the RV-designated area, instead of the partially flooded 'hiker/biker' patch. This seemingly innocent decision didn't please the park's 70-something matriarch, who stormed over from her hidden trailer to demand the full vehicular fare of $25. After I explained that I didn't wish to sleep submerged below the grass line, she offered me the site for the standard cyclist's rate and toddled off back into the woods, visibly pleased with her interjection.

The pain was agonising that night. My mind was not yet accustomed to reminding my body not to roll onto its side, and I woke over and over again, with a sharp burning sensation on the left side of my chest. It was just fleeting and disappeared as quickly as it arrived, but was energy-sapping and enough to pull me from sleep each time.

The next morning, over a delightful breakfast within the sun-dappled woods, I elected to sleep indoors for a week if the price was right. Even if it didn't do much in terms of my recovery, it would at least grant some reprieve from the strain of pitching and packing away the tent.

Olympia was ideally located 90 km away, and I cruised towards it with a steady tailwind, alongside the finger-like Hammersey and Little Skookum inlets and the edge of Oyster Bay. Chez Cascada was the only hostel in town, according to a quick Google search on my phone, so I checked into a dorm room that had two other guests.

'Wow! Is that your bicycle?' said a greasy-haired man with a pockmarked face who was sitting in the corner. 'I bet she's got miles on her. You know, I've got a bike too, but I don't care to cycle it much, 'cos those roads are so dangerous. Still don't stop me from carrying her around, though. Look, she's right there outside the window.'

Bob was a shaky 45-year-old ex-cocaine addict with an infectious zest for life. His interest in my trip was exclaimed through a series of 'wooooaaahs' and 'jeeees'; after several minutes' talking, I found him to be an affable character and roommate, if a little distracted.

'Hey, come here, I want to show you this song on YouTube. It's called "Mummer's Dance". I bet you know all about it, being Irish,' he yelled at me while I unpacked. 'It's like, traditional Irish stuff, so haunting and eerie – makes me wonder about life, you know. And I've cried to it as well, I'll tell you that.'

Once the song was over, he began loading videos of F-15 and F-35 fighter jets, explaining that his fascination grew out of his service in the Gulf War.

'I was in Iraq, but they never sent me out. The damn war was over so quick, I didn't get a chance to serve. Probably for the best, really,' he told me. 'I'm better out here, travelling without any particular place to be.'

He was a drifter and seemed to enjoy this transitory existence. He said it kept him 'steady and entertained'. The same seemed to apply to Gene, the other guest, and Bob's temporary travelling companion.

Gene was a little older than Bob and had sad eyes. He'd been on the road for a year without plan or direction. He said he was, 'bored of what retirement offered', and instead of settling for that, he travelled from distant family member to family member, stopping off wherever his interest was piqued. His tone of voice was laced with regret or pain – maybe a combination of both – and he sighed loudly after almost every story he told. He was gentle though, and intrigued by both Bob's and my fascination with riding bicycles all day long.

'At least he cycles the damn thing,' he jeered Bob.

'Ah shut up, Gene, I bet you can't even get one mile on one,' was the answer.

I invited both for dinner in town as I was on the hunt for live music and dingy bars, but they wanted to turn in early. It was in Olympia that Kurt Cobain wrote most of Nirvana's *Nevermind* album, and I felt it appropriate to see if he had left his imprint in any of the local watering holes. As it turned out, he hadn't, at least as far as I could see.

Hair salons, banks, and restaurants took up most of the street frontage in downtown Olympia. The eateries all offered 'epicurean delights', and jazz played softly below the buzz of a talkative, semi-casual clientele. In Vancouver, I had shaved for the first time since leaving Ireland, and had bought some new clothes from REI in Seattle, so I figured I might just fit in. Unfortunately, the reality of cycling for the majority of daylight hours meant that, by the time I arrived, unpacked and showered, most businesses were closing and the streets edging closer to desertion. After three laps of the compact downtown district, my search for a dive-bar proved fruitless. It seemed that Olympia was early to bed at just 10 p.m. and I figured that was about right for me too.

The landscape of central Washington was entirely unexpected. From all the stories of rain I'd heard, I imagined I'd ride into a temperate climate and lush green vegetation, but I instead found a browning agricultural landscape, where cattle appeared to outnumber people and birdsong replaced the noise of passing cars. Around Centralia, the road lilted up and down with great regularity. As I chased the rolling horizon, grain silos peeked out from behind finely cambered hills and tractors came and went from comely farmsteads. I cycled alongside the Chehalis River, whose innumerable ox-bow lakes confused me as to which direction its flow would take next. The temperature was rising now, forcing me to remove outer layers of clothing until I was down to just a short-sleeved thermal top. It was as hot as the initial days back in Alaska, and it felt wonderful. The towns of Napavine, Winlock, and Vader were pleasant rest stops where locals would stop to offer directions, even though they had no idea where I was heading.

'Longview ain't that far now,' a dusty farmer in a clattering pick-up told me in Castle Rock, speeding off with a wave.

'You want a lift to wherever you're headed?' another said outside of Kelso.

My countryside breather was broken by Longview, a town I could see and smell from 10 km away. White plumes rose from smokestacks and drifted northwards, becoming more foul-smelling by the mile. Longview was also the first place – and the last as it happens – where someone attempted to steal my bicycle. Normally, I would bring it inside a supermarket when shopping and ask the security guard to keep it secure while I took five minutes to pick up necessities. However, in Longview's Safeway supermarket, the nervy manager was afraid of what I felt was an unlikely lawsuit.

'Just last year, an old lady sued us because she tripped on her shopping cart,' he told me. Staunch in his opposition, he asked me to leave the bike outside. I did so reluctantly, but checked back before the aisles blocked my view and saw a young man attempting to stroll off with it. As soon as he noticed me running out in panic and anger, he let go, threw it against a wall, and jogged into the car park.

I spent the night in a motel and had an overpriced pizza for dinner. My ribs were still aching but not as much as before, the bed rest helping. I saw that Áine was on Skype and we chatted into the night. In her big news, she had been offered a job in Tajikistan with Save the Children. It was a dream position, but not a dream destination. As her application was for the job and not the country, the proposed location had come as a shock.

'I'm not sure I want to go there,' she said. I could see how uneasy she was, twitching anxiously on the screen. 'I thought they'd send me to Central or South America, on account of my Spanish.'

She was upset and confused. Temperatures in Tajikistan could fall to −30 °C in the winter and reach 40 °C in the summer, and she'd need to learn basic Tajik and Russian. The job was based in the country's third-largest city, and with language skills taking time to learn, she would have difficulty making friends. It wasn't that any of this necessarily bothered her – Áine being a person who loved new experiences – but just that she was expecting something else. My words did little to help, and I knew they wouldn't in the long run. Sometimes words aren't what is needed: it's presence that matters. I slept uncomfortably, wondering just how many more such moments might arise in the coming months.

The next day was a race to meet a boat and beat the sunset. The Columbia River – at 2,000 km long, America's fourth-largest waterway – drains into the Pacific Ocean about 80 km west of Longview. The only way of crossing it into Oregon is by bridge at its gaping mouth or via boat at Puget Island. I dashed along the Columbia's banks, navigating several steep and winding climbs with huge, overhanging rocks above. I made the penultimate sailing of the day, just as the ropes were being untied from the dock at Puget Island. A heavy autumnal haze hung in the air between the ferry and island; soon the grassy banks disappeared into it.

In Astoria, 30 km away, I met US Highway 101, renowned for its 2,500 km of coastal splendour as it runs through Washington, Oregon, and California. My first sight of the Pacific Ocean came the next day in Seaside, Oregon, just a little south of Astoria. I sat with an ice cream under a statue of Meriwether Lewis and William Clark, the pioneering nineteenth-century explorers who completed the first crossing of the western United States close by. I watched the waves break onto the white sand beach and thought about the last ocean I had looked upon – the Arctic, frigid and still at the top of the world. The warmer Pacific waters looked quite different, energetic and purposeful in their rhythm. I pressed south to Cannon Beach, a sheltered strip of expensive houses and cafés attached to a gently-inclined beach which reaches 200 metres out into the Pacific. William Clark was the first

European to arrive in the area in 1806, and it was on this beach that he famously bartered for 140 kg of whale blubber with a group of Native Americans of the Tillamook tribe. Today, a wooden whale commemorates the amicable meeting between Clark, Sacagawea (the expedition's Native American interpreter and guide), and the indigenous Americans.

Given that I would spend the coming weeks on the coast, Pacific sunsets were a delight almost every evening during this period. Cannon Beach offered my first taste of these, and the golden sun setting behind Haystack Rock, a 70-metre sea stack in shallow waters beside the beach, was mesmerising. I wasn't alone in appreciating it either – couples strolled arm-in-arm, families walked their dogs, and others like myself ambled on the sand; all stared idly westwards.

My ribs were healing and the pain easing day by day, but I remained in discomfort any night I found myself forced to sleep in the tent due to hotels being scarce or too expensive. It was becoming unaffordable in any case to continue paying even $40 for hotel rooms, so I began experimenting with emails to motels, hotels, and B & Bs along the coast, enquiring about a discount or perhaps even a complimentary room. I didn't see it as greedy or cheap, but I was cognisant that it might come across that way. I was just hopeful that human charity could stretch to hosting me in any of the rooms unlikely to be sold in the low season. In return for such generosity, I promised to post my thanks online through Facebook, Twitter, and on the blog. With a few thousand people following the cycle, and the vast majority of those in Ireland, most accommodation places were aware this wouldn't generate a single sale, but they seemed to appreciate it all the same. So, when Hostelling International in Portland sent an email, donating a free two-night stay in a large double room, I was incredibly grateful for this, the first such act of kindness since I had sustained my injury.

'Hey there, by any chance are those pannier bags yours?' a man asked me on one of my trips at the hostel between the bike and room.

'Oh, oh yeah. They are.'

'On a long one then?' he asked. 'Me, I'm coming from Alaska, headed to Argentina on the Pan-Am. Started in Prudhoe, ending in Ushuaia,' he said, before introducing himself as 'Bob'.

Many months previously I had received an email from an Australian called Bob Stanley who went under the nickname 'Buff3y'. I'd learn later this name had stuck after his pithy attempts to get fit at the gym: to honour the failure, his friends had decided to keep it. Buff3y's e-mail had been short and to the point, indicating he'd be leaving to ride the Pan-American around the same time as Lee and I, and hoped we might meet along the way. Now, we had.

Buff3y was instantly likeable. He was self-deprecating and sarcastic, and in no rush to reach Ushuaia. After all, he was in his mid-30s and had spent the past few years in Afghanistan working in development. This was his extended vacation, a chance to ground his body and mind once again.

'This ride is like my meditation after Afghanistan,' he told me over a coffee. 'Never watched the clock once while I was over, but I suppose I don't have to now either.'

He was a well-seasoned tourer too and in the late '90s had cycled across Central Asia, from Pakistan to the Netherlands.

'Was attacked in Bishkek on my birthday that time, course I was buggered drunk and nearly dragged into a bush until I whacked the guy,' he told me in his typically dry manner.

With Buff3y, most things were consigned to humour. He didn't take himself too seriously and liked a few pints, so we got on well over two days spent frequenting one craft brewery after another. I didn't mind the closeness at all, even though I had of course been waiting to be alone for a time just prior to this – and this was most likely because I knew I could call a halt to it at any time.

'What'd you think of the Dalton? I nearly bloody died on that thing. Three days out, I had to stay with this old lady in backyard Alaska so she could feed me eggs for a day, 'cos I hadn't any food left,' he said.

'I loved it. That was some incredible road, but an absolute pain to ride, especially when you're setting out. But the appreciation for it only comes after you've got through it,' I answered.

'In what way?'

'Well, at the time, when you're actually there, you can see how great things are, but you've also got to just plod through them. The joy comes in thinking back on it. That feeling is stronger after the event, once the gruelling days are over. When you're not cycling, you can almost stand back from the scene and look at it again. All those shitty days, the really hard ones – you can feel some achievement in them from a distance, I guess.'

Buff3y didn't indicate that he agreed, but I could tell he understood what I meant. Instead we drank to how 'bloody hard' those 'shitty days' were, and how 'bloody hard' we were to get through them.

I started to create my own schedule on days off, and my time in the cities – where I generally stopped – was just spent writing blogs and newspaper articles, answering emails, and phoning home. Needing to reach the €100,000 target in charity donations for The Carers Association meant trip promotion activities took up much of my time. If I had two days off, I would usually spend the morning and afternoon of the first day writing to potential sponsors, which included everyone from airlines to outdoor gear manufacturers, asking if they could support the cycle in return for logo placement on our jerseys, plugs on the radio, and testimonials for their products. It wasn't tough to get a supportive response, but it seemed impossible to secure a deal. However, *The Tom Dunne Show*, a nationwide radio show on Ireland's Newstalk FM, invited me to do a spot every two months, to tell trip stories and renew the call for businesses and people to donate and follow my travels. *The Gorey Guardian*, my local newspaper, also published my diaries every six weeks and built awareness around my home county. Each one of these commitments took preparation and time, which I was happy to invest, once I had time away from the bicycle.

When I reached Portland, the very first of our video diaries aired on Setanta Sports, an Irish satellite sports channel. The five-minute diaries would be going out several times a day between regular programming. Since these began in Alaska, viewers at home were seeing what had happened three months ago. This was to give us enough time to film the ongoing parts of the trip and then FedEx the footage home on USB keys to the television production company. Although many tourers I later met were of the opinion that sharing such a trip on a grander scale than just a blog would effectively take away from the individual's experience and sense of control, I was eager for others to know about what we were doing. For one thing, our account might just give someone the push to do something similar in the future – in the way that Göran Kropp's book had done for me.

However, the fact that Lee and I were now both cycling solo was bound to upset the original premise and proposed narrative of the trip and corresponding film, which was supposed to feature two cyclists happy to stick each other's company all the way to Argentina.

Buff3y was heading south to Eugene, Oregon, where he had an appointment with the manufacturer of his bicycle. Even though I could have joined him and taken the opportunity for some sustained road companionship once more, I opted for the Oregon coast, where the climatic difference from the interior of the state is dramatic. I rode for eight hours and pedalled 145 km southwest of Portland, only to meet thick, temperate forest and saturated air in the last 30 km. A noticeable weather pattern began to emerge as days went by; on the mornings I left Lincoln City, Waldport, and Reedsport, the dense mist would clear within an hour or two after sunrise, until the last wisps of low-lying cloud dissipated under the heat of the sun. The cool and sunny aftermath of these very early mornings was quickly becoming my favourite time of day, and so I pledged to depart just after sunrise from then on.

At Cape Foulweather — so named for the extreme winds and rain experienced by Captain James Cook on his third voyage around the world — a magnificent grey whale breached the water's surface, just a kilometre offshore. Its powerful, arched back caressed the water with a choreography surely unmatched in the aquatic kingdom. An interpretation board at a lookout point told the story of the 10,000 km annual migration these whales undertake from the Arctic Bering Sea to the warm waters of Mexico. Like me, they would be travelling around 100 to 120 km per day and were headed for the balmy Baja Peninsula, and so it is likely we departed the northern limits of the continent at the same time.

It was in Florence, Oregon that I rekindled another Arctic connection.

'Long time no see, Ian!' shouted Rick Olson as I rode towards him on Main Street.

'It surely is, there's been a bit of distance between Deadhorse and here, hasn't there?' I replied.

The first and last time I had seen Rick was at Prudhoe Bay General Store, 101 days previously.

'I bet you're glad of the beaches and sunny weather instead of dreary Prudhoe,' said his wife, Becky, who had come to join us.

Seeing Rick was a pleasant reminder of how far we'd come. He had been there, wishing us well as we rode onto the Dalton Highway and could relate to the strangeness of beginning a bike ride in such a place. For me, Deadhorse would always be special precisely because it *wasn't* for very many others. For those who earned a living there, it meant hard work and being away from family. For Lee and I however, it was tied up with a romantic notion to depart the northernmost city in the Americas, and Rick had hinted at an understanding of our perspective. His time was limited in the Arctic anyway, with his duties almost served.

Upon leaving Florence, US 101 swings wildly in and out from the coast. Sudden and unreasonably high climbs pinched my leg muscles until they ached. Every 20 to 30 km a river would run across my path to flow hurriedly into the ocean, often leaving sand spits curling into the breaking waves. This section of my route was also frequently intersected by the State Parks, which represent one of America's finest institutions of preservation for areas of natural beauty and historic significance. The very first one ever designated was Niagara Falls State Park in New York in 1885, but today there are almost 8,000 under state administration. Oregon and California have some of the highest numbers of these; the former's coast is full of well-tended examples of what the State Parks were always intended to be. Their campgrounds are of immense benefit to cyclists, as the hiker/biker sections offer $5 pitches in relative security, often with a wash block, so I took full advantage of the peaceful camping, the picnic tables for dinner and breakfast, the sinks to wash my clothes in, and the trees on which to dry them.

In Gold Beach, southern Oregon, I met Rob Fletcher once again. Our last moment together had been at a gas station at Jake's Corner, a crossroad junction not far from Whitehorse, Yukon, where Rob had promised 'to catch us up', but we had never seen him again. Now, after a fortuitous exchange of emails, I learned he was in Gold Beach.

'I couldn't do it mate,' Rob told me as we strolled the empty main street. I understood where he was going with this. The crossroads, I believed, was almost a metaphor for his experience out here. 'You remember me telling you that? I didn't know how to change a tyre tube before getting over here.

I'm a bit of a silly bugger, really!' he said.

Rob never intended to catch us after Jake's Corner. What we failed to notice at the time was that at the junction there had been a road that wound its way to Skagway, a small fishing town 160 km west in a sheltered glaciated valley, hidden away from the rest of Canada. Skagway also supported itself through one particular industry – cruise liner tourism.

'When I found out I could catch a boat to Prince Rupert, I said, "Fuck it!", and headed that way.'

I asked him whether he had planned it or whether it was spur of the moment.

'Umm . . . well, you know I really liked riding with you two, but after that burger in the gas station, I said to myself, "Hey, Rob, what sort of cyclist eats burgers and chips for lunch and then rides 80 km up and down mountains?" So I thought I should quit right there.'

Rob's experience so far was similar to many I would eventually hear. He had left a good work and personal life at home, where he was 'pretty damn settled', as he put it, but was now out here, somewhat dishevelled and exceptionally confused as to why he kept pushing on by bike and boat even though he really didn't want to. Feeling that as a solitary traveller, Rob might have liked some company, I offered to ride with him out of Oregon and into my fourth and final US state, California.

Whilst US 101 hugs the perimeter of the great Redwood forest, the Newton B. Drury Scenic Parkway cuts right through the middle of it. At the parkway's entrance the barrier was down and there was a sign that read: 'Road Closed Due To Treefall'. Taped to the metal bar was also a small note: *Hi there, although cars not allowed, cyclists can still make it through! We went a-ways in and all seems ok. Enjoy – Trudy and Martin*. The ever-intrepid cyclists, I thought. Rob and I dragged our bicycles under the barrier, hopped on the saddles, and pedalled into the past.

Diary: 29 October 2011, Orick, California

These trees are spectacular. They are just majestic and have an aura of another time. Some are over 1,000 years old and the vegetation surrounding them looks Jurassic – big, green, leafy plants around with the dinosaurs. Droopy mosses and hanging ferns line the banks by the edge of the road, and there's a kind of reverence in the air.

The echo of birdsong rang through the still air, and a legion of damp brown giants, ancient in every twist and knot of their skin, took breath immemorial. We didn't dare speak; there was no time or need for it. Our necks were craned upwards to make out the naked light of the sky attempting to break through layer upon layer of thin green needles. Each tree was a stately individual, but we were aware of being amongst family, and one of the few such iconic groupings left on the planet. It had never felt so good being on a bicycle, in a place cars couldn't reach. There was a poetic justice in it, for the reason many are disappearing is in part due to air pollution. With an untainted atmosphere and a purity of silence around, it was as if they could breathe a little easier.

The Redwoods are an incredible species. They are the largest and tallest trees on earth, while they have a lifespan up to, and sometimes beyond, 2,000 years. Northern California and the eastern Sierra Nevada range are the only natural Redwood habitats remaining in the United States; one other rare variety exists in central China. A typical coastal Redwood forest contains more biomass per square foot than any other ecosystem in the world, including the great rainforests of South America and Central Africa. These forests are quite literally, teeming with energy and life.

The world's tallest tree, according to current knowledge, is in Redwood State Park, where we now cycled. Named the Hyperion Tree, it's almost 116 metres (380 ft) high, and is roughly 800 years old. It was an infant in the early thirteenth century, when King John sealed the Magna Carta; it reached adolescence by the fifteenth century, when Christopher Columbus discovered the New World; it acceded to maturity around the Great Fire of London in 1666. Compared to many of its neighbours though, it's just enjoying the stretch of middle age.

As we left patches of characterful forest and entered others, Rob, a tree surgeon by trade, was transfixed. He became my arboreal tour guide through northern California.

'You have any idea why there are so many trees down around here?' he asked me. He answered his own question before I had time to ponder. 'It's the road, you see. We've disturbed their roots and they've become weak, along with the soil.'

I wondered how many had been uprooted from their homes. It seemed a savage irony that putting a road through the forest was supposed to build a conservation ethic and an appreciation for our natural resources, and yet this very act had ended up destroying hundreds if not thousands of this endangered species. This was perhaps another place where humans shouldn't be, at least by car, and perhaps not even by bicycle. I imagined how wondrous would it be, to get in by foot, with only water, food and spirit in tow, and experience this grandeur exactly as it had been for the greater part of its existence?

We rode on in the direction of Eureka, one of the largest towns in northern California. During that day, I bumped into Buff3y at a gas station near Trinidad. He was with three others – Dave, an estate agent I had met a few days before, and Angela and Philip, two Germans cycling the West Coast. Rob had gone ahead of me with more eagerness than I'd witnessed before – possibly as he was searching for a hotel.

It was a game of road tag between the three of us until San Francisco. I met Buff3y and Rob again at Burlington campground amidst a grove of beautiful Redwoods. One by one, more touring cyclists arrived until there were 10 of us. Of those, half were attempting the Alaska to Argentina ride, including Karl and Felix, two Germans Lee and I had met at a campground in Tok, Alaska. There was also Maria, cycling from Seattle to Guatemala, Dave, headed from Portland to San Francisco, and Helen, travelling nowhere in particular.

The following morning, I woke desperately hungover. To mark Hallowe'en, we had plundered three bottles of whiskey, four bottles of wine and countless beers. The sun streaming through the Redwoods pierced my eyes and fuelled a thumping headache. I was however, by all accounts, the best of the bunch. By the time I left, Buff3y hadn't emerged from his tent, but I later learned he made it just 6 km further along the road before giving up to sleep it off in a nearby hotel. Rob stayed with him and maintained that although he too was in bad shape, he could've continued – except for the fact he now 'despised' cycling again.

To aid recovery, I loaded up with a greasy fry in Myers Flat. I'd need a ferocious amount of calories to engage the day's climb, the longest in over a month. Sneaking up the pine-covered coastal mountains overlooking Leggett, US Highway 1 is merciless in grade and elevation. Although I completed 110 km out of the day's 145 km in the first five hours, it took me over three-and-a-half more to ascend those final 35 km. One can never underestimate the debilitation gifted by a night of partying, and what appeared a manageable hill at first, rather hastily turned out to be a sorrowful slog around switchbacks that disappeared into impenetrable forest at each turn.

Mountain climbs – despite the inherent challenges they present – are however gratifying for the most part. There's always a top, and this, more often than not, means a descent. So, as Highway 1's serpentine obsession was left behind in a sodden mist at the summit, I accepted my reward. After 20 minutes bolting through the semi-blackened forest, with the sky turning the deepest navy before ushering in the black, I emerged at the ocean, where the sun's burning red disc had abandoned day for night.

Northern California is a good example of how the sea can cast its designs on land; it is tamer perhaps than Washington State and Oregon, where there are sea stacks and huge rocks visible above the waterline hundreds of metres out into the sea. The beaches are long and gently graded, so the breaking waves crawl and bubble rather than crash and foam. Further inland, square-fenced fields enclose grazing sheep, horses, and cattle on terrain that slopes forever towards the water. More than once, I came upon a passive cow in the middle of the road, wandering from one pasture to the next. The temperature was mild and pleasant from mid-morning to evening, with a subtle haze and light breeze that prompted me forward at both ends of the day. On a couple of occasions, cars stopped as their drivers handed me cereal bars, water, and fruit. Somewhere past Point Arena lighthouse, a couple from Winnipeg, Canada pulled alongside me, asked where I was going, and gave me a punnet of strawberries for my efforts. Two years later, Peter, the husband and his son would come to stay in my home in Ireland during their own cross-country tour.

My approach to San Francisco was, sadly, a masterclass in poor planning and execution. The route from Bodega Bay – the setting of Alfred

Hitchcock's *The Birds* – to the city itself should have been a predictable 115 km ride, with ample rest-spots over a mellow landscape. Somewhere around Point Reyes Station however, I missed my turn east towards the main highway into San Francisco, and instead continued south on the Shoreline Highway, around the peaceful Bolinas Lagoon and onto Stinson Beach, before I realised I'd made a mistake. It was 3 p.m., and although I had now added a few extra kilometres to the day's route, it shouldn't have been a problem. As the highway rose steadily for a full 30 minutes, I came to a plain surrounded by small grassy hillocks and with no city in sight. Consulting my map, I reckoned that San Francisco should have been right in front of me, with its downtown skyscrapers commanding the horizon. Only then did I grasp the fact that I'd actually travelled west and was now skirting the Marin Hills, indicated by an empty, pale-green blotch on my map with too many contour lines to count. On the other side of these lay a city of three million people, yet I couldn't hear a sound nor smell a scent of any of it. So I pushed on, resigned to the climbing, the delay, and the prospect of a night-time arrival. Two hours later, after a ride that twisted up mountainsides and dropped into nettle-strewn valleys, I was relieved when the hills finally made way for a broad vermillion sky and bustling Sausalito, an affluent suburb of the great city.

After 8,000 km of problem-free pedalling, I knew it was time to service my road-hardened bike. Considering the distance we had covered together, the mountains overcome and potholes evaded, I felt a touch guilty that I hadn't even christened it, or given it an ounce of formal identity. But in terms of possible names, nothing had ever struck me as ideal – nor did I think too much about it. I reflected though that it was remarkable that, after such a distance, not even a puncture or broken spoke had dented the bike's perfect record. But I was about to hear a very familiar story.

'You see this here? This whole thing is about to crack open,' said Marcello, who was changing my chain set and tyres at Mike's Bikes in the SoMa district of the city.

I could see a six-inch crack along the inside of the rear wheel rim, a problem indicative of too much tyre pressure or weight on the bike. It was almost identical to Lee's on the Icefields Parkway, the only difference being that mine was internal and couldn't have been seen, unless I changed a tube.

'You say you're carrying 30–35 kg? Well, you stick enough air in there to stop the tyre dragging, and it's probably forcing the rim apart,' Marcello explained. 'Could just be a bad part too, but she's gotta come out regardless.'

I left the bicycle in the shop and then walked to the Mission District to meet Elizabeth Creeley, a San Fran native, bicycle enthusiast, and freelance journalist: I had organised to do an interview with her a long time ago, as part of the documentary. Elizabeth took me on a walking tour of her neighbourhood, showing me examples of how city bike planning has eased traffic congestion and given more reality to the notion of a sustainable city. On Valencia Street, there were as many bike stands as shops, and cars had been demoted to second-class transport. The entire road was taken up with single-speed bikes, beach cruisers, and top-end racing machines, all pulsing side-by-side on smooth, wide bicycle lanes.

We strolled to Balmy Alley, an unmissable side street with the most concentrated collection of murals in the city. Indigenous Mexican and *mestizo* (people of mixed European and native American descent) artists now living in the United States have used the alley's walls to express a history of the marginalisation faced by their families and community. More recently, Guatemalan, Nicaraguan, Tunisian and other artists have contributed their work to the bare concrete.

'This is a prime example of feelings that exist behind closed doors here,' said Elizabeth, pointing to one of the most striking representations. 'You can read the fierce political and social anger that speaks from it.'

One mural depicted Mohamed Bouazizi, the Tunisian man who set himself on fire in protest against political evils in his country. The incident inspired the Tunisian Revolution and was very significant in terms of the wider Arab Spring movement. Other murals captured the essence of destruction caused by Hurricane Katrina. Yet another depicted the life and times of Michael Jackson.

Getting an insight into such a city as San Francisco is always better with a guide, and Elizabeth was truly that. She told me, for example, about the frenetic atmosphere stirred up within the immigrant Irish community there, when Gerry Adams – the leader of the Irish Republican political party, Sinn Féin – had visited the area some years before. 'Political activism towards a reunified 32-county republic doesn't just occur at home in Ireland, but here the immigrants are as alive and kicking,' she told me. The fact we were sitting outside a bar called The Napper Tandy – the name of an eighteenth-century Irish revolutionary – wasn't lost on me either.

We ended our afternoon people-watching in coffeehouses that now occupy former residential housing sites. Gentrification has taken hold in some of the Mission District's busiest streets, and art-house coffee shops are a prime indicator of it. Elizabeth and I joked about the Apple Mac and mocha latte hipster culture that now pervades, but came to the conclusion that it should remain in evidence, so we can continue to poke fun at it.

Mexico, really just down the road in terms of the distance I'd already covered, was beginning to occupy my thoughts. An acquaintance of mine knew the Vice Consul at the Irish Consulate in San Francisco, and I decided to meet him and discuss what should be of concern to the solo cyclist. I had been told in no uncertain terms that I should fly to La Paz at the southern tip of Baja California, and continue from there, but even then, *only* if I had to go there at all.

'The place is like a warzone. I wouldn't even go on holiday there, let alone ride a bike through it,' said the Vice Consul.

'But aren't the drug cartels just concerned with themselves, eliminating each other? I've heard there's no need to fret over it?'

'There are hostages taken every day in Mexico, people being murdered in major trafficking states – and the border is a battleground between cartels and the Feds. I can't tell you nothing will happen, but I can say that there's a far greater chance of trouble on that side than here,' he asserted.

I decided however to listen instead my own common sense, which told me that all those cyclists who had successfully crossed Mexico, with only extreme kindness to worry about, had to be a better litmus test. Surely, I thought, there was a greater danger of my being hit by a car than encountering violence in Mexico? So I parked these concerns at the back of my mind for now, and decided to think about it once more in San Diego.

On my fourth day in San Francisco, emails arrived from the three people I had been hoping to hear from. Buff3y had come in one day ago; Rob Fletcher was trucking his way in, with a story we 'just had to hear'; and Marcus, the young German I advised on bike touring in Vancouver, was somewhere downtown.

Outside BB King's Blues Bar, where we all agreed to meet, Rob turned up, smiling and with a cigarette stuck to his bottom lip.

'Where's the bike, Rob?' I asked and gave him a hug.

'Sold it.'

'What?' I laughed in disbelief.

'You know, mate, I can't cycle. Going to buy this nice Norton motorbike and continue on that instead. Yeah . . . That'll do the job.'

As BB King's was closed, we soon found ourselves in a jazz bar far too opulent for dirty tourers, and there Rob explained his decision to the assembled party.

'You remember that big fucking hill out of Leggett? That broke me. No more,' he said. 'To make things worse – when, believe me, they could not have gotten any worse – I stopped for a cigarette after the climb. In the ditch, I noticed this spider watching me.'

Buff3y began to laugh. He knew what was coming next.

'I wanted to see him move, so I picked up a twig, got on my knees, and rubbed the ground with it in front of him. He didn't do anything for a minute, but then he ran at me and ran back again. He wasn't that big, so I figured nothing had happened.'

Buff3y had quietened a little.

'Here's the best part,' Rob said. 'About two minutes after, I start vomiting violently, passed out, shit myself, and woke up in an ambulance!'

When we all calmed down, Rob told us the doctor said it was probably a Brown Recluse spider, which must have nabbed his hand in the split second when he charged.

'A sign from above,' Rob proclaimed, looking up. 'In a stroke of luck though, the guy who found me on the road came to the hospital afterwards, and said he liked my bicycle a lot. I told him to take it then for a grand. And he did.'

When it was time to go, Rob said he'd 'catch me up', just like in Yukon, but I think he knew he never would. Buff3y wanted to stay a few more days, so we set San Diego as a meeting point, by which time Lee and I would have reassessed whether continuing together was a wise idea or not.

I planned to make Los Angeles in just over a week and without taking a day off, but on the way to ride shorter days, so I could explore smaller towns in a leisurely way. Within two days, I made it to Monterrey, a prosperous seaside community with one of the world's most impressive aquaria. It was enchanting to saunter through glass exhibition cases filled with jellyfish, crabs, sharks, and seahorses, as well of shoals of herring and much more exotic life forms. The centrepiece was an underwater kelp forest: growing over four inches per day, it is fed by Monterey Bay seawater, which adds natural movement to this living museum.

By this time, acute pain in my ribs had been replaced by stiffness, and I resolved to begin camping regularly once again, at least until I crossed into Mexico. However, as I left Monterey, an unexpected invitation arrived from the manager of Post Ranch Inn, a hotel about 80 km down the road.

Four hours later, as I struggled up the steep driveway of the inn, a neatly-dressed man with gelled hair and a beaming smile came out to greet me.

'Mr Lacey, I presume?'

Wiping the viscous mixture of sweat and sun-lotion from my eyes, I confirmed it was indeed I, the filthy cyclist.

'We've been expecting you. Champagne or sparkling water?'

'Sorry, what was that?'

'Would you like champagne, Mr Lacey?' he repeated.

'Ah . . . sparkling water would be great, thanks,' I said.

Roses, Persian wall hangings, and polished mahogany furniture adorned the lobby I was guided into. Bryan, the Reservations Manager, had received my email a few days before, and was more than happy to offer this tramping cyclist a private bungalow overlooking the captivating Big Sur coastline, 200 metres above the ocean.

'We were impressed with your challenge and thought one night under a roof would make your travels through the US a little easier,' Bryan explained. 'Our rooms usually cost $600–2200 per night, so we've reserved a special bungalow for you.'

Damp and smelly, dressed in torn bicycle shorts, and sporting a mangy ginger beard along with salt stains on my shirt from sweating, I felt rather out of place. All around were the elite of California's high society. Every so often I'd catch a wisp of lavender in the air or look out to see a Lamborghini pull up. I hadn't been checking the star ratings of the hotels I e-mailed each morning, instead just sending a general enquiry to each of those listed in the local Chamber of Commerce directory. Never would I have had the temerity to take a chance on something so different to what I was used to, and so I actually felt terribly embarrassed, waiting in the lobby to be driven to my room.

At dinner, sitting at a candlelit table and surrounded by doting couples, I wasn't sure how to hold myself. I wrote in my diary to distract my attention from the surroundings. However, one of the diners took an interest in my presence.

'Is that a novel you're working on?' said an elderly man in a tweed jacket with slicked back hair.

'I'm just taking some notes,' I replied. 'Maybe it'll be something more in the future.'

Before he had a chance to quiz me anymore, the waiter arrived. I nodded politely as he elucidated the contents of my Celery Root Agnolotti with Parmesan Brodo and Garlic Confit.

My uneasiness wasn't merited, as the hotel had treated me exceptionally, but I guess the anxiety was acceptable considering the $200 meal and $30 glasses of wine I was able to enjoy, all without placing a hand in my pocket.

I felt refreshed the next day, and as I hurtled downhill and out of the grounds, I thought about the previous evening's proceedings. I promised my ribs that we'd go out on a high and no longer look for complimentary lodging. I'd just hit the jackpot and there was no value in being greedy now.

Between Carmel and San Simeon, California, exists a 140 km area of inexpressible coastal beauty, known as Big Sur. Here, the Santa Lucia Mountains sweep down to the sea, leaving only the tightest of space in which to squeeze in a road. Experiencing this particular stretch of exquisite land is best done on bicycle. The sound of waves crashing into the steep rock cliffs 100 metres below is a reminder of what shaped it. Coves and crescent beaches no more than 20 metres long are everywhere and visible from the highway which curves its way about the rock face above. Below, waterfalls plunge from rock terraces onto the sand, where portly seals lie loafing in the midday heat.

At San Luis Obispo, a dry desert breeze stole in to replace the sea air. In similar fashion, industrial agriculture had now replaced forest, and seasonal immigrant workers – the majority from Mexico – had supplanted the affluent communities just a few hours north. The land was flat, so cycling was easy and the new rear rim on my bike held up well, delighting no doubt at panniers now 3 kg lighter.

The *Los Angeles Times* carried a short 'What's Hot and What's Not' travel feature on *350South* in October. PR work we knew nothing about was being continued by the production company in Ireland; they had finally found some traction with a reasonably prestigious newspaper. As it happened, we were seen in the final analysis as both 'hot' and 'not-so-hot', the former an honour bestowed upon us for merely hopping on the saddle; and the latter because of our apparent failure to update the blog enough.

The article had caught the attention of a family in Westlake Village, just north of Los Angeles, and they were open-hearted enough to invite us to stay with them. Warm and motherly, Brenda Skelly was a psychologist of Irish ancestry with more than enough wall-mounted photographs of Ireland to prove it. She visited when she could and was adamant that her two children should embrace the culture and custom. Brenda was married to Dave, a successful Hollywood producer and screenwriter. On the night of my arrival, an episode of the acclaimed television series *House*, which he wrote, was due to be viewed. Friends and family gathered in the Skelly living room for a more sedate and sociable Hollywood experience than we might tend to imagine is the norm, but I was downright excited by the entire affair. Dave paused the show every few minutes to give a commentary on various scenes and explain twisting plot lines and the effects used to build atmosphere. He even included some of his children's teddies as props in his expositions! As soon as the show concluded, the phone rang off the kitchen wall, with family and colleagues offering their opinions and insights on the episode.

'You know Dave, it was much better than last week's, such tension there at the end. Great job, pal,' one person said in a message recorded on the answering machine.

'Hugh seemed really into that one,' declared another, referencing Hugh Laurie, the actor playing the show's main protagonist.

Both Brenda and Dave asked me to stay more than one night, but Lee had arrived in San Diego and I was eager to sort out our travel plans, so I headed off early the next day.

On Las Virgenes Canyon Road, a wind that couldn't make up its mind which direction to blow from tossed me left and right into the traffic. Such is the uncontained sprawl of Los Angeles that I aimed for the bike paths after Malibu, which would take me through the city in one-and-a-half days.

That time was full of chance meetings and rare encounters. First there was Darren Moore, a local eco-architect and former Discovery Channel presenter, who I got chatting to in a roadside pullout. He invited me to give a talk about my travels to 8- to 10-year-old school children in Muse School, an alternative learning initiative begun by film director, James Cameron's wife. In the two hours I spent there, I stitched together a speech about sustainable living in relation to bicycle touring and met Mrs Cameron too.

Along the Venice Beach boardwalk, I discovered male and female bodybuilders weightlifting on the sidewalk, roller-skating grannies, and Rastafarians flogging their breakthrough debut albums. The pulse of this particular beach life was infectious and overwhelming at the same time, and I felt I needed several ice-cream breaks to etch into my memory the Disneyland of colours and noise within the space. Every ethnicity must have been represented; at one moment I could smell Middle Eastern dishes, and North African ones the next.

The superbly designed maps of the American Adventure Cycling Association became invaluable in piloting my way through the chaos that the Los Angeles street system threw up. Despite sticking to the highlighted and safest routes on these maps, I found that motorists were vociferous in their opposition to my presence.

'Get off the road, you're gonna be killed!' one driver roared out the window.

And yet the dangers presented by the mass of traffic in Los Angeles were nothing, compared to those of the relative calm and serenity of Big Sur, where I had two near-misses. One involved an overtaking car that clipped me with its wing mirror, and the other, a jeep careening wildly around a corner in the fog – fortunately, the driver hit the accelerator and swerved back into his lane when he noticed my bright lights and yellow jacket.

In Torrance, Barney, a road cyclist in his mid-60s, came to my assistance.

Barney had a hunchback, veiny legs, and a face that wrinkled up to form deep creases when he smiled. A former national racetrack champion and friend, he mentioned, of the young Bob Dylan, he said he'd take me through the suburbs and across the Los Angeles River until I could find a way to Long Beach. Barney spent most of the time talking about his drug addiction in the '60s and '70s, and shed some light on what New York's Greenwich Village music scene was like during that era.

'The music was good – great, even – and everyone was taking something. That was the scene alright, always changing, always fun.'

He donated his water bottle to me, and I promised to send a photo of it to him from Mexico City – a point far enough away to highlight the great distance between the two megacities, but close enough that Barney would still remember who I was.

I was soon free-rolling to San Diego and looking out to see surfers bobbing on the water at Huntington and Newport beaches, as they waited for their waves. I spent 24 November – Thanksgiving – in Oceanside, a dimly lit, centreless city, south of Camp Pendleton Army Base, where I managed to get lost as I cycled across it. I celebrated America's biggest holiday in a Denny's restaurant, simply content at not having to cook for myself, and I opted to stay at a cheap motel.

A couple of kilometres before Cardiff – which was just a three-hour ride from San Diego – I received a text from Buff3y, who was now nearby. We met up in Starbucks, drank two lattes and cycled towards the city together. It was only a few hours before I'd reach the terminus of the west coast highway, and I could sense the impending loss of independence once again. One-and-a-half months previously Lee and I had parted ways, and in the interim period I had found an equilibrium and sense of control in travelling solo. We had spoken via email, and tentatively agreed to carry on together, but I knew that this was only important if we were to continue filming for the TV production company, but likely not for our individual happiness.

'I don't see the point,' Buff3y said, breathing heavily on a climb. 'You want one thing, Lee wants another, and there's no middle ground in that. If it's not working, fuck the TV guys and just enjoy this.'

He was right and his words resonated with me. Yet, once more too fearful to follow my instincts, I knew I was leaning towards giving it another shot;

I still had hope we could work things out.

Palm trees and red-tiled stuccoed houses welcomed us to La Jolla. San Diego rose in the distance, and so we crunched through the miles – first to Mission Beach, and then residential Point Loma before reaching downtown San Diego. An Asian couple snapped some photos of Buff3y and I in front of the enormous aircraft carrier, USS Midway, after which we went in search of a hostel in the Gaslamp Quarter.

Three full days passed before Lee came into town. He was staying outside the city with a friend, disinclined to come into the crowds unless he had to. Talk was genial but reserved. It was still little tense, but easier than I remembered.

'So, are you comfortable with us travelling together again?' I asked him after a while. I instantly disliked my own tone. I wasn't talking to a stranger, but somehow it felt that way.

'Yeah, I guess so. We said we would, so we should, right?'

'Let's see how it goes and get used to it. I'm sure Mexico will be out of the ordinary anyway. Better with two, eh?' was all I could say.

It wasn't inspiring or confidence-building, just short and to the point, with a consensus reached within a mere 30 minutes. We barely even mentioned all the various experiences each of us had had over the last seven weeks, but agreed to meet up in some days' time to continue.

Rob actually caught us up as promised – but in a rented car this time. He was charging through every possible mode of transport to get south, apart from the one he set out on. We all visited San Diego Zoo, world-famous for its conservation and animal rehabilitation programmes. But I loathed seeing the black bears in restricted exhibits, pawing at fake stone walls and without curiosity or fear or anger in their eyes, especially since, not so long ago, we had been passing them in their natural habitat in the wilds of Canada.

At night, I'd Skype Áine, who was now in Tajikistan and settling into a freezing winter. Usually upbeat, she sounded downcast, if not completely unhappy. There were some good things too. She had made friends with some expatriates in the capital Dushanbe, and travelled up there on the weekends from her posting, to party and make connections.

'It's just going out on Fridays and Saturdays,' she told me. 'So at least I've that to look forward to, but the electricity and Internet cut out most evenings here and then comes back at crazy times, like 3 a.m.'

She was sleeping under three blankets and in her clothes, such was the cold that crept into her room. I tried to hold back my descriptions of 25 °C heat, golden sandy beaches and palm trees, but when I didn't manage to, at least she laughed. Áine's sense of humour could never be beaten. I missed her terribly and told her as much. It had felt too long already, but I suppose at some deeper level, I was becoming accustomed to our circumstances, along with the knowledge that, since I had cycled merely one-third of the way down the Americas, it would be some time yet before we could be together again.

Buff3y, Rob and I wandered the streets of San Diego together for four more days. It was a city that didn't take itself too seriously, evidenced by all-day 'Happy Hours' and mammoth groups of people surfing midweek. Buff3y was flying to the Maldives for a wedding on the day Lee and I would leave, so there was no chance that three could be company. Rob had decided to fly home to Oxford to save some money, before coming back out to ride a motorcycle into South America. He knew all too well that each of these proclamations would likely be met with a mixture of doubt and encouragement from Buff3y and I. But we both appreciated the fact that Rob remained a true dreamer.

Although I felt a degree of anxiety about the impending departure, there was so much to be excited about too. We were just hours from another language, and the chance to absorb Latin culture, enjoy different food, ride through cactus deserts, and experience the delights of Spanish colonial cities. It was about to get cheap too, and a whole lot hotter. Any worries about the border had subsided, and a sense of new adventure kicked in. I bought some Spanish language books and sent home a jacket, base layers, and a pair of shoes. In instead came flip-flops, sandals, and an awful Hawaiian shirt. We'd be leaving familiarity and routine, and exchanging it for things we couldn't anticipate or imagine, but which we knew were far more coveted and valuable.

5
New Beginnings

San Diego, United States to San Juan Teotihuacán, Mexico – 3,096 km

WE WERE WITHIN SIGHT OF Mexico before we lost it again. With our backs to a scorched hillside and the faint noise of a busy freeway somewhere in the middle-distance, we checked the maps once more.

'Maybe the airfield is over there,' I said, pointing at the hill. 'If it is, then that's west. Let's just head the opposite way, hit some traffic and ask how to get to the border.'

We were riding in the company of Darren Scott, the eco-architect I met near Malibu. He had expressed interest at riding into Mexico and back to the United States in one day, so I encouraged him to come along. That morning, he had driven from Los Angeles to San Diego, bike in tow and ready for an international day out.

Despite the prominent Tijuana Arch being in plain sight, it took us three hours to locate the turnstiles that allowed us into the immigration complex. Officials stamped our documents efficiently, asking all the requisite questions about our intentions in Mexico and if we would be coming back.

'Hopefully not on this trip, though I do love the place,' I said to the pudgy guard.

Expressionless, he handed my passport back, pointed to the door, and 60 seconds later we were in a new country.

As expected, Mexican border control was a more laid-back affair. We shuffled between dusty windows, passing white sheets of paper to disinterested officials, paid our $20 visa fee and were off.

Darren accompanied us into downtown Tijuana, where we scoffed fish tacos and enchiladas, washed down by Corona beer. The city centre was calm and orderly, with people shopping, banking, and chatting on street corners. I spotted a group of elderly gentlemen wearing wide-brimmed felt hats, and mariachi music played from the restaurant's speakers – the first real cultural indications we were in Mexico. On the surface, Tijuana didn't seem to correspond to the negative media portrayal of borderland Mexico, or even the picture the Irish Vice Consul in San Francisco had hinted at. I knew we were only 30 minutes in, but sometimes one's intuition – which at this point, for me, was subtly optimistic – has more of a bearing than second-hand forewarnings on how one first perceives a place.

Luckily, Lee and I would have a roof over our heads for the night, but it was still an afternoon's cycle away. A former work colleague from The Wilderness Society in Denver had generously offered us his family holiday villa in Medio Camino, 35 km south of Tijuana, so we set off at 2 p.m., after saying goodbye to Darren.

Advice from other cyclists suggested we should err on the side of caution on Baja California's roads. As a general rule, the road, of which there was soon to be just one, was narrow and had no shoulder. Trucks, commuters, American holidaymakers, and motorcycle traffic all used this single artery to travel south through the 1,250 km peninsula – and we would be the lowest common denominator in this parade of vehicles. As we departed Tijuana, two roads shadowed each other: Federal Highway 1D was a four-lane toll road that prohibited cyclists, yet it contained a sizeable shoulder; Federal Highway 1, on the other hand, was much smaller, windier, and significantly more dangerous. We had been given a tip that, somewhere outside of Tijuana, it was possible to cycle under a marked underpass and drag our bikes up a steep bank until reaching a break in Highway 1D's railings, where we could then ride safely and attempt to avoid the *policía* – but we never did find it.

In the following days, I noticed only minor visual differences between Mexico and the United States. The scenery was undeniably similar. Beach hotels were strewn along any available ream of sand, and the roads were in immaculate condition: it felt as if we were riding on linoleum. The vehicles however were of an older and more down-at-heel vintage. Dingy mini-vans and pick-ups would shudder out black smoke in town traffic, but every now and again a sleek sports car would race effortlessly by. Often, these would pull into gated communities hidden behind sandstone walls perched above the ocean. For now, it seemed that we were in a transition zone between two very different worlds and, until the United States could be referred to as being far away instead of nearby, that would endure.

Socially, our interaction with locals was limited at first, but grew gradually as we became adept at remembering and pronouncing *hola* (hello), *muchas gracias* (thank you) and *no entiendo* (I don't understand). As Irishwoman, Dervla Murphy expounded in her 1965 book, *Full Tilt: Ireland to India by Bicycle*, language is only a small part of communication. If you want to eat chicken and don't know the word, squawk and act like one, flapping bent arms pressed to your sides. Not only will you get the chicken, but the comedic value will also break down barriers. I kept this in mind, as our paltry Spanish was sure to limit us during the initial weeks and months.

In Ensenada – the last major city until La Paz, 1,400 km away on Baja California's southern tip – we stayed at a *casa de ciclista*, which literally translates as 'a house for cyclists'. The semi-detached brick building was empty and without heating, water and furniture, apart from some ragged mattresses leaning against the wall. *Casas* are so-called, because one or more of the family members is a cycling enthusiast and wants to help fellow riders out, by providing a room and bed. They're not advertised, but knowledge of them spreads through word-of-mouth in the touring community. This house had no family attached, but was open in memory of Valdo, a Brazilian touring cyclist who died of a heart attack 400 km south of Ensenada some years before, halfway into his cycle from Brazil to Alaska. Valdo was travelling to promote peace in the world, and his recumbent bicycle, adorned with stickers from the countries he had pedalled through, with the poems of remembrance above it, was a haunting tribute.

Baja truly begins after Ensenada. Crawling up and away from the coast brings with it scrubby grassland and mountains that pierce the horizon all day long. Settlements dissipated until only small farm holdings remained, and it became difficult to determine which way the road would turn, as it proceeded directly into a landscape of thorny hills that seemed impenetrable, at least from the distance at which we were viewing it.

As we still weren't sure just how safe it was to camp, I proposed that we spend a couple of nights in motels until we developed a sense of how secure wild camping would be. Lee wasn't eager to sleep indoors, because of the expense and the increasing space we were afforded in the outdoors. And so, each evening like clockwork, as shadows grew long on the road, this debate became our subject of conversation. With 30 or 40 km between villages, once we passed them, we wouldn't be going back, so it became imperative to agree early on what we'd do. In truth, I had become a little more used to sleeping inside, and this did affect my decision-making, in that I was an advocate for paid accommodation for several days at least. Setting us back no more than 70 pesos ($5) each per night, I didn't see any harm in it. But to avoid confrontation, we aimed to mix it up every other night.

Adapting to a shared routine came easily this time around. We would do our shopping in gas stations, family supermarkets, and *tiendas*. The latter is a type of roadside family stall, which from the outside often appears to only sell crisps and fizzy drinks, but on the back shelves you can usually find pasta, cooking oil, toothpaste, and toilet roll. Variety was not a virtue of the *tienda*, but if you were forced to live from them, you'd just about survive.

Cooking went back to basics too. We could ascertain *atún* was tuna and *carne* was beef, while the smiling cartoon animals on the front of canned goods would confirm our suspicions in the event of uncertainty. With a full set of kitchenware each after the split in Seattle, we were now preparing our own meals and often at different times. Sometimes Lee would go for a walk while I cooked, or I'd assemble the tent while he cooked. This lack of synchronisation of activity and times started to become more apparent as we cycled through an increasingly barren and windswept Baja: only then I began to notice how our separate food stores, maps, cycling paces and preferences for rest stops were indicative of our evolution from a team to two individuals.

Five days after leaving San Diego, our environment had morphed into an unaccustomed world. Stopping for water on one of the hundreds of exquisitely sculpted prominences of bare rock gave us the chance to view a vista that incorporated visions of the American Wild West and a Martian landscape. Cacti were the sole inhabitants of the valleys and ridges; the only resident of the broad blue sky was the crescent moon. Lee often remarked how beautiful it was for its apparent emptiness, and he was right. Yet, in amongst this, somehow disguised between the brush and sand, live the coyote, rattlesnake, and salamander. Too harsh for humans, the desert is a prime habitat for species tougher than us, those able to adapt to waterless plains, searing days and frigid nights.

Notorious for its fearsome wind, the central region of Baja is a battle to ride and once again a tangible indicator of why almost no one lives in the wildness of its expanse. The gales picked up in intensity near El Rosario, as Highway 1 turned east to cross the peninsula in search of the Gulf of California. We were carrying 12 litres of water, one full bottle of stove petrol each, and enough food to last three days.

The wind began by whipping in from the side, shunting us dangerously out into the road. Then it would curl around behind us, giving a brief push and a short reprieve, before swiftly and angrily facing us off from the front. It stole our words away as soon as they were spoken and scoured our faces with the moving desert sand. Our speed dropped to 6 km/h, three times slower than normal. We could no longer tell if a truck was approaching from behind, as the sound was unable to reach us. We'd repeatedly check over our shoulders, scanning kilometres behind for that quick flash of sunlight off an approaching cab. We'd shout in warning to each other if a truck were close, and when it passed, the vicious pull of its slipstream would draw us to the middle of the highway, the roar deafening our ears.

At the lonely outpost of Guayaquil – a forlorn collection of wind-lashed outhouses in a stretch of endless desert – we drank tea in an old lady's house that also served as a trucker's rest stop. No more than a dark room with rattling windows, and sooty kettles and pots hanging above the wood-burning stove in the corner, it was marked as a town on the map, such is the vacancy of this part of Mexico. Three kilometres past Guayaquil, we happened upon a grove of leafy trees, each about two metres high. It was the first concentrated patch of vegetation we'd seen all day, and although it was just 3 p.m. (with sunset to be expected at around 5 p.m.), we sought refuge within it. It was the perfect windbreaker and once we were inside, it was impossible to sense the howling gale turning the sand into dust devils just 20 metres away. Close by, a herd of inquisitive cattle, somehow braving the elements too, kept us company.

Early camping was forced upon us because of the short daylight hours, but this gave us the chance to occupy ourselves with other things in the evening. We finished dinner by 5 p.m. and then took a short wander around our back garden for the night, clambering to the top of the nearest hill in search of a view, if there was one. The temperature dropped quickly after sunset, so we layered up with thermal leggings, extra-long sleeved shirts, and our insulated jackets. The only reason to remain outside any longer was the stars, and how incredible that sky at night was. Thousands upon thousands of shining pinpricks were cast in layers across the darkened ceiling; the swirling arm of the Milky Way, the constellations of Orion, Gemini and Cassiopeia, and the nebulous blue Pleiades spread across our field of vision. There was nothing – not the sound of a single car, or, when we were lucky, the gusting wind – to disturb our lying down and looking up. Eventually the cold won and we retired to the tent to read by headlamp. I hadn't read enough books while on the road, but I intended to right this during the long nights of our time in Mexico. *The Kite Runner*, which I had begun in San Francisco, was the first due for completion.

> ### *Diary: 6 December 2011, 3 km south of Guayaquil, Mexico*
>
> *The desert was in spectacular form today, and even with an incessant, end-of-the-world type wind, I was in the mood to appreciate it. Giant cacti three times our size were growing out from between the rocks. The cows here, funnily enough, are scaring Lee! He thinks they might charge at him but they couldn't be more passive! Getting in so early is fantastic. We've so much time to wander and read and not rush to sleep, meaning we can buffer cycling with actual relaxation.*

The following day I noticed that my rear wheel hub (the part in the centre of the wheel which connects the spokes to the rim) wasn't catching properly when I pedalled. In essence, it meant that, as I spun the pedals around, I got no forward motion in return. When it eventually did lock in, I was able to power forward once more until I had to slow my revolutions, such as when going downhill. It would then disconnect again, and only after a few minutes would it reengage. On and on went the issue, until we were forced to find a dry riverbed to camp and try to figure it out.

The next morning we rose with the sun at 6 a.m., and I went to see if I could uncover the problem. I had absolutely no idea what I was looking for, but took out some spanners and Lee's chain whip, released the wheel from the frame, and removed the cassettes from the hub with great difficulty. The problem didn't appear to be anything external, and I hadn't the equipment to poke around internally with the hub itself, so I put everything back together.

'Could be inside the hub, bearing issues or something else,' Lee said.

'Yeah, seems to be. Can't ride on like this though, it would be stupid and I'd get nowhere.'

I had two options. I could get a lift to the next town south with a well-stocked bike shop and competent mechanic – but by my reckoning, that would be La Paz, 980 km away. The other scenario would be to return to San Diego, where I could take my pick of mechanics and explain the issue in English. As the $450 hub had a lifetime guarantee, I opted to return north. This also meant I wouldn't miss any of the road in Baja, and could hopefully return to this exact spot to continue.

Lee asked if he should come with me, but I told him to carry on and enjoy Baja at a slower pace. 'I'll catch up with you in La Paz. If I can get back tonight, have it fixed by Monday and get a bus back here for Tuesday, I should just be about five days behind,' I said. Lee agreed with this plan, but said that he would at least wait with me until I found a ride back to San Diego.

An hour passed and not one of the dozen or so cars, minivans, or trucks which had passed during that time acknowledged my outstretched hand and thumb. As hope was fading, a blue dot on two wheels appeared 200 metres up the road, moving in our direction.

'Problem, fellas?' said the cyclist and came to a stop.

Andy Peat was from Scotland but had left San Francisco a couple of months previously on his way to Argentina.

'Rear hub's gone, so I'm going to head back to San Diego and get her fixed. My name's Ian, by the way,' I said and shook his hand.

'Ian from Ireland?'

'Accent gave it away?' I said attempting to be sarcastic.

'Well, yes – but no. I met your mate Buff3y back in California. Camped a night with him near LA.'

It all seemed rather opportune. I didn't want to leave Lee alone in the desert, but now he would have Andy, or so I hoped. I somehow managed to get my hub connected again, and the three of us set off to a point on the map marked as Chapala. The *Guía Roji* map Lee bought in San Diego covered the entirety of Mexico, but regularly had towns marked where there were none. It was a little disconcerting when it came to planning for supplies in isolated regions of Baja, as luck would determine whether we would be able buy food or water. However, Chapala *did* exist – although it consisted of just two buildings, one of which was a ramshackle wooden store, selling coffee and vehicle lubricants. The outside was littered with polystyrene cups and oil cans; behind the building a grey dog tied to a post barked incessantly. I arrived there ahead of the others, having been forced to keep pedalling at speed once my hub locked in; they decided to take things at a more leisurely pace.

By the time Lee and Andy got there, I had built the foundations of friendship with a 25-year-old Mexican tomato truck driver named Jesus Orlando Ibarra. Jesus spoke English, but barely. As an illegal immigrant in the United States for five years, he had basic conversational skills and just enough to understand my explanation in a poor blend of English and Spanish – which I had been learning from a book mounted on my handlebar bag for the past four days – of exactly what had happened. Jesus agreed to give me a lift, and I said goodbye to Lee and Andy (who had now arranged to cycle together), secured my bike and panniers in the sleeping cabin of the 18-wheeler truck, and we shot off towards Vizcaino, 200 km south. Jesus was collecting a trailer full of Roma tomatoes there before driving back to Tijuana, from where they would be imported into the United States. I was happy to do the southern part of the journey with him, in the knowledge that we'd be returning north afterwards.

Jesus wore a sleeveless denim jacket, Ray Ban sunglasses, and was twice my size, even though we were the same age. He was from Sinaloa State, and had returned to Mexico one year previously, in a more comfortable manner than he had left – in 2006, it took him and three friends four days to walk from Sonora State in the north across the Arizona desert to a town where some acquaintances lay in wait. From his explanation in broken English, I could ascertain that it had been a journey fuelled by the hope of better money, but not necessarily a better life. His family and girlfriend at the time still lived in

Mexico, and his social ties and security were here too. He wanted Mexico to remain his home, but a higher income would bring the possibility of buying his own house and putting a future child through school. However, as with that of so many others, his luck had run out, and deportation papers for him were processed. Now Jesus found himself driving a truck back and forth to the country that had expelled him.

If riding a bicycle was terrifying in Baja, driving a truck there was equally so. Unbridled fear came across me each time we passed another vehicle.

'Look . . . mirror gone,' Jesus said at one point, pointing to the driver-side wing-mirror.

It had been ripped off by an oncoming semi. The road was so narrow that when a truck passed us, Jesus would have to quickly and skilfully steer the truck off the road and back onto it in one rapid movement, just to avoid being hit. The sharp compression of air between carriages sounded like a gunshot, and behind, in the passenger-side wing mirror, stones could be spotted flying up from the sloping gravel verge we had swerved back from. This pattern repeated itself all day long, until the futility of worrying about a crash finally sank in, and my anxiety simply dissolved into a sleepiness that came upon me with the advancement of nightfall.

We left Vizcaino again at 11 p.m., having just heard the news that one of Jesus' friends, a fellow driver, had been killed on a mountain road known as 'El Espinazo del Diablo' in central Mexico. Directly translated as 'The Spine of the Devil', the road already had a deadly name for itself and Jesus backed this up by telling me that his friend's lorry had crashed over the edge and down into a valley. Happy and talkative earlier in the day, Jesus now looked pale and forlorn.

On the way back to Tijuana, we stopped for burritos in a fluorescent restaurant, where a dubbed film starring Denzel Washington was playing. The tables, chairs, and walls were coloured red and white – the colours of Tecate beer – as with every other building and roadside diner in Baja, it seemed. Jesus and I ate in silence and then promptly left for the border, in a convoy of trucks carrying lettuce, sweet peppers, and other vegetables.

The following day at 4 p.m., I said goodbye to Jesus in a truck yard just east of Tijuana. The smell of burnt rubber and gasoline hung heavy in the air.

'Send me a mail and keep in contact,' Jesus instructed me. 'I want to tell you about Dani, my new girlfriend. She will visit from America soon. I'm very excited.' He certainly looked it, his eyes shining with the mention of her name. I promised I would, and slowly wheeled my bicycle out of the yard and towards the United States once again.

San Diego was much the same as before. I quickly established that it would take one week to have the new part ordered and installed. During this time for the most part, I wrote blogs and took photographs. To be in the United States again felt like a step backwards, to a place all-too-familiar – a regression of sorts, where city life was too organised and predictable. I had just left the desert, and had now been transported back far too quickly to its antithesis. It was this rapid change that generated a lag in my mind, accustomed as I was to the pace of a bicycle and the gradual shift from complete emptiness to scattered houses, then to suburbs, and then to town or city.

However, I did take the chance to connect with some of the Irish community in the city, who had organised a Christmas party, to which I was invited. An evening of singing Irish rebel songs and talking to people with familiar accents was a nice brush with home at this time of year, one which was always a big occasion for my family.

Meanwhile, Lee was almost in La Paz so I had a lot of catching up to do, but he was fine with me starting from Chapala again, if I could manage to reach such an obscure station in the desert.

I met Buff3y, who had returned from the Maldives, and we cycled out of the city and into Tijuana once more. After some time together, I was sad to see him pedal away, as I knew what a good cycling companion he'd be. But I understood that he – just like myself – was often more comfortable alone.

An argument with the bus driver of the Tijuana–La Paz Express, about my wish to be dropped off in the middle of the night at Chapala, required the handing over of extra pesos to both the driver and bus attendant. To their credit however, seven hours later I found myself watching the tail lights of the rickety bus disappear into the cool night, as I set off to blindly pitch my tent in the spiny land behind the store I had left one week ago.

Towns came and went, as I then rode three consecutive 140 km plus days. My legs felt strong and I enjoyed every minute of the scenery and people. As I crossed the border from Baja California Norte (North) to Baja California Sur (South), I was aware that there was a greater military presence in evidence. Although the peninsula's two provinces are considered among the safest in Mexico, armed soldiers still man small barracks every few hundred kilometres. The Spanish language book wrapped in its plastic pocket on my handlebar bag generally forced a laugh and a largely unintelligible conversation with the soldiers, whereupon they would decide to stop searching my pannier bags for contraband.

Undoubtedly one of Baja's gems is the palm oasis town of San Ignacio. Not in my wildest imagination did I believe such a place could exist amidst heat, dust, and dryness. The land had originally been occupied by the indigenous Cochimí of southern Baja; in 1706, a Jesuit mission was founded there. The mission was abandoned in 1806, but what remains to this day are a late eighteenth-century church, plaza, and some delightful side streets. Bounding the entire sleepy enclave are thousands of palm trees fed by a trickling river and natural spring pond. Realising it would be a shame to pedal on, I found a $10 hotel room, and lounged in San Ignacio's square for the evening, where a youth concert was taking place.

Passage from the Pacific to the Gulf of California was finally complete when I reached Santa Rosalia. In the main square I met Salvatore, a Spanish cyclist I had encountered fixing his tyre a couple of days previously and whom I now agreed to split a room with.

In 2005, Salvatore left Granada, Spain to travel the world by bicycle. He hadn't stopped when I bumped into him on the 20 December 2011, and had no immediate plans to either. He had come from Africa but had already journeyed through Southeast Asia, Central Asia, Europe and North America. His repertoire of experience had included getting lost in Indonesian jungles, living with Kyrgyz families, and being severely beaten in Russia. However, it was the central lesson of the last story that had the most emotional impact on me.

'Fear and intuition are bound together. You cannot separate them, nor should you,' Salva began.

'However, intuition is your friend and you need to listen to it. Call it what you want. Call it the voice in your head,' he continued. 'When I first went to Russia, I entered with fear. I was scared approaching the border. Within an hour a dog had bitten me on the bicycle, and I knew something bad was happening. But, I continued anyway and didn't listen. Then, a few days later I was attacked by bandits and, only for a passing car, the first in three hours, I would never have been rescued.'

Salva then decided to leave Russia through Vladivostok and cross to China.

'I waited until I felt a sense of difference come over me and went back to Russia again. This time everything was fine, as I paid attention to the signs, and my intuition about the place. Of course, you can't understand it fully, but everyone has been somewhere where something doesn't feel quite right, or you are aware of a change or danger coming about.'

He then told another haunting story about Peru. He had been travelling with his girlfriend and stopped a passing pick-up to ask for directions to a campsite. 'The pick-up had maybe eight or ten Europeans in it, many in the back. They were going to climb a mountain in the Cordillera Blanca, but I saw this ghostly look in one of their eyes. He knew I could see it, something troubling. News came the next day that seven of those climbers had died on the mountain. The guy I noticed didn't listen to what his fear represented,' Salva recounted.

Now Salva was toying with the idea of crossing to mainland Mexico and cycling to Copper Canyon to see the Rarámuri tribe, a people known for their long-distance running and isolated living. 'I've heard that bandits sometimes dress up as police there, so I'm wary. This is the type of decision I need to be ok with.'

Salva left a strong impression on my attitude to travel, and I rode out of pretty Santa Rosalia with more questions than answers. Even when we spoke about Alaska, where he had also cycled, he spoke of it not being 'adventure' in the true sense of the word. 'There's always a safety net,' he'd say. 'Always a passing car.'

I agreed. He wasn't trying to dilute any sense of journey or travel being important in itself, but I could see he meant adventure really only happens when things go wrong or are thoroughly unexpected. He had enough first-hand experience in this for me to consider it a statement worth pondering, however I was sure I would discover elements of truth in it through my own encounters.

> **Diary: 23 December 2011, south end of Bahía Concepción, Mexico**
>
> *More interesting chats with Salva this morning: he really is a fascinating character and knows how to tell a story. He spoke about humans being animals too, and getting caught up in city life and not connecting with nature as a way of destroying our animalistic instincts. He believes strongly that the more we remove ourselves from what is natural, the more we lose these traits. His stories seemed to back this up, but I think I'll be contemplating them for a while to come.*

A strong tailwind whisked me along Concepción Bay; it was Christmas Eve and one of the best days on the bike thus far. I felt festive, even though it was 20 °C and I was sweating heavily throughout the morning. I played 'Fairytale of New York', 'Driving Home for Christmas' and other holiday songs on my iPod, and every so often a pick-up would overtake me, with its driver and their family in the back throwing their arms aloft, shouting, '*Feliz Navidad*' (Happy Christmas) as they moved by.

The bay was a greenish-blue and, carved out of its softer rock, were pristine white strands. One blustery night I camped in a thin gully that hooked down towards a beach; I woke up chewing sand at breakfast the next morning, and rooting it from my clothes as the day progressed.

The seaside town of Loreto deserved at least two days' exploration and therefore would be my home for Christmas. It was the first one spent alone, but I had sunshine and an ocean view to make up for it. With Mexico being a steadfast Catholic nation and very family-orientated to boot, the streets were empty but some shops remained open. For dinner I cooked potatoes, vegetables, and bacon over my stove in the bedroom, but the mush it coagulated into drove me out of the hotel in search of something slightly more palatable.

The cobbled alleys that surrounded the Mission of our Lady of Loreto were especially charming and flowerboxes burst with colour, brightening the impressive stone church. Loreto was the first Spanish settlement on the Baja peninsula, and therefore showcased resplendent mid-eighteenth century colonial architecture. I met two ladies from Oregon at the jetty, and we chatted for an hour while tall masts clinked and swayed in the breeze. Only on Christmas Day am I totally comfortable doing absolutely nothing, so that evening I ate chocolate and crisps, drank almost two litres of coke, and watched Christmas movies into the night on my laptop.

I stayed one more day to make the most of a fast Wi-Fi connection, and spent it Skyping my parents and my sister. I also dedicated as much time to Áine as possible. Unfortunately, she hadn't received the Christmas present I had posted to Tajikistan and I suspected she wouldn't either. Her best friend had also sent some gifts, including a chocolate Lindt bunny with a red ribbon and bell around its neck. When Áine received the package a month later, all she found was the gold foil wrapper and bell rattling at the bottom of the box, with the chocolate nowhere to be seen.

The only present I received that Christmas came from an elderly Mexican man I met outside my hotel. Watching from across the street, he had seen me come and go with my bicycle for two days. When I checked out on 27 December, he moved as quickly as his legs could carry him, and handed me a large black sticker of Loreto and a souvenir key ring of the seventh-century Maya city of Palenque.

'You must go here,' he said, tapping the key ring.

'I'm planning to, it looks beautiful,' I answered in poor Spanish.

'Good, you will love it. Safe journey, friend,' he said, and waved me down the street as I pedalled out of sight.

Just 300 km separated me from La Paz, but I needed to work hard to get there in the three days as I'd planned. I suffered an awful headache for the first two, and it coincided with tough drags up and over red-coloured mesas. Dehydration hadn't been an issue for me for some time, and it was always difficult to predict when it would set in. The big sun above me, the arid air, and the sea breeze combined to dry up any perspiration from my brow. Sweat is a direct and obvious sign you are losing water but I didn't realise just how much I actually was, because I couldn't feel it. However, when I stopped for a drink at a dusty lay-by near Ciudad Insurgentes, I noticed salt marks along my sleeves. I took my top off and the back was streaked white in perfectly contoured lines: it looked as if the black was tie-died white. It was 3 p.m., and I had only gotten off the bike once to pee since morning; I was only three-quarters of the way through one 800 ml water bottle. I downed a Gatorade in a gas station an hour later, but it was too late, and I shivered all night long, suffering through sleeplessness and then bad dreams in a damp motel on the outskirts of the city.

The next day I placed myself a comfortable 120 km from La Paz after riding exactly 120 km the day before. Earlier, I had made two attempts to tear down a section of barbed wire fence next to the highway, before a third was fruitful. The great irrationality about Baja California Sur is that for the immense desert wilderness it is, almost the whole thing is fenced off, five yards from either side of the road. This makes finding a suitable campsite extremely tricky, as you're not just battling the fence, but also safety issues. Unless you find a gap in the wire as well as a nearby mound or some vegetation high and wide enough to shield a tent from passing cars, you're in sight of the road. When I did unearth three wooden poles and untangled the thick barbed cable thread between them, the soil directly behind was infiltrated with cactus spines, some the length of an index finger.

On I went, with darkness descending. One hour later I rode two kilometres up a sandy access trail that connected to an outlying ranch. About 10 metres from the verge was a collection of wiry bushes and cacti, which would partially screen my tent from the road, should any vehicle come this way.

Poles and tent pegs out, I erected my little green shelter on a patch of sand I had meticulously cleared of spines. No sooner had I zipped the flysheet closed than I saw my 10-litre water bladder lying on the soil, with a fat spine through its centre and a shallow puddle around it. I found it just in time for there still to be just enough water for dinner and breakfast, but with nothing for the next day.

In the morning, I awoke rigid on the ground. 'Not again,' I mumbled, and got up groggily. I was flat on the surface and could feel stones under my back. Another spine had pierced the corner of my inflatable sleeping mattress. 'Fix it in La Paz,' I muttered, and rolled out of the tent to a gloriously cool and bright December morning.

After breakfast, I carried my panniers, patched water bladder, dry sack, and bicycle carefully to the road. There and then, I realised I'd been punished for the third time. My rear tyre was flat. A rich green four-inch spine was wedged tightly into the sidewall. Upon closer inspection, there were over 10 more spikes through the tube, which needed removal by my teeth as they were lodged so deeply in. It had taken over 8,500 km and 166 days to suffer a flat tyre, but it was Baja that eventually beat me.

La Paz looks inviting from the far-off hills that overlook it, especially after a sprint finish. The palm-fringed city tucked tightly into the bay was a fitting end point for the trans-peninsular cycle. It has a stringy beach that stretches for two kilometres, with hundreds of thatched parasols to lie and read under. The streets are indefinable as either commercial or residential for the most part, as both types of buildings intermingle once away from the seafront. Although most Mexican towns centre around a cathedral or a main plaza, the Catedral Nuestra Señora de La Paz occupies an indiscriminate location beside some coffee shops, a petrol station, and a couple of pharmacies. It's still an impressive edifice, but most definitely somewhat lost in the midst of busy streets.

When Lee returned from a few days on one La Paz's outlying islands, we met up in my hostel and talked about the rest of Mexico. From his demeanour, I knew he had something to tell me.

'I think it's best we split, for good this time,' he said straight up, just a couple of minutes into the conversation.

I was happy to hear it, and as Lee had told me in Bellingham that he had thought about us splitting up but would likely not have been able to act on it, now at least he was happy to communicate how he felt.

'I think that's a good idea,' I said.

'We have a lot of fun sometimes, but, you know, at other times we don't connect. We're just different people, and probably want to cycle in totally competing ways as well,' he added.

Simple as it was, that sentence captured everything we knew.

'Things were never going to be perfect and we understood that. And at least we gave this a go, tried it together, you know,' I said back to him.

Everything was finally clear-cut, out in the open, and without regrets. I suspected the time he spent cycling to La Paz with Andy, and reuniting with a couple he had travelled with in California, had influenced his decision. He had friends on the road and companions to move south with; they were people he liked and felt comfortable around.

The freedom I felt after talking in La Paz was a genuine one this time. Before, it had been only partial, because my mind was tied up with the weight of worry and the suppression of my negative feelings about cycling with Lee. This dissipated almost immediately after we spoke. I was now on my own, both physically and most importantly, mentally. Although I might travel with others for hours, days, or even a week or two, control over where I'd sleep, what I'd eat, where I'd go and how long I'd take to get there, was now unconditionally mine.

> **Diary: 3 January 2012, Pichilingue, Mexico**
>
> *Sitting here on the beach in Pichilingue. Said goodbye to Lee today – no hassles and no sadness. A little apprehension though about the next stage, as it's really just me now. Mainland Mexico is a place of new beginnings and a launch pad for exploring countries with every choice and turn up to me.*

Instead of hanging around, hoping to hitch a ride on a private yacht to the Mexican mainland – as many economising cyclists did – I opted for Baja Ferries. The overnight sailing would take me to Mazatlán on the west coast of the mainland, and from there, I had a rough plan to cycle southeast towards Guadalajara and on to the colonial city of Morelia, after which I'd visit the Reserva Mariposa butterfly forest and then navigate my way through the enormous web of highways, satellite towns and neighbourhoods that make up the largest metropolis in the western hemisphere: Mexico City.

Touring cyclists often frequent two other routes from Mazatlán. One of these heads due east, up into mountains and pine forest, through what is often referred to as the 'Colonial Heartland'. The cities of Durango, Zacatecas, Aguascalientes, Guanajuato, and San Miguel de Allende are worth seeing, if colonial history and warrens of cobbled streets is your thing. The other less frequented route is a coastal path through Puerto Vallarta, a sandy playground for rich city folk, and Zihuatanejo, the beach retreat where

Andy Dufresne escapes to at the end of *The Shawshank Redemption.*

My decision to take a path in the middle of these routes was influenced by two factors. The first was the fact that I'd met a couple at a taco stand in La Paz who had offered to show me around Guadalajara. The second was my wish to see the Reserva Mariposa butterfly sanctuary in the highlands of central Mexico, where one of Mother Nature's greatest migrations comes to an end – or just begins, depending on how you look at it.

For 300 km south of Mazatlán, the road is flat and the air is dry, often polluted with the stench of road kill. This smell was to be a constant accompaniment on my journey until I reached the Andes, the concrete guttering of the roads a home to the decaying corpses of dogs and cats, as well as cows and even horses.

Sugar and tobacco plantations abutted the highway for large portions of those 300 km, in a territory which was beginning to feel quite distinct from the United States. Tortillas inevitably replaced bread rolls, but otherwise I kept faith with my tuna, tomato, cheese and avocado lunch, now a staple meal and reliable source of energy. New brands of biscuits appeared in mainland *tiendas* too, so I'd generally devour a packet a day for just 3 pesos (20 US cents). The price of everything was falling. Water, pasta, fruit, cereal and coffee cost just three or four dollars per day if I rationed well, but I never scrimped on food, always bearing in mind the number of calories I needed.

I did, however, routinely forget to drink sufficient water. On the climb to Tepic, 900 metres above sea level, I suffered both minor dehydration and heatstroke. I limped into town hours after dark, feverish and weak, having badly underestimated the time it would take for the climb over the coastal mountains.

The following afternoon, as I nursed a headache at Café Diligentes – a brown, leather couched, smoke-infused coffee shop purportedly patronised by Tepic's intelligentsia – four guys about my age struck up a conversation with me.

'Is that your bike?' one asked in English, gesturing outside. 'Where are you going? Mexico City?'

I said I was, but that the ultimate destination was quite a lot further than that.

'Nooooo, that's crazy, surely impossible! If it's true, then you must be hungry? *Are* you hungry?' another one said in crisp English, pretending to fork imaginary food into his mouth.

Later that night I was sitting in a simple, mustard-coloured living room, sharing pizza with my four new acquaintances and their wives and children. Jarco, Victor, Meza and Sentero were all childhood friends from Tepic, but just Victor and Sentero, whose house I now was in, still lived in the city. Jarco and Meza would come home once or twice a year for a reunion, as well as to see parents, grandparents and cousins.

'Family is important. You should try to see them as much as possible, no matter where they are,' Jarco began telling me. 'In Mexico, family means everything. Even us, we are friends but family all the same. If you pass through any towns where we know people, you'll be welcome to stay.'

As the tequila flowed and their wives put younger children to bed, we sat around like old men, emerging philosophical about life and happiness. My new friends were interested to know why I was undertaking the cycle and what I was sacrificing. I told them, as clearly as I could, that for the most part I didn't know why I left a faultlessly happy and fulfilling life at home, but that I suspected it was something to do with a desire for movement, to counter the ease of staying still, and to see other places beyond the pages of a book or computer screen. It was the first time I'd said that to anyone on the road, perhaps the first time I'd even truly realised it through my many days spent downhearted and lonely from missing Áine. Jarco said that the need for exploration and discovery was within all of us, and I agreed it probably influenced me to leave when I needn't have.

They then wanted to hear stories from the trip, so I offered up anecdotes about bear encounters and using the woods as my bathroom, the latter of which they found hilarious.

'No trees in Mexico, friend. You must shit in the fields with the *vacas* [cattle]!' Sentero shouted and refilled our glasses.

Minutes before I motioned to leave, Victor began to tear up. He was the only one without a wife, and was worried he might never find one. According to the guys, his emotional side was apparently a feature of his late-night drinking, but nonetheless they put their arms around him for comfort. 'I'm expected to marry, but I just want someone to have a life with,' he said. He spoke gently, struggling to find the correct words in English.

Even though I was an absolute stranger, the guys didn't see it that way, and certainly not Victor, who stayed teary until Jarco's wife – a typical Mexican *mamita* – told him to 'man-up'. I eventually found the strength of will to leave, well past 2 a.m., with a heavy head from tequila and, at the guys' insistence, with the addresses of friends of theirs, who might host me through the remainder of Mexico. As would happen unfailingly in Latin America, its people could brighten the most mundane of settings, and thanks to my new friends, the very ordinary town of Tepic would remain in my memory as a special place indeed.

From central Mexico until south-eastern Panama, a procession of smoking volcanoes emerge, like lighthouses marking the flow and curves of the land. Leaving Tepic, I rounded the deep green Volcán Sanganguey, an extinct volcano guarding the highland town. By early afternoon, the mighty Volcán Tepiltic and its sheltered crater lake came into view, and just two hours later, I cycled past the iridescent lava fields of Volcán Ceboruco.

In the market town of Ahuacatlán, an enthusiastic hotel owner called Andrés Moreno offered me a night's free accommodation in a decadent room befitting an upscale country lodge. Hearing about my journey, Andrés was overwhelmed – this was real wonder, from a man who wished so much to travel. His hotel guestbook, which he protected as if it were an ancient parchment, had the signatures of 15 to 20 other 'human-powered' travellers, who, like me, he had commandeered on the streets and invited to stay. The majority had been cyclists, but some were walkers and others, runners. An Irishman called Tony Mangan had slept there for a night just two months previously. I knew about Tony: he was an ultra-runner, who was completing a marathon each day around the world. Despite several email exchanges and attempts to convene, unfortunately he and I failed to meet up further south,

'Great man, Tony, impressive,' Andrés would repeat, smiling at the relevant page of his guestbook.

Understanding Western concerns and perceptions about modern-day Mexico, Andrés believed I'd feel safer cycling through the states of

Nayarit and Jalisco with a police escort. I assured him I had thus far only ever been met with warm hospitality from Mexican people, but Andrés wouldn't take no for an answer.

Before I left Ahuacatlán with a police jeep and two officers with shotguns, Andrés insisted I should meet the mayor, whose door was apparently always open to the town's residents. After ceremonial handshakes, photographs, and accepting the offer of a fizzy orange drink, I left the town hall and tackled a 9 per cent gradient out of one valley and into the next. The jeep chugged and revved at 7 km/h behind me. It was a painfully slow climb, and an audible strain on the overheating vehicle. At times, the driver would stop, turn the engine off and wait until I travelled about 300 metres up the road. I'd hear the clinks of the engine cooling down in the searing heat. Then, three or four minutes later, a loud growl would rattle the air and the jeep would begin its crawl up behind me again, stop, and repeat the process once more.

One-and a half hours later, at the top of the mountain, I was introduced to my next escort. Destined for Amatlán de Cañas – a town I could see 10 km away through the early morning haze, buried within a vale of golden cornfields – these four officers, all wearing white polo shirts, jeans, and baseball caps, guarded me with Kalashnikovs. My Spanish wasn't good enough to have a conversation – or tell them it really wasn't necessary to chaperone me – but they didn't seem to mind. In fact, they seemed to enjoy the apparent privilege of protecting a visitor to their home territory, and in that, I felt it was an honour to spend whatever little time I was given with them.

As we continued, I raced down the other side of the mountain, taking hairpin bends like the breakaway leader in a Tour de France mountain stage. At the bottom, I returned to the normal, lethargic touring speeds I was accustomed to. As I decelerated, the police pick-up pulled up beside me.

'Gatorade – good!' said the chubby officer with a delightfully trimmed moustache, and handed me a bottle of it, grinning.

'*Gracias*!' I replied, and the pick-up swiftly returned to shadow position directly behind me.

Well separated from the *autopista* (motorway) on the other side of the mountains, the valley I moved through now was rich in colours and sounds. I had originally chosen this route because it would offer me my first opportunity to be in something approaching agricultural Mexican countryside where I could count on being almost entirely alone. Of course, now that I had my protectors, that wasn't the case, but I didn't mind at all.

In Amatlán de Cañas, an annual festival was taking place. The police pick-up driver signalled towards the plaza as we came close, and waved his arm from the window for me to stop when we arrived. Walking with my bicycle amidst a crowd of extra police, intrigued locals and several photographers, I was, yet again, at the town hall. The mayor greeted me with pat on the back and some mumbled words in Spanish. He had his mousey assistant pour me a coffee, and then motioned to a young man in a blue-buttoned shirt to come forward. Before I could ask if anyone spoke English, a Dictaphone was pushed under my nose. I intimated that I would struggle with whatever interview was about to take place, but no recognition seemed to register with them.

In the opening question, I thought I heard the verb '*gustar*', so I took it to concern how I liked Mexico. In a roundabout and broken manner, I muttered – or at least I thought I did – something to the effect of: 'I like Mexico very much and I think the people are friendly. The police especially, are very nice.'

Everyone remained quiet; the Dictaphone was still poised right in front of me. I thought they wanted me to say something else, so I said the one thing I knew how to correctly in Spanish. I had spoken it innumerable times at this stage.

'*Quiero ir a Argentina por bicicleta.*' ('I want to go to Argentina by bicycle.')

The room, now full, erupted. Everybody but the mousey assistant was laughing, with hands on heads. I guess the idea of pedalling to the town on the other side of the mountain was wild enough, let alone the notion that someone would willingly ride 27,000 km for a reason he couldn't explain, although that was purely for lack of linguistic ability.

At about 4 p.m. on the Nayarit-Jalisco border, my final escort of the day was waiting. Normally at this point in the afternoon, I would already be preoccupied with looking for a campsite or hotel, but I had come so far that I was stuck almost equidistant between Amatlán de Cañas and the next village of San Marcos. More dangerous than Mexican bandits was the looming darkness, so I rode on, with a dogged determination to make town. However, once the stars became visible, adrenalin and a sense of panic kicked in. After an hour dodging potholes by the headlights of the police car, I finally reached San Marcos. I decided to rent a room in the centre of town, close to the police station, where I was asked to turn up at 7 a.m. the following morning to set off again.

Guadalajara was 110 km from San Marcos, so I woke early to make a break for it. Two policemen were already outside my door, and after brief pleasantries we set off, bumping along country roads in the soft daylight. About 60 km from the city, I convinced Roy and Reyes, my fourth and final team of defenders, that I'd prefer to continue on my own. The two-lane highway, bordered by maize and sugarcane plantations and which fed into the heart of Guadalajara, was horrendous to navigate, and had some perilous sections of road within tunnels, where the hard shoulder simply disappeared, leaving me amongst the stream of traffic.

Isis and Marcus, a couple I met whilst scoffing fish tacos in La Paz, had given me their phone number, so I was thrilled when they confirmed I could stay with them for a few days. Isis, from Mexico, and Marcus, an Italian, fed into the stereotypes both nationalities are associated with. They fought passionately about everything, but made up lovingly, instantly forgetting whatever the problem was. Isis was the boss, and Marcus knew it. He'd throw his hands to the air, shouting and moaning at her decisions in the flamboyant manner only Italians can triumph at. Although they ran a fast-food shop near the university, they knew where to find the best authentic Mexican food I'd tasted so far. They introduced me to a taco stand selling *gringas*, a type of flour tortilla filled with *al pastor* (grilled) meat, cheese, and spices. At night, I visited the cathedral with them, its Renaissance-style exterior lit up handsomely. We took in some more eccentric activities too, such as paying for a canary in a cage to predict my love life by picking cards from a box that had been filled with seed. After the bird managed to convey a message of sorts to me, to the effect that 'I wouldn't find love until I truly knew myself' – or something along those lines – its keeper asked that I pay more money to hear more of my fortune. At this point, Marcus started to turn red with anger, and had to be pacified by Isis. It was nice to be in company again after many days alone and without conversation, I thought.

The old centre of Guadalajara is discreetly captivating. Centred around Plaza de Armas, several gardens and bushy pedestrian boulevards buffer the old town from the intensity of life outside it. Many multi-national corporations have relocated their Latin American headquarters to this, Mexico's second city, and there's a definite air of self-assurance on its streets. As a transitory blow-in, I base this observation solely on an evidently young population, a heaving arts movement, a high standard of civic maintenance, an obvious sense of pride in historical spaces, and of course the proliferation of Starbucks coffee shops, this representing for me a rudimentary cross-cultural indicator of some people's disposable income.

A remarkably progressive aspect of Guadalajara's personality is its innovative practice of 'Car-Free Sundays', when tens of miles of city streets are closed down to vehicles, and only open to walkers, joggers, performers, cyclists, and just about anyone else off of four wheels. I left on a Sunday and was able to ride 15 km through the city centre and suburbs, unimpeded by cars and traffic lights. Parents played with toddlers, dance groups practised hip-top and hula moves in the parks, and elderly couples sat eating ice creams on benches. Marcus, Isis and their friend Jose Juan cycled with me to the *autopista* and we said goodbye at a junction where the road veers east towards Morelia and onwards to Mexico City.

My thoughts on the journey from Guadalajara to Morelia were again dominated by Áine. It had boosted my confidence to hear that Marcus and Isis spent three to four months apart each year, when he would return to Italy to work and see family. However, what began as just a physical distance between Áine and I had now grown into a conversational one. How many times could I tell her about the wonderful places I'd seen and people I'd met, without her doubting how seriously I took our relationship? I was afraid of being *too* happy during a call, in case she should think I wasn't missing her, or didn't want to share my experiences with her. It was another inconsequential mind game for me to play with myself – no doubt a product of spending so much time in my own head – and, I told myself, one that made little sense to dwell on.

A night in a fetid $5 motel room in Panindicuaro marked my six months on the road. The cycle was going to take far longer than the 350 days I had initially planned – simply running my finger from Alaska to Mexico on a torn Americas map I kept with me was assurance enough of that. If anything, it would be another seven to eight months, at least. Although it wasn't a race, it felt like it to me, because I knew Áine was waiting. Balancing this consideration with the desire to see the world by bicycle, and at a pace conducive to doing it justice, consistently plagued my mind, but I knew it must be achievable at some level.

Realising all of this, I made the decision to visit Áine in Tajikistan. I wanted to see her desperately. I hoped, as much as one could, that letting her know I was committed to us in person, and by action, would make our time apart easier and more bearable. So I booked flights from Bogotá, Colombia for 17 March, St Patrick's Day. The decision to travel from Colombia on that date required detailed route planning, but the life of a touring cyclist being what it is, I was aware that I could easily fall short of my destination. There were new challenges and new terrain ahead – bigger mountains, worse roads, unmarked distances on maps, and a boat journey around the marshy, guerrilla-inhabited forest of the Darién Gap separating Panama and Colombia.

As I approached Morelia, the temperature rose uncomfortably. A suffocating heat and smell emanated from the black asphalt of the road, and my tyres looked exhausted as they turned over the sticky surface. I was riding through the state of Michoacán, an area of huge geographical variation. This band of Mexico is strewn with oddly-shaped lakes that roads wind neatly through. At an altitude of 2,000 metres the vegetation is mostly pale green brush, starved of water. At higher elevations conifer forests dominate, while lower down it's possible to encounter mixed tropical and broadleaf forest. As for recent history, Michoacán played a seminal part in the Mexican War of Independence in the nineteenth century, and it was here that the Jesuit priest, Miguel Hidalgo y Costilla led his army to victories against the Spanish, effectively ending their centuries-old rule.

Morelia is another example of an astonishingly well-preserved historic centre. The Plaza de Armas, built in the sixteenth century, is almost unchanged to this day, and provides a space for local and national festivals to take place. Surrounding the Plaza are stone portals, backed by graceful, colonial-era buildings. Exploring the old quarter was best done on foot and each street had qualities distinct from the others. Rose gardens, petite coffee shops situated down sloping back-alleys, and cast-iron balconies overlooking cobblestone courtyards were all magnificent aspects of a city steeped in a terrific sense of history.

My Spanish was improving to the degree that I could now ask about the attractions and sights best viewing, but this was done mostly for conversational practice: Morelianos were cordial and chatty, and didn't fail to direct me to what I'm sure were intriguing areas of the city – but I never did understand everything that was spoken between us. Instead, I just wandered and took photographs of whatever looked characteristic of city life, such as the Mercado de Dulces, an indoor market selling every colour and variety of local sweets and jellies. I bought a half-kilo bag of purple and red fruit-shaped candy, and ambled to the town's seventeenth-century aqueduct, where university students were hanging out, lazing in an adjoining park.

On my second and last evening in Morelia, I carried out a purge of unnecessary gear, clothes and other items that I hadn't needed since my last clear-out in San Francisco. I was afraid of another rim failure, and was mindful that three or four crumpled mountain ranges lay ahead before I got to the Andes. One by one, I emptied my four pannier bags onto the hotel bed. First I went through my clothes. Tattered items like old socks, a pair of fuel-stained shorts and two faded T-shirts – victims of the incessant sun – were thrown out. I considered passing some of this to a second-hand clothes shop, but felt it would be an insult, handing in things so road-beaten. Next, I scoured the inside of my cooking and camping pannier. Useless plastic forks, a cracked food container and a spare fuel bottle were put aside. The pannier holding tools and repair equipment suffered the worst fate. I ditched extra gear cables, a couple of spanners whose function I wasn't even sure of, as well as cable ties, a bungee cord, and one of my two spare tubes. My burst water bladder was also discarded. Instead I would start carrying extra two-litre plastic bottles, as I didn't expect to be very far from people again for quite some time. In truth, I never really was anyway, and I could always flag down a car if need be. In total, I shed 2.5 kg of baggage, a substantial weight. Items that might be of use to others, such as the spanners and fuel bottle, I left by the bed, with a note I hoped would indicate that they were giveaways.

Over the next two days, I climbed from a height of 2,000 metres to over 2,500 metres, and ended up in the mountainside hamlet of Angangueo. The altitude gain brought a wintry air with it, and disguised the fact I was getting painfully sunburnt on the top right-hand side of my head, from my eye to my ear. I had ditched the highway towards Mexico City and turned south, climbing steadily into patchy forest where the clearings were covered with short, mossy grass more akin to the horse pastures of the Himalayas than central Mexico.

Angangueo was exciting for what lay on its doorstep. The Reserva de la Biósfera Santuario Mariposa Monarca – or Monarch Butterfly Reserve and Sanctuary – is quite simply one of the world's most magnificent and awe-inspiring natural wonders. Every year, when the warm North American summer creeps to its close, one of the planet's greatest natural migrations begins, as 60 million to 1 billion monarch butterflies leave their homes east of the United States and Canadian Rocky Mountains, and commence a 4,000 km journey to the pine and Oyamel fir forests of Michoacán state. After spending several winter months at an altitude of between 2,800 and 3,600 metres, they travel north once more in February and March, returning to their ancestral homes in North America. No one individual completes the entire round trip: the journey is concluded between the two to four generations of butterflies which live and die during its course. It isn't yet known what exactly guides the monarchs north and south, but it's believed to be the result of an inherited compulsion. Other theories include the butterflies having some kind of internal compass or map, which obliges, and enables them to travel the staggering distance between North America and their highland dwelling in Mexico.

The science is moving in itself, but nothing can prepare the visitor for this astonishing cradle of nature. Millions upon millions of monarch butterflies wake with the morning sun's heat and delicately rise upwards towards the forest canopy, fluttering in the sunlight. The noise from their wings, when all else around is completely silent, sounds like soft rain on welcoming leaves. Their red, black and yellow colouring looks like perfectly blown stained glass. As you sit in the grass, butterflies land on your head, arms, legs and feet, in the hope of finding the warm surfaces they crave, while hundreds of thousands collect so thickly on tree branches that these bend towards the ground and lose all resemblance to actual vegetation.

Like much of our world's natural magnificence, the monarchs and their habitat are under threat. Illegal logging, agricultural pressures, and climate change have affected the colonies to great detriment, while the financial advantages brought by tourism don't trickle down through all levels of local communities, meaning the success of conservation efforts is rare. In this age of human dominance and unfaltering 'progress', the future of the forest and its winged inhabitants remains unclear.

On many occasions during the journey I had felt truly privileged at being able to look into someone else's world – and descending out of that pine forest was one of the most important of these. At night-time, when humans depart the forest floor, the butterflies huddle together for warmth and survival. They cared not that we were there. Yet I pondered how we should learn from this. Peering into nature in such a way was like looking into an exhibition case in a museum. We were a part of it, yet we weren't, and the disconnect between their environment and ours never seemed so great.

Instead of cycling through the smog, pollution and treacherous traffic created by Mexico City's 20 million inhabitants, I opted to stop somewhere on its outskirts, in the hope of finding a willing person or family to take care of my bicycle and gear while I visited the capital. The satellite town I chose was San Juan Teotihuacán, which lay about 255 km from Angangueo, on the calmer, north-eastern boundary of the metropolis.

San Juan Teotihuacán is known principally for the enormous pre-Columbian archaeological complex of Teotihuacán to its east. The site encompasses the remains of a 2,000-year-old city, which by the first century AD was the largest and most populated urban centre in the Americas. Today it survives as a collection of residential buildings, avenues, temples, plazas and pyramids, one of which – the Pyramid of the Sun – stands as the third largest in the world.

Although the details of Teotihuacán's early history are still unclear, there is no doubt as to its influence upon the Mesoamerican region, a belt of ancient cultures and city-states stretching from what is modern-day central Mexico to Costa Rica. It is believed that Teotihuacán was established around 200 BC, but the identity of those who founded it is unknown. Some archaeologists suggest that the Toltecs – the intellectual antecedents of the Aztecs – may have been the city's first architects and residents. However, based on colonial-era texts, this seems unlikely, as the Toltec civilisation flourished much later. Others advocate for the early Totonac culture that had eventually centred on the eastern coast and mountains by the time of Spanish arrival in 1519.

Whatever the genesis, it's agreed that, by the end of the first century AD, the city had become a powerful player in Mesoamerican politics and culture, and may have had between 150,000 and 250,000 inhabitants spread over around 30 km². In the succeeding centuries, cultural exchange led to Teotihuacáno ideologies and architecture spreading south and east into Guatemala, where the Maya civilisation held sway. Indeed, long after Teotihuacán collapsed around the sixth or seventh century, its artistic motifs endured in Maya city-states.

The reason for its decline is as mysterious as its beginnings. Some experts hypothesise that repeated sackings and consequent burnings ultimately brought this once-supreme city to ruin. Arguments have also been put forward citing internal strife and even climate change, in the form of severe droughts around the middle of the sixth century. Backing this up are the increased numbers of juvenile burials in evidence, as well as the clear signs of malnutrition demonstrable in the uncovered remains.

With just the morning sun for company, I walked along the Avenue of the Dead. There was not a soul around and the dusty thoroughfare was eerily silent. I imagined what it would be like walking through a deserted London in millennia to come, identifying St. Paul's Cathedral, Buckingham Palace, Westminster Abbey, and Leicester Square. It was analogous to this, but instead of those contemporary and well-trodden sights, here I could see the Temple of Quetzalcoatl, the Court of Columns, the Plaza of the Moon, and the Pyramid of the Sun. What is familiar to me in the twenty-first century was once as familiar to the ancients in the third, fourth and fifth centuries, I thought.

I climbed the steep steps to the summit of the Pyramid of the Sun, and sat down on the flat lime-plaster base. The immensity of the complex can only be appreciated from a vantage point such as this. Directly to the north was the Pyramid of the Moon, built to mimic the form of Cerro Gordo, the mountain several kilometres behind it. To my east was the San Juan River, which runs right through the site, and may have been part of its well-planned canal architecture. To the west were the stone remains of upper-class residences, where elaborate murals still exist, pointing to the affluence of this particular neighbourhood. And to the south was the Citadel and Temple of the Feathered Serpent, the political and artistic centre of the city. It was here that artisans produced the unique orange-coloured Teotihuacáno pottery often exported to other city-states throughout Mesoamerica.

It was 7 a.m., cool, and without a noise on top of the Pyramid of the Sun – but most striking of all was the dense discolouration of a naturally blue sky, distantly to the south. Under the grey haze that lingered over the tapered valley stood raging modern urbanity in all its glory. What an extraordinary bridging of histories, I felt, as I looked on from the now silenced but once great pinnacle of the ancient Americas' most powerful city, towards its modern, heart-pounding and always sleepless successor.

6

South by Southeast

San Juan Teotihuacán, Mexico to La Mesilla, Guatemala – 1,677 km

'IAN!' I HEARD SOMEONE SHOUT from a kerbside restaurant. 'Is that you?' I turned around and searched several rows of tables.

'Ian! Over here!' I heard again, and saw a familiar face smiling at me.

It was Bob Byington, an American expatriate originally from Chicago, but now living and working in Mexico City. I had first met Bob on the Baja Ferries' sailing from La Paz to Mazatlán, and we had exchanged contact details in case I was looking for a place to stay in the city. A few days before, I'd emailed to let him know I'd soon be arriving. However, I was still surprised he had picked me out of the crowd in a city of 20 million people.

'Good to see you, Ian, good to see you. How have you been? I received your mail and your bed is made up,' he said. 'Please meet my dear friend, Jorge. He's a teacher friend of mine from the university,' he added introducing me to Jorge, who was picking at some chicken.

'Great to see you too, Bob. I can't believe you spotted me through all these people.'

'Well, you know, only the *gringos* come to this part of town, so it wasn't that hard,' he replied. 'Plus, you've got that red Irish beard!'

I was delighted Bob had invited me to stay. As always, a local connection was better than any other, and meant I could attune myself to the city and its geography much more easily.

Bob lived on Isabel la Católica, a busy street in the city's historic centre. His apartment was in a 200-year-old stone building, whose innards were a den of narrow archways with dark wooden beams overhead. The roof of his apartment opened out onto a lovely streetscape; in the corner was a granny flat that he had converted into a spare bedroom.

'This is yours, for as long as you want,' Bob said, laying one of my bags in the corner. '*Mi casa es su casa.*' ('My house is your house.')

The roof was the most attractive aspect of his home, as I could be a voyeur into city life, three floors below. Across the street, in a building with wrought iron balconies and yellow plastering, was one of many bars that occupied second-floor space in the downtown area. Mexican college students, a growing middle-class, and what I identified as Mexican hipsters often frequent these flamboyantly decorated watering holes – and Bob expedited my introduction to this one.

'I had a very different idea of what the city would be like,' I told him as I looked back at my granny flat from across the street.

Bob put his beer down, wiped the froth from his top lip, and leaned forward. 'There's a general view, that Mexico is just a handful of things. People hear about the drug troubles, they hear about mariachi, a lazy lifestyle, and too much tequila. Things they can easily box up. Who hears about this side of it? The students, the music in these bars, or the counter-culture that's alive here,' he said.

'I guess not many, apart from those who see it first-hand,' I answered.

'Exactly! You have to witness it. There's so much energy in this city, it's overwhelming at times. And the energy doesn't have to be youthful: it comes with the past and traditions of Mexico,' he said, drinking the remaining beer in his glass.

Bob was right. There was something intriguing about this place that I couldn't quite pinpoint, but just felt in the bricks and mortar, through the noise of the students frantically chatting, and the atmospheric shadows cast on cobbled streets. I was just a few hours in, but the capital – or D.F. (*Distrito Federal*), as most call it – was already growing on me.

The Zócalo is the beating heart of Mexico City, and perhaps the whole nation. This echoing plaza is focused upon a tall flagpole at its centre, from which the Mexican flag billows in slow motion. The National Palace, the Metropolitan Cathedral – the largest in the Americas – and the ancient Aztec Templo Mayor flank what is one of the world's biggest plazas. As the government is centred on the Zócalo, it's a popular gathering place for protests, as well as for concerts and festivities.

Close to Zócalo is the site of the city's foundation. According to legend, the god Huitzilopochtli informed the Mexica people (later known as the Aztecs) that they should build a great city on the site where they would see an eagle perched on a cactus with a snake in its beak. This very configuration was in fact seen on a small island in Lake Texcoco in 1325, and there the Mexica founded the city of Tenochtitlan, later renamed Mexico City after the Spanish conquest.

Hernán Cortés ordered the rebuilding of the city in colonial style after its sacking; eventually Lake Texcoco was drained, with the modern capital occupying the space it left. Today, it is divided up into *colonias*, or neighbourhoods, and makes up one of the most populous urban areas on the planet. However, it's not all Mexicans, as the city has considerable Latin American immigrant communities too, as well as Europeans, Americans, and Canadians. Indeed, by some estimates, the latter two expatriate populations total almost 1 million people.

Bob brought me to La Opera, one of Mexico City's famous *cantinas*. These bars, consisting of just a few simple tables and chairs, are emblematic of 1940s and 1950s Mexico. They are places where elderly waiters in immaculate uniforms serve tequila to a typically male clientele, while mariachi music sounds from ageing record players. La Opera is uncharacteristically the opposite of such typical *cantinas*, and features smooth leather booths, plush curtains, and brass bar rails. It was here that Pancho Villa, one of Mexico's foremost revolutionary generals, supposedly galloped in on his horse and put a bullet hole in the ceiling.

'Look over there,' Bob said. 'See the hole? The great Pancho Villa came through these very doors, they say.'

Of course, times have moved on, and hence La Opera has shed the traditional cantina feel. Instead, a young socialite class now makes the most of its fashionable history and elegance.

'Many of the cantinas have changed, but the barmen haven't, I bet,' laughed Bob, eyeing the perfectly trim waiter in a white suit behind the bar.

'Where can you find the old-style places, then?'

'Oh, you'll see them just walking around. Poke your head inside and if you find some old guys playing cards or chess, you'll know it's the right place.'

Bob was a university professor of English, but loved history, so he was in his element showing me around. He was also studying mindfulness and practiced yoga every morning in his bedroom, which had no door, but just a bead parting. His room was covered in trinkets and draped with reddish wall hangings and had an ambient *feng shui*.

I had several long conversations with Bob during the three days I spent in the city, largely focusing on elements of the cycle I was struggling with.

'It seems your trip will be defined by how you handle the long-distance relationship with your girlfriend,' he told me over lunch. Bob could sum my own feelings up succinctly; he seemed to have a natural ability to read my thoughts and repeat them to me in a much wiser manner than I could analyse them. 'You can't think of the past and future too much. You've got to enjoy what's there as you travel. To be truly content, you have to accept lack of control, but that doesn't mean to say you should give up maintaining your connections.'

Bob spoke softly and thoughtfully. Usually when I came to a new place, I was eager to first see it alone and form my own impressions, rather than have somebody narrate the scene. However, as Bob had travelled through South America and Europe years before, he didn't try to act as a guide, but more as a companion to my exploration, often reciting and laughing at anecdotes about Mexican culture or a place in which we found ourselves.

'This is Zona Rosa, the gay quarter,' he indicated – as if I needed confirmation.

Same-sex couples strolled hand in hand, perusing bookshops and clothes stores. Occupying 24 blocks of Colonia Juárez, Zona Rosa is famous for its nightlife and eccentric atmosphere. Even during the day when we visited, the streets were packed with locals, tourists and hordes of businessmen from nearby Paseo de la Reforma, a street peppered with big banks and international corporations. Zona Rosa began its life as a bohemian neighbourhood in the 1950s, which today has extended to become an area synonymous with a thriving gay community, intellectuals, and artists. More recently, a Korean population has established itself in the area, adding a new cultural dimension. A number of oriental eateries have since opened up, and menus have diversified to offer an extensive selection of eastern cuisine alongside the traditional *birria* (meat stew) and *cabrito* (roast goat meat).

On my final day in Mexico City, I took some time to wander the city alone. I walked from Bob's house to the Palacio de Bellas Artes – a brilliant white art nouveau edifice constructed from Italian Carrera marble. It's one of Mexico's most important venues for cultural performances and best appreciated when viewed from the main entrance, while standing in Alameda Park. I picked up a coffee and walked along Paseo de la Reforma to the Angel of Independence column that serves as a roundabout and a memorial to the beginning of the Mexican War of Independence. Nike, the Greek goddess of victory, flies resplendent at the top of the column, clutching a laurel crown to signify victory and a broken chain representing freedom. Just west is Bosque de Chapultepec, an enormous 1,700-acre green lung in the centre of the throbbing city. After an hour reading under the trees, I ambled 1 km to the Museum of Anthropology. The museum was the one attraction I was committed to seeing, as I had heard its exhibits were an incredible insight into what is a fascinating and complex ancient history.

The Maya, the Aztec, the Mixtec, the Olmec – the museum's staggering permanent exhibition shows each of these Mesoamerican cultures, neatly packed and wonderfully presented under tinted lights: a physical depiction of humanity's ancient intellectual development.

The Aztec Sun Stone, which was found under the Zócalo in 1790, is the centrepiece of the museum's display rooms. The stone is 11 ft in diameter, 3 ft thick, and circular in shape. Carved into it are cosmological motifs sacred to Aztec civilisation, including the four previous 'suns' or 'eras', each of which ended with great destruction. Other rooms contain similar cosmological artefacts that etch a sense of curiosity into the visitor's mind.

Bob had been the kindest host and a very accommodating one, but, as I was eager to push further south and catch my flight to Tajikistan, I refused an offer to stay longer. I collected my bicycle and panniers from the family-owned hotel in Teotihuacán where I had left them with the owner in an act of blind trust. My promise was that I'd stay an extra night in the hotel, to add to the one I had taken after visiting the archaeological complex there.

'Let's go, let's go,' this man said on my return, and guided me towards the stairs that led on to the roof. I asked him where the bicycle was but didn't get an answer.

We ducked under white bed sheets drying on a line which stretched diagonally across the top of the building. Rusting pipes and old oilcans littered the rough concrete floor. The owner opened the door of a small outhouse, where some unused washing machines were stacked and I saw the bike crudely jammed in the corner. The front wheel was turned back on itself and, wedged underneath it, the panniers which held the majority of my clothes, tools, and cooking and camping equipment.

I was livid but acted as normally as possible, and made three trips between the roof and ground floor to collect everything. How stupid had I been? Anyone could have taken the bicycle or my gear, as the stairs was also accessible from the street. My things didn't look expensive, but they were – this was all I had, the entirety of my physical possessions. That wasn't even the point, as, if the bike had been stolen, it would just have been too demotivating and costly to try to replace it, that the journey would effectively have been over. I left, annoyed with myself, while reasoning it was a lesson learned, at least.

After several days away from cycling, I knew to expect a slow acclimatisation to a touring rhythm once again. However, as I rejoined Arco Norte – the mega-highway north of the capital that cyclists are forbidden to travel on – I was particularly off-form. Symptoms of these particular days included a stinging lactic acid burn in my legs, a loss of appetite, and a desire to stop early and sleep it off. However, my body was too acquainted with movement and the constant expenditure of energy within regular and set daylight hours to stay put for long. This physical effort was countered when touring with a steady calorie input through a limited and rarely changing diet, normally consisting of oatmeal for breakfast, chicken, beans and salad for lunch, and pasta for dinner. I would seldom cycle less than five days in a row and on many occasions, reached up to eight or nine consecutive days before resting. So when I did stop and get up or go to bed late, walking instead of cycling, eating different foods and drinking less water, I found that, when returning to the routine of the road again, my body was more inclined to laziness than action.

Diary: 1 Feb 2012, Tecamachalco, Mexico

Up at 4.50 a.m. this morning, to do the Tom Dunne Show on Newstalk FM. Found it a little tough to remember all the interesting bits between here and Baja, when I did the last interview. Was in late last night too, as I met a guy who had lived in the US for 17 years before being deported recently and we stayed up chatting. He was so eager to go back [to the US], as he wants to study engineering and must be only in his early 20s. Hearing quite a few of these stories now, and it's hard not to feel for people who really want to stay the course there. For so many, all roads point north.

After an early lunch on my way to Tlaxcala, my lethargy was cured by Mexican generosity. A family pulled up beside me, handed a bag of mango juice out of the window and drove away. Three kilometres on, I found the mother, father, and small daughter flagging me down, pointing across the highway and into a restaurant. I rode down the gravel entrance and dismounted the bicycle, perfectly aware I was about to be fed, whether I liked it or not.

Plates of rice, potatoes, and beans materialised within seconds, followed by tacos with *barbacoa* (barbequed meat) and an assortment of vegetables on a small tray. A baby bowl of fried chicken then appeared in front of Nellie, the delightfully happy daughter. Soon after, a stocky middle-aged man arrived on a motorbike, hopped off and sat in beside us. He greeted me, but made little conversation, perceptibly more concerned with the danger of his food going cold than the entertainment of a *gringo* pulled off the road. I gathered that the man on the motorbike was the brother of the car's driver and that this was the usual meeting place for the two.

There was precision to the manner in which they consumed the food and the side bowls of soup. Chicken legs, cow parts and what I loosely understood to be goat meat were picked out of the greenish stock and sucked dry. When the table was clear, they paid for this, which was in fact my second lunch of the day. Then they motioned me outside for photos to be taken. The couple stood up against a wire fence, child in arms, and posed for photos from every possible angle. We had hardly spoken, but they had been content just knowing they had provided me with a meal. Then they were out of my life again, as quickly as they had entered it.

The topography returned to flatland once again, strikingly reminiscent of central Baja but with superior hues of vegetation. On my western horizon was the puffing, snow-capped Volcán Popocatépetl, a reminder of the violent forces beneath my feet. A year-and-a-half later it would erupt spectacularly, creating a 3 km plume of ash visible from Puebla and even Mexico City.

I was now travelling towards the mountainous states of Oaxaca and Chiapas, strongholds of Mexico's indigenous ethnic groups. At least one-third of the states' collective population are speakers of indigenous languages, and almost half of those do not speak Spanish. What allows these people and their ways of life to survive is the inaccessibility of the landscape around them. Apart from their obvious natural beauty, mountains are in this sense also protectors and guardians of culture and an intangible heritage, and, for me, this is what gives them a personality surpassing their aesthetic appeal.

The valley succeeding Tehuacán had crisp and sun-drenched panoramas, as the road turned south towards the city of Oaxaca. Barley fields were set alight by the evening sun, sharply contrasting with the uneven land coloured a thousand shades of green, which lay beyond them in the distance. I had left the main highway and was cycling by little farms and villages along empty country lanes. I had been told I could find the village of Zinacatepec on the far side of the open valley, but the road was not signposted. Curious farmers walking the road pointed towards the hills, saying, '*Por ahí, por ahí*' ('Over there, over there'), so I followed this general direction.

In Zinacatepec, I paid 200 pesos ($9) for a room in the Gran Hotel, the town's most expensive accommodation. Most Mexican hotels I stayed in didn't have heating facilities and Gran Hotel was no different, so I washed under a steel pipe spouting ice-cold water. At night, I'd usually cover myself with the sleeping bag and whatever woollen blankets were provided, to stave off the chilled air that filled the room after sunset.

Although it was past 8 p.m., the plaza in Zinacatepec was a hive of activity. Gabriella, the 15-year-old daughter of the Díaz family who owned the hotel, was told to bring me to the market where I could buy food for the next day. Gabriella was extremely well-educated and fortunately had an excellent grasp of English.

'I want to be a doctor, like my father. I think, yes, I know – a surgeon!' she exclaimed. 'I can only do this if I get over 90 per cent in my final exams. Then the government will pay for me to study.'

I asked her why she wanted to be a doctor and she paused a moment, searching for the right words.

'I want to help my country. Doctors are important people and help others. This is a good way to help Mexico,' she said with perfect pronunciation.

We chatted for 10 minutes in the market before I suggested we go back. I gave her my copy of *Kim*, the Rudyard Kipling classic, and explained that it might be a little above her abilities for now, but when she could read and understand the majority of it, she'd be as good at English as any native speaker. Two days later I received a Facebook friend request from her, as she had tracked me down online. Her newly updated profile picture was one of her and me, taken with her mother's phone as I departed, but now with love hearts and red ribbons photo-shopped in around us. I was more than a little taken aback, having had no idea that young Gabriella might have seen me in this light, and I felt a certain degree of relief that I had left town before her father had a chance to see the image.

Highway 135 D hooks right and embeds itself into the base of Cerro Verde, a mountain of splendid pyramidal form. I crossed a huge, white arched bridge that stemmed both sides of a canyon, and the road then began its ascent. I sat back and settled into motion, inching my way along the arid valley wall. To my right, over the guard rail, a sloping area of cacti sat soaking up the morning heat. Ahead was a seemingly never-ending corner that brought me no closer to respite. After 20 km, the highway levelled off and Cerro Verde dominated the view behind. A small, unpainted *tienda* was open, serving soft drinks, plastic-wrapped baked goods and bags of crisps. Jagged cavity blocks framed the entrance where a door should have been, but I presumed crime was infrequent up here, so the need for protection and privacy was of little concern.

I knocked on the counter and a scruffy man in oily jeans and a Notre Dame jumper came to my attention. I ordered a Pepsi, cake and a bag of crisps for the ride. Inside, a woman, who I presumed was his wife, three kids covered in dirt, and an older, stoic-looking man sat quietly around the television. It was hard to fathom how someone, anyone – a family, even – could live up here under a barren hillside, amongst the rocks and scree, and tens of miles from neighbours.

Diary: 3 Feb 2012, Nochixtlán, Mexico

What a day up here! At the tienda the man said there was just 6 km to go until the road dropped – it did, but then went up and down all day long in a weird landscape with nothing in it but the odd petrol station. I took a break at each one, so basically every 10 km, to get some chocolate and water. Have heard from the woman at this motel that Andy Peat was here recently and camped in the back garden. Seem to be shadowing cyclists here and there, and wonder are others doing the same with me?

By 3 p.m. that day, I had covered the grey and forgettable plateau in front of me. It wasn't without hardship though, as short drops were countered by abrupt and steep climbs. The chain and gears of my bicycle remained locked into slow turns on the many ascents to the top of the mesa. Aside from the challenges presented by topography and weather, my mental and physical wellbeing was usually determined by one or two factors. Fitness was one of those, and it seemed to come and go in waves that were now easier to predict. I understood that racing into a morning's cycle wasn't a good idea, as I would burn up energy early and risked feeling rotten if I didn't achieve a 'decent' number of kilometres by lunchtime. Decent to me was at least half of what I intended to ride during the day, as it was always comforting to know I had less distance to go than I had already travelled. Even though I was chasing a plane in Bogotá, there was no point in ruining the space between with unattainable targets and pressures, so I eased this by rising earlier and leaving while the sun was low in the sky.

The second, and perhaps most important factor of influence on my mood, was the degree to which I interacted with others. The more social I was, the less time I had to withdraw into my own mind and overthink relationship issues with Áine. We were speaking as regularly as always – three to four times per week – but our conversations were not as long as they used to be.

'I guess I'm just used to it. I've got to stop thinking about how I miss you and just get on with things here,' she told me over Skype.

I could see how our relationship was entering another stage, as Áine – more practical than I – had accepted the firm reality of life for the foreseeable future and forced her thinking to change, to make my absence less painful.

'You don't know what will happen. You can't tell me you'll come home feeling the same,' she said before I left Ireland.

'I know I can't,' I told her honestly. 'But there's no reason either to think I won't.'

Half the world away, Áine was right to protect herself from undue distress. I couldn't seem to do the same, and no amount of Skype calls could address this. My only hope was to arrive in a mid-winter Tajikistan, with her as happy to see me as I would be to see her. However, despite short periods of dampened spirits, the majority of my days were positive and taken up with just getting over the next hill and finding a place to sleep at night. Cycling was as good a meditation for the soul and mind as anything else, and this is perhaps the activity's most understated wonder.

Red rock country rushed in from the west and soon swamped my thin corridor of asphalt. The land closed in, to form a tunnel like an Olympic luge or bobsleigh track; the road twisted sharply into and around high, red soil banks with green grass on top. I raced downhill at breakneck speeds, leaning into corners like a motorbike rider, more confident and controlled than ever in steering my 45 kg machine. The sight of the ground passing under my feet reminded me of static from an un-tuned television set, while the strap of my front pannier bag dragged poker straight in the wind.

For a touring cyclist, downhills are the reward for climbing, and some are incomparably special. Experience tells you whether it's to be fleeting or not, and this gives you time to appreciate it as it opens up in front of you. As Oaxaca neared, I sensed one such descent ahead. The colour between my map's contours transitioned from heavy browns to light ones. The road lost its eager uphill incline and levelled out. Every tree I could see in the distance was at a lower elevation, to which I was surely headed. I put in my headphones and turned the volume up, searching for some AC/DC that would serve as soundtrack to an immense descent. I saw where the highway's crest ended, as those on a rollercoaster see the end of 'up' and the beginning of 'down'. I rolled towards it and then plunged into the semi-circles and spirals of the earth at 20–30 km/h, the wind roaring past my ears making all other noises inaudible, even those of cars flashing past, on their way uphill on the other side of the road. After 10 or 15 minutes, the road's gradient receded, but we maintained a downward slope, thus easing me out of the thinner air. Of course, what's gratifying for the southbound cyclist is hard work for those plodding north. True to fashion, I'd soon again be on the receiving end, and it reminded me what Lee had said after the Atigun Pass in Alaska: 'It's all up, down, up, down until we reach Ushuaia. Can't get away from that. We start at sea level and will end there too.'

Apple orchards indicated the presence of civilisation and within half an hour I was in Oaxaca. Curving around the foothills of interlocked mountains, the city's layout and architectural style are reminders of Mexico's lasting colonial legacy. The outer zone is a jumble of car garages, supermarkets, fried chicken houses and mobile phone shops. However, at its heart are alluring low-rise, greenstone buildings dating from the early sixteenth century, surely as manicured as they had been right after their construction. As I roamed the side streets, looking for a reasonably priced *posada* (guesthouse), I bumped into Urs Etzenspurger, a Swiss touring cyclist. He was standing on a street corner, scratching his goatee and looking profoundly confused.

'Hey man, where are you going?' he said to me as I cycled past.

As he didn't have a bicycle, I suspected he was a regular tourist, so pulled off the road and onto the footpath to answer. 'Hey, I'm looking for a *posada* here. Trying to get something cheap but with Wi-Fi if I can.'

'Cooool, man,' he said in a thick Swiss-German accent.

Urs, as I'd later notice, always elongated the first word of his replies and more often than not ended them with 'man'.

'Do you know of any near here?' I asked him.

'Couple of us cyclists are at Posada Vicky, about five blocks from the cathedral. No Wi-Fi, though.'

'Oh, you're a cyclist? Nice. Where are you going yourself?'

'Ushuaia man, end of the world or whatever,' he told me with a vacant expression on his face, before a smile burst through and he began laughing.

'I've been cycling these craaaazy roads, never on the motorway. Mexico's so great, don't you think, man?' he asked me.

We chatted for about 30 minutes and it surprised me to realise our stories were very similar. Urs had begun his journey in Mexico over one year before, travelling as slowly as possible through Central America. There he met a Pan-American cyclist, who was heading from Ushuaia to Anchorage. Urs, liking the sound of this, pedalled back to Mexico with him and then they flew to Alaska. His new cycling partner's belief was that he'd encounter the most favourable seasons if he completed the trip in two halves, first from Ushuaia to Mexico City and then Anchorage back to Mexico City.

'Stupid idea,' Urs said. 'Who wants to do that? It's not the same, but I thought how super great it'd be to start in Alaska and just ride to Argentina anyway.'

Somewhere in Montana, as Urs and his partner tackled the Great Divide Trail – a route roughly following the Continental Divide – they fell out and decided to split up. Urs indicated that things had become too competitive and disingenuous.

'I'd get to the top of a climb and wait for him, and then he'd arrive and be pissed at me because I was faster. What could I do? You can't enjoy stuff that way, man,' he said. 'Plus, he was always taking these stupid photographs of himself on the bike, looking like a warrior, wanting people to say, "Hey, you're soooo cooool!" That pissed me off, you know.'

Urs told me there was a group of cyclists meeting later that night in the plaza, and invited me along. It would be the first time since southern California that I would spend time amongst other tourers, and, as it was Urs' birthday, we'd be on the hunt for mezcal, a drink similar to tequila but made from the local agave plant.

My memory of that night is sketchy, to say the least. However, the outstanding moment of inebriation came with stuffing orange segments into the waiters' mouths and dancing the cha-cha arm-in-arm in La Casa de Mezcal. Photographic evidence is the only proof this ever occurred, but I'd be shocked if that was the pinnacle of our exploits, considering the fearsome hangover of the following morning.

Apart from Urs and I, there was Jorge, a Spanish cyclist on a similar route, and Emilie and Rafael, two French friends riding from the United

States to an undecided terminus in Central America. The majority of our conversation was lost within the noise of Spanish dance music at a club we paid an extortionate amount of money to enter. Jorge, who was the quietest of the bunch at the outset, turned into the zaniest, perhaps as he had the language to express himself more easily to natives and unfortunate waiters alike.

Nights such as those never helped my ulcerative colitis, which had been in remission for over two months. However, I felt basically healthy and the trip was far from being under threat, as it had been in Alaska. I'd learned that the only way to remain problem-free was to take my prescribed drugs three times daily. As my medication was now running out, my mother had organised, through a friend, to have a staff member at the Mexican Embassy in Dublin post three months' supply to her grandmother, who lived in Oaxaca.

Roberta Montero was as lovely as a grandmother could possibly be. She plied me with 7-Up and biscuits, and I stayed chatting well beyond the limits of natural conversation. Roberta sat in a comfy armchair that dwarfed her body, and had a permanent grin on her face. Her pleated dress was pale blue and blended into the wallpaper. She wanted to know what I thought of Mexico, and Oaxaca in particular, but there was only so much I could describe with my inadequate Spanish.

'Very beautiful, I like it a lot,' I repeated on several occasions, intonating the words differently each time, to mask the fact I was just regurgitating them.

After an afternoon of broken conversation and poring over photographs of the extended family, I thanked Roberta for keeping my medication and gave her some locally made chocolates and sweets to share amongst her grandchildren. It was a paltry gift in comparison to what she held for me, but she seemed delighted and asked me to write a letter from further down the road and tell her how I was getting on.

Jorge the Spanish cyclist was on the lookout for a cycling companion for a few days, and he proved to be the most interesting and sociable of people to travel with. The reason he set out to cycle the Americas is long and complicated, but it centred on the break-up of a 16-year relationship. Although Jorge told me it was a mutual decision, he had hurt in his voice when explaining it. He was travelling to relieve the pain, unlike me, who was travelling in spite of it – and that I suppose is why we connected so easily.

'I have lived my whole life with objectives and rules, and always meeting them,' Jorge said at camp the first night, over the noise of our stoves and sizzling pans. 'Now, right here, I don't want them anymore. I will go by bike into South America without any town or city as a target, and spend time wherever I want.'

He was deeply empathic and not afraid to speak openly. Restraining emotion and feeling is one of the greatest hindrances to thoughtful conversation, as far as I'm concerned, but as long-distance cyclists are so often alone, these barriers often lift immediately with others in the same circumstances. In truth, I had been hesitant to go mile for mile with somebody else after the difficulties of paired travel with Lee. However, Jorge understood my experiences as I related them to him and, as we favoured travelling by ourselves for the most part, there was no pressure to stay together.

Since Lee and I had parted ways, my enjoyment of travel had increased enough to realise that I preferred an unaccompanied touring lifestyle. As I found it, strangers are happy to approach one, but with two, are more cautious. Your outlook on people and places changes immensely too, and freely, since one's perception isn't shadowed or influenced by others'. Everything just appears clearer and more in focus. So I was glad to have found this happy medium in Jorge.

Diary: 7 Feb 2012, El Camarón, Mexico

Jorge is so cool to travel with. He loves his photographs, so stops while I cycle on, and then catches up. Then I might take a quick break and meet him a few kilometres later. Very relaxed and easy. The Geological Survey of Mexico team we met on a back road gave us six litres of water and spoke for ages about the area and the work they are doing, building some reservoirs. Bought a heap of different food for dinner tonight with Jorge – it's going to be a feast!

Jorge and I cycled for three days together. The first took us to a wild campsite in the damp hills near the town of El Camarón. We had completed almost 100 km, with 35 km of that a single, snaking descent in a bitter February cold. Our route was taking us to the coast – the only viable option, as the highlands of south-central Mexico are largely roadless. The next day, we continued a downward trend and settled for sleep in a field off a farmer's track. The sandy, briar-infested shortcut we followed would cut the distance we'd need to cover on the traditional *autopista*, but pushing through sand and labouring over scattered rock beds was the back country telling us to slow down.

Dining with Jorge was a lesson in culinary creativity. His amalgamation of many diverse and seemingly unsuited ingredients into something colourful and exotic conjured a sense of wonder in me. I used avocado for the first time at dinner, and that was just on crusty bread with some chopped tomatoes, mayonnaise, and egg. I was in heaven. Jorge had bought *salchichas* (sausages), powdered soup, an assortment of vegetables, and a papaya as big as my head. As constituent parts, they were very little, but together, they masqueraded as a Michelin-star meal. To achieve such wonders, the only things required were time and a little imagination, two things I vowed to put to use more often in my cooking efforts from here on in. After all, pasta mixed with tuna and cheese had lost its taste after 208 days on the road.

We spent our last day together on a heading towards Zanatepec where a 'Warm Showers' host family was waiting. Warm Showers is a service just like Couch Surfing, but specifically for bike tourists, and connects travellers with a bed and, of course, a warm shower. Other cyclists had warned of severe north-easterly headwinds in this, an area of Mexico where the coast deviates from its traditionally south-eastern bearing and into the direction of the gales. Testament to this fact, and taking advantage of these natural conditions, wind farms were everywhere on the horizon. Soon after the hulking wind began whistling through our wheel spokes, we took turns at being windbreaker in front, while the other stayed in the calmer slipstream behind.

In Santiago Niltepec we pulled into a gas station and bought a litre of apple juice and some moist cakes. After a morning of physical and mental struggle, all you can do is keep quiet, eat your lot, relax a moment, and move on again. At this point, we only spoke to discuss why it was that Mexican gas stations seemed to employ one person to constantly water the forecourt. Religiously, one man with a hose in his hand would amble up and down the concrete, splashing it with water until the whole thing was covered, then, after a brief bathroom or smoke break – too close to the pumps for comfort – he would reappear at the far end and start the process again. Jorge even asked one of these individuals what the point was, to which the timid attendant replied that he didn't know, but didn't believe it was a waste of water either.

In Zanatepec, Jorge and I slept in the converted outhouse of a teacher's home. Rodrigo Martínez and his family had prepared fish, potatoes and salad for dinner, and we chatted for a couple of hours about the idiosyncrasies of Mexican, Spanish and Irish culture, including such things as the watering of forecourts.

'Why do people not know how far the next town away is?' Jorge asked Rodrigo, who spoke excellent English.

I wondered this too, as earlier in the day, when Jorge had suffered a flat tyre, we had stopped at a small shop by the roadside to fix it. When we asked a large, middle-aged man, who wrestled with his flagging trousers that fell below his waist every time he moved, how many kilometres it was to Zanatepec, he responded: 'More or less, 5 km. No, 10 km. Yes, yes, it's very far.'

Preceding a sentence with *más o menos* (more or less) was, as we had established at this stage, an indication of having no clue whatsoever. It turned out that Zanatepec was a healthy 40 km away.

'Mexicans don't judge distance by numbers, but by time,' Rodrigo explained. 'They actually have no idea, but instead are prepared to give the even wrong information, so not to disappoint you.'

I could think of no greater distress than riding 5 or 10 km and not only not finding the expected town, but also being told there once again that it was '5 or 10 km away'. I did appreciate the local effort to please, but very soon realised that this national quirk of character was in evidence throughout much of Latin America.

Jorge stayed another day with Rodrigo and his family, while I decided to ride on towards San Cristobal de las Casas, a mountain valley town two days away. I suspected Jorge had found some comfort in the Martínez home, as he took a great liking to Rodrigo and also his mother, who lived in a separate building at the rear of the house. One evening he was quite emotional when he returned to our room after having talked with her after dinner.

'She reminds me so much of my mother, and grandmother. She is so frail and Rodrigo tells me her mind is not so good,' he said. 'I am going to spend time with her, give her a new face to speak with.'

This show of feeling and human compassion was typical of Jorge, and I knew I'd miss him.

There are two ways to reach San Cristobal de las Casas, and cycling opinion is split on which is the better. After the last big town before Guatemala – Tuxtla Gutiérrez – the cyclist can either fight with an extreme, 25 km switchback climb and an increase in altitude of 1,100 metres, or opt for the long-haul 45 km, and 1,700 metres rise. In general terms, choosing the first means you're going for maximum discomfort over a correspondingly shorter distance, while favouring the second indicates a preference to spread out the climb at a more bearable gradient.

I usually much prefer to get the climb 'done', but in this case, chose the 45 km route because there was an ample shoulder on the road, and a spectacular view and descent onto the plains to the south. As soon as Tuxtla disappeared, the climb began, and I sat back into a five-hour slog. The clattering of low gears joined the flapping of fan belts and beeping of horns, as beside me coachloads of tourists overtook convoys of trucks, until the highway veered north and the wine-bottle green flatlands below were no longer in view. Enterprising locals, taking advantage of the pedestrian pace of travel, had set up tens upon tens of stalls selling bananas, chocolate bars, soft drinks and coffee for those drivers needing a rest.

It was a relief to arrive in San Cristobal before dark and I set about scouring the undulating brick streets of this pretty mountain town for a hostel. The walls of the surrounding hills enclose San Cristobal so snugly that it feels concealed from the rest of the country, and almost lost in time. The indigenous Tzotzil and Tzeltal populations dominate an ethnic population that embraces several other prominent groups, evident from their distinctly more rounded and tanned faces and the multi-layered style of dressing on the streets. Wandering for just an hour, I could already sense stylistic variances in people's way of dressing. Some women wore long dresses with waistbands, and shawls draped over their shoulders. Others adopted ordinary T-shirts and combined them with ankle-length skirts of symmetrical stitching. The facial shape and character of some was very different than that of the nationally dominant *mestizo* and their skin considerably darker in colour. Indeed, many of the state of Chiapas' ethnic groups are descended from the Maya and share with them not only similarities in skin colour and dress, but also language.

Cultural and political assimilation into Mexico has been a contentious issue for the indigenous of Chiapas and, while taking a coffee in TierrAdentro Café and Restaurant the next morning, I could see why. The café is affiliated with the Zapatista movement – a leftist group of mainly indigenous membership in Chiapas. The name originates from Emiliano Zapata, an agrarian reformer and leader of the Liberation Army of the South during the Mexican Revolution of 1910. Of primary concern in Chiapas is the Zapatistas' demand for indigenous control over their own land and resources. Tensions came to a head in 1994, when a 3,000-strong army stormed San Cristobal and six other state towns, declaring a revolt against Mexico and its neo-liberal politics. Although the revolt ended peacefully, anti-Mexico sentiment still runs high in the town and wider southern region.

Although I loved visiting colonial towns in Mexico, I enjoyed San Cristobal in particular, as it had a lived-in feel to it, which some of the others didn't. The buildings were rarely higher than two storeys, and so always had sunlight drifting across their facades. Colour coordination wasn't pursued to any great length, and rows of terraced houses mixed all sorts of pastel shadings. The layout was Spanish-influenced but didn't feel obviously so, and the cobblestoned streets maintained a quaint character.

It was a pity then that I had to leave San Cristobal no sooner than I had arrived. Speaking to Áine about the next month's trip to Tajikistan, I realised I needed a Russian transit visa to be able to make the fourth of my six flights to get there. The only place I could realistically get this done was the Russian Embassy in Mexico City, and so, irritated at my own bad planning, I had to board a bus and make the 20-hour trip back to the capital.

It was three days before I travelled back to Chiapas, as the process of issuing a visa had involved all the expected bureaucracy. My bicycle had been kept safe in a Warm Showers hostel, so I was unfazed at leaving it this time. To occupy my time in the city, I rewrote old blogs that had been lost to a malicious virus on the 350South website some weeks previously. When I finally arrived back in San Cristobal, I received an email from Jorge who had triumphed over the mountains earlier in the day. Emilie and Rafael were also in town, so we did what we did best together, and went out for the night, dancing until our bodies were worn from the physical release, and contaminated from the mezcal. It was by no small miracle then that I managed to leave the following day. I was still reeling from the night before, but I was on the road out of Mexico.

With a new playlist loaded on my iPod, my next goal was Comitán. When I eventually passed through San Cristobal's boundary, the smell of wood smoke broke through forest clearings and all was quiet again. Soon, I was coasting downhill and counting villages as I went, such was my speed and their frequency. The colours and sounds of indigenous Mexico sang from the roadside, and to me, the whole area seemed to have more diversity in its sights and sounds that day than a full week's worth of travel through any other combination of the country's states.

Whilst I breathlessly chugged up 100-metre climbs and gratefully accepted the descents after, I was happy to be simply a passing observer of the life around me. Beautiful women in brightly coloured and intricately patterned clothes made their way to market; utterances of native languages could be heard from fruit vendors, mechanics, and others touting ceramics and crafts as I braked on the downhill, all the while employing evasive manoeuvres against reckless combi-buses hurrying people from one country town to another. The Sunday markets in Teopisca and Amatenango del Valle were wild and alive, with strolling groups of fresh-faced girls in purple and saffron attire. Under stilted houses, chickens pecked seed from the grass, while adjoining farm lots housed cattle and pigs, some of whose young had escaped through fence cracks to rummage in the undergrowth.

My last night in Mexico was spent in a clean and comfortable $15 hotel. I didn't know what Guatemala would offer in terms of accommodation, so I splashed my final pesos on as much comfort as I could afford. A warm bedroom, stacks of bed covers, complimentary hand soap and a towel were the luxuries I got in return. The noise of motorbikes and music kept me awake during the night, but despite the sleep deprivation, I woke with a building excitement. I'd be in Guatemala by the evening. Not wanting to delay this transition a moment more, I set off on an 82 km run to the border town of Ciudad Cuauhtémoc.

Truthfully, Cuauhtémoc wasn't really a town at all, but more an assemblage of immigration service buildings, such as livestock inspection units and various customs posts. Behind these, and illuminated by the setting sun, tall pinnacles of bare rock jutted skywards. I knew these were property of Guatemala and would shortly mark the beginning of the Central American leg of my trip.

I called to the immigration post, presented my passport for inspection, and waited for an exit stamp.

'You have papers?' said an official, who looked like he'd been sewn into his navy blue uniform.

'Papers?'

'Yes, papers. You had white papers when you entered Mexico. I need them for your exit,' he answered.

'Ohhh . . . the receipt for my visa, you mean?'

'*Si*,' he answered glumly. 'Please, now.'

At this point my papers were probably fluttering in the breeze, blowing through a landfill somewhere in Baja California. I had thrown them out in a weight-saving measure over a month ago, not realising I'd need them again. I tried appealing to the official's better, less sullen nature.

'I don't have them. But you can see I paid for my visa because I have an entrance stamp,' I told him. 'And I'm sure to be on the system?'

'Yes, but no papers mean no exit,' he said, getting impatient.

'Well, I don't have them, so what can I do?' I said, hoping he'd take pity on me this late in the evening. I was the only person in the building and assumed he'd be a touch humane, considering I'd cycled the length of the country.

'No stamp – no exit,' he growled once more.

Although I hate doing it, I figured a bribe – or 'penalty', as I translated it in Spanish – was the only way out of the situation.

'Do you think, maybe, I could pay a penalty for not having it?' I said.

'You need to pay the fine of 294 pesos (US$22), the same price as your visa,' he responded.

'Great, can I pay this now – here?'

'No, you need to pay it in a bank and come back with the receipt. The bank is in Frontera Comalapa.'

Frontera Comalapa was 23 km away, over some charred hills and huddling in a nondescript valley. But it was 5 p.m., and I had no intention of making the 46 km round trip. Plus, the bank would be closed, so I couldn't depart until morning anyway. I tired one more appeal, but to no avail. My attempt to earn favour had failed dramatically and this one, merciless old border guard would just not grant me some desperately needed charity.

'Feck it,' I said, as I sat outside on the concrete windowsill. 'I'm off!' I decided, and rode on towards Guatemalan immigration 8 km away.

The guard I now hurriedly pedalled away from had told me Guatemalan officials in the town of La Mesilla wouldn't stamp me in unless they saw a stamp confirming my exit. He also explained that, if somehow they did, I'd have to pay a $200 fine the next time I tried re-entering Mexico.

Darkness fell like a heavy blanket upon day, as I skulked up a 5 km hill to an immigration post perched nervously on a cliff-edge.

'Hello, where are you going?' said an ungainly man in a torn polo shirt. He was wiping a sandwich stain from his pants.

'La Mesilla. I'm very tired, lots of mountains,' I said.

He looked through my passport. Another official asked if I wanted a map of the country, but before I could answer that I did, he spread on the table a map so magnificently large it could have been used as a groundsheet for my tent. He pointed out all the popular attractions, old ruins, and towns with the finest *'chicas'* (girls). He was an obvious authority on the last point, and considerably more enthused speaking about it than about ancient Maya cities.

After noticing the first official had conducted several sweeps of my well-worn document, I told him that I didn't have an exit stamp from Mexico, and explained the reasons why. My apology lasted for about ten seconds before he stopped me.

'Friend, friend. No problem, no problem,' he said grinning, and clarified that he just wanted to see what other countries I'd been too.

'*Bienvenidos a Guatemala,*' ('Welcome to Guatemala') he announced, and inked a big blue stamp in my passport.

I liked the place already.

7
The Small Places
La Mesilla, Guatemala to San José, Costa Rica – 1,690 km

WHEN CROSSING NATIONAL BORDERS, I always imagine the possibility of sweeping cultural changes being immediately in evidence, and the wonder associated with this prospect remains as strong as when I was a child, staring at the world map on my bedroom wall. And so when I rode up Main Street La Mesilla then, I hoped something would flash out and overtly inform me that I was now in Guatemala, and a new geographical region. Perhaps people would have different accents, or different facial features, or the buildings would be new shapes and sizes?

Most things, however, appeared at first view to be the same as in Mexico, except that I now used quetzals instead of pesos, and *tiendas* were called *abarrotes*. Aware that border towns can sometimes be unsavoury places, with aggressive hawkers and currency exchangers badgering from the moment you enter, I decided to hold off setting out to discover this new nation until the next day.

It turned out that La Mesilla was actually quite a pleasant place. It rolled up along the hillside, and a bustling clothes market lined the streets. Before the morning sun found its full intensity, I strolled either side of my hotel for half an hour each way. I noticed several Mexican registered cars parked on the street: possibly families taking advantage of the cheaper food and domestic goods. A couple of kids sped by me, crouched on skateboards, giving a wave and a '*Hola, gringo*' as they flew downhill, while two men struck up a conversation with me, interested to know why I had come to visit their town when many didn't.

Leaving La Mesilla, I plod uphill for a few kilometres before descending to a gurgling river at the edge of a near-vertical valley. Ahead lay blue-grey mountains that closed in to form a 'V' shape, their walls obscured by a light haze and the whole scene looking distinctly like a superimposed backdrop from a Hollywood movie set. I expected to climb out of the valley, following the river until the road separated from it, and then to make a big final push to the top, this the usual way to get out of one. Instead I was treated to a gradual uphill ride, propelled by a light tailwind. I followed a short diversion where I saw an orange sign crudely marked with the word '*Peligroso*', which alerted me to the danger of falling rocks. The dirt path then dropped suddenly down an embankment and ran behind some exposed grey-brick houses with galvanised roofs. There entrepreneurial old men in straw hats were collecting a 'toll' from cars, semi-trailers, and motorbikes, in return for permission to drive through their land until the main road resurfaced.

By late evening I arrived in Huehuetenango (pronounced *way-way-teh-nango*), the largest city in the highlands of western Guatemala. The ride in was accompanied by the screams of 'Goodbye, goodbye!' from local children dressed in shabby football jerseys, who chased me along the road. The houses they emerged from looked rundown, and on another level from the worst I'd seen in Mexico. Hardened mud tracks led from the road to these small clay houses that had roofs secured by steel cable laced through a number of wooden posts. A few scraggly bushes were attempting to flower in the yards and dozens of children hung around, kicking deflated footballs and chasing chickens. It was a colourful scene, but I wondered how many of those kids had access to education, decent healthcare, or running water. On this, my first day, I had already spotted the widespread presence of international development agencies, their logos painted on the sides of school buildings and etched into plaques in front of numerous local clinics. But I wondered what the trickle-down effect of all the investment was having in the end.

As I'd been told that safe wild camping space would be a rare commodity in much of Central America, I decided to try to sleep indoors at night as often as possible: for $4–$7 per night, a bed and a cold shower were well worth the expense. Huehuetenango had many low-price hotels within that moderate budget. It also had a grand open square corralled by some government buildings that were decidedly weary-looking, but that still retained an aged charm of their own. In the middle of this square was also a 40-foot flagpole with a gigantic national flag snapping in the blustery wind, a common feature of most large towns in Mexico and now, it seemed, in Guatemala.

Over dinner that night, I read up on the local history and found out that, until recently, Huehuetenango was the epicentre of a sad and cruel history. It was the birthplace of one of Latin America's most violent dictators, Efraín Ríos Montt, who served as President of Guatemala from 1982–83, in a regime supported by the US through covert CIA activities. During this short term, Ríos Montt oversaw a military campaign against anti-government guerrilla groups and one of genocide against indigenous Maya, whom he suspected of harbouring sympathies towards them. A UN report years later documented widespread human rights abuses, including massacre, rape, torture and the ethnic cleansing of these indigenous minorities, many of who still live in the areas around Huehuetenango. It's tough to tell how long it takes for such scars to heal – if indeed they ever do – but, given the warm welcome I received when chatting to locals in the town, it was hard to imagine such atrocities occurring so recently in the tranquil hills surrounding it.

When I cycled through the country in February 2012, the Guatemalan courts were still in the process of pursuing charges of crimes against humanity and genocide, but the following year Ríos Montt was convicted and sentenced to 80 years in prison. He was already 86, so justice unfortunately would never truly be served. Worse still, an overturning of the decision months later set things back further once more. Ríos Montt will now see his trial resume through appeal in 2016, so the anguish for those who lost family members and lives rolls on.

After Huehuetenango I cycled an easy 85 km to Cuatros Caminos. Literally translated as 'Four Ways', this is a heaving crossroads set 20 km from three other cities. It is also a place almost unrecognisable as a town or settlement. I was unsure if anyone actually lived there, as all I passed were gas stations, dingy hotels, *abarrotes*, fast-food joints, and car garages. It was a blemish on otherwise scenic countryside, terribly ugly and filthy. I also couldn't escape it, as every ATM rejected my bankcard, leaving me with just enough money for a bedroom in a motel that smelled overpoweringly of mould and fried chicken. It was, thus far, the most undesirable place I had ever laid my head. I slept hungry and restless, waiting impatiently for the next day when I could desert Cuatros Caminos for what I hoped would be a distinctly contrasting environment.

Unfortunately, this wasn't to be easily the case. Around mid-morning, as I faced into a climb which curled a full 180° around a brown mountain valley scattered with simple homesteads, I began to notice a severe rubbish problem. Plastic bags, cigarette packets, babies' nappies, and full sacks of household waste were just dumped on the roadside. The stench in some places was insufferable; the panorama of distant working communities set against the mountains was tainted by it. In amongst the mess, I came across a puppy that had been probably hit by a car. He was still alive yet unmoving. Originally I thought he was just resting, sitting on all four paws, but moving closer, I could see the blood and his failing, tired eyes. I gave him some water out of my mud guard, which I cleaned and he could easily drink from. I stayed with him for a time, until some people came down the road; when I showed him to them, although they didn't really understand my exact words, they were clearly able to interpret the scene. I left the puppy with them, but don't know what happened to him – there was little else I could do at that point.

This wasn't the first time I'd come across injured animals, and seeing them in pain was tougher than any mountain climb or bad day in horrible weather. I had noticed from the saddle that animals here – from dogs to cows to goats – were routinely tied to trees with only a yard of space to move and live within. This treatment seemed totally harsh and unfair, especially in such a hot and unforgiving climate.

The topography of Guatemala is quite different from any part of Mexico I had travelled through. It is true mountain country, and nowhere is that more obvious than at Lago de Atitlán, which the English novelist Aldous Huxley once described as, 'the most beautiful lake in the world' and, 'too much of a good thing'. This ancient, near-circular body of water lies in the crater of an extinct volcano and is hemmed in by three others, which rise arrestingly to the north, east, and west of it.

I could sense the lake's presence behind the misted trees, which followed my descent to the water's edge. A smaller regional road had taken me from the main highway and almost immediately I found myself on a 17 per cent downward gradient that burned the rubber from my brake pads. At corners I pulled in to allow the rims to cool. After 45 minutes and 12 km of coasting, I rounded a gravel bend and saw a chink of light through the green. Minutes later, after another sharp corner, daylight ruptured through the remaining vegetation until at last, extending left to right across my view, I saw blue, rippling waters. Around Lago de Atitlán, the mountains rose uninterrupted to the sky, clouds deferring their ascent and resting heavily on their slopes.

Along the roadside, men emerged from the woods, blackened and dirty, with machetes in hand and dragging carts of firewood. Farmers were working the slopes, planting corn and onions in the rich volcanic earth. Daily agriculture and primary industry were very much alive in this perfectly picturesque scene, which was reminiscent of Constable's English countryside paintings, but with the obvious Guatemalan inflection.

My next stop, San Pedro, was teeming with backpackers.

'They all think they'll find enlightenment or something here,' one expatriate pub owner told me.

'Why's that?' I asked him.

'I don't know. Aren't beautiful places in poorer countries always attracting these kind of people?' he answered. 'No harm in it though, adds a bit of colour, I suppose.'

Westerners had well and truly taken over San Pedro. As I wandered the narrow streets, bongo players and guitarists walked by in groups, singing songs of rejoicing and of new beginnings. Incense wafted from shops selling homemade soaps and woodcrafts sculpted from local materials. I could hear German, French, Russian, English, American and Australian accents almost everywhere I ate and drank. I was offered weed at least twice daily, and given discount coupons for lakeside yoga as I tucked into my tofu and bean curd curry.

That particular curry however soon induced a severe bout of food poisoning and for two days, I lay awake in bed vomiting into a bucket. When I went to buy water and paracetamol, I got sick again. I vomited at the hostel door, at the hostel gate, and in the lane astride the hostel. It was a truly appalling scene over the 200 metres I hobbled to and from the store. The stomach pain was worst: it felt as I if I had torn the lining from throwing up so much. The only saving grace was intermittent Internet access that allowed me contact – albeit, terribly slow – with the outside world.

I had been advised to avoid the road on the south side of the lake, because bandits had been known to rob tourists and cyclists. So, once the sickness subsided, I boarded a *lancha* – a small wooden boat – to Panajachel on the far side of the water, and cycled over the volcanic hills at the same degree of ascent as I had come in at. From the top, I could see white and grey dots in the distance: towns spread evenly around the lakeside, trapped elegantly in a sort of lost paradise. Further along, the road had been damaged by landslides and flooding rivers to such an extent that I had to pull the bicycle and gear across it. I had been told that the water was four feet high and that I'd be swept away if I dared cross it, but very soon I realised the extent of local exaggeration. The water, as it happened, barely reached my ankles, and so I plodded on happily, making a note to take such information with a pinch of salt from now on. I wanted to make Antigua by nightfall and learned it was a town as equally frequented by foreign soul-searchers as San Pedro.

The colonial centre announced itself with the appearance of well-worn cobbled streets and the sound of ringing church bells. The sky was a russet red behind Volcán de Agua, as I bumped and shunted over the lines of stone and grout, and through throngs of wandering tourists until I found a hotel. In the light of evening, Antigua was incredibly beguiling. The rustic churches, portal alleys, bright flower boxes and even a McDonald's – camouflaged behind carved wooden signs and a polished stone edifice – fit in well together.

I wrote as much as I could in Antigua, and began to recognise a common theme in my diary entries – that of appreciation. I pondered if it was possible to stay fresh and open to new places and people, maintaining the enthusiasm to engage with them throughout the trip? Seeing so much that is new each day surely had an effect on such enthusiasm. Was there, I wondered, an art to travelling, or was it at the end of the day just a collection of experiences to be noted in a mental scrapbook in the present, only truly appreciated in the future?

It was hard to remain mindful each and every day, and some passed by without any due reflection at all, to be confined to just an ordinary memory or two. Indeed, these 'ordinary' memories were overwhelmingly the norm, and I somehow knew that it was those that were most important to be aware of – the long days just riding from A to B, sweltering in the blistering heat on a two-hour climb, and finding a motel to cook and sleep in, before sweating it out until morning came for me to do the same all over again. Although I had a desire to constantly see new places, it just so happened that the more I saw, the more their impact on me was diminished. Often I felt that each new sight had to be at least as beautiful or unique as the last, if it was to truly captivate me. Little did I know that these days, especially the difficult and unexciting ones, would become as the English adventurer Alastair Humphreys put it, 'the moods of future joys'. After all was said and done, looking back on them would be the foundation for permanent wanderlust and that itch to get moving again.

Diary: 28 February 2012, Pedro de Alvarado, Guatemala

I perhaps don't have the same enthusiasm for places as when I began. And I wonder, do I truly look forward to them? I was obviously delighted to be at Lago de Atitlán with all its beauty, but I was aware that its effect on me was not as powerful as it would have been on the first day of my trip. It's not easy, coming to grips with the fact your explorative soul seems to become numbed with the more you see. I think that if I were with someone, maybe Áine, it would be better. But when I think of sharing with another cyclist or person other than her, I don't get the same sense of excitement. After seven days in Guatemala, I know I'll hit El Salvador tomorrow, but will I appreciate and revel in the differences? Am I just passing through places? How can I say what is truly unique between one country and another? I guess embedding oneself in an area provides that opportunity and the chance to gain a thorough, continuous understanding of each new place. Otherwise it's more like a kind of travel voyeurism.

After Antigua, the road winds downhill in a long southern arc around Volcán de Agua until Escuintla, where it bears directly east towards the border with El Salvador. The wind and its random gusts made it difficult to handle the bike, and it felt too unsafe to take advantage of the 25 km descent. But only for the restricted pace, I'd never have seen coffee farmers and their labourers in the fields sliding down the volcano's slopes.

'Take me home, gringo,' a woman in Escuintla had yelled at me. 'I want to go to America now!'

In Guatemala, passers-by automatically assumed I was American. At an *abarrotes* outside Escuintla, the shopkeeper was baffled I was from Ireland, a country he had never heard of.

'*Holanda* (Holland)?' he said.

'*Irlanda*,' I replied. '*Irrrrrlanda*,' I added, emphasising the slight difference in sound and explaining it was close to England.

'Ohhhh, *Holanda*!' he answered, quite happy he had met his first Dutchman.

More often than not, conversations followed this path, until I brought either sports or Guinness into the equation.

'Roy Keane, the Manchester United footballer. He's Irish,' I would say. Satisfied with the link between my heritage and Roy Keane, they would proceed to ask about the Irish weather, what people did for a living, and whether the women were as pretty as in Guatemala – to which it was customary to always say no. Now and again, when my brain was in gear, I could easily guide the conversation away from these subjects and on to questions of family, life in the country, and even politics, the latter of which never failed to garner an emotive response. Politicians, without fail, were the bad guys, and their cronyism in the capital didn't go unnoticed, developed or developing world aside. It was on such concurrence of opinions that brief roadside friendships were forged.

As soon as I dropped from the rugged highlands into the coastal plains of south-eastern Guatemala, the temperature rise was staggering. I began filling my water bottles with Gatorade to increase my electrolytes, and consigned myself to a battle with the humidity. It had been just four hours since I had left behind a clement Antigua, but the remaining 70 km to the border would be fraught with a heat I was unused to. This stifling air was altogether different from Mexico, and marked the beginning of a succession of long, hot and sweaty days in the saddle.

HALF THE WORLD AWAY

Entering El Salvador was smooth and painless. After having my passport stamped and receiving good wishes from the officer in the Perspex box, I was on my way. For about three hours, the landscape was flat and desperately monotonous. The morning heat grew and fumes from passing trucks and cars lingered stagnantly in the air. According to my map, I was due to turn south and reach the coast, where the road, seeking the path of least resistance over a millennia-old lava field, would then ease into a pattern of switching north for a few kilometres, then east, and then south again back to the coast. Over and over, this would repeat itself, with hundreds of rivers flowing south from the blank space on the map, which marked the volcano.

The ride was a grim exercise in patience. At first, I pedalled alongside the coast, where waters crashed against the cliffs 20 metres below me. When a river would come rushing from the forest, the road would turn left and up the ridge until such point as a bridge would cross the river, the road then returning me downhill to the Pacific Ocean. Where no rivers ran, I'd repeat the loop and ride along the inner edge of a lush and thin peninsula, generally meeting a small village in the crescent where it ended. The road would sweep through it and branch back out again, along another isthmus to the sea.

Such terrain makes for great surfing, I was told in El Zonte. The beach town was a surfer's paradise, but yet to be fully exploited by the community. I met a Dutch girl who predicted that, in less than a decade, Americans and Europeans would begin cascading in.

'This place has a point break as good as any other. It's as close to perfection as you'll see in Central America,' she told me.

Although I wasn't a surfer, the scene was storybook. From the palm-fringed white sand beach, the sun grazed the horizon as slowly as I've ever seen it, leaving behind the most remarkable crimson afterglow that silhouetted the faraway trees, while those still surfing on the water saw out the embers of the day. El Zonte really was worthy of this sort of romanticising, I found myself reflecting, aware that very soon it might not exist with such striking character.

I took my lodging in a converted shed priced as a $6 room. There were cobwebs hanging in every corner, and a rusty fan blew steel-smelling air at my face throughout the night. A wooden desk and a lone bulb poking through the ceiling were the only other semblance of décor in evidence. Outside, I could hear the waves meet the shore and because of the beauty in such simplicity, I felt lucky to experience it. There were just two restaurants on the beach, serving seafood and other meat dishes, along with some local drinks and fruit shakes. However, further along the coast, in towns such as La Libertad and El Tunco, I would find that development had taken hold. One painting on the wall of a 5-star residential development read: 'Welcome People of the World', and I wondered if such open arms would be met with anything but determination on the part of an exploitative few to impose a sense of exclusivity on what was once there for all to enjoy.

On the road beyond La Libertad, multi-coloured local buses, motorbikes, and pick-ups hurtled by, along with trucks packed with sugarcane – their smoky contrails were littered with slivers of the sweetly scented cane, which splattered on the highway, giving something for the dogs to sift through. An hour later, the air turned grey, shockingly polluted from the traffic streaming eastwards from San Salvador. On the advice of just about every traveller who had passed through the country, I avoided the capital, as it held little touristic appeal and was reputedly quite dangerous. In El Zonte, a local shop owner had told me that people still pay protection money to criminal gangs such as MS-13, who actively recruit young people in the cities of El Salvador to carry out retribution killings and drug smuggling. Indeed, the country has one of the highest murder rates in the world, along with its neighbour Honduras. My instinct told me to skip a visit, so I paid heed to it. The coast was always prettier to look at anyway.

Since southern Mexico I had been exchanging emails with André Lanwehr, a German cyclist en route from Anchorage to Ushuaia. We had shared a room briefly in San Cristobal and intended to stay in touch along the road, and it was at the Posada Don Quixote in Usulutan on a muggy March evening that we reconvened.

The Posada was an odd place, as not only did it provide accommodation to travellers, but also beds and medical treatment to sick people. It was a clinic of sorts, but I never saw any high-tech equipment, intravenous drips, or actual treatment rooms – things you would expect to exist in such a place. The sterility and smell of the bleached white interior was undoubtedly that of a hospital, and not that of a hotel, however. As I carried my bicycle and pannier bags up three flights of stairs past patients being shuttled around on gurneys by masked attendants, I couldn't help but sense a surreal world close in around me.

I eventually located André in an upstairs bedroom, trying to get his laptop to connect with the hotel/hospital Wi-Fi.

'Ian, it's good to see you. Welcome to Usulutan!' he greeted me.

'Good to be here. Do you need a doctor too? I have a sore backside after that seven-hour ride,' I answered. 'Are you hungry? There's a pizza place up the street: I'm about to buy everything they have.'

André was eager for company on his journey. Unlike me, he had rarely spent time cycling with others, and liked to take the opportunity to connect where possible. He was an accountant by trade, but had left his job for the 'great Pan-American trip' as he described it. He came from a small town called Greffen in western Germany, and was by this time a local celebrity because of it. As I discovered, we were quite alike, except from the age gap: at 33, André was seven years my senior. He knew a little about bicycles, but not a lot. He liked to drink at least three or four Coca-Colas a day, preferred cooking plain and simple camp foods to get full as quickly as possible, and didn't mind splurging a few dollars on a motel room to beat the humidity of night-time outside.

To break the tedium of riding with the heavy congestion through urban areas, we planned to travel together for 450 km, to Granada, Nicaragua. As the official Pan-American Highway is generally a chaotic intercontinental thoroughfare in Central America, cyclists tend to avoid it unless necessary. In truth, there is no real point sticking to 'the longest road in the world' just because of a title. In fact, from Deadhorse to Ushuaia, an incomprehensible jumble of road types and designations means the route is malleable and it's not necessary to stick to those officially identified as part of it. Departing Usulutan, however, we had no choice but to ride the Pan-American as it was the only clear path on our maps to the border with Honduras, and so we scuttled onto it, balancing body and bike nervously on the one-foot shoulder, awaiting our next opportunity to leave it.

André kept a swift and steady pace, which I liked. He didn't dawdle – and there was no reason to, on this sweaty avenue of industry and community in transit. Buffering the baking asphalt from the countryside beyond it were immense swathes of household rubbish on each side of the road, with only the occasional gap for fruit and vegetable vendors in dusty lay-bys. The red and white colouring of Esso service stations signalled our chance to take a break from the bedlam, and refuel in our own way with Coca-Colas and chocolate. At one such station, we got chatting to a man who had spent the past two decades in the United States, working as a roofer everywhere from Alabama to Chicago. At present, his primary income was a regular remittance sent by his two brothers, who were naturalised US citizens living in New York. In El Salvador, remittances of this kind being sent into the country amount to $3 billion per year, and to say they are one of the most crucial forms of financial support propping up this fragile economy is a grand understatement.

André and I found a mid-priced twin room for $10 in a hotel in Santa Rosa de Lima, 16 km from the border. The ground floor was a grotty bar with torn green pool tables and wall-mounted televisions showing football and car racing. We needed to carve a path through the hive of drunken activity and not once, but twice, I was groped by one of the frisky, red-faced male customers. The room was a typical low-cost purchase; it was just wide enough to fit two beds, both of which had stained sheets, but at least an attempt at washing them had apparently taken place. There was one chipped black locker, with a towel that felt like sandpaper on top of it. Perfectly placed in the middle of the towel was a bar of complimentary, unbranded soap. In the corner, near the ceiling, a fan blew warm air towards us; beneath hung a small rectangular mirror with signs of water damage around it. It was however a perfectly suitable habitation for the night for us, and reflected in its fittings our own state of wear and tear.

As I settled in to sleep, I became abruptly aware of how small Central American countries were, compared to their North American neighbours. This was my third night in El Salvador and I'd leave it for good in the morning. In just 72 hours, I would have pedalled through the most densely populated nation in the region. Guatemala, too, consisted of a border-to-border cycle in just seven days. Tomorrow, I'd pedal across a narrow section of Honduras and perhaps enter Nicaragua, a distance of just 158 km. It took almost seven months to ride through the US, Canada and Mexico put together, whereas on this leg of the journey, I would have travelled through the same number of nations in just 11 days.

Despite the apparent speed at which I was cycling, I knew my effort to reach Bogotá, Colombia for my flight to Tajikistan was in vain. It was now 2 March, and my ticket had been booked for 17 March, meaning that 15 days, 2,000 km and a boat trip from Panama to Colombia still separated me from the Bogotá plane. The only option left was to book a connecting flight from San José, Costa Rica to Colombia to bridge the gap.

The closer I came to the date, the more my excitement was building at the prospect that I'd soon have two whole weeks with Áine. She had been more animated on the phone of late, and this was encouraging, as I was naturally the worrier of the relationship. It would also mark the approximate half-way stage of my journey, and I intended to do everything to reinforce the belief that if we could cope with the separation for this long, we could survive the rest too.

It was at this stage that the TV production company emailed to inform me of the cancellation of the filming project. Funding couldn't be sourced to enable them to send a professional film crew over, and therefore the final product they intended to develop would never materialise. In truth, I was relieved. Once I had informed the executives that the original 350-day target couldn't be met, the filming no longer hindered my progress or enjoyment. Now I didn't have to film things I didn't want to, such as the video diaries. I also didn't need to send footage home, hold Skype meetings, and so on – although I still did some personal filming. However, the TV company felt that this loss of a 'hook' made continuing production pointless. As I had originally sought a TV deal for the purpose of raising money for The Carers Association, I didn't really care that the project had now been scrapped, since I had discovered meantime that in practical terms it didn't help me greatly in my fundraising efforts. Now I would be able to concentrate on other more effective approaches, such as doing radio spots, blogging and local fundraising initiatives.

In other ways too, the cancellation of the TV project was the best thing that could have happened. Apart from the production team's wish for Lee and I to talk about our ongoing concerns and frustrations with each other, as they had been keen for us to do in Canada, they also expected us to meet specific deadlines and organise meet-ups with online followers on the road south, thereby putting us under pressure to ride big distances some of the time. It felt almost as if we were under some sort of obligation to create an atmosphere of tension, especially for example, when crossing borders or riding through isolated stretches of road in Mexico and Central America, where bandits were sure to be lurking in the undergrowth, waiting to prey on vulnerable, defenceless cyclists such as ourselves.

In essence, the TV people were in search of drama, and without it – and Lee – the story-arc was redundant. For my own part, I had been growingly increasingly uncomfortable with a premise that required an artificially dramatic aspect to everything we experienced: I knew I'd be doing a great disservice to the people and cultures of these nations by portraying every foray into their towns, cities, and even homes as somehow inherently dangerous. And on even more of a personal note, why would I sacrifice the authentic experience of a wonderful, memorable, and perhaps life-changing journey for the sake of someone else making money from a partly dramatised version of the story? I understood what the world of TV production needed, but day-by-day, it was becoming increasingly clear to me that this tour couldn't, and shouldn't, deliver that. The executives listened to my concerns and understood them, but we both knew it was time to end it.

The one-day ride across Honduras was the longest of the entire trip so far. Through a sporadically hilly and thirsting landscape, we covered 148 km in over eight hours. Our Coca-Cola index – measuring which country was cheapest, based on price of a bottle of coke – indicated that we were now in the most economical nation, with Coca-Cola at just $0.60 for a half-litre.

A single day in Honduras isn't of course a long enough time to explore any aspects of the country, but in those 24 hours we didn't see a particularly pleasant side of it. There was an unidentifiable atmosphere of hostility in the air – remarked upon by other cyclists too – which was hard to pinpoint or elucidate upon. Unlike in Guatemala and El Salvador, where a wave in greeting from children and adults alike was a common occurrence, here, most just stood and stared at us, craning their necks in a long turn to acknowledge our presence, expressionless and ominously passive. It was an otherworldly feeling that caused us a sense of unease, not so much because of actions taken, but because of the general ambiance, and the impenetrable silence our attempts to interaction were often met with.

Our arrival in the border town of Guasaule came late, after over an hour-and-a-half ridden in total darkness. Two-foot wide potholes, deep enough to crack a wheel, impeded us to the extent that we had to drop our pace in the final 8 km, as weak lights illuminated the road. There was only one *comedor* (restaurant) open, so we gleefully gobbled up fried eggs on rice before closing time. Flies took every chance to land on our plates for their own feeding purposes. Moths swarmed the lights, mosquitoes circled our heads, and cricket-like noises came from the shrubs across the street. We were in the centre of town, at night, but every minute form of life was out and in evidence, the humidity of Central America sustaining them around the clock.

André and I passed through Honduran border control at 7 a.m. the following morning, and crossed the Río Guasaule, where Nicaraguan and Honduran currency exchangers and mini-van drivers stood, scratching their heads and waiting for business. Some rested against lampposts, holding out until you came close enough, before rushing over to offer the 'best rates'. André became frustrated with the harassment.

'These fucking guys! You stop for one second and they're all over you.'

He was right to be wary. At the Nicaraguan immigration booth, five or six men had stood near us, inspecting his bicycle, pulling at the panniers and pressing the bicycle computer. I went over to make a presence felt, but I suspected they were probably just making fun of the *gringos* who preferred the hardship of cycling to the comfort of a bus. Where possible, to avoid changers' charges, we would take local currency from an ATM, but as we had been told there weren't any, we exchanged Honduran lempira for Nicaraguan córdoba with a man holding the biggest calculator I had ever seen, and for a rate we couldn't quite comprehend but trusted nonetheless.

Nicaragua instilled a sense of positivity almost right away. Once we had cleared the medley of hawkers at the border and passed through Somotillo, the first village 3 km away, the landscape became exquisite to behold.

HALF THE WORLD AWAY

Diary: 4 March 2012, León, Nicaragua

I really felt wonderful today, even though we had 80 miles (132 km) to do. The road was slightly undulating, as the slopes of the volcano stretched to meet the low-lying land around. Fields of sugarcane, maize, and cotton lined the roadsides and the place was extremely open, not like the claustrophobic highways and landscape of Honduras and El Salvador. The people were relaxed and friendly, to the extent that 'gringo' was not once shouted at us. Instead, they rode with us; two workers chatted about their lives and carried machetes on the back of their rickety bikes. I like the working atmosphere here, and the men in the fields. It's cleaner too, not as much rubbish around. It looks like the roads are being repaired.

As we progressed towards León, there was such an incredible assortment of colours everywhere. White, fluffy cotton plants grew beneath the smoking charcoal top of Volcán San Cristobal, which pierced a wispy sky. Every now and again, the cotton fields were broken by acres of conical golden haystacks, organised in rows of military precision. We rounded Volcán San Cristobal and stopped at Chinandega for lunch at a service station. It was clean and crisp inside, the customer service attendants in white, surgically clean uniforms with nametags. There was a sandwich bar and fast-food counter, the shelves were stacked with Lay's crisps, Mars Bars, Snickers and a variety of familiar snacks. The cars at the pumps were shiny and many of them new. A few buildings were even three or four storeys high, painted and sitting tidy. It appeared that this was a very different economy to the one we had just come from.

León's cathedral was dazzling as we arrived with the late afternoon sun at our backs. Two roaring alabaster lions stood fearsome at its entrance, which was bordered by two sets of double pillars holding up a second floor with a sculpted frieze. Either side of the door were larger bell towers of chipped yellow plaster that gave the building an authoritative presence.

León is Nicaragua's second largest city, with a population of close to 200,000, but it feels little more than a town. Several downtown blocks are the relics of crumbling colonialism, and continue to radiate an elegance conditioned by the slowly passing centuries. The city is home to revered composers, poets, and giants of Nicaraguan literature, and is the intellectual heart of the nation. Its sister cities, contemporaries in history and culture, are Oxford in England, Gettysburg in the US, and its namesake, León in Mexico. Crossing the main plaza, we saw fresh-faced youths carrying books underarm – a hint at the large student body here. It all felt like a gratifying finish to what had been a wonderful day, one filled with cycling ease, good company and wonderful scenery.

We might have stayed in León longer, but I had an offer of a free hotel room for two nights in Granada, 140 km away. The owner was Gerald Webb, a native of my hometown in Ireland, who had read about our trip in the online edition of the local newspaper. On an extended holiday many years before, he passed through Granada and had fallen in love with the location and people, subsequently buying an old city-centre villa, which he converted into a boutique guesthouse.

The wind had picked up during the night and by the time of our departure from León, it was rattling telephone lines and unlocked gates. The sky, however, was clear, menacingly indicating an impending storm. At breakfast, the hostel owner told us this type of weather was a common feature of the region, as north-easterly winds raged over Lago Nicaragua and Lago de Managua during springtime.

Twenty kilometres from León, we took a 90-degree change of direction onto Highway 28, a new road bordering Lago de Managua. At the junction, we picked up another cyclist: Chad, who was from Alaska. He had no maps, and generally no idea where he was going.

'It's all new to me. Why do I need maps?' he said. 'What's down this road anyway?'

'It goes to Granada, following the lake. It's supposed to be pretty nice, if you don't mind this bloody wind,' I answered.

'Ok. Well, I was going to go the other way. Didn't know there was a lake over there. Mind if I tag along?'

The three of us started into an unrelenting headwind in the form of a breakaway group in a bike race. At first André took the lead, with Chad in the middle, while I rode behind. Every three or four minutes, whoever was at the rear would nip out and force his way to the front, taking the brunt of the wind's muscle. I grinned at the exercise and our unwieldy movement, for we were far from racers, laden down by bags weighing perhaps 100 kg together. There was no way to speak, as the howling gale whisked our words away before we could form them. After an hour the lake emerged, but we could only take cursory glances at it, instead, having to concentrate on simply staying balanced.

Close to Managua, Nicaragua's capital and a city we opted to bypass as quickly as possible, we met another cyclist, called Dominik, who was from Germany. We found Dominik in the shade of a bus stop, sweating profusely. He joined us reluctantly, maintaining that he was 'too tired and unfit' to keep a pace, but André intervened with a few motivating words in German, and soon we were four.

The wind surrendered to the concrete sprawl of Managua and we entered a period of brief respite. However, our foursome was about to be broken up, as Chad suffered multiple punctures of his rear tyre and was practically riding on the rim. The damage was substantial enough to require at least an hour's repair work, so Dominik, wearing a sickly pallor, agreed to stop to help Chad and find a hotel for the night. It was 6 p.m., and we had just an hour-and-a-half of sunlight remaining, but André and I decided to push the final 45 km and make the meeting with Gerald.

Highway 4 from Managua to Granada bobbed and weaved over the hills and ridges at the base of Volcán Masaya, before a 6 km ascent up the main crest. It was an energy-sapping ride and André struggled to keep going, further frustrated by the fact a teenage boy had stolen his rear bike light when he stopped for water. After André had pressured him to pull the light from his pocket – where we had seen him stash it – the boy took two steps back, pulled out the light and smashed it on the ground in front of us. Curses and fist-shaking ensued, before I encouraged André to forget about it and put his energy into reaching Granada, to avoid another panicky night arrival.

With the last of dusk departing, we panted over the highest point of the volcano and then drifted graciously into a 9 km downhill on the wide, unlit highway. With the lights of passing cars brightening the surface, we crouched into aerodynamic postures and took advantage of the lights on the road. Soon, Granada came into view as a yellow blotch in the valley below. The enormous black patch to its north was Lago Nicaragua, Central America's biggest lake and the ninth largest in the Americas.

It took some time to find Casa del Agua, Gerald's guesthouse. But when we did, we realised it had been worth the work. Crystal-clear waters filled a pool in the centre of the tiled atrium. On the walls hung old-timey maps of Nicaragua and a second-storey red slate roof sloped down either side, where a tall mango tree overlooked the central space.

'In case you're wondering what that almighty bang is during the night, it's the tree dropping fruit onto the roof,' Gerald told us. 'You can pick them out of the pool for breakfast if you like.'

There was a real palatial feel to what was in fact a small villa. André and I sat around with Gerald for an hour, drinking beers, admiring the rich ornamentation, and basking in the cool air of the Granada night. The wind that streams in from Lago Nicaragua keeps the city pleasantly cool, and has just enough energy to billow curtains and shuffle grounded leaves. Gerald was insistent that we venture out to try some Flor de Caña, aged sugarcane rum famous to Nicaragua. But instead of a traditional watering hole, he took us to O'Shea's Bar on the Calzada. It was one of the more traditional Irish pub offerings I'd come across on the trip, perhaps because it was actually owned and run by an elderly Irishman. Tom O'Shea brought us out three plates of fish and chips, and a couple of pints of Guinness. The Flor de Caña would have to wait for a while yet.

The Calzada is Granada's main tourist strip, and it tapers down to the shores of Lago Nicaragua. Along it are souvenir stores selling tacky wares, expensive French and Italian restaurants, a handful of ATMs, and a grouping of Westernised bars such as O'Shea's. It's the typical agglomeration of all that is touristy in Granada, and thankfully the majority of it is encapsulated just here. The rest of the city is a raucous buzz of normal Central American activity within this architectural bubble of colonialism. Street markets open up early, pedalling shoes, knock-off clothes, fruits, and vegetables. The pong of chicken bubbling in broth wafts around street corners, and every other shop appears to sell mobile phones and their accessories. When the shops close up, the streets empty and all that is left behind is damp cardboard and the squashed remnants of fruit skins on the footpaths.

Close to the lake promenade, I noticed the smell of excrement drifting inland over five or six street blocks. The lake was a wonderful sight, but it was sullied a little by poor waste management, as Gerald later told me.

Strong waves and frothy foam charged towards the shore and, had I been Chad from Alaska – without maps or any real sense of where I was going – I might have assumed it was the sea, if I had come across it without warning. Way off to the east rose a volcano skimming the bottom of the clouds – but the smell of pollution moved us off before we could explore its form and features much further.

With my flight so soon, I needed to make ground towards Costa Rica, and I said goodbye to André, who had decided to stay a little longer and visit the island of Ometepe in the centre of Lago Nicaragua. Five days had passed so quickly – one pleasant aspect of shared travel – and in that sense, I regretted having to leave. So I continued on my way, following the lakeshore with full exposure to the wind. To my right were green fields, absent of any crops or grazing animals. To my left was the water, but every 20 to 30 km, the road would veer away from the lake. In the space between, a glistening wind farm grew from the soil – a community of giant, swirling turbines, making huge 'swoosh' sounds, as their clean-cut blades cut the air above me.

Before I passed the eastern limit of the lake, where the border between Nicaragua and Costa Rica lies, I bought three mangos, a bunch of bananas, tomatoes, some avocados and a melon from a lady selling fruits on the roadside. Stacked in terraces on her wooden stall, they were the freshest I'd seen yet. It cost just $3 for the horde, and I swore not to be tempted by the supermarket variety again.

By late evening, I was in Costa Rica. Another country was upon me, and it seemed I'd had barely enough time to figure out the last. From Granada, I had covered 132 km and now stopped in a town called La Cruz, just off the main highway. It was hidden behind some stout hills, and occupied a prominent point over the surrounding plains, which could only be seen from the local schoolyard. Very little was happening in La Cruz, so I immediately checked into a hotel of which, similarly, nothing was going on. The owner warned of a severe storm to come the following day, and made several attempts with his hands and body to indicate I would fall off of the bicycle if I rode through it. After a cold shower and rinsing my shirts and shorts, I walked to the nearest supermarket for crisps and some coke. I had already cooked a dinner of peas, beans and pasta on the stove outside the hotel, where the wind had kept blowing out the flame over and over, until I sat with my back to it, protecting the burner. The aisles in the supermarket were gleaming from fresh buffering, and there were two sections dedicated to frozen goods. There were all sorts of American brands, like Hershey's chocolate and Powerade energy drinks. A bakery with large stainless steel ovens in the rear had the remains of the day's bread and cakes. I ended up putting more than I needed into the basket, and watched in horror as the sweet-faced checkout girl totted up a total of $23 for some chocolate bars, crisps, peanut butter, soft drinks, the cakes, and a small packet of washing-up powder. I thought of the fruit seller, 20 km back over the border in Nicaragua, and felt I might have been robbed on my first night in the country.

The hotel owner's forecast was right. Leaving my room at the Cabinas Santa Rita the next day, I could sense the wind warning me to remain inside. I rolled downhill from La Cruz and rejoined Highway 1, the Costa Rican leg of the Pan-American Highway. As I had several days before my flight from San José to Bogotá, I had decided to take the longer route to the capital via the Nicoya Peninsula, which bulges out of the north-western mainland, before turning back parallel to it. My guidebook described it as, 'a hook-shaped, beach-fringed and sun-drenched' strip of land that, 'has featured extensively in the history of Costa Rica'. I didn't tend use guidebooks so much except for accommodation options, but the expanded description of the peninsula was enough to push me west for a few days' exploration on its sandy back roads.

The wind howled with a nightmarish strength on the way to Liberia, where I would take a regional road towards Nicoya. The trees swayed from side to side; branches scattered the road and trucks shook as they thundered past. I crept into Liberia after three hours and just 30 km of cycling, and stopped in McDonald's, too lazy to make my own lunch. Afterwards, I crossed the busy road and followed signs for Highway 21 to Santa Cruz. The wind was now coming from behind, and pushed me along with such energy that I struggled to put force into the wheels. But after 10 km, I noticed a faint noise as the wheels spun. 'Ding, ding, ding', it went, with regularity. I thought it might have been dirt caught between the brake pads and the wheel rim, which would eventually find its own way out. Several kilometres down the road at a junction called Buenos Aires, the noise was still audible.

I dismounted the bicycle at a petrol station to inspect it. The frame looked good. So did my panniers. The mudguards weren't touching the wheels, nor was the hub clicking when I rotated the pedals.

I checked the wheels at the distance of a few inches.

'Aha,' I said to myself, spotting a broken spoke in the rear wheel. 'About time my luck ran out.'

The spoke was the least of my problems, as I found out. Directly above it, glimmering in the sun, was a three-inch crack in the rim. On the opposite side too, another fracture stared back at me. Knowing all too well that in this part of the world, well-stocked bike shops were only found in big cities, I realised there was no possibility of carrying on – I'd only do further damage and probably find myself stranded in a tiny beach town on the Nicoya Peninsula off a bus route, and a couple of hundred kilometres from proper repair. Not that the former fate wasn't entirely unattractive, but I did have a flight to catch.

A sympathetic cashier at the petrol station – understanding my predicament, after inspecting the damage first-hand – told me to relax while she sent for help.

'My friend, José. Five minutes. He'll come with a truck,' she said and ushered me onto the forecourt, where I sat on a plastic chair counting the weeks since exactly the same wheel issue had occurred in San Francisco.

Punctual as you like, José arrived exactly five minutes later. The rusted green pickup pulled into the station, sputtering smoke, and I was beckoned to the driver's window, where José sat, grinning. He was going to take me back into Liberia, where I could board a bus to San José and scope out the scene for a reputable bike shop.

'Twenty dollars,' signalled José.

'Twenty? That's too much. Liberia is 10 km away,' I said.

We bargained for a few more minutes and all I had received was a two-dollar discount, so I passed on principle of paying over the top. José shot off, blowing up a cloud of dust as he careened onto the highway once more. I didn't mind paying for the petrol, and a little more in appreciation money, but that price was extortionate. The bus ride to the capital almost 300 km away wouldn't cost half of that, so I was happy to cut José loose.

The cashier, who remained kind despite my rejection of her acquaintance, told me a local bus would come by in about 10 minutes, and that if I stood patiently in the midday sun, I might have a chance of boarding it. Punctuality obviously ranks highly on Costa Rican public and private transport services, because exactly 10 minutes later the bus rolled to a stop adjacent to the petrol station. This time I was charged $2, so I squeezed my bike and panniers into the aisle and sat wedged between them and the door.

Seven hours later, I arrived in San José and booked myself into a hostel close to the bus station. I had five days until my flight to Bogotá, so I searched the Internet for a bicycle shop with a big showroom and lots in the way of online marketing. I figured with these criteria in mind, I would at least be given a wide selection of rims and spokes to choose from, and as it happened, I was. Rodolfo Soto Rivera, the owner of Ciclo Los Ases and a former Costa Rican race champion, took the bicycle and assured me it'd come out in better shape than ever. He spoke perfect English and was able to suggest a few things that might help relieve pressure on the rim in future, such as monitoring tyre pressure and fitting better spokes.

'Go and enjoy your trip. Your bike will be here when you get back. I'll drive to Customs for you and pick up the part you need imported,' he told me. Rodolfo proved to be a true gentlemen and capable mechanic.

I had four days left, so I spent the afternoons walking the gridiron streets of the capital and the nights partying with a mismatched group of hostel residents. There was Andre, a mid-20s Costa Rican man, who was in love with a local pole dancer named Esmeralda, and whom he insisted I see perform; there was Lucho, a bald, late-40s Argentine painter who also worked mornings in the hostel, and 30-year-old Johnny, another painter, but this time from the unlikely artistic haven of Cardiff, Wales; then there was Kevin, an early-50s, scraggly-haired man from Los Angeles, who was a former electronic engineer charged with designing the guidance systems for Tomahawk missiles in the United States. Although each one had very different pasts and presents, they were all bound together by a common reluctance to talk about them. For each, San José was a seasonal sanctuary from whatever life they lived either side of it. Both Lucho and Kevin visited for five months of the year and just, 'hung out, chilling', as they put it. Andre came anytime he wanted to escape Tamarindo, his home on the Nicoya Peninsula, because sometimes, as he said: 'It's just too much – too much noise, too many tourists, too hard to think.' Johnny, like me, was just passing through, but had decided to stay for an indefinite period of time, as he had recently broken up with his long-time girlfriend, and San José was to be therapy, in a sense.

Our tiny community appeared to be a microcosm of greater foreign immigration trends. Costa Rica is a country pulsing with new development and middle- to high-society arrivals, especially in the capital and on the coast. The United States' influence cannot be understated and as far back as Baja California, I had met people driving from the States to Costa Rica, in search of summer sunshine, beaches, surfing, and a tamer pace to life. At the border separating Costa Rica and Nicaragua, I had rubbed shoulders with individuals, couples, and families on visa runs from the southern provinces, looking for another month's extension. Even though they needed to exit and re-enter the country once a month, they'd already built seaside homes or bought ranches inland. I met a pastor from Virginia and a farmer from Wyoming, who both owned land and raised families in Costa Rica. The downtown bars and upmarket coffee shops were full of foreign blow-ins from Europe and America. There was a truly staggering volume of foreign settlement.

San José was more an exercise in social observation than touristic engagement. In fact, I couldn't really find much to do there, except go to the cinema daily before heading out with the hostellers. But the time passed quickly and before I knew it, my best clothes were clean, my bags were packed, and a taxi booked to Juan Santamaría International Airport. I can't say it was just excitement building – nerves were present too. I was a little daunted. Although it was easy to quantify how much time Áine and I had spent apart and think that it was not that long at all in the grand scheme of things, it seemed far longer, considering how far I'd come on a bicycle in the interim. I remembered phone calls from the tent in Canada, from payphones in the States, and on Skype in Mexico; so much had happened before and after them, such a wealth of new places and experiences in comparison to my normal daily life, that what was just in fact seven months appeared to be so much more. I knew that, without this being experience shared with Áine, it was also somewhat lost experience in terms of our relationship. Such was my vague analysis at the time. But for now, it was important to put these thoughts aside. I had six flights to catch, halfway around the world.

It was time to go to Tajikistan.

Ian (left) and Lee at Prudhoe Bay General Store.

Our first camp by the Sagavanirktok River, Alaska.

Caribou on the Dalton Highway with pipeline behind.

40 kg of gear on the bicycle at Coldfoot, Alaska.

Lee climbing a long gravel drag on the Dalton.

Lee, Ian and Eddie Brosnan in Fairbanks.

Meeting with Amaya and Eric (worldbiking.info) who had been cycling around the world for 5 years (and still going!).

The Terminal Range in British Columbia.

Afternoon arrival at Mt Robson, the highest mountain in the Canadian Rockies.

Riding the Icefields Parkway in the Canadian Rockies.

Ros Bartley filming Lee atop the Whistlers in Jasper.

Dave Wodchis, our fantastic host in Vancouver.

Occupy Wall St protestors (mother and daughter) in Seattle.

Beach sunset in Bandon, Oregon.

Redwoods camping with Karl (left), Rob Fletcher (centre), Buff3y (second right) and Felix (far right).

Balmy Alley murals, San Francisco.

Big Sur coastline, California.

Lee and I at the Mexico – US border.

Baja California desert.

Jesus, the truck driver who drove me back to Tijuana.

Salva Rodríguez, round-the-world cyclist, Baja California.

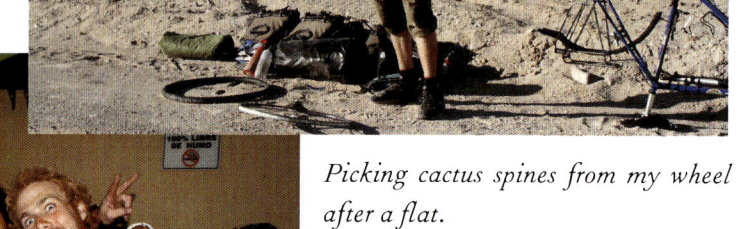

Picking cactus spines from my wheel after a flat.

Jose Juan (left), Marcus, Isis and I sharing some cervezas in Guadalajara.

My first police escort in Ahuacatlán, Mexico.

Monarch butterflies in the amazing butterfly sanctuary, Mexico.

Sunrise on top of the Pyramid of the Sun, Teotihuacán, Mexico.

Partying with Jorge (right), Rafa and Emilie, and Urs (centre) in Oaxaca.

Lago de Atitlán, Guatemala.

Cycling past Nicaragua's volcanoes with André.

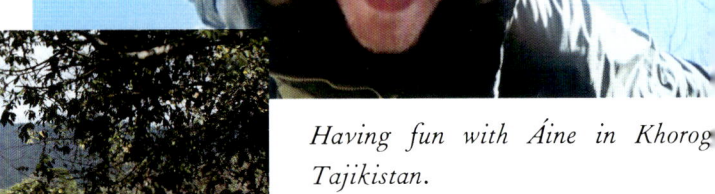

Having fun with Áine in Khorog Tajikistan.

A rest after dragging the bicycle up steep hills in Nicoya, Costa Rica.

Having a beer with Urs on the way to the San Blas Islands and South America.

The windblown palm trees of the San Blas Islands.

Locals, including Jesus and Cristi (left), offer incredible hospitality in Sahagún, Colombia.

On the way to Yarumal, Colombia, these kids made me carry their schoolbags home.

One last look into Colombia near Ipiales.

Crossing the equator in Cayambe, Ecuador.

Remarkable views over Alausí and the Andes in Ecuador.

After 18,000 km and 11 months, I bump into Markus Höfle again.

The muddy, rough track from Vilcabamba into Peru.

Todd (left), Lucho (second right), Lance (front) and Jean-Luc at the casa di ciclista in Trujillo, Peru.

On the way to Cañón del Pato and the Cordillera Blanca, Peru.

Never-ending switchbacks up to Punta Olimpica Pass.

One and a half day's climbing to reach Punta Olimpica Pass, the highest pass in the world's second highest mountain range at 4,950 metres.

Friendly locals on the east side of the Cordillera Blanca, Peru.

Lago Huachacocha, Peru – one of the prettiest and most remote lakes I've ever seen.

Sunrise at Machu Picchu, one year after leaving Deadhorse, Alaska.

Freezing campsite close to Lake Titicaca.

Arrival at 3,330 metres, La Paz, Bolivia.

Revisiting Áine's past at Fundación Arco Iris, La Paz.

Naked and liberating cycling over the Salar de Uyuni, Bolivia.

The Andes lie ahead on my crossing from Mendoza, Argentina to Santiago, Chile.

Boat crossing to Parque Pumalín on the Carretera Austral, Chile.

Lago Negro, Chile.

Volcán Corcovado near Chaitén, Chile.

Entering Aysén Province on the northern Carretera Austral.

The 'dead forest' on my second day attempting to cross roadless terrain between Chile and Argentina.

Stunning scenery in the Patagonian wilderness, Argentina.

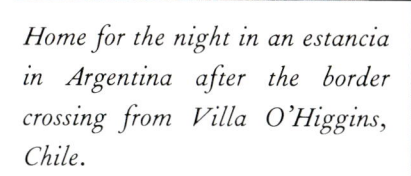

Home for the night in an estancia in Argentina after the border crossing from Villa O'Higgins, Chile.

Riding towards beautiful Mt Fitz Roy in Argentine Patagonia.

Perito Moreno glacier near El Calafate (look at people in front for perspective).

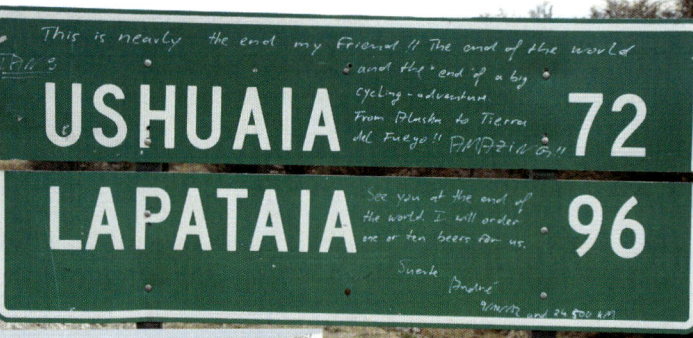

André leaves an enthusiastic note near Ushuaia.

The very last climb of the journey up Paso Garibaldi, 3 hours cycling from Ushuaia.

Arrival at El Fin del Mundo after 27,369 km and 452 days on the road.

8

Crossing Continents

San José, Costa Rica to Medellín, Colombia – 1,843 km

I couldn't see Áine, but she could see me. The blackened windows at Dushanbe International Airport were for one-way viewing only, a fact I learned after answering my phone to hear Áine's giddy voice on the other end. Five minutes later, as I waited for my entry visa, I turned around as I heard the sound of someone running, the distinctive shuffle of a rain jacket accompanying quick footsteps across the tiled floor. Before I had time to comprehend what was going on, Áine had launched into my arms. I could smell her hair, and I ran my hands through it as we kissed. By the windows, previously stern airport officials were now laughing, as she had broken through the security barrier to make it through. Whatever nervousness existed within me had been blown away in a fraction of a moment.

From that instant at the airport, I knew that things would be ok. I had had plenty of time to think that they might not, that an odd estrangement might creep in after a while, or we'd forget how to talk with each other. It had been eight months and five days since I last saw her, that time both of us had been crying at the departure gates in Dublin Airport.

After a brutally cold winter in the capital, snow lay thick on the ground. In the distance, encircling the southern and eastern limits of the city, the Fan Mountains were carpeted white, as if a soft blanket had fallen upon them from the sky, to cover all but the highest peaks. The crunch underfoot was a stark change from the searing road surfaces in Costa Rica. As we walked to her apartment, I noticed how people here were dressed to resist and survive, unlike the shirtless farmers working in Central American cornfields. Even

Áine herself was wrapped up in a duffel coat and woolly hat, bracing for the final chapter of the winter season.

We walked the neighbourhoods she had described on the phone, going to the cafés and restaurants she would hang out in. She had booked two weeks off work to see some more of the country, so we planned a jeep trip to Khorog and the Pamir Mountains in the southeast, this range the neighbour of Afghanistan's legendary Hindu Kush. The rocks and valleys, rivers and glades were the stuff of fables and ancient travel, the land of Marco Polo and goat caravans, and now we'd be exploring them together.

The winter had been tough on Áine. Her accommodation in Kurgan-Tyube — Tajikistan's third city — was basic. She slept in a dimly-lit room in the compound where she worked. The water pipes were often frozen through winter, the blankets were pitifully thin, and the bitter cold had led to a semi-permanent sleeplessness. Her nights were usually spent reading by torchlight, as the electricity would more often than not be turned off.

What I had missed most in Áine was her humour: it was matchless. We would spend a great amount of our time together in self-deprecating conversation, mocking each other and making fun of odd habits and idiosyncrasies. On our journey to Khorog, it was good to be back at it, jibing each other as a form of endearment, although perhaps confusingly so for the three Sri Lankan diamond traders we were sharing the jeep with.

Every now and again, we'd speak about the end of my trip and arrangements for coming home. I told her I was aiming for a September finish, this being the earliest I was comfortable riding through the waning Patagonian winter. I could sense her angst, as that was another six months away and we wouldn't see each other again in between. I attempted to reassure her that we were over the worst of it. I hated speaking about the trip in an apologetic tone, yet it was the only way of making it clear that I didn't take leaving her lightly.

'Well, you've got to finish now and I'll be home in August, so we can go from there,' she said in a tone of confidence rather than hopefulness, which was comforting.

Those fleeting conversations were hard to broach, especially when they impinged upon the special moments we shared in the present. In Khorog, with mountains of astonishing beauty all around, we cozied in together by the heat of a gas burner, keeping each other warm. These precious times were paradoxically some of the hardest to enjoy, because we knew they were temporary – even though it went unsaid.

The majority of our time during those two weeks was spent in nobody else's company but our own. We played table tennis in one of Dushanbe's few city parks; shopped in old communist warehouses, retro-fitted as modern malls; escaped the biting cold in smoky pizza houses with Russian soap operas playing on the big screens; we took in a couple of expatriate parties. We were as normal as always, and it felt like home. My lack of companionship on the bike was mirrored by Áine's relative isolation on weekdays, when she worked away from the capital. Spending this much time together now was a very welcome tonic for what sometimes could be a lonely existence for us both.

'Where will we go, what'll we do when we get back?' I asked her.

'Africa? South America? But you could be tired of that by then!' she said.

I loved her desire to travel as much as anything else. We'd frequently argue about the best places to live, and the right times to live there. Since we started seeing each other just two years and five months earlier, I had spent time in the United States and she had lived in Spain. Now, it was Tajikistan. The problem was that we were always apart, so the next time, we promised, we would be with each other. People often wondered how we could possibly stay in a functioning relationship, considering we had been separated longer than we had spent time together. Even now, it's difficult to put into words, but every couple is unique and for me, Áine was – and still is – my soul companion. Distance and time could always threaten that, but remaining mindful of this one truth, in which we shared a strong belief, was surely the best way of keeping it alive.

On 5 April, I left Dushanbe at 10 p.m., with a heavy heart. Áine cried as I passed through security and I followed suit on the other side – just as we had done in Dublin. When the wheels of the plane left the ground, the distance between us was as great as if I were back in Costa Rica. Then, as the lights of the capital twinkled and silently faded away through the saturated clouds, and we banked westwards towards the other side of the world, I felt foolhardy once again.

Diary: 10 April 2012, San José, Costa Rica

Where to start? I had the best time. It passed so quickly, that I feel as if I wasn't there at all. I can remember so much but the time is nearly non-existent in my head. I felt horrible leaving Áine again. At the airport, she had that face I adore, one that makes me cherish being around her. I still think, why the hell am I here, and know it's an unanswerable question. We got on as ever before and laughed so much; there was no strangeness, and I love that. After five minutes we were the same. She ran to me through the arrival gate and that was the most amazing feeling. Being so wanted by somebody, even though you decided to leave, makes me feel so fortunate. I think, from this visit, we are still strong and every day is one closer to her now.

I rose at dawn to make my second attempt to reach the Nicoya Peninsula. Instead of continuing east from San José, I felt the need to return to Liberia and pick up where I previously left off. I was still of the belief that if I was going to ride the length of the Americas, I should do it without missing a mile, unless I was forced to.

My bicycle was in a wonderful condition after Rodolfo's repairs in the city. A new, thicker rim had been fitted, and strong spokes threaded into it. I was carrying less gear too, after giving away and discarding unneeded items, such as a pair of trousers, some electronics, toiletries, and two books. I would now travel with much less food, and transfer some weight to the front panniers to relieve stress on the rear of the bicycle.

By lunchtime on the first day back, I was labouring and had become dehydrated. I pulled in to rest at a bend in the road, where it descended into a fragrant valley filled with green and yellow flowering bushes. I instantly fell asleep and woke up an hour later, to the howling of some local teenagers in the back of a pick-up. I thought about Áine throughout the day, as I pushed hard to reach Samara, a beach town protected by a hooked cove. These thoughts made cycling much harder, as I couldn't help imagining the vast distance still to go before I could see her again. I certainly didn't want to reinstate the thought processes that had plagued me before my visit to Tajikistan, which had centred around losing Áine because of my absence and the separate lives we were living. And so I decided to simply accept that my feelings were a product of the recent separation, hoping they'd become quieter and more akin to background noise in the future.

After Samara, the first true dirt roads appeared. I had already cycled over poor surfaces throughout the trip, coping with sandy stretches around road construction in Canada and muddied tracks connecting highways in Mexico, but to come across dirt highways that were permanent fixtures was new. These surfaces, and the regions they exist in, are the first signals of true remoteness; they hint at a time when all travel occurred in such conditions. The freedom and sense of escape most long-distance bicycle tourists describe, and cherish, is found on tracts of road such as these, where all that exists is the bicycle, its rider, and the sounds of nature layered upon the crunch of gravel. There is a perfect stillness to everything.

At Puerto Carrillo, just 20 km from Samara, the topography became almost impossible to negotiate, with 60- to 80-metre climbs coming in waves, at grades of 18 per cent. As I pedalled uphill, often skidding on the loose stone surface, the front wheel of the bicycle would lift off the ground unless I laid myself forward over the handlebars. This is the limit of anyone's cycling ability, and I realised that the only way forward was for me to get off and push. Of course, this solution presented its own challenges, as there was little grip on the dirt surface for the bike or my shoes. So I resorted to unpacking the bicycle, carrying the panniers to the top of the climb first, and then walking back down the hill to wheel the bike up.

I spent an afternoon in the jungle heat, hauling bike and bags over the hills of Nicoya, recovering from each summit attempt with a quick siesta at the top. Eventually, the land flattened and the sea came into view. I passed signs pointing down sandy roads to Playa Islita, Playa Corazolito, Playa Bejuco, Playa Javilla and Playa Coyote. These beaches were ubiquitous and uninhabited for the most part, and I was sure I could've set up camp and hidden out for days without encountering another soul. Although this is one of the least visited areas of Costa Rica, it is one of the most exceptional. I skirted by farmhouses and grazing cattle, cycled through ankle-deep streams that crossed the road here and there, and got an unrestricted view onto those gently inclined beaches which beckon the Pacific waters with a graceful welcome.

By the navy hue of nightfall, I could see the lights from Cóbano, 6 km ahead. I decided to push for it, as I was almost out of water, and badly wanted a shower after a day of constant sweating. On the approach to town, a family of howler monkeys swung from branches across the road, mothers carrying babies on their backs. Further along, others could only be heard but not seen; the open forest was coming alive.

Costa Rica's biodiversity borders on the magical, and near the town of Quepos – across the Gulf of Nicoya – is an enchanted sanctuary where this wonder can be experienced. Parque Nacional Manuel Antonio is home to 109 species of mammals and 184 species of birds. In this space of just under 7 km^2, you will find squirrel monkeys and white-headed capuchins, green iguanas and black spiny-tailed varieties, toucans and woodpeckers, sloths and dolphins. The noise inside the park is incessant, but always changing. Monkeys swing overhead, tanagers whistle by, and hawks circle above. A white sand beach runs alongside a skinny isthmus into the ocean. Located in amongst several settlements on the coast, the sanctuary is a smaller, and well-preserved example of what exists plentifully in the mountains of central Costa Rica. As presentations of biodiversity go, it's a remarkable natural exhibit.

I lingered just a day in Quepos. After almost a month off, my legs were still eager to pedal and re-educating them would require a series of steady days of riding. After a breakfast of *gallo pinto* (rice and beans), I rode back onto the Costanera Sur Highway and enjoyed an undulating coastal road and tailwind. Sea stacks – natural rock formations – were embedded deep in the blue waters and positioned all along the coast; a brisk wind kept me from overheating. Every now and again, enormous palm plantations would block the sun and offer some reprieve from it, which seemed ever-present, despite a sky half-full of clouds.

Climbing into Uvita, I noticed the familiar reflection of Ortlieb pannier bags up ahead. I wasn't travelling particularly fast, and so was surprised to catch up with their owner at the crest of the hill within just five minutes. As I approached, I noticed sweat stains all over his red T-shirt, and a pool of it at his feet. The rider was Steve, a 60-year-old native of Birmingham in the UK, who was travelling from Mexico City to Panama City. Every year, Steve takes six months to cycle a different part of the world, while for the other six, he lives on his barge somewhere amidst the tangle of middle-England waterways.

'Best way to see the place,' he told me in a pronounced Brummie accent. 'I've gone from Buenos Aires to Colombia, ridden the coast of Norway, and next I'll do something in Africa.' He searched for breath in between sentences, still wearing an expression of pain after the ascent. 'Haven't met too many of us types so far, always good to get company. I'm not the fastest, so people tend to pass me by.'

We agreed to cycle into Uvita and grab some lunch. Steve bought some pre-packed sandwiches and I came back with a two-litre bottle of coke.

'Bloody good stuff! Can't go without the sugar,' he said, leaning for the bottle.

I told him about the Nicoya Peninsula, and the country roads being largely unoccupied. He wanted to know why I cycled through there, if I had already reached San José and had the bike fixed.

'Did you really want to see it *that* badly?' he asked me.

'Yeah, I did. But I guess I felt I should too, and am glad to have done it. I have this idea that I should . . .'

'Ride every inch?' he said, finishing my sentence.

'You could call it that. I don't see why not. I started as far north as I could get, and am going to finish as far south as I can, too.'

'You seem like a good lad,' he responded, taking a bite of his sandwich. 'It's just that sometimes I meet these people – and believe me, after 20 years of touring, I've met a lot of 'em – who are determined to ride every fucking inch. I call them the 'EFI club'. I've seen a lot, who get angry with themselves if they don't do it, as if they won't win their badge of honour on completion. Got to show off they've done it.'

I explained to Steve about how I wanted to get as far as possible, without taking a bus or hitching a ride. It was an added achievement in my mind.

'Well, we're all different. Just don't let it affect your travel. And by the sounds of it, if you want to get back to see that girlfriend of yours, it's probably going to take longer than you think.'

Steve had the touring years on me, and there was wisdom in the forthright way he spoke about it, yet he was adamant too that no matter what happened, as long as I considered what was *really* important and made a decision based on that, then there'd be no regrets.

'Look at it this way. What's the point of riding ten days into a headwind – and it will happen where you're going – with nothing around to see?' he said, while finishing his sandwich. I had some food for thought when I left Steve, who decided to catch a boat tour in Uvita instead of carrying on.

My first night in the tent in over two months was spent at La Ponderosa Bar and Restaurant, just outside the town of Cortes and a short ride from the Panamanian border. The owner had graciously offered a patch of grass under a big tree at the rear of the restaurant. I cooked on the steps of an outhouse, and watched as ants formed orderly lines to feed on anything that bubbled out of the pot. During the night, the noise outside the tent was incredible. Although I was surrounded by a couple of residential buildings, and the closest forest was on the other side of the road, there was a captivating, cyclical hum all around. I could hear scuffling in the leaves, squawking from the trees, and the noise of crickets and tiny reptiles in the grass. Earlier, over tea in the restaurant, I had read that Costa Rica comprises 0.1 per cent of the planet's landmass, but contains 5 per cent of its biodiversity. This cacophony was audible confirmation of that fact.

When it rains in Central America, it pours, and the next afternoon, the skies opened. The last time I had felt rain on my skin was in Santa Barbara, California, so when storm clouds rolled in, leading with a plume of dark grey, I took cover in a driveway sheltered by the overhanging forest canopy. The wet season was just beginning and I expected this to become a common occurrence, but I also knew that the brunt of it could be avoided the further south I travelled. One hour after the first drops landed on the road, the storm had vanished, with the only tangible evidence of it a slick surface and cool breeze.

Anticipation was building, as Panama – the last country I'd visit in Central America – was just 30 km away. I knew little about it, except that it had a humpback shape on the map, the Panama Canal ran across it, and wide-brimmed cream-coloured hats were one of its famous exports. I was, however, surprised at the level of friendliness I encountered as soon as I crossed the border. I was escorted half a kilometre to an ATM by a cheery couple who wanted to ensure I had enough currency to make it to David, the next biggest town. Then, at a supermarket, the security guard put the bike in a storeroom for me, telling me not to worry as he had a gun to protect it. Later, in Pension Las Americas – a guesthouse that reeked of faeces – Omar, the hyperactive manager, offered me a papaya- and rice-based drink free of charge, because I was the first Irish person he'd ever spoken to.

Whatever route I took through Panama, I would inevitably end up in Portobelo, a Caribbean port village to the north of Panama City. It is from here that private sailing boats, from yachts to catamarans, cross the narrow sea to Cartagena in Colombia. The need to sail between both countries is one borne out of inaccessibility and safety, as separating them is the Darién Gap, an area of dense swampland and forest that both governments have for decades decided to leave undeveloped and wild. Road construction is too expensive and the environmental damage would be immense, and so those wishing to cross the continents either fly or take a boat. It is possible to navigate the gap in an off-road vehicle with a competent driver and sufficient supplies, but this is also incredibly dangerous. Even if one was determined to make it through purely for the purpose of adventure, the presence of an armed FARC militia from Colombia, with a history of kidnappings and assassinations, makes it very much ill-advised. In 2000, two British rare plant hunters were held hostage for nine months before being released, and this is just one of countless harrowing stories that have begun – and sometimes ended – in the Darién Gap. Therefore, true end-to-end Pan-American travellers are given their pardon when arriving in Portobelo, in recognition of their prudence and level-headedness.

I had booked a place on a catamaran for 25 April, my birthday, and with this date in mind, I made haste from La Concepción to David, and then from David to Tole. The highway was tight and winding, and it felt as if 18-wheel trucks exclusively occupied the lane closest to me. There was nothing to see either side of this road; the greenery that existed in Costa Rica had disappeared within kilometres of the border, to be replaced by single-storey concrete buildings and a sweep of burnt land.

Ironically, just days after meeting Steve from Birmingham, my own 'every fucking inch' rule was broken for the first time since Lee's wheel issues in the Canadian Rockies. After a puncture, I realised I couldn't inflate the tyre, as the tube valve wasn't long enough to attach to the pump.

The new rim installed in San José was too wide, and only at a gas station could I chance getting air into it.

> *Diary: 18 April 2012, Santiago, Panama*
>
> *I'm a tad frustrated right now. I got a flat at sunset and couldn't repair it, so checked my map for the closest town – which was Tole – about 4 km away. Two Panamanians stopped, and I put the bike in the back of their van, asking them to drop me to Tole. Of course, they misunderstood 'Tole' for 'Hotel' because of my bad pronunciation. After 10 or 15 minutes, I asked where the town was and they said about an hour away. At that point I realised what happened but couldn't ask them to turn back. Instead, I ended up deflated on arrival to Santiago, 85 km further along the road. Should I get a lift back in the morning or just keep going from here?*

After the unfortunate mistake caused by my mispronunciation, I was now being hounded by the preposterous thought of going all the way back the following morning. The route was hill-strewn, so, I asked myself, what would be the point? What would I achieve by turning around again to cycle a road I had already travelled? Nothing – apart from being able to say I had pedalled the entire section. Even then, who would care? Nobody should, except for myself, it seemed. I stopped to analyse the reason for my thinking. I came to the conclusion that, by not cycling every kilometre, I might become susceptible to laziness in the future. If I skip this part, maybe I'll do it again and again, when things get tough or the landscape is boring. In essence, I posited that what I was dealing with was the fear that, in tough periods ahead, I might give in to alternative transport. But I didn't have time to gamble with at this juncture, as I risked missing the boat to Colombia – so I decided to carry on from Santiago, and not be so hard on myself because of an honest mistake.

Panama in April is unrelentingly hot. The horizon wears a permanent haze from a stifling heat rising from the road, but the sociable locals somehow make it easier to bear. In the midst of many baking afternoons, I'd be flagged down to explain what I was doing; others, who didn't require my presence in person, would give me a wave or a beep of the horn. I hadn't witnessed such camaraderie between cyclist and driver since Mexico, a country I had felt would be extremely difficult to top in terms of highway hospitality.

Just east of Santiago, the Pan-American Highway takes one of its very few surges north, and follows the humpback shape of the coastline. Since Panama narrows suddenly at this point, the road shifts back towards the Pacific, avoiding the mountains in its way, and taking in some wonderfully underdeveloped beach towns and villages. I ventured towards Nueva Gorgona and soon found myself on black sand beaches and the Gulf of Panama.

After a night in a beach shack, so close to the sea I could hear the waters lapping as I fell asleep, I woke, intending to ride just 70 km to Arraijan on the outskirts of Panama City. I soon crossed the Bridge of the Americas and watched as bulky container ships, yachts, and fishing boats sailed in from the glistening ocean and along the Panama Canal. Unquestionably, this was one of those moments of reflection for me, and I thought about the 16,198 km between Alaska and here, and all the things that I had experienced in between. Although I was over halfway in terms of distance travelled, in my mind the Panama Canal was the true marker of the second half of my journey.

I paid a visit to Miraflores Locks, one of three locks along the canal's 77 km length, from Pacific to Caribbean oceans. I had hoped to be able to watch a cargo ship passing through, but I was too late. Instead, I wandered the impressive exhibition room and watched an audio-visual presentation, with black-and-white footage showing people hammering, shovelling, digging – and eventually celebrating – in or around 1914, when the canal was completed.

This canal is a marvel of human engineering. Without it, ships would need to sail south to Cape Horn and round the tip of South America in order to cross either the Atlantic or Pacific oceans. Noting how profitable a transoceanic canal would be in this case, the French began construction in 1881 under Ferdinand de Lesseps, the man behind the Suez Canal. However, the hardship involved in carving a channel across swamp and tropical rainforest had been dramatically underestimated, and, with 22,000 men to lost disease or accident, the project failed dramatically. Later, the US acquired rights from Colombia (of which Panama was then a province), and moved ahead with a more workable plan, which included the damming of the Chagres River, resulting in turn in the formation of Gatún Lake. Since Gatún naturally provides a 33 km stretch of water to the Atlantic Ocean, this means that just over half of the canal is actually canal proper. Almost three decades after work began, the finished project at last opened, on 15 August 1914. Since then, over 820,000 ships have passed through. Only since 1999 has this happened on the say-so of the Panamanian government; before this, the US exercised full control. Now however, thankfully for Panama, the tax dollars remain entirely in the country.

In the same way that the French originally underestimated the difficulty in digging through the isthmus, so did I, in cycling across it. The uncompromising nature of the topography I had to navigate meant that the likelihood of an incredibly rare ocean-to-ocean day was slim, and I knew I'd reach Portobelo only after darkness had fallen. After bypassing the busy port of Colón, my route changed to a north-easterly direction for the final leg of this long ride. Over the shoreline, a crimson sky burned low before the blackness descended. In the golden hour of sunset, I watched as the Caribbean rushed onto stony beaches and palm trees rustled in the breeze between hundreds of fishermen's huts.

In Portobelo, I spoke with a few locals roaming the unlit streets. They directed me towards a guesthouse overlooking a small alley near the main square, where the dim yellow glow of restaurants was the only hint of life. The guesthouse owner, a finicky old lady with hair tied in a large bun and an apron slung around her waist, directed me upstairs. As I was her only customer, she led me to 'the best room', which was small but clean and located at the end of a narrow corridor with a panorama over the town. It was just big enough to store the bicycle and panniers between the bed and the wall, but was perfectly suitable as the final place I would sleep in Central America. Not long after I settled down for the night with a book and some crackers, raindrops started to fall. First, there was just a soft pattering on the roof, and minutes later, a full-blown downpour. The noise became hypnotic, pounding the slates above me and the galvanised sheds around the property and across the town. I don't think it lasted long, as, after futile attempts to stay awake, I nodded off into a deep sleep with the light on and a group of bugs circling it.

The morning broke, with sunshine and a comfortable warmth. Portobelo was quiet even during the day, but it did have some interesting colonial ruins scattered about, which I went looking for straightaway. In my eagerness I got lost at the waterfront where fishermen were arriving with the early catch, in slender, one-person boats. In amongst the languid Caribbean residents coming to shore were clusters of backpackers on the hunt for private yachts to Colombia. As it is the only means to reach South America bar a plane journey, Portobelo – normally, I would imagine a sleepy community – has become a fulcrum for inbound and outbound Pan-American travellers. Location is everything, of course, and Portobelo's position close to the tropical, palm-fringed San Blas Islands – usually included in the passage – is an added attraction to offset days of seasickness and general misery on what can be terribly rough seas.

In Captain Jack's Hostel – Portobelo's backpacker base – I encountered a familiar face coming through the door, just as I was leaving. Wearing a long red poncho, and otherwise rain-soaked wherever it didn't cover, I heard him before I saw him.

'Fucking rain, man,' he said to nobody in particular. 'Can't go five minutes out there without getting totally wet. I thought this was the Caribbean.'

Urs looked as dishevelled as the last time I had seen him in Oaxaca. His beard was dripping wet and knotted, and he looked thoroughly downtrodden. But he lit up when he caught me grinning at him.

'You know, I left here five days ago on this other boat, but the captain was always drunk and he crashed it on a reef or some shit,' Urs told me over hamburgers upstairs. 'Then there was an argument with his wife and these other guys, and they wanted the drunken captain to turn around, but he wouldn't, so we had to tell him to do it or we'd report him to the police. Fuckin' crazy, man. We were halfway to Colombia and this shit happens.'

Urs always had a story, and I couldn't figure out if unfortunate things always occurred when he was around, or he was just good at recounting normal events in an absurd manner. His upbeat Swiss-German timbre and wild gesticulations added to the show, if not actually making it. He still faced the issue of finding a boat to Colombia though, for his second attempt at crossing. So I went off to ask Jepi, the captain of the catamaran I was booked on, if there was any more space. I was able to come back to Urs with some good news.

'You serious?' he shouted.

'Yep, looks like there's room for one more lazy, dirty bicycle tourer.'

'That's amazing, dude. This is gonna be some crazy fun. We better start toasting Central America now then!'

Of all the tourers I met on the road, Urs was unequivocally the most stress-free. He didn't care so much what road he took south, just as long as it was actually in the direction he was heading. Because of this attitude, he embraced many facets of travel others didn't – such as the daily uncertainty of whether he'd find a bed to sleep in or not. He tended to ask a lot of questions of those sharing time with him in conversation. This was evident on the second day of our boat crossing, when he remarked that only a handful of us (there were 18 in all, mostly Europeans, Americans, and Australians, with the majority being between 19 and 26 years of age) had taken time to talk with the deckhand, a Panamanian man in his early-20s, who prepared our meals, washed up after us, and made our beds each night. Urs couldn't understand how people who called themselves 'travellers' didn't bother to say anything other than 'thank you' to this guy.

'We're here for five days, right? So why don't they ask Ricardo about his family, his work, or other things?' Urs asked. 'It's rude, man, don't you think?'

I agreed. We were all confined to a 50-foot catamaran, and every passenger knew the rest of those on board by name, nationality, and travel stories. But three to four days in, some still forgot Ricardo's name. It wasn't down to poor Spanish skills either, as the majority had a rudimentary level of the language, and enough to attempt conversation.

I told Urs about a friend of my mother's in Ireland. In the early 1960s, he had crossed Canada, the United States, and Europe, riding boxcars and hitching lifts. He slept in farmers' barns and repaid them with labour. His stories were fascinating, not just as it was a different era of travel, but because his approach to it was dependent totally on hospitality.

'I guess travel now is different to travel then. There was probably more exploration in it, because so much of the world was difficult to reach, or at least so expensive to travel to,' I said to Urs in conclusion.

'What do you mean?'

'Well, things were left up to chance an awful lot, I think. Or at least, circumstances were more likely forced upon you,' I said. 'Look at us. We're paying $500 for a five-day cruise. We have times to eat, times to sleep, expensive outdoor clothes, travel insurance, iPods, iPads, and very little to do except eat and rest.'

I wasn't saying that people didn't forge adventure in their own terms, but we could make it as easy as we wanted – even Urs and I.

'There's a philosophy in it, I guess,' Urs said. 'Anyway, we're the lucky ones, man. We get to travel by fucking bicycle!'

The journey to Cartagena was dominated by seasickness. From the moment we broke away from the coast and into open waters, I began to retch. Our French-Moroccan captain suggested we place bets on who would get sick first, and the winner would get a six-pack of beer. I was the third of us to empty the contents of our stomachs: I threw up all over the starboard rigging in the middle of dinner, watching nauseously as the moon bobbed up and down on the horizon with the swaying of the boat.

By the third day I had adjusted to the catamaran's motion over the water and was thankful we weren't on a yacht, which would, I had heard, be much less stable on the ocean. At night I slept on the roof over the mess hall and kitchen. I wrapped up in a sleeping bag when it became chilly and stared up at the dome of the night sky. It was magnificent and it was with this canopy that I fell asleep each night, unless a rogue rain shower woke me, in which case I'd jump downstairs and into the covered living area, where five or six others were normally passed out on the soft cushions.

We moored at the San Blas Islands for one-and-a-half days. The archipelago, less than 10 km from the mainland, is made up of almost 400 islets not more than a metre or two above sea level. To the passive observer, they all look quite the same – white sand beaches slipping into pristinely clear ocean water, and flanked by palm trees that moved in unison with the light wind. However, the Kuna – an indigenous people of Panama and Colombia – occupy around 50 of the islands. They wear brightly coloured dress and live a subsistence lifestyle for the most part, with fishing of crucial importance. To supplement a basic income, some Kuna charge a levy to swim to their island, and a worthwhile one it is, to be able to take a break from the boat and touch terra firma once again.

On the afternoon 28 April, a shout rose up from Jepi, saying that if our eyesight was strong enough we'd be able to see South America ahead in the distance. I could only make out two white dots; three hours later, those dots had grown into apartment blocks, as Jepi cut the engines and the cat came to rest in the water outside the city of Cartagena.

Urs and I high-fived each other, and untied our bicycles from the metal guardrail surrounding the catamaran. They had been wrapped in thick blue plastic sheeting to stop corrosive salt water getting into the drivetrain, and looked unharmed as we loaded them into a small dinghy that would take us to shore.

Our first steps on South American soil were unsteady. We suffered with land-sickness, and the buildings, cars, and roads seemed to sway up and down in the same manner as the ocean we just left.

'It feels so good, to actually be here, don't you think?' said Urs.

It really did; I was ecstatic. We were in South America – the land of the Andes, great salt lakes, majestic colonial cities, mountaintop empires, rain-soaked gravel roads, Patagonian pampas, and El Fin del Mundo. We cycled without a clue as to where we were going, and talked excitedly to each other through lanes of cars with unusual number plates, shop windows with unfamiliar names displaying familiar wares, and well-groomed plazas and squares. There seemed to be a certain light and spaciousness in Cartagena that made it instantly agreeable, even though we were still outside the heart of the old city. We rode for 15 minutes to the Getsemani district, where a woman walking her dog had suggested we'd find plenty of cheap hostels. At Hostel Casa Viena, we paid for a room to share, and had a shower for the first time in six days, something all 18 of us on board the catamaran had been looking forward to with a building desperation. Later, we went to meet the others at a salsa bar inside the colonial city walls, and got lost in a night of music, drink, and dance.

Diary: 30 April 2012, Cartagena, Colombia

Cartagena really is a gem of a city. I absolutely loved it on first sight, and my heart was beating with the beauty of its historical centre. The plastered buildings are a rich yellow; the colours are deep even at night. The buildings are only two- or three-storeys high, and they all seem to have a memorial plaque outside, commemorating someone or other. As soon as we walked in, there was a smell of bread and sweets, and old men stood selling churros con chocolate behind their carts. Earlier, Urs and I went out to the walls to watch the sunset. There were old cannons pointing out to sea at each hexagonal bastion. It's a pretty romantic destination and I'm sure I like it more than the other colonial cities. Even though it's touristy, that doesn't take away from much of its charm.

Cartagena deserved some traditional sightseeing so I got to it over four days there. I walked under the Puerto del Reloj (Clock Gate) each day and strolled down either Calle (Street) 32 or Calle 34, both of which led deep into the old town. First on my list to see was Plaza de Bolívar, named after Simon Bolívar, the Latin American politician and activist, who led five South American nations including Colombia to independence from the Spanish Empire. The square was quaint and as quiet as a church, with lots of tall palm trees; beneath them were benches and green spaces to rest on. It felt like a small Spanish courtyard, not just because of its diminutive size and its design, but also because of the slender white portals that border it, every second one housing a café or fashionable restaurant. Close by was Cartagena's cathedral, which stands in the middle of a spacious square where students and families gather. The bell tower is visible from the edges of the city but is better appreciated up close; the medieval grey stonework offers a striking contrast with the brilliant white archways of another palatial building across from the cathedral.

Sights such as these were the big draws, but on every other street and alleyway there was something to match them in terms of beauty or interest. Flamboyant plants and vines hung over wooden balconies, while vendors sold clothes, fruit, and an assortment of breads, in any open space they could find. Museums were housed in the lavish residences of the expelled Spanish aristocracy. The entire old quarter pulsed with the energy of the ages and it was impossible to be bored within it. Often, the most pleasurable thing to do was just sit with a coffee and watch the streets wax and wane with people, or pick up an *arepa con queso* – a toasted flatbread filled with butter and cheese – and walk the city walls.

Urs left a day before me but was heading in the same direction, so I was sure we'd meet each other in Medellín and Popayán, cities we both planned to stay in. Although it went unsaid, I think he preferred to travel alone, just as I did. And considering we had spent the past 10 days at close quarters with each other – even though all had passed very well between us – it was nice to set out alone into Colombia.

The morning I departed Cartagena, I received an email from Lee. He said he had finished cycling for the moment and instead had taken up teaching in Quetzaltenango in Guatemala. He reckoned he would probably stay for six months, maybe longer. Either way, he was happy and content to leave the touring life for the time being. I got the impression this was what he had desired all along – to be able to stop for as long as he wanted, or even live for a while in a place that he liked. As we hadn't maintained much contact, I didn't know where he was or if we would cross paths on the road, but I realised that this might be one of the last times I heard from him while we were travelling.

As I left Getsemani and the old town of Cartagena behind, I navigated my way onto Highway 90, which took a south-easterly direction for 20 km, before gently edging south and turning into Highway 25 all the way to Medellín, 640 km away in a high Andean valley.

Before I cleared the congestion of outer Cartagena, a man on a motorcycle pulled up beside me and gestured for me to stop.

'Where are you going?' he asked, as cars and other motorbikes rushed by on the dual carriageway.

'Medellín, I'll get there in five days,' I answered.

He then put his hand inside his jacket, fidgeted for a moment, and pulled out 2,000 Colombian pesos (US$1) from an inside pocket. He handed me the money and apologised that he didn't have any more. Then, riding back into the traffic, he wished me a safe journey. The encounter lasted all of 30 seconds, but it was a random act of kindness that would set the tone for the following three weeks.

Next I travelled 110 km through a permanently saturated portion of northern Colombia. Streams, rivers and lakes crossed the road with such frequency that bridges were always visible ahead. By evening I reached San Onofre, after a small climb from the main road and into the well-laid out and clean town.

'Hey, man,' I heard someone shout as I stopped to get my bearings.

A burly, dark-skinned man with a plain mustard-coloured polo shirt came walking towards me. He had been sitting with some other men on a wall which enclosed a small square.

'Hey, man,' he said again. 'Are you looking for a place to stay?'

Usually I'm wary of anyone soliciting for hotel business, as it often results in being taken to an overpriced, substandard hotel run by a cousin or friend of the person asking. Here however, in a non-descript provincial town, I couldn't imagine there were enough tourist arrivals to suggest that the soliciting was part of anyone's business model.

'Yes, a hotel or hostel. Somewhere cheap and close to the plaza,' I said.

'No problem, no problem. I know a place. In fact, it's my mother's and just down this street. By the way, I'm Tulio,' he said, with a wide smile that stretched from cheek to cheek.

I walked with Tulio for 10 minutes to a three-storey building bearing a sign with the name 'Rosarita' on it, which I presumed to be a reference to his mother. I paid $5 for the room, and Tulio said he'd show me a nice place to eat that was as cheap as I had suggested. He spoke excellent English, and so over a dinner of rice, spaghetti, meat, vegetables and a coke – which cost just 5,000 pesos (US$2.50) – I asked him how he learned it so well.

'I'm a tour guide in Cartagena and am used to bringing foreigners like you around the city,' he told me. 'But I've given a lot of that up. I sell cocaine now, to foreigners just like you!'

Tulio spoke and acted with apparently harmless intention, and I was intrigued about how a coke seller conducts business. He talked openly about it, and as Colombia is heavily associated with the production and export of cocaine, it was fascinating to hear him speak of it in the same way as if he sold apples and oranges.

'I sell coke at 5,000 pesos per gram. The purest stuff you'll get,' he said. 'In Cartagena, you'll get backpackers who'll pay big dollars for it, but I keep prices steady. It's not right to rip people off for it, you know.'

'Where do you get it?'

'Oh, a friend has connections and they get it from high in the mountains and deep in the jungle. Secret places, but not so secret that *policía* don't know, you get me?'

'Do you . . . want to try the product?' he asked, lowering his voice.

'Thanks, but I'm good. Don't think it's gonna help me pedal that bike tomorrow!' I said.

'Oh man, it's exactly what's going to help you ride it. I bet it'll get you to Medellín much faster!'

We walked back to the hotel and sat on the steps with a beer. He explained he had two children, but that they were living with their mother now. He didn't say much more when I asked where exactly they were, but was more jovial when changing the subject to his new girlfriend.

'Man, you should see the curves.' He waved his hands into an hourglass shape to reinforce his point. 'She's one of two, though. I gotta make sure I have options.'

His mother knew exactly what he was talking about, and leaned out of the kitchen window to scold him, her finger pointed like a dagger at him.

'*Si, si, si, Mama,*' he shouted back.

It is a strange point of the machismo culture of some Latin American men that they can talk big about all the young women they've got on the go, or the 'disobedient' wives that have left them, yet still transform into guilty-looking boys as soon as their mother disapproves of something they do. Their respect for women seems to extend only to their mothers, and not much further.

I was too tired to stay much longer, but Tulio insisted I chat for a moment with his now good-tempered Mama. When she emerged from the kitchen, she didn't have much interest in conversation, but instead began to stroke my hair as I downed the end of my beer.

'She likes your hair,' Tulio told me, as if I couldn't gather it already.

If that wasn't strange enough, Tulio's brother arrived home soon afterwards and once pleasantries were exchanged, he began scrolling through the extensive collection of porn on his mobile phone. At this juncture it all became a little much, so I bid them goodnight and went to my room, where I hoped to think other thoughts and fall asleep as quickly as I could.

For the next two days, the landscape was rather uninspiring. It was flat, with a few short climbs and dips each day, but nothing that would bear remembrance. Near Sincelejo however, a car passed, parked up on a wide grassy verge and signalled for me to slow down. Out climbed a middle-aged man and his two children, a boy and a girl. They opened the boot and then poured out some orange soda into a plastic cup and tore open a packet of crackers to share with me. José, the father, was a lawyer and told me to be vigilant in this part of Colombia, insisting that I should take care where I stayed and with whom I talked. He was a serious man, bordering on sombre, with a face that frowned with worry and contemplation as I described my route through the country. With each town and city I mentioned, he crossed and uncrossed his arms, interrupting me from time to time with information of how to remain safe there. His mood lightened when I spoke in English to his son, who I could see was eager to practice, and after a few moments, José insisted I continue so that I could arrive at my destination in daylight.

'My country is your country,' he said leaving. 'Stay safe.'

Later in the evening in Sahagún, two men on mopeds escorted me around town as I searched for a cheap hotel. On my behalf, they explained that high prices would not do, and when an hotelier suggested charging above what I had said I wanted to spend – usually between $5 and $10 – my new minders would say that we should leave and look elsewhere.

In the morning, after an overnight costing just $8, three men on motorbikes stopped me just as I was merging onto the main highway.

'Where are you from?' one asked.

'Where are you going?' said the other.

'Where is your family?' enquired the third, an elderly gentleman in a thatched hat.

By the time I had answered these questions, a large crowd of people had gathered by the roadside. From the elderly to the young, each and every one wanted a photo taken with me. What puzzled me most was that they weren't interested in the photo being taken on their phones, but instead wanted me to capture them on my own camera. Men with big bellies mounted the bicycle, bursting into laughter as I took picture after picture. They pressed the brakes, changed gears and knocked on the steel frame as if exploring the workings of a bike for the very first time. Then they insisted I pretend to ride their motorbikes. Twenty minutes passed before they began to disperse. It was beginning to get very hot, so I took one family up on their offer of breakfast and rode back into Sahagún and to their house.

Jesus and Cristi brought me to their grandmother's home, which was located on a peaceful side street with a dusty path outside it. They cooked eggs and tortillas and made coffee. We struggled with language but they seemed delighted to have me in their home, none more so than the grandmother, whose name I didn't catch, but whose expression I won't forget. She shied away from their efforts to get her sitting near to me, but became protective when Jesus jokingly asked me to marry his daughter, Juli. Grandmother might have appreciated the novelty of catering for a *gringo* in her home, but wasn't quite ready to let her favourite granddaughter run away with him.

In every village and town I passed through in northern Colombia, the people took an endless interest in my reason for being there. I wondered if it was the recent cessation of FARC violence or the decades-long civil war that contributed to this. Tourism was just picking up again, and travellers were beginning to regain trust in a country familiar with a great deal of bad press. In this part of Colombia, visitors were anything but regular. Unless you were on a bicycle, you didn't stop in places like Sahagún. Tour buses push the 600 km from Cartagena to Medellín in one day and only stop for meals in pre-determined restaurants that rarely connect with urban and rural life. Even if they do, you just have half an hour to take it all in. The beauty of the bike is that in many ways, it is everything other forms of transport are not.

The Andes would subtly provide me with a final chance to reflect upon the relative ease of the past nine months. After passing through Caucasía, which sits on the banks of the deep and brown Río Cauca, I could finally see Colombia's first hills coming into view. Initially they are just crumpled mounds of earth, and the road moves through them effortlessly. Then, as mists begin to rest heavily in the valleys between them, the land very soon rises momentously to the sky.

Diary: 8 May 2012, Yarumal, Colombia

Today I climbed from 130 metres to 2,230 metres. It was quite an ascent, starting immediately after rounding the corner in Valdivia and turning away from the river. All I can say is that it went up and up and up. It was tough but as usual, when I'm in the rhythm, it's far better. I did a 55 km straight climb and finished at 4.15 p.m., after an 8 a.m. start. The green was beautiful and I eventually cycled into the clouds before Yarumal.

On my way to Yarumal, there was a captivating floral smell to the forest, and its deep green colouring of shrubs and trees and grasses told a tale of health and life. Río Cauca, a muddy and commanding river, gradually became string-like at the bottom of the mountain. Along the road were houses and wooden shops selling everyday items; they used every last inch of land available, as directly behind them was an immense drop into the river valley. Very soon it grew colder, with the temperature falling into the low teens as I moved into thinner air. As I sat into 8 km of switchbacks, I wondered how people even got up here in the first place. What brought people so high into the clouds?

Yarumal, for example, sits at 2,265 metres above sea level, and clings on for life on a mountainside in an ostensibly uninhabitable landscape. The weather is most often gloomy, with grey clouds lingering in this gently inclined pocket of the Andes. However, what is most impressive is that people have lived here for quite some time – since 1787, if you consider the official date of foundation. Before roads, rough horse tracks were dug in the soil and stone to enable access to the town, which is at least 30 km from the nearest area of level ground. It's remote more because of its setting than in terms of its actual distance from other communities. Nonetheless, the toil and work involved in getting to such places and in then shaping them into liveable spaces was something that continued to astound me.

Emphasising just how isolated Yarumal was for so much of its history is the unfortunate statistic that it has the largest population of Alzheimer sufferers in the world. *La bobera* ('The stupidity') – as it's known locally – is so widespread that Yarumal is now the focus of several clinical trials concerning a rare form of the disease passed down from just one eighteenth-century Basque settler. This particular genetic trait infiltrated and then spread through the community to the extent that a significant proportion of people there have a strong chance of inheriting it. Yarumal's inaccessibility and seclusion then for so long, in a lofty Andean environment, ensured the propagation of the condition within a small population and until recently kept outside awareness of it limited to a local and regional context only.

As I proceeded through the countryside, the distinctive sound of truck engine breaks indicated that Medellín was not too far away. I was ready to descend sharply at any minute: according to my map, the close-packed contour lines would soon give way to a tamer valley bottom.

'Jesus!' I whispered to myself, as I looked over the edge of a reinforced steel vantage point.

To my right was Highway 25, which disappeared behind bluffs, only to reappear again further along my line of sight at a slightly lower elevation. Throughout the entire valley, I could hear the reverberation of sticky gear changes of heavy vehicles and see black smoke billowing from exhaust pipes behind the drivers' cabs. Ahead, and extending to my far left, was a giant hollow in the mountains. In the soft curve of the valley perhaps 700 metres below, I could make out some villages; birds soared halfway between that level and mine. I attempted to gauge what size these villages might be, by counting church spires; as I did so, the sun fell behind the mountaintops, throwing some of them suddenly into shadow.

Within 20 minutes, I had exchanged life at 2,200 metres for an altitude of 1,400 metres, and felt better for the extra warmth. As I made my way into the city along the raging highway, which had a very slim hard shoulder, I thought I felt a flat tyre. The drag on the road increased, the bicycle became sluggish and wobbly, and I had to push hard to pick up any speed. If it was a slow flat, I reckoned I could make it to a hostel and change it that night, but after a couple of minutes it was becoming too onerous to ignore, so I glanced over my shoulder to pull in. What I hadn't expected to see was a small Colombian boy, perhaps 10 or 11 years of age, crouched low on his bicycle and holding on to my back rack to take advantage of a free ride. Beside him, a friend pedalled quietly on his own bike – until they realised they'd been caught, and rapidly scuppered onto a side-road. The temerity of the action impressed me, and reminded me of an event from the previous day when four young school children, walking up a steep incline I was labouring to climb, had tied their bags onto my panniers and told me to leave them five minutes' up the road, at a white house with a blue gate.

Medellín was lit by gloomy yellow streetlamps in the midst of darkness, so I picked the first hostel from my Lonely Planet book and made my way there. Right on time, as usual, and with his trademark smile, Urs greeted me, coming out the door. He was off to find a Chinese restaurant, so I hurriedly checked in and the two of us headed to the La Candelaria district, the cultural and touristic hub of the city.

In the 1980s and 1990s, Medellín was said to be the most violent city in the world. At the mercy of the Medellín Cartel and its leader, Pablo Escobar, the city was a focal point for Colombia's booming cocaine industry, and often served as centre stage for violent clashes between feuding rival drug gangs. During this period, the Cartel controlled 80 per cent of the world's cocaine supply, and Escobar had accumulated a personal worth of $25 billion. Only with his death in 1993, did the murder and serious crime rates fall.

As I considered the facts and histories outlined in guidebooks and online during my time there, I realised that it was hopeless to try to imagine what Medellín must have looked and felt like just 20 years ago. The polished downtown skyscrapers, the easy-going street atmosphere, the university students hanging around city parks, and most of all, the sincere and wholesome welcome given to me by Colombian people: all of this had replaced my imagined vision of its darker past. I found myself wondering also about how quick we are to cast judgement on a place or a country without really knowing it. 'Oh, you can't go there' or, 'You'll get yourself killed in those places' – how many times had I heard such warnings before and during this trip? Naturally, caution should be well observed, but such superficial labelling shouldn't be the determining factor in where you travel, and by what means. In reality, I was unlikely to meet violent criminals here, and yet they are the only ones we hear of. And for its part at least, it seemed that my bicycle had become as disarming here as it had been in Mexico, helping me forge a path to chance encounters and friendship, as other cyclists had done before me.

Medellín was a perfect break from cycling and, as I wasn't so interested in being a typical tourist, my exploration of the city was done at a slow and leisurely pace. The place had all the usual city amenities I had experienced time and again – wide and airy boulevards, plenty of cheap eateries, live music in the college district, and a moderate enough climate, meaning that I could walk there without breaking too much of a sweat. If anything, Medellín seemed like a city that meant business, literally. For a valley barely 3 km wide, it had an immense number of skyscrapers, with corporation logos glinting over their top floors. It was also a city for socialising, and, the night before my departure, I was glad to hear that Buff3y was in town and up for some storytelling on the steps of the Parque Bolívar. He was in fine form and had just spent two weeks learning how to salsa badly in Cartagena – he loved the place as much as I did – and would leave Medellín soon if his legs would allow him. It was a pity that Urs, Buff3y, and I couldn't have set off together, but we each had different plans moving south, and perhaps dissimilar climbing abilities, once the Andes set in for the long haul.

With a blazing sun on the rise the following morning, I wedged my sunglasses as close as I could to my eyes, and rode off into the 9 a.m. brightness. The wind whisked parting clouds across the sky, over tall buildings and beyond the stocky end of the valley. It looked like there was a lot of space up there over the crest, where trees replaced people, and streams the maze of roadways. It was towards that – the top of another crinkle in a giant fold of the northern expanse of this immense Pan-American mountain chain – that I channelled my energy, as I set off into what I expected to be an eternity of climbing.

9
Valleys and Mountaintops

Medellín, Colombia to San Ignacio, Peru – 2,251 km

IN CARTAGENA, I HAD RECEIVED a message from a Facebook follower, saying that the town of Santa Barbara, 55 km south of Medellín, was a worthwhile place to see. On account of a stubborn headache that was worsening the further I cycled from Medellín, I decided to make Santa Barbara my target for the evening. It was a rather short day, compared to the 110 km daily average I now maintained, but suggestions from past travellers are always worth heeding.

Santa Barbara was full of activity. Chatter burst out of crammed restaurants and bars, facing onto streets full of commerce, banter, and colour. It seemed as if there was a market in progress, but there was no centre to it. The entire town, including groups of youth, young families, individuals and elderly couples, were out in force with the same vigour as if it were a festival weekend. It was a welcome sight, and one of my favourite things to do on an evening such as this was to walk around amidst the animation of local life.

Emerging from my hotel, I noticed, on the far side of the street, a slightly chubby man wearing a khaki jacket, with a camera slung over his neck. When I had first entered the hotel, 30 minutes previously, I spotted him watching me but he hadn't said a word. Realising that he had now caught my eye, he crossed the street between speeding bicycles and women pushing carts of brightly-coloured flowers and pot plants, and put his hand out to shake mine.

'I want to be the first to welcome you to Santa Barbara,' he said, appearing delightfully happy. 'I am Gustavo, and here we are so glad to host travellers. Please, let me buy you some coffee.'

I was a mere nine days in Colombia, but I had already become used to this direct and uninhibited kind of welcome, and knew far better than to turn it down. Gustavo motioned towards Parque Central, a plaza with a slender, three-storey white church at one end, and lots of stalls selling fruit juices and unidentifiable deep-fried meats at the other.

My new acquaintance chose Panadería Monterrey, a bakery at the edge of the plaza furthest from the church, as, 'they had the best cakes in all of Colombia', according to him. Countless meetings such as these were, I knew, motivated by the desire to get some English practice, but Gustavo's purpose was simply to tell me about Santa Barbara and its beauty. His English was extremely good and he was adept at recounting the town's history, architectural styles and attractions for the visitor, all of which were things he was truly passionate about.

'Santa Barbara, I must tell you, Ian, is a wonderful place,' he began. 'I think to appreciate it in the right way, you must stay many days. This church here, I have photographed many times. Its face is so lovely, don't you think?'

I told Gustavo I agreed wholeheartedly. It was a pretty structure, although had he not explained it was a church, I might have mistaken it for a municipal building. It was rather chunky and didn't have any great grandeur, but it was imposing and acted as an anchor for the rest of the town.

'I will give you this,' he said, handing me a key ring. On it was a picture of the church that Gustavo had taken years before. 'Tell me, Ian, what is Ireland like?'

He knew three things about Ireland already, namely that: it was very green, agriculture was important, and there was some connection to England. I told him as much about the country's history as I could and he nodded intently, hanging on every word. At the mention of any possible similarities between Colombia and Ireland, he felt compelled to stop me and say that we were 'brothers', and he would love to visit someday. An hour later Gustavo's wife arrived, and we shared some *café con leche* (milky coffee). The conversation flowed easily and we talked about my trip, his work as a carpenter, and things I had to see in the rest Colombia.

'Of course, you have everything here. The mountains, the cool weather, a quiet town, and lots of opportunities to marry – why would you leave?'

He was adamant that we share breakfast the following morning, and we agreed to meet early at the *panadería*. Bakeries in Colombian cities have clearly become more than just a breakfast hangout, but places to stop for lunch and to gorge on sweet breads, cakes, and chocolate biscuits. The next day, Gustavo was already waiting for me at 7.30 a.m., and proceeded to take plenty of photographs, most of which were of me eating my eggs, rice, and a *banuelo* (deep fried bread), in full cycling attire and with tables of other curious customers looking on. He told me to return someday, because he wanted to take me on a tour of the countryside; after which, of course, I would then be obliged to do the very same for him in Ireland.

From Santa Barbara, a 16 km downhill road leads to the Río Cauca and its damp and foggy valley once again. The vegetation seemed prehistoric, with ferns the size of my bicycle sitting motionless, all along the valley floor. At La Pintada, a little village hugging the side of the river, there was a major traffic jam: a rockfall the night before had blocked the road, claiming the lives of three people, one in a truck and two in a car. In the river, I could see the exhaust of the truck, sticking out about a foot above the water line. Emergency services were rushing to move boulders up to five metres wide from the road, to open up another lane of traffic. Being on such a slender machine, I was waved on – I could just about fit through the gaps in the fall. On the far side, a lonely and deafeningly quiet Highway 25 was all mine.

In the Colombian Andes, the average elevation for cycling hovers in and around 2,000 metres. I found that the general pattern when passing through the range was to ride up one side of a mountain or valley and descend into another, before repeating the process again. However, as I moved steadily onwards, the daily elevation gain (i.e. the number of metres climbed each day) was increasing, as the topography became more challenging and intense, with longer descents into river gorges and more gruelling ascents to mountain passes. I was now negotiating 15–20 km climbs over 800–1,200 metres of elevation gain: a substantial increase from what I encountered in North and Central America. I was spending two to three times as much time riding uphill as I had been – the equivalent of 3–4 hours per day – and this usually took the form of one or two extreme drags towards the clouds, and oftentimes actually within them.

One saving grace during this time in southern Colombia was the Valle del Cauca: a broad, high-elevation valley which extends over 240 km from Cartago to Santander de Quilichao. Two 130 km-plus days through a coffee-growing region brought me to its head, and the openness of this segment of Colombia encouraged my hope that I might start camping again, after three weeks without pitching a tent. Until this point, I had made a deliberate choice to sleep in motels attached to gas stations – not only was I happy to spend $5 for a bed, but the attached restaurants were typically open until midnight and would give me the opportunity to have a chat with staff or other passers-through.

Close to the town of Zarzal, I approached security personnel at a commercial fruit farm to ask about the possibility of camping on its grounds. Despite a desire to offer space inside one of the large metal storage sheds, these guys didn't want to get into trouble with their bosses. Insistent on providing help, however, three workers in blue overalls escorted me into town on motorbikes, taking me first to the police station and then to the fire station, but no one in either place seemed interested in offering me a corner in what were sizeable and safe compounds. My chaperones' efforts were finally rewarded at a comfortable motel however, where the owner was warned in advance not to overcharge the gringo, as 'he doesn't have enough money', and 'might say bad things about Colombian people'.

The valley soon unfastened itself from the nearby mountains and emerged entirely flat and light green in colour. Along the faraway slopes were family-owned coffee farms and some industrial plantations, where assiduous workers tended the fields under the sun: farm implements flashed in the afternoon sun, as men and women angled them to the light above. Despite my susceptibility to high-mountain vistas, I had to concede that there is much that is worthwhile seeing too, in the life that plays out on open land – especially in countries such as Colombia, where so many are still involved there in such an active way.

Diary: 15 May 2012, Candelaria, Colombia

The Río Cauca is seemingly directionless in this valley. It swings in and out from the middle, just like the pictures of elderly rivers we used to learn about in school geography. Since before Medellín, this river has crossed my path three times and wherever I meet it, there seem to be boundless numbers of people. It's used to irrigate the farms and threads towns together.

Today Marcela, a stunning Colombian girl, pulled me over on her moped and brought me for coffee. I am beginning to forget just how many times people have helped me out or wanted to buy me something. Most have mentioned that it's important to treat visitors well. What a nice thing to think and act upon!

Copper-coloured freight trains rattled by, clinking on the tracks as I veered east and away from Cali. They were making their way towards a blanket of smog that discoloured the sky and indicated the country's second largest city was close by. After visiting Bogotá briefly on my way to Tajikistan and spending several days in Cartagena and Medellín, I opted instead to take in the 'White City' of Popayán, one of the last big settlements before Ecuador.

The valley closed in from both sides to a sharp, claustrophobic end, where I rode, despite a building stiffness and discomfort in my right knee, in a landscape very different to that further back. The terrain was bumpy and dry, and it felt as if I had been shrunk down and the desert sand dunes enlarged. Shallow streams were behind every bend and scurried across my path. The road twisted and turned, cut back on itself and took a strange perambulation, which was dictated by the contours and obstacles of the landscape. It struck me that this was an area in which no town could establish itself: there would be little room for people and buildings here.

I never anticipated having such difficulty in riding the 145 km stretch from Candelaria that morning, and I was so tired on arrival in Popayán that I didn't realise my fleece top and sandals had fallen off the panniers they were strapped to. I was so exhausted, in fact, that when I saw Urs approach me in the main plaza, I didn't really react much to his presence and marked this up as a warning against such overly-ambitious, under-researched days in the future. In any case, Urs showed me to his hostel, where I booked a large single room for two nights, with the intention of sleeping until my body was thoroughly rested.

Popayán is a dazzling and captivating place, to which the moniker 'White City' is aptly applied. Its historic centre is almost entirely whitewashed, with residential, commercial, and government buildings all painted a brilliant white. Beneath this superficial brilliance, these structures are superbly preserved, and shine in their simplicity of design. Dark wood panelling around windows and doors complements the terracotta roof tiles and spotless finish of the paintwork. One reason for the remarkable state of upkeep of the city centre was a 1983 earthquake, which razed most of Popayán to the ground. The subsequent restoration works are now complete, and this is a major factor in giving the city its polished look.

Popayán is also home to a rich culture of gastronomical creativity too. Its *tamales de pipían* (tamales with potatoes and peanut sauce), spicy soups and local varieties of *empanadas*, corn snacks and stews are all famous throughout Colombia. Urs and I decided to walk beyond the main downtown area and over the Humilladero Bridge to find a place selling the typical southern food we'd heard so much about. Luckily we didn't have to walk too far, and for $3 ate a dish of fried potatoes, chicken in a peppery sauce and a vegetable soup, which too was loaded with spices.

'I'll miss this when we're done, you know,' Urs said on the walk back.

Urs had mentioned on more than one occasion how disappointed he'd be when he reached Ushuaia, because that would mean a return to the realities of the life he had left behind in Switzerland. He was also missing Carolina, a Uruguayan girl he had a fleeting romance with in Mexico, and who was waiting for him to finish.

'I think I start to feel like you, man,' he joked. 'Always missing your girlfriend. Sometimes I think, should I keep cycling the badass mountains of Peru at all – or just go to her?'

Not one for dwelling too long on emotions, he answered his own question almost immediately after asking it. 'Badass mountains, always!' he exclaimed. 'Always gotta be the mountains. Wait until you see the Cordillera Blanca in Peru, and you'll know.'

I could see that he was engaging with a stage of separation and uneasiness in terms of his relationship, very similar to what I had gone through in Alaska and Canada – but Urs wasn't quite as positive as I had been when it came the future outcome.

'I bet maybe she doesn't wait for me, which is ok, you know. It's a long time to be gone.'

He had commented before about how I was too time-driven and unable to rest, without knowing where I'd be on the map a week from now. Completely aware of this, I had accepted the rising and falling levels of anxiety associated with it as something to manage, rather than extinguish altogether. If in my mind I couldn't find the balance between what lay ahead and what waited at home, I knew I'd only lag behind and draw out extra days into weeks and then months, to the point where I would be fortunate to get home for Christmas.

Urs and I would frequently discuss the merits of applying a certain type of philosophy to bicycle travel, and whether there was any use in it. We'd argue over whether doing particular things and living in a certain way could bring a better sense of connectedness to the people and places around you. For instance, should a tourer sleep in the tent as much as possible? Should we depend on the generosity of strangers to such a high degree? Should we always take the road less travelled, and draw away as much as possible from the familiarities of home?

Personally, I had come to the conclusion that travel would only be enjoyable as long as I retuned myself to the original aims and enthusiasms of the journey every now and again, while also remaining aware of the other commitments I had made. Some days, there was a desperate urge to wild camp and others, not so much. Recently, during my time in the mountains, a good sleep and cheap restaurant dining trumped a sticky and broken night of sleep with roughly cooked pasta, cheese and vegetables for dinner. Although I didn't like gravel roads all the time, I did always revel in the peace and tranquillity many offered, and so I would split my time between traversing their rugged beauty and cycling on the highways, which would enable me to pick up some speed. By taking the thin yellow road on the map as opposed to the thick red one, would I, I wondered, get to know another side of Colombian life and its people?

In any given country, one thing I wanted to determine was how its people – Colombians, Panamanians, or the Kuna of the San Blas – were distinct or connected; I wanted to learn as much as possible about their lives by travelling openly and freely without the constraints of self-imposed pressures. I did realise that, without limitations and time constraints, I would have ventured 'off the beaten path' more, and maybe also taken some extra rest days. This sense of restriction bothered me somewhat, especially departing from a place I didn't really want to leave. As Rob Fletcher had said in the Redwood forests of California: 'You'll always go somewhere new, you'll always meet unexpected people and their lives probably won't be different because you went down this road or that. The most important thing is doing it by your own compass and without any sense of regret.'

I hadn't read much about southern Colombia before arriving there, and it was with much surprise that I became enamoured with it within just a few hours of riding uphill out of Popayán. I left the drab brown hills behind and now, in their place, was a wholesome new palette of greenery, extending over mountain plateaus and valleys of rushing rivers. El Bordo was the first town I encountered in this new terrain; and its precarious location at the bottom of a sweeping massif was visible from the swooping downhill leading into it. As I coasted in a U-shape from a pass to a river punctured with sand banks on its bed, my speedometer read 35 km/h – a pretty nifty speed on a touring bicycle.

The next day I rode 65 km to Remolino, and positioned myself at the base of a 50 km ascent into Pasto, Colombia's southernmost city. After a horrible morning's climbing with stomach ache, I topped out on a stony mesa, and rolled by a couple of shops with forlorn faces behind the counters. They laughed when I told them I was heading to Pasto, and informed me that it was surely impossible on a bicycle, gesturing that the road was too steep and would go on for 'many kilometres'; these pronouncements were accompanied by a waving motion intended to represent the series of hills I would encounter. After some *gaseosas* (soft drinks), I left this chilly outpost, chased by a couple of resident dogs. I soon passed through a sheer canyon wall, part natural formation, part human earthworks. I then sat into a sweaty climb on broken surface that resulted in my third puncture of the trip – this one relatively easy to repair, fortunately. About eight or nine kilometres further on, the road eased to a more manageable incline, and the highway entered a tunnel cutting under a mountain. As I progressed through this tunnel, the light ahead of me slowly expanded from a distant, monochrome dot into a diffuse spectrum of colours, and then eventually pure, brilliant daylight, where I was astonished by the vista before me: a vast expanse of lower elevation mountaintops, which cascaded into the distance under a blue sky. Carving out the only sensible path through these mountains, the road zigzagged slowly uphill again until it was barely visible, and eventually vanished around a mountain spur.

> **Diary: 22 May 2012, Unknown village, 40 km north of Ipiales, Colombia**
>
> *I'm sitting on the roof of a hotel, in a town I don't know the name of. The sun is just going down and it's giving a smoother sheen to the hills here, one that the midday sun can't replicate. Being outside at the close of day in places like this is an amazing feeling, especially in Colombia. There's not a soul around, which means there's almost zero noise. There's not so much to report today apart from the scenery, but I'm glad to say I didn't have comida corriente (set lunch) as usual, but instead a Mister Pollo burger and chips – the first Western food in ages! I remember a time when I was excited at the prospect of rice and chicken, and ordering pollo a la plancha (grilled chicken) for $2, but I think I've had my fill.*
>
> *I'll miss Colombia – Ecuador has a lot to live up to! Tomorrow I'll ride out of here and cross over the border – very excited about that, and in no time at all I'll be in the southern hemisphere.*

I intended to reach the Colombia–Ecuador border early, in case I ran into issues crossing it. A few websites I used to search for cycling information and tips had posted that some cyclists had been asked by border officials for bike papers and proof of ownership. Apparently, only bribery or good fortune had allowed them passage through – and so I had my game face ready, in case of questioning.

Ipiales is more a border city than border town, and although there's not much to see in it, on its outskirts there is a wonderful combination of man's engineering ability and religious zeal in evidence. Las Lajas Basilica, built between 1916 and 1949, is an odd yet fascinating insight into just how far faith will drive a community in their efforts to build an edifice to it. The basilica sits deep inside narrow gorge walls, which have been carved out over millennia by the Guáitara River; the river makes an ever-more ferocious noise, the further you go into the canyon. The story goes that in 1754, a local woman named Maria witnessed an apparition of the Virgin Mary and the baby Jesus, in a cave close to the site of today's basilica. Not only did she report this holy apparition, but also that her deaf-mute daughter, Rosa, who was with her, had begun to speak for the first time in her life. Months later, Rosa died from illness, so Maria brought her body to the cave, asking the Blessed Mary to resurrect her child, which she did. News of the miracle soon spread, and days later, inside the grotto, a mural of the Virgin Mary, Jesus and the saints, Francis and Dominic, was found on the walls. And thus began the community's intense devotion to worship.

It was only in 1916 that it was decided to build a church in place of the original shrine, and that local contributions made it possible for construction to begin on the basilica, and a 50-metre high, stone-arched bridge over the river. The building has four floors and rises triumphantly in the middle of the gorge with a grey-and-white brick spire. Today it's a popular pilgrimage location, and there were hundreds of solemn worshippers present when I arrived there, after a 200-metre descent from higher land into the depths of the canyon. I walked around for half an hour, visiting the original grotto and picking up an 'I Visited Las Lajas' sticker for my bicycle. I was conscious however of needing to reach Ecuador with daylight to spare, so I raced back up the canyon and left this impressive feat of religious fortitude behind.

Diary: 23 May 2012, Julio Andrade, Ecuador

I made it! Five-and-a-half-days from Popayán, but in Ecuador at last after 87 km. I'm camped in a local school, after the more-than-accommodating nuns who run it let me put my tent up in the yard. It was great today and I'm delighted with the scenery. The first valley was long and a golden-green colour (if that's possible!), and waterfalls were crashing down on all sides. I got one last look into Colombia, but when I arrived here, it was different again and there's a pastel colour to the fields.

I'm feeling wrecked after Colombia and my quads are aching quite a bit. The acid burn in my legs each morning lasts for a few hours, and my body is aware there's a new test ahead. This is country 11 of 15, but the real deal is ahead. My elevation now is around 3,000 metres but with no effects on breathing – I got slowly acclimatised. It's pretty cold, close to freezing, and the mist of my breath is filling the tent. Have a socket on the outside wall though, so I'm settling in for a movie night in the schoolyard!

Cycling in the rain is always unpleasant, but a 30 km downhill ride in a violent thunderstorm, with sodden socks and shoes, and inside layers dripping from the condensation under a rain jacket, with a severe wind-chill factor from hurtling along at 30 km/h at 3,000 metres above sea level – this is in a different bracket completely. In Costa Rica – the last place I encountered such rain – it had at least been warm. However, cycling in such conditions high in the Andes is not just a lesson in forbearance, it's also quite dangerous. The rain meant that the connection between my brake pads and the rim became slippery, and so when sharp corners appeared unannounced through the fog, I struggled to control the bicycle and the back wheel would skid from under me. This took total concentration, especially on a road that cut like a fishhook into an area of sparsely vegetated open ground, at least 1,300 metres below where I had begun the morning.

When I reached the far end of the road, the storm had eased and I could at last open my eyes fully again, after two hours spent squinting through the pelting rain. I rode into a town called El Junta, where people were coming out of hiding after the deluge; every eye was upon me as I shivered up the main street, looking like a drowned rat. Colombian and Ecuadorian restaurants have a nice policy of leaving all sorts of mixable drinks on their tables for their customers – such as coffee, hot chocolate, fizzy drinks, and high energy solutions. I pulled into such a place, far away from the crowds, and ordered two cups of hot milk, into which I mixed some coffee and hot chocolate, while my outer layers dried on the radiators. I drank this, along with two baps which each had a single slice of cheese, and fortunately it was enough to revive me again. When the rain stopped, I set off again, embarking on an ascent alongside the Chiota River, in a dry rock desert that resembled the tablelands of Utah or Arizona.

On the approach to Ibarra, a city occupying a bowl-shaped mountain valley, a series of switchbacks slowed me to a crawl. I needed to regain the elevation lost earlier in the day, but because I was shadowing the river, the ride was a lot longer, if less taxing. About two-thirds of my way up, a truck slowed to my speed and a man popped his head out of the window. Introducing himself as Graham, an Australian living in Ibarra, he was nice enough to offer me a space to camp at his garden nursery in the city. When I got there however, I couldn't find it despite following his directions. Instead, I settled for the Hotel Imbabura, a regal establishment charging below average prices in the heart of the old town.

Pepe, the stately owner, is quite a famed fixture of Ibarra, but I didn't know that at the time. It looked as if I was the only guest, which was a surprise, because the building had an attractive and lived-in opulence to it. The interior was borderline dusty, like a museum which has been closed for the winter; the floorboards creaked loudly as we walked. Pepe took me upstairs and gleefully showed me the corner room, which was bare and musty but had two large double beds, heavy-knit blankets, and a big window looking onto the surrounding rooftops. The hotel's two floors overlooked an open, central area that was filled with hanging plants, ivies, and a few exotic species of flowers.

Pepe set about telling me of all the wonderful attractions around the city, such as the Cotacachi protected area and some beloved local lakes that I should definitely visit. Such was the fluency of his oration that I suspected he had given it many times. He kept reiterating however that I mustn't miss the artisanal market in Otavalo, which takes place on Saturdays and brings in indigenous people from the countryside to sell their wares. As I'd arrived on a Thursday, a smaller version of it would be taking place, and Pepe indicated it was still well worth seeing.

When I rode into Otavalo, the street sellers had already marked the spaces out and a few were open in the Plaza de Ponchos. Encouraged to buy local,

I haggled with a man for a woven top made out of alpaca wool. It looked like the perfect warmth-preserver for the big downhill rides I'd encounter in the Ecuadorian Andes, and would allow me to relegate my synthetic down jacket to the panniers. We finally settled on $15, which I thought was a fairer price for him than for me, as I soon saw others advertised for half the cost – but at least it was better than buying one in a department store in Quito.

I ambled for an hour, watching Otavaleño men and women shopping and selling at the market. As it was a popular tourist spot, I wandered along some backstreets until I came across a food market, which announced itself through a viscous waft of chicken and spices. Even in such a smelly and dank environment, the men's embroidered long ponchos and women's subtly-toned dresses somehow remained clean. These Otavaleño faces had typically indigenous features: plump, round cheeks, small noses with dark eyes and raven-coloured hair. I realised at that point that in South America thus far, I had really only been meeting people of *mestizo* descent, but now, in the mountains where more ethnic peoples lived, I would surely cross their paths more frequently. I was incredibly pleased at this prospect, as their expressive style of dress and ethnic features made me feel that I was now really in South America – the original South America. I had to remind myself that the colonial presence – one that I noticed mostly in the architecture – was just a drop in the ocean of the longer history of the continent. And that the history of the colonial period hadn't been an entirely peaceful one either, especially for the ancestors of those people I now walked and talked with.

By early evening, I had reached the Equator, where I paused for 20 minutes at the commemorative structure, which lies just off the main road. A long, thin orange pole rises 10 metres out of the ground and is simply marked, 'Cayambe, Ecuador 0°'. A steel line representing the Equator is embedded in the pavement and runs away from it on either side, before reaching nearby fields, at which point it abruptly stops. As nobody else was around, I cycled back and forth across this line until the novelty wore off. Then I duly proceeded into the southern hemisphere, quietly thanking the north for all it had given me.

I wasn't far from Quito now, and, after a stay with the *bomberos* (firefighters) in Guayllabamba, I wrapped up the 1,200-metre ascent in two hours. I did this in the company of two other cyclists. First came Guillermo, who asked me to come to visit his bike shop in a town that I could see atop a 300-metre cliff ahead of us. Bursting with excitement, he insisted that I race him to the top, but when I explained that carrying 35 kg on a heavy bike was no match for a fit mid-50s Ecuadorian on a lightweight racer, who was used to high-altitude, Guillermo drew in behind, put his hand on my back and, rather kindly, sought to push me up. A little later, at his chaotic repair shop, I met Oswaldo, who offered to lead me into the city. One hour later as we pedalled, out-of-breath, over the final rise, Oswaldo left for home, while the horizon in front of me dropped back to eye-level and I could see Quito unfurling before me.

Quito is the highest official capital city in the world, at a breathless altitude of 2,800 metres. Although La Paz in Bolivia has 650 metres on it, it is the nation's administrative capital rather than its official capital city, so the purists don't count it. Understanding that you are at altitude can be difficult without any other physical markers – such as a valley bottom that you know is 1,000 metres below you, or seeing the ocean in the distance when you are at the summit of a 500-metre high hill. Otherwise, the only other indicator is the physical effect it has on your breathing. By this stage in my trip, I was of course already well acclimatised to the thin air of the Andes, and so wasn't greatly aware of any difference in my breathing.

When I arrived in Quito, I tried to gain some sense of its altitude by imagining that I was standing by the ocean and staring up the face of an almost 3 km high vertical wall of rock, which in my mind, resembled the face of El Capitan in California's Yosemite National Park. I found myself wondering what I'd be able to see of the top of such a structure from sea-level, and figured perhaps only the very tallest buildings would be distinguishable to the naked eye.

To thoroughly appreciate the geography of Quito, it's best to take a trip on the TelefériQo, an aerial tramway which rises from the edge of the city and leads up along Volcán Pichincha to a hill called Cruz Loma, whose summit is 4,000 metres above sea level. From Cruz Loma, you can get a 180° view of the capital, over 1 km below. On the sunny morning I visited, the air was just that little bit thinner, and as I walked around, the effect of the altitude made itself clearly felt, mainly because I'd arrived there much faster than I would have on the bike, which would have given me time to adjust. Two vantage points on the hill, 10 minutes apart on foot, offer remarkably different views of the Guayllabamba Valley in which Quito rests. The first point gives you a direct line of sight into the city, which runs north to south in the lean valley. The business district, airport, and some large parks are visible, in amongst a sprawl of white and grey buildings, as well as the major roads which course through it. The other point presents a vista onto what looks like a fertile farming valley to the southwest, where smallholdings and patchwork fields of varying greens populate the hill slopes. Looming over it all with iridescent intensity is the perfectly snow-capped Volcán Cotopaxi.

At ground level, Quito impresses as much for its cultural assets as it does for its natural features. Along with Krakow in Poland, Quito made the first raft of UNESCO World Heritage Site nominations in 1978, by fulfilling the requirement of 'outstanding universal value' through cultural merit – and it's easy to see why. The city's historic centre is replete with the architectural manifestations of an interesting past. A personal favourite for me was the Monastery of Saint Francis and its adjacent square. The monastery's construction began just weeks after the city was founded in 1534 and took 80 years to complete, but evolutions in architectural style imposed themselves on its exterior and interior over the succeeding centuries. Outside, the façade is ordered and symmetrical, with two bell-towers overlooking the stone entrance. A terracotta roof slants over the remainder of the beautifully simple double-storey whitewashed edifice, to protect an inner courtyard of palm trees and exotic purple flowers. A small entrance fee buys a tour of the grounds and a visit to the art collections, and the chance to see the Church of San Francisco, a room gilded in gold. For me, the most appealing feature of the complex was outside the main building, where a cobbled square was humming with locals and visitors like myself, drinking coffee on the brick walls.

I told Áine about the plazas, churches, and markets that I had rambled through, and she was always keen to know a little more. I was used to explaining things in as much detail as possible, hoping that she'd be able to form her own image a little better, and take from it some connection to what I was doing and seeing. Beyond telling her about the mundanities of my day-to-day life – which was largely an exercise in repetition – places such as Quito gave me an opportunity to reveal something fresh and new to her and added an extra dimension to our conversations. It was a chance for her to enter my world for a short time, in the same way as I entered hers when she told me about any new experiences of her own.

At the southern end of Quito, Volcán Cotopaxi pierces the sky. There is so much captivation in a name, I thought, as I rode ever closer to its base on my way out of Quito. One of the first mountains to inspire a sense of wonder in me, I remember reading about it in childhood geography books, and how I marvelled over its distinctive and somehow otherworldly name: *Co-toh-pax-ee*.

The volcano stayed in view for most of that day, but by evening it had disappeared under the horizon. I finally reached the smoggy town of Latacunga, after a rough six-hour cycle dominated by a total absence of energy and any kind of will to pedal onwards. My breathing was too shallow and seemed too fast to keep up with; I felt as if I was in training for a marathon and that this was my first day of training. It was rare to encounter such awful days on the bike, but when they came along, simply waiting it out until the next day was the only thing which would help. I constantly tried to analyse the reasons for such fatigue. Perhaps my daily diet of rice and chicken was a factor? Maybe it was the two days off? Or was I just feeling down and this was affecting me physically too? As I write this now, I look back with fondness on the Ecuador leg of the journey – but my diary entries at the time said something different.

> *Diary: 24 May 2012, Ibarra, Ecuador*
>
> *I had very little energy [today], and mostly it was a combination of my mental state and the physical energy factor, but I'm not sure how they tie into each other. I wasn't happy and just wanted to be with Áine.*
>
> *Diary: 30 May 2012, Latacunga, Ecuador*
>
> *What can I remember about yesterday? It was another tough day, and I didn't feel great. There were plenty of aches and pains and a general lack*

of will for cycling. I'm feeling a little demotivated at the moment – more so than any time before.

I had felt low on several occasions over the previous two or three weeks and I had nothing to pin it on, except missing Áine. Of course, banishing negative thoughts had proven futile, and I was finding it difficult to get to the place of acceptance about the situation for which the moment called. I knew these feelings were taking a toll on my physical health too, and also affecting the quality of my day-to-day experiences. It seemed as if there was just a small grey cloud that never lifted, as I travelled through the mire of some days in the Andes. When left inside my own head for too long, I felt that the colour of the places and interactions with the people was somehow dulled, processed through my own gloomy internal filter. All I knew was that I didn't feel altogether happy or content. I was stalled in a state of mind, where only certain things would lift me throughout the day – such as lunch breaks in unexpected places, playlists on my iPod, or the thought of a good bed and a book at night. Others – such as the remaining the distance to be covered in a day, or missing family at home – would leave me feeling listless. And yet, writing this now, almost one year later, I tend to only remember those days as positive and, but for my diary at the time, I'd have little recollection of the creeping despondency which wouldn't leave me alone.

The Andes are the spine of Ecuador; in amongst them is a string of soaring volcanoes, the most famous of which is Chimborazo. A low mist was covering its slopes when I passed over the ridges at its base, so I couldn't see the summit of what is the furthest point on the planet away from the centre of the Earth. Although at 6,268 metres, Chimborazo pales in significance to Mt Everest's 8,848 metres, it holds this novel record because the Earth bulges at the equator due to the force of its rotation. It is therefore only Ecuador's highest mountain, rather than the world's.

Past Riobamba, the road climbed steadily up through farms and lakes; the hills looked as smoothly cambered as a potter's wet clay. I stopped to chat with some broccoli pickers near La Balbanera, a town which is the home of Ecuador's oldest Catholic church. A humble building, it could hold perhaps 50 people at most, and has a plain white stone altar, some modest stained glass windows, and rows of wooden pews.

As the kilometres ticked by, a brisk side-wind periodically caught my back and nudged me further into some gorgeous grassy knolls that were set just wide enough apart to accommodate the two-lane road and a railway track. After exactly seven hours in the saddle, I had covered 103 km and descended a further 5 km to Alausí, where the fog was so thick that condensation formed into droplets on the hairs on my arms. In the town's fire station, I was offered a neat space on the upstairs floor to roll my mattress out. But sleep would wait, as I was determined to indulge in an *aloo gobi* curry in what must be one of Ecuador's only rural Andean Indian restaurants.

The part of Ecuador I was now entering was home to some of the wildest mountains and climbing terrain in the country and, from a lookout over Alausí the next day, I was able to appreciate this fact. To reach it, I endured an hour-and-a-half of coaxing my tired legs along snaking switchbacks under a light morning sun. At the top was a gap in the cliff face, where the road plummeted 15 km over 900 metres. To my right was a small area of flat ground where long grass rustled in the breeze, and below this, in the valley's corner, lay Alausí, so quiet and somehow so vulnerable in this very early morning. To the west, there was another fearsome drop off the valley edge – known as *El Nariz del Diablo* (The Nose of the Devil): here the Ecuadorian railway goes through some of the most precipitous descents to be found in South America. Perhaps the setting, the time of day, or even my own mood contributed to the magnitude of my amazement, but this was certainly one of the most incredible sights I had witnessed in South America so far.

Diary: 2 June, 2012, Tambo, Ecuador

I had been told the route out from Alausí was easier and with more of a downhill incline than another one on the far side of town – but it didn't feel that way. However I doubt it would have had such spectacular views. All day, the road ran slowly through the mountains and, as it was Saturday and most cars were off the road, the sounds of farm animals could be heard over everything else. Cycling is a little more meditative here now.

The discomfort of the heat has subsided, as I'm at around 3,000 metres, and I can move without sweating or having to stop so often. I often wander off in my thoughts, only to be brought back by another spectacular sight or the noise of a village buried somewhere almost improbable in the hills.

Even along the length of my particular Pan-American route, it seemed that the power of coincidence knew few limits. If I hadn't been so fresh and alert, having only cycled a leisurely 40 km, I wouldn't have believed my eyes when I caught sight of Markus Höfle — the softly-spoken Austrian cyclist I had met in Whitehorse, Canada — standing on a street corner in Cuenca. I recall Markus saying at the time that he planned to travel more slowly than us, and to complete the journey to Ushuaia in 18 months — so I was more than astounded to come across him, deeply absorbed in a Cuenca city map, 18,000 km and 11 months from our last encounter.

'I knew we'd meet again,' he told me later that night, while devouring bolognaise. 'Isn't it incredible how far you have to travel and lose contact, before bumping into people?'

It really was. Although a lot is down to the fact we had the same destination and were on similar paths, it should be much easier to disappear in amongst the road network, towns, and even cities like Cuenca. Markus himself had just arrived but intended to stay a few days while I would be leaving in the morning, meaning I would have missed him except for the fact that he was standing around looking for a hotel.

I asked him how he was finding Ecuador.

'Oh, I love it. I think everyone does. It's a special country and the people are wonderful, don't you think?' Markus always spoke slowly and with such lightness of tone, putting deep consideration into what he was saying. 'Cuenca is a milestone for me in another sense as well, but I don't think I mentioned it to you in Yukon, did I?' he continued.

'No, I don't think so.'

'Well, you know this is my third attempt trying to get from Alaska to Ushuaia. The first time I became sick and had to go home. The second, I made it to here before hearing that my father was very ill, and so I had to return home to Austria. He didn't live much longer. When I make it out of here, I'll have gone as far as those two times. And this time, I aim to make the end.'

Markus preferred being alone but liked interludes of cycling with others, and we had more in common that just that. In fact, we had even met the same people, including Jorge the Spaniard whom I cycled with in Mexico, and André the German that I spent almost a week with in Central America. Like me, he also had suffered from a lack of motivation on many occasions.

'What's the point if I don't want to be here?' he explained. 'Travel means very little unless you are invested in it, but we must always adapt to changing circumstances.'

He understood his own nature whilst on the road, and his inherent vulnerabilities, but so far he had only imagined returning home a few times. It was Peru, he thought, that would really liven things up: Markus was also a mountain climber. I imagined that the Cordillera Blanca – the world's second highest mountain range – might offer a spiritual refuge for him, if his interest in the ride waned.

It was one of the most enjoyable nights socialising I had had during my trip, and once I left Markus, I found a fresh outlook on the road ahead. Sometimes validation of your own feelings, or listening to others who were in similar places of self-examination, can give you a most-needed lift, and help you to reassess or place in perspective your own emotions and thoughts.

Cuenca was a city that needed a week of exploration, rather than just a day. It had two cathedrals – the 'Old Cathedral' and the 'New Cathedral'. The latter has three big blue domes, and is visible from just about any rooftop in the city. It's so colossal that when it was first built in the late 1800s, 9,000 of the city's 10,000 inhabitants could fit inside it. Around it are pleasant streets with colonial houses, small parks and gardens, fenced off for private residents. Quite uncharacteristically, I had had my fill of colonial architecture for the time being, so I decided to make my way to Vilcabamba instead, a town famous for a very unique reason.

Residents of Vilcabamba will claim they've earned the area's nickname of 'the Valley of Longevity'. It is said, most notably by locals, that the town has seen a fair number of centenarians in its time, including some in fact who are purported to have reached the ripe old age of 135. Such claims encouraged the first scientific studies of the phenomenon in the early

1970s, when a team of French researchers were sent to verify or disprove the assertion. However in 1973, *National Geographic* magazine featured the people of Vilcabamba in their cover story, and no longer were they hidden from the world. The French team, still working, didn't reach any firm conclusions, other than to say that diet and lifestyle may be a factor in the apparent health and demographic of the valley's people. Even a Nobel Prize winning chemist, Dr Richard Laurence Millington Synge, claimed that the plant life in the area contained some remarkable medicinal qualities, such as strong antioxidants. Later studies, aimed at determining the correct age of residents, have cast doubt on the validity of the villagers' claims, however. In many cases, it appeared that the locals were exaggerating and, after analysis of interviews and other scientific data, it was found that there wasn't a single person over the age of 100 in the area.

Nevertheless, people – most of whom are foreigners – have flocked in their droves to Vilcabamba, in the hope there's something special in the water, ground or air – all now subjects of ongoing scientific research. When I arrived three days after leaving Cuenca, I noticed little different from other small towns, except a few young-looking, hemp-wearing travellers hanging out in a small agglomeration of western-styled coffee shops in the deathly quiet square. Despite the exposure resulting from the reputed longevity of its residents, the town is still just several dusty streets, where people go about their daily business in a fertile agricultural valley.

I did, coincidentally enough, feel thoroughly relaxed after two days in Vilcabamba. The lack of anything going on and the languorous pace to local existence made me totally at ease with doing absolutely nothing. I was surrounded by a wonderful bunch of people at the Hostel Valle Sagrado, which included Urs, Eric and Lydie, a Swiss-French cycle touring couple, and Shyam, an Indian man also travelling by bike, as well as Christoph and Paul, two long-time residents of the hostel.

It was Christoph who provided each evening's entertainment, with stories of how he turned up in Vilcabamba. He had been working as an on-board air courier, a job that required him to carry valuable packages across the world, from one person or office to another. On one occasion he had apparently flown from Frankfurt to Tokyo, solely to re-check in a bag for a famous composer, who didn't want the hassle of doing it himself. Christoph had been to the United States 155 times in just four years, and on some occasions, had been carrying little more than a bag of screws.

'You know how stupid I sound at immigration, when they ask me, "What's your intention in the US?", and all I can say is, "I'm carrying ten very special screws to Los Angeles for a speaker system",' he told us.

It was an episode of major air turbulence which had brought him here, in fact: on a flight to the United States, he had been frightened to the point that he vowed never to fly again. Instead, he travelled south and settled in the first place he felt at home in, which just happened to be Vilcabamba.

Paul meanwhile was a poet, seeking solace from a crazy world he didn't want to be a part of. He was the typical visitor to Vilcabamba, a soul-searcher looking for peace and contentment. Every day, he wrote poetry and walked in the hills around town, seeking inspiration for his next piece of writing. Like many of the visitors I met during my stay, Paul had specific reasons to be here.

> *Diary: 7 June 2012, Vilcabamba, Ecuador*
>
> *I could have stayed a week here and been happy. The town seems to have a resistance to becoming overrun by travellers, even though there are quite a few. Our hostel was a place of laziness and we could only get food when the owner – a large lady who seemed perpetually discontent – came back from visiting family. Perhaps the reason the town is not seeing more hotels and restaurants and other tourist services open up is its inaccessibility. There are no buses for backpackers here. And after this, the road turns to mud and it's 250–300 km (3–4 cycling days) before tarmac again, in a very remote section of Ecuador. Tomorrow Urs, Eric and Lydie, and I will leave separately, and hope to catch up later, since we all know we've very different paces on gravel and dirt climbs, of which many lie ahead.*

It was another 180 km until the border with Peru, which was indicated on my map by two crossed flags, but with no sign of a town, apparently. Just 3 km from Vilcabamba, a profound silence fell and the road began rising. At the hamlet of Yangana, I pulled in for a lunch of rice and eggs with a coffee full of sweetened milk. It was the first town in southern Ecuador where I hadn't seen any *cuys* (guinea pigs) rotating on a spit over hot coals. Apparently, it's a long-running joke in northern Ecuador that the southerners are animals and less evolved, because they've a penchant for their roasted rodents.

After lunch the wind appeared behind me on a climb tucked under a dark stone cliff face with patches of moss and water streaming from its uppermost layers of rock. I was on the edge of the Parque Nacional Podocarpus, a protected area which spans two long spurs of the Andes. With its rich-smelling, damp peat soil, I could sense that it was teeming with life both above and below the ground. I had even read that jaguars roamed within this and so didn't mind that I would, before long, be veering away from it on a long stony descent into the village of Valladolid.

In Valladolid I scoured the streets in the rain, looking for a place to sleep. A local policeman, who would later offer to find cocaine and a woman for me, brought me to the only accommodation open and swiftly left as soon as I turned down his other offers. The condition of the road into the village made me question if people ever left Valladolid. It was as depressing a place I'd come across: tens of empty streets with discarded steel girders lying around, and half-finished concrete foundations collecting rainwater. No one could deny the haunting beauty that existed around it, even under the rainy sky, but the dark clouds now made the town itself look even gloomier than it perhaps was.

At 6 a.m. the next morning, listening to the rain falling upon the roof above me, I just wanted to turn around and fall back to sleep. But I reckoned it was about time that I got some experience of such murky weather, after managing to avoid so many rain showers this far on account of fortuitous days off. Setting off, it wasn't long before the road turned from mud to a slushy combination with the soft gravel that had been laid by road crews. Less than one hour in, I removed the mudguards, as a stony mush was clogged between them and the wheel, making it impossible to pedal. Soon the force of mud between the rim and brake pads was causing the wheels to jam, so I removed the back pads too, and put a new set in the front, much tighter this time, and with less room for mud to gather.

At noon, the heavens opened with a thundering rainstorm, and my waterproof socks – which I wore with sandals to keep my shoes dry – were soaked through, my feet swimming in a shallow pool of cold water.

Nobody else was out here anymore, and there was a welcome absence of wind, so the only audible sound was of raindrops falling into the deep brown puddles and splicing off exposed rocks.

I crossed several knee-deep streams on foot before arriving in Progreso, a tiny mountain town with enormous character. In a trip record low, I paid just $1.50 for a night in the basement of a family's home. There were two rooms down there, and I was confident I was the only guest they had had for weeks. My main concern at this point was the first match Ireland would play in the European Football Championships the next day. I couldn't possibly have imagined being more isolated from a television than I clearly was in Progreso, but some friendly locals were able to advise me that I could go to Zumba, 20 km away, where someone might have cable TV.

As a muddied foreigner on a bicycle is a rarity in Progreso, the local kids soon learned of my presence and were quick to find me outside, updating my GPS tracker. I wondered if they'd ever been to Quito, or how long it would be before they had reason to. Having no idea whether people travelled for pleasure or business in this part of the country, I loaded a 40-second video of the capital, taken from the top of Volcán Pichincha.

'Ohhh-ahhh,' they giggled, impressed with the view. Some clips I had recorded while stuck between mini-avalanches in Tajikistan got the same kind of response, but I was hard-pressed to describe in Spanish what they were looking at, and where it was.

The next day, I caught the match in Zumba's bus station. It was a 3-1 defeat to Croatia, so I dealt with the disappointment by riding with purpose to the border with Peru. I found it at the bottom of a poorly surfaced road, strewn with large rocks and smaller stones: a collection of tin-roofed houses, two or three shops and a makeshift guard post. Across a bridge spanning the little Río Canchis – the official border – coffee beans were drying in the sun. There was nobody in official immigration attire around, so I asked a woman in one of the *tiendas* where I could get an exit stamp; she duly pointed to the restaurant across the street, where two uniformed guards were four beers deep.

'*Si, si . . . Pasaporte?*' one answered when I requested a stamp, holding out his hand for my documents.

We walked to the adjoining building and I signed the immigration book, which had just two signatures in it this far for that day – those of Eric and Lydie. For each of the other days, I saw that there were just two or three signatures. It didn't surprise me either, as the road leading to the border was in such a dreadful condition and better suited for a four-wheel drive, if anything at all.

I then crossed the bridge, past the drying coffee beans, and was told to wake the Peruvian border guard, who was taking a nap. Some enthusiastic older locals encouraged me to throw rocks at his window, if he didn't wake up. With no answer to my knocking, I launched a small stone about the size of a cashew nut at the window and then several more. Eventually, a groggy, bare-chested man lifted the glass and told me to meet him in 30 minutes at a building he pointed to, across the road.

'I need a shower,' he shouted down at me, and then roared profanities at the two old men who had suggested the stone throwing.

It took all of five minutes for him to enter my details on the computer and for me to answer his question as to whether I was carrying anything illegal into Peru. Satisfied, he stamped me in and I went on my way, while he returned to his house.

Instantly, I found myself appreciating the efforts of the great, the wonderful road engineers of Peru. What had been gravel and stones in Ecuador was a slick, pre-asphalt treatment here; most pleasing, however, were the gentler grades. In three hours and 45 minutes to the border that morning, I had ridden just 28 km and had been intensely frustrated by the constant jolting and slipping of the bike on sandy areas of the surface. I was in terrible form, a unique kind of displeasure only this type of cycling brings.

Now, as I curled around the mountain, following a river into Peru, I noticed just how much easier it was to complete a revolution. It seemed that, instead of getting over whatever hill or topographical obstacle lay in front of them as quickly and directly as possible, Peruvians had a policy of going the long way around. The drags weren't as steep or short, so they carried on a little longer. This meant that there wasn't a slow up and fast down, but that I could keep a steady pace through it all. At dusk I happened upon San Antonio, a one-street village not marked on the map. There, a family offered me their only son's room for the night: he was studying in university, and they had no problem hosting a stranger.

The next day, in the village of San Ignacio, I stopped for a *sanduche con queso* (grilled cheese sandwich) and an ice cream in a wide octagonal plaza tiled in marine blue slates. I sat and wondered about all the other experiences bicycle tourists might have had here. Who had stayed? Where had they slept? What did they do? In all my reading of the ongoing blogs of other cyclists – some of whom were behind and some ahead of me – I'd remember place names from stories, but the same places might have little impact on me when I passed through, because I didn't have any memorable experiences there myself. One person had apparently stayed for four days in San Ignacio and had fallen in love with it.

It was all a game of chance, really. Enjoyment and memorable experiences could come from just picking a name off a map as a place to rest for the night, or from setting a certain mileage goal for the day. Others could come from meeting the right people at the right time, or even from breaking down somewhere, to be helped by a friendly passer-by. As I looked around the vacant plaza, finishing my ice cream while the sun cast a pale light on the edges of the buildings and, further away, on the nearby hilltops, I was filled with wonder at the prospect of all the chance encounters and experiences still out there, ready to fall into my lap. Never was this feeling more alive than with the anticipation of a new country, and I was excited picturing all of Peru ahead of me.

10
To the Lost City

San Ignacio, Peru to Cusco, Peru – 1,565 km

I FLAGGED DOWN A PASSING taxi just 20 km out of San Ignacio, and with that, willingly opted for public transport over the bicycle for the first time. Exasperated at the state of the road and my inability to ride with any joy on it, I travelled the next 75 km to Jaén – the capital of Peru's Cajamarca region – in near silence, apart from some sporadic and broken conversation with a middle-aged woman, my co-passenger. For the entire journey she held her daughter tightly to her chest, letting her sleep softly under the ruffles of a small blanket. We talked about potato farming, school, and fish caught in the east of Peru and served in her restaurant in San Ignacio. They were the best tasting fish around, she told me, but her cooking was the real reason people came to eat it. We swapped numbers, and I promised I'd text her from Machu Picchu, as she'd never been and would be pleased to know I had reached it by bicycle.

The road days since Vilcabamba had beaten me into submission. Loose gravel, rocks, and steep descents, where I persisted in falling off the bicycle and into the ditch, were enough to leave me pining for some asphalt or even compressed dirt once again. I didn't want to miss any of the road by choosing just not to ride it, but sensed that another day of bad form and cursing the dreadful highway wasn't worth the effort. My conversations with Markus, and memory of Steve in Costa Rica, also played into the decision, and I finally broke ranks from the 'Every Fucking Inch' club.

To its credit, Jaén was a good place for me to stop and think a little about my schedule in Peru and make a provisional target timeframe in which to get through it. I estimated it would take at least two months, but knew that another four weeks on top of that was just as likely. First of all, I had to cycle across the Cordillera Blanca mountain range and then ride at an elevation of 3,000–4,000 metres towards Ayacucho in the south. Then, turning east towards Cusco, five immense climbs lay in wait. Peru was going to be tough, very tough. As I'd found, the rich rewards in reaching the mesmerising beauty associated with these countries were often proportional to work put in, and Peru would be the poster child for this principle. But despite failure to make it a full day on the bike on just my second day in the country, I was curious about what I could prove to myself for the duration of my time there.

Highway 3N was immaculately sealed for the next couple of hundred kilometres, presumably because spacious valleys ran through a barren and scrubby landscape. The sun shone from dawn until dusk, reflecting off exposed grey rocks and sandy soil, while every now and again, what looked like rice paddies would appear in any available flat areas alongside the interlocking mountain spurs. My route through this peculiarly fetching environment led towards Trujillo, a large city near the coast. Instead of travelling immediately inland to Chachapoyas – famed for the nearby pre-Columbian ruins of Kuelap – I wanted to stay at a well-known *casa di ciclista* in Trujillo that has hosted upwards of 2,000 cyclists through the years.

It had been a long time since I had taken a rest day in a small town. Bigger urban centres and cities were always handier, giving me a chance to restock the panniers with food and call home on a faster Internet connection. In Pucará, I booked in for two nights at a $12 per night guesthouse that had cable television. The main reason for stopping was that Ireland were playing Spain in the European Championships the next day, and only on cable TV could I watch the match. In the end, Ireland lost, but I won. The pace to life in towns like Pucará, which must have had no more than 500 people living in it, is borderline drowsy. People are more inquisitive than in big towns, and heads turn as if in unison as you walk by. They are what some may deem 'uninspiring', in that they have little to do but just watch normal life go by. However, towns like these are the real Peru – not the Cuscos and Limas that cater for foreign tourists, with upscale hotels and restaurants, guided tours and regular transport – and as such, give a better glimpse into the daily life of a country. Two women working in a restaurant were happy to talk with me while they flipped *carne asado* on the grill, joking about my beard and generally dishevelled appearance. On the streets, I found the kids were more likely to call me over than in the other Latin American countries thus far. They were direct and confident in engaging me, unlike the children in Colombia and Ecuador who would usually shy away when I spoke to them. Their skin colour was fairer than that of their more northern neighbours, perhaps, I assumed, as a result of a greater degree of integration with their past colonial rulers.

Between Pucará and Trujillo the road goes through two distinct phases. First it bumbles up along a valley, twisting here and there as if disinclined to escape it, before topping off at a pass called Abra Porcuya, just over 2,000 metres above sea level. Then it descends rapidly through a cold, misted forest to emerge into a desert environment 30 km later. The arid conditions persist all the way to Trujillo, but I earlier stopped at Chiclayo and took a bus to Trujillo instead. This was one section of the road I had never intended to ride, as violent muggings of bicycle tourists had been known to take place near Paiján. Some of the victims had lost their wallets, but others, their entire possessions – as well as the ability to recover from the experience and find within themselves the will to continue on. Viewed from the top floor of the air-conditioned bus, it looked like an incredibly unappealing stretch anyway. In a desert-like heat, the long, straight highway was littered with plastic bags, household waste, and drink cans. Emaciated dogs roamed in packs around derelict houses, in what were clearly desperately poor villages, barely surviving between the shifting sand dunes. It was a side of poverty I hadn't seen in quite some time – since Guatemala perhaps – but there at least, the people were smiling and appeared happy with their lot, even if it wasn't much. Here, every face was marked with a permanent air of despondency.

Diary: 16 June 2012, Chiclayo, Peru

Eleven months on the road today. 70 km done on a smelly highway with a strong stench of dead dog. Today, however, I felt slightly jaded. Perhaps it was the fact that I got sick last night from whatever I ate. I was pretty out of it, and then just threw up in the bathroom, locking the door just in time before vaulting for the toilet bowl. I felt far better after it, but the room was stuffy and there were flying beetles whacking off the walls and windows. I stopped at the Museo Tumbes Reales de Sipan, which was laid out very well, and showed off the ancient Sipan culture – nice gilded work, pottery and information on social organisation, metallurgy, agriculture and customs. But I've seen so many such displays now that I can't tell the cultures apart!

The famous *casa di ciclista* was more ordinary than I had expected, for a place with such reverence attached, and which has been hosting cyclists since 1985. It consisted of just three downstairs rooms and two more upstairs. Lucho, the owner and a former Peruvian cycling champion, brought me into one of the bedrooms on the ground level, a cluttered space with a mattress on the floor, and boxes of papers and books on a desk in the corner. Although Lucho was happy to answer questions surely asked countless times over the years, he needed to get back to work, so left me with a key and plenty of time to wander about the establishment. Upstairs it had a cold shower and a small balcony, where travellers could stove-cook breakfast, lunch, and dinner. It wasn't a home as such, but just a free space for touring cyclists to dwell in before moving on. Lucho lived in another building down the street, along with his son Lance, named after the seven-times Tour de France winner, Lance Armstrong – who the following year would be stripped of all of his titles after admitting to doping. Earlier in the day, I had noticed that Lucho had pictures of Armstrong decorating the walls, and signed memorabilia impeccably ordered on his shelves. I wonder what he thinks of it all now.

The most impressive item in the *casa* was the guestbook, signed by the majority of the 2,000-plus people who had stayed here. Stories, advice, pictures, and expressions of thanks were left inside. Some names I recognised from my pre-trip research and others were unknown, but together, they represented hundreds of thousands of hours of bicycle travel from Trujillo to Ushuaia, Prudhoe Bay, Europe, Africa, Asia and Australasia. It was a fascinating centrepiece of travelling history, and a repository I was eager to ink my presence into.

One of my primary concerns in Trujillo was my laundry. I had been embarrassed by my stench on the bus from Chiclayo, and desperately needed someone to industrially clean my clothes. It's rare to be in such an enclosed space and smell so foul, but I was down to a single T-shirt and a pair of stained pants. A laissez-faire perspective on personal hygiene is definitely one of the road's most unfortunate gifts.

I brought my clothes to the dry-cleaners and then continued into the plaza, stopping for coffee and cake along the way while reading about local history. Trujillo was founded in 1534 and named after the hometown of Francisco Pizarro, the Spanish conquistador. It was in fact one of the first colonial cities to be established, and as such is laid out in an orderly manner with plenty of squares, churches, and wide streets enclosed within city walls that were based on those in the city of Florence, designed by Leonardo da Vinci. Of most interest to me however was not Trujillo, but Huanchaco, a seaside town close by. All along the beach there, laid up against the walls in a row, were *caballitos*, slender reed boats with pointed fronts that have been used by local fisherman for thousands of years. On these boats, it's possible for the fishermen to ride the waves back to shore without much labour, and so it has been suggested this mode of sea transport was the progenitor to surfing. Indeed today, Huanchaco is a World Surfing Reserve due to the quality and consistency of the waves there.

I spent a glorious half-day wandering around Huanchaco, almost all of it at the seaside. It was the first time I had seen the ocean since avoiding the Darién Gap on the catamaran sailing between Panama and Colombia, and as always happened, I felt a sense of freedom, as I watched its salty crests turn to a shimmering azure where it met the sky. I might love the mountains more, but the ocean is a close second because it grants a sense of calm unlike most of the natural world's earthscapes.

Back in the *casa*, I met Todd and Adie, an American couple from Seattle who were settling in for several days. They were delightfully easy to talk with, and I learned that they travelled when they liked, worked when they had to, and had an open and adventurous attitude to each and every road they pedalled down. They were moving north, and had come from Chile and the Carretera Austral, about which they could not use enough superlatives.

'Oh, well now, let me tell you something, that is just an incredible piece of the world right there! Oh yeah, you'll enjoy it, but let me fill you in on the boat situation,' Adie began.

She pulled out maps and told me which boats were running when, and gave suggestions on the best ways to cross Chile's fjords at different times of the year. 'Now, if you keep going like you're going, you'll be too early to get the ferry at Villa O'Higgins – it only runs from November – but I bet you could cross at Chile Chico,' she continued. 'Todd, Todd honey, you think Ian can do that?'

'Oh, you bet. I think that road will be open, maybe a tough ride but if you can get through Peru, you'll get through anywhere. Tell me, what way are you thinking of heading from here anyway?' Todd questioned, and went on to describe the multitude of possible routes from Trujillo to the border with Bolivia.

I could have spent all night talking with them, but as soon as they felt hungry and primed the stove outside, I left in search of a meal I wouldn't need to prepare. I also in fact didn't want to be around when the couple upstairs returned, as they had been fighting each evening so far. As far as I could grasp, the woman was Lucho's sister and she had a perennially vicious temper, but perhaps it was merited because her husband seemed to always be drunk. On one occasion, Todd had had to comfort him after midnight, when in a sobbing rage, he stumbled up the stairs, clattering every table, chair, and bicycle in his way. When they weren't fighting, they played Britney Spears songs – and only Britney Spears. To my mind, the latter was more reason to vacate the premises than the domestic issues, so I hurried out, resolving not to come back until midnight.

As I soon learned, Todd and Adie's advice was invaluable. I was heading to the mountains – 'the real mountains', as Lee would call them. 'If it doesn't have snow on it, it's not a proper mountain,' he had told me in Canada, after I said I liked the look of the Appalachians.

From Trujillo I would take the main highway south; 70 km along this, I would turn off onto a private dirt track owned by an energy firm, and head inland. This was to be a shortcut into an area known as Cañón del Pato, a deep gorge that swallows up the Río Santa in vivid geomorphology. I would then reappear on a sliver of flat ground near Caraz, and take a mountain pass over the Cordillera Blanca, where some of Peru's most inhospitable and adventurous cycling terrain awaits those game enough to ride it.

As soon as the dirt track appeared, just south of the town of Virú, it became obvious this wouldn't be an easy way to travel, but it was a relatively soft introduction to what I heard would become bone-shuddering further along. One minute short of seven hours riding, and with 98 km covered, I met a brief stretch of pavement that began just before Chuquicara and ended immediately after it. A police officer invited me to sleep in the corridor of his station, on a mattress usually reserved for those on night shift. The town hugged a curve in the road beside the Río Santa, and could be walked from end to end in about three minutes. There was one restaurant open, but it wouldn't serve food until the next scheduled minivan passed through, so I hung around outside, flicking through photographs on my camera and talking to a few men who had bags of crisps on long poles that could be pushed through the windows and sold to the passengers of any van that didn't stop. They told me that several such vehicles came by Chuquicara daily, taking those from the foothills of the Cordillera Blanca to Trujillo. As the road had been blasted from the canyon and never paved, it could take almost six hours to travel 230 km. Watching vans lumber by while I slogged carefully along on the bicycle, I was glad to be outside and not indoors, tightly pressed against the windows and smothering in the heat, while looking down at harrowing drops into the river.

The softness of dawn light is perhaps the best to ride in, so I skipped out of Chuquicara early to have it all to myself. From the coarse and folded rocks around me, I assumed that this was the Cañón del Pato, but it turned out to be its precursor. This area was however far more remarkable than I had expected, based on what people had told me about it. When the asphalt ended, the road bent around another of the innumerable mountains and then narrowed to occupy a place by the side of the Río Santa. This river gurgled away, as if in its infancy, while grey rock walls as old as time itself flanked it on either side. Scree from the frozen nights and warm days had collected in pockets of the canyon sides, and much more lay at their base. Clusters of green plants appeared sporadically, and when the wind blew through the gorge, dust and rock litter was cast up into the air and illuminated by the sun's rays. I kept shouting, '*Ola, quién está ahí?*' ('Hello, is anyone there?'), and allowing the words to echo back at me, knowing very well that nobody was. In some sections the road had been mined from the rock, and it passed under immense overhangs. In others, short, narrow tunnels were hewn through blocks of rock the size of 10-storey buildings.

By the time I reached Cañón del Pato, nightfall was upon me; the high walls of the canyon had stolen half an hour of my daylight. No wonder too, as they were just eight metres across from each other – a space so tight, it begs the question as to how anyone could engineer a road through it. A succession of tunnels made for dangerous night riding, and when I happened upon the Huallanca hydroelectric plant, I banged on the steel gates and asked for a place to sleep. Apart from three wooden shacks I had seen at lunchtime, this was the only evidence of human existence I had come across all day. The dam wasn't even visible from the road, but instead masked in the canyon's belly. The security guard turned me away for safety reasons and surreptitiously nodded at the security cameras, while whispering that his boss wouldn't be pleased. It was just the second time on the entire trip that I had been told I couldn't pitch my tent where I had asked. I returned to the lightless road, and considered sleeping in one of the tunnel enclaves between the road and the river.

Eric and Amaya, the bike tourists I had stayed with near Whitehorse, Canada, had told me at one point: 'When you think things are bad, really bad, something always comes along to make it better.' Since then, I had remembered those words periodically, and now, when I felt the gravel give way to the sweet and noiseless embrace of asphalt, I finally believed them. It wasn't shelter, nor was it night turning to day, but it was a sign that people were around. Just 10 km later, with the time approaching 8 p.m. and my head torch beginning to fade, the faint lights of a personnel camp for the hydro plant came into sight. By 9 p.m., I was huddled inside my sleeping bag, outside the bunk block, with the playful resident puppy poking his curious nose underneath my flysheet.

Diary: 23 June 2012, Huallanca Hydropower workers' camp, 20 km from Caraz, Peru

This was something else, a day I loved! The road was rough, the land was rough and it was a rough ending. Total darkness for at least two hours after that 6 km climb into the canyon and the slow drop back out of it. They say it's where the Cordillera Negra and Cordillera Blanca ranges meet, and if so, it's a scary place to find yourself with only a head torch for safety. I can't see them now, but outside the tent, giant mountains are standing tall! I'm so thankful for the kind folk here who sneaked me in past the management, who initially didn't want me around. Let's hope the pup doesn't give me away!

I don't know the name of the first mountain I saw in the Cordillera Blanca, but it stays in my mind as the first real sighting of the range's splendour. It may have been Alpamayo, known not for its prominence or climbing heritage, but distinguished for its beauty. Like the Matterhorn in the Swiss Alps, or Everest in the Himalayas, this is among the favoured peaks, a frequent ambassador of the Cordillera Blanca, and my map suggested that what I was looking at might well be it. Conical, wholly ice-covered and scarred by striations, it's a mountain high above the others, and is steeped in local folklore and legend.

As it had been in Canada, such mountains of snow and ice brought me an intense joy. With them framing my lines of sight, the scenery could never be bland or boring to ride through. Unlike the deserts or plains, oceans or lakes, they are to most of us entirely inaccessible. They make no noise; they stand silent and unmoving in the face of storms and windless days. At the northern end of the cordillera, only a few raise their summits above the undusted peaks to their front, but once I rode onto Caraz and further along the ridgeline, they emerged from the untouched middle to the foreground. Clouds gathered in wisps around their peaks, trying to navigate east to west over them, and floating weightless into waiting valleys on the other side.

Caraz was my base for three days while I figured out which direction to travel next. I had two options. The first involved cycling south into Huaraz, the climbing capital of the Cordillera Blanca, and then proceeding east and across Peru towards Cusco. The other possibility was to cycle over the nearby Punta Olimpica Pass – the highest pass in the range – and take a gravel country road into the rolling alpine hills on the far side. I had enjoyed the peacefulness of the ride through Cañón del Pato, so I opted for this tranquillity again. This would be a chance to stray far away from the Pan-American Highway and cut into the great highlands of central Peru, where alpacas grazed on the shores of lakes believed to be inhabited by Incan gods, and stillness reigned supreme.

Before leaving Caraz, where the daily market was in full swing, I travelled by local taxi to Lago Llanganuco, an emerald-green lake that stretched short but wide through a glaciated mountain valley. The taxi dropped me off at almost 4,000 metres above sea level and told me I'd find a car to take me back in an hour or so, coming from the other side of the mountains. The scene comprised only three obvious elements – the lake, which had tiny ripples blowing across it, the dark grey valley walls, and a beige dirt road running along the lake's edge. However this was perhaps the most remarkable lake I'd ever seen. As I walked along the shore, I met a man, who had been a passenger with me in the taxi for a short distance earlier. He greeted me in English, speaking with a hint of a British accent.

'I studied in Scotland for some time,' he told me when I asked about it.

I wanted to know why he was up here.

'Many reasons. I'm on a pilgrimage of sorts, and I'm going to swim in the lake. I live in Lima, but I come here every year.'

'It's a long way to come for a swim,' I responded.

He took a moment to look right at me while composing his answer. I noticed a feather in his white fedora. 'Well, sometimes, you do things in the name of memory, and sometimes in the name of habit. This – why I'm here today – is a little of both.'

He was a man that would hold your gaze while talking, like a wise character from an old Arabian tale. He brushed back his black curly hair, and asked me what I was doing in the mountains. I told him and he smiled at me.

'I imagine you're on a pilgrimage of sorts too?' he said.

'I'm not sure really, it wouldn't be the first word that comes to mind. But pilgrimage usually has an end destination and involves a challenge to get there, so in that regard there are similarities. But that's probably the furthest it goes. When I'm done, I might see it differently.'

He shook my hand and said it was time for his swim. Fifteen minutes later, on the other side of the lake, I saw him dipping into the water and wading out to the middle, turning the soft ripples into larger swells, leaving with me only a greater sense of mystery as to what he was doing up here under the quiet of soaring mountaintops.

I left Caraz with July just a few days away, and not a sign of summer temperatures in the air. Technically though, it was still winter, as I was in the southern hemisphere, but around the equator and at lower elevations at least, seasons aren't like home. It was cold and frosty, and most mornings I would wake to a heavy mist and the need for thermal leggings and a jacket.

In Yungay, the last town I would meet on the western side of the Andes until I reached Santiago, Chile, I stopped for fried eggs, bread and rice – my staple breakfast. Then, setting off eastwards, I gradually curled up and around semi-forested hills, until there was little vegetation left. I could see the treeline thin below the ice of the highest peaks Chiqllarahu and Huascarán – the latter being Peru's highest – which pointed into the deep blue heavens above me. After 22 km, the road ascended in a well-proportioned rise that didn't involve as much stinging in my calves as had been inflicted by the 7 km/h battle from Yungay. I was at 4,000 metres and the road – with nobody on it but me – persisted alongside a small river, which was cut sharply into mossy banks. In the distance, about 7 km away, I could see the asphalt ribbon taking a curt right-hand turn, as it entered into tens of switchbacks stacked above each other along the mountainside, then disappearing around a corner where the valley closed in. If I craned my neck, the peaks of previously unseen mountains came into view behind the road and I couldn't imagine how it would find a way through them.

Behind a scattering of boulders 300 metres from the road, and out of sight of any traffic that might pass, I pitched the tent slowly and collected water from the nearby stream. It was far too late to attempt the climb – and even if I did, I was unsure whether there would be any flat ground available for camping. Huascarán to my left was basking in the last streams of sunlight, glowing golden despite the whiteness of its snow. By tomorrow afternoon, I needed to clear the valley and find supplies on the other side, but the pass would require at least another 1,000 metres of vertical ascent.

As the sun fell, the cold set in. I was still cleaning pots in the stream and boiling water for the next day, when I felt the bite in my fingers and saw my breath clouding thickly in the air. The water, shallow, with a bed of copper-coloured stones underneath, was rushing along the exposed soil banks. Some hate camping in the cold, but I've found it to be the best of all. The chill keeps you alert – unlike the heat, which tires you – and fills you with appreciation for the warmth of a sleeping bag, the softness of a good air mattress, and the uninhabited and wind-protected patch of ground you occupy for the night. Sleeping under Huascarán, the giant of Peru, with only a trickle of water in earshot and some hot tea to take to bed, was the essence of a kind of simplicity I had come to love, away from towns and the disturbance of people.

Reaching Punta Olimpica Pass was a worthy test of patience. Between 9 a.m. on the first day until 4 p.m. the next, when I finally got to the top, I had only been climbing. On the switchbacks, I stopped every 10 minutes for roughly 30 seconds, to catch my breath – the only way to recharge my legs and inhale enough of the thinning air. I ran into a road construction crew dressed in high-visibility orange, and was told I would have to wait for over an hour before I could pass, as the surface was undergoing repairs. In my panniers I had just one piece of bread, an avocado and an orange, and the delay meant I'd be unlikely to reach Chacas, the next town, by evening. Twenty minutes into the wait however, a gorgeous brown-haired girl allowed me and three other cars to proceed, and so I was able to round the mountain edge where the road had seemed to disappear the previous night. To my astonishment, I could now see that it continued upwards as a mucky track towards what looked like a man-made incision in the rock high up above.

Only for the help of another construction team, I would have run out of food and energy. As I lay with my back – padded by my large dry bag – against a small tongue of ice that had slid down onto the road from a mountain saddle, they approached with a dinner of chicken, rice, and soup. They asked for some photos, which on later inspection were breathtaking shots of the valley behind us; my previous night's campsite was a mere speck in the distance.

At 4,950 metres' altitude, I dismounted the bike, my backside sore and my lungs empty. I set the bicycle against the wall, took the orange from my pannier and ate it slowly under the massive sliced rock behind me. The sky was broken into every shade of grey. After a couple of minutes without movement, I began to shiver. The pass was proving to be a trip high, in terms of both altitude and emotion. I was 50 metres short of 5 km into the sky, and would probably not ride to such a height again. I was in the heart of the Peruvian backcountry, and just in time to experience it before the road was sealed and a proposed tunnel built through the mountain, which would dispense with the need for that last hour's work in reaching the top.

Now the race was on to Chacas, and after a harrowing descent on a road that dropped tremendously steeply to a small lake, before meandering down the course of an ever-strengthening river, I could finally see flickering lights emerging from the darkness. I was guaranteed gravel roads for at least a week now until I came near a bigger town, but I felt ready for it. Whatever temporary frustrations came about from rattling along such roads would, I knew, be tempered by the serene and grassy landscape, sprinkled with farmsteads and horses grazing the fields. It was just like Switzerland, although I was jolted back to reality every time I received a smile and wave from a Peruvian country-dweller, pushing a handcart or tilling their plot of land.

Three days of alternating between high Alpine meadows and plains of rocky debris eventually brought me to Huari, at the southern end of the Cordillera Blanca. I had travelled an average of 35 km per day on terrain I very quickly began to fatigue on. These were the worst roads I had ever seen; they were made up of compacted rocks and sand, which meant that when I wasn't shuddering over the surface, I was slipping and skidding. I took a rest at Lago Huachococha, where I met a man walking from one village to the next for work. It would take him two days, he told me, and he'd sleep under a blanket for his night outside, just hoping it didn't rain. Each time I encountered someone like this, distance and time seemed somehow less important and I was reminded that, although the road could be bad, it would always end.

I plodded south towards Huánuco and a sun-drenched vale surrounded the Huallaga River. Days were turning a shade warmer, but I could only feel this when the breeze died down. By mid-afternoon, a haze would form and the sound of buzzing insects would come from the hedgerows. Highway 3N then turned due south and gained elevation once more, en route to Cerro de Pasco. This road is just one of three that cut lengthways through Peru, the others being the Pan-American on the coast and another, which ventures in and out of the Peruvian Amazon. In a nation as large as this, it's evident just how restricting the Andes have been to infrastructure development and improvement, and when this does take place, it's entirely determined by the availability of rivers and valleys large enough to accommodate it.

> *Diary: 2 July 2012, Cerro de Pasco, Peru*
>
> *A sign announces Cerro de Pasco as the highest city in the world, at 4,380 metres – I did 3,089 metres of that today. It was absolutely freezing when I arrived over the moors at 7 p.m. My hands were numb and I couldn't feel the handlebars. I'm now feeling quite ill and might throw up: the altitude and hard days are wearing me out. It's so cold in the mornings and drops to minus temperatures at night, with a sun at midday that can't seem to heat the air but which will burn your skin. It will only be much further south that things heat up again.*

Peru's geography makes for an intriguing cycle through the country. On the coast you've got the desert and bone-dry air; the interior is high, mountainous and cold; and in the east is jungle, where a handful of indigenous tribes maintain their traditional ways of life, in relative isolation from the rest of the world. It is a country of ancient societies and new, rural subsistence and urban dynamism. It's tamed and untamed, depending on where you look. From one area to another, I thought I could pick out in people's facial features the small nuances that perhaps hinted at a particular tribal origin in the past. I didn't have the words to ask about such matters, however, and so the mystery remained just that, a fact which somehow kept me in high spirits as I cut across the Peruvian *altiplano* (high plains) by Lago Junín and in the direction of another neck of the Andes. For others riding down the middle of Peru, or even in from the Amazon, there would undoubtedly be a story of people and places, customs and lifestyles, very different to what I had encountered.

In La Oroya, 137 km from Cerro de Pasco, the morning's good form was sullied. La Oroya is Peru's copper and zinc mining capital; it has the unhealthy distinction of being one of the world's most polluted places, because the smelting operations produce an assortment of noxious substances, such as cadmium, indium, selenium, and tellurium: too many '-iums' make for a rather insalubrious place to live. However to its credit and despite all the industrial activity there, the town is hemmed into an impressive cul-de-sac of furrowed rock walls.

I hadn't spoken with any other travellers in weeks, and my only other fleeting conversations had been with hotel owners and the ladies in eating places who served up *milanese de pollo* (breaded and fried chicken) and other chicken-centred recipes at lunch and dinner. I didn't know when I would next cross a bicycle tourist's path, as the country offered many more route options than Colombia and Ecuador, with roads criss-crossing the mountains. Buff3y was still in northern Peru, and Marcus – who I had met in Vancouver and San Francisco – was already in Cusco: these were the only two people I knew in the same region. All I did was ride, albeit at a slower pace than before because I recognised that very soon, full climbing days were all I would have.

From the road's changing colour on my map, I knew that it would soon disintegrate into foundation layers for a future highway. Such a change in conditions has the potential to hugely alter journey planning, as well as access to shops for food and water. It's quite possible to increase speed on asphalt, even on a climb, but almost hopeless on hard-packed gravel and dirt, because often there are too many protruding rocks and potholes to avoid. Two hours after Huayucachi, I hit a torn-up surface 70 km before I had expected to, and with almost 230 km left until the city of Ayacucho. Ten kilometres later, the washboard began; perhaps a cyclist's worst enemy, this is up there with sand and headwinds, but the funny thing is that when you experience one of these, you find yourself almost wishing for one of the others. I could feel the bike's steel frame bearing the brunt of the pressure induced by what felt like thousands upon thousands of mini-speed bumps. Alongside the road ran a railway track with a generously slight incline; it would often disappear to take a circuitous route around a mountain, before returning again to match my course.

I had felt ill since Cerro de Pasco. For the time being, my main symptoms were the kind of shivering and fatigue I would normally associate with a recurrence of my colitis. So, when I ran to relieve myself beyond a mound of earth adjacent to the road, all the while gazing desperately into the depths of a sandy-sloped ravine, I could sense that the colitis was edging back. The ebbs and flows of weakness and high energy were always indications that my system wasn't coping with the stress of a disease, which flared up every now and again, as if to remind me it was there. I had been through this before and so knew to increase the dosage of my medication, and drink plenty of water to stay hydrated. I also vowed to take a good deal of time off wherever I next felt comfortable.

One saddening feature of the environment I was now journeying through was the river running through it. The Río Mantaro gushed for the majority of its course, close beside me, until it stopped abruptly, where a mid-sized dam blocked its path. On the other side, no more than 10 metres away, I could see a weak stream that dribbled pathetically around boulders that had no doubt previously formed eddies and whirlpools in a once surging waterway. The culture of damming rivers in Peru is a disturbing one. For those like the Mantaro, the first earth-movements and concrete foundations laid by human intervention heralded the death-knell of an ecosystem and of all those depending on it, humans and animals alike. What has been in existence for millennia is ended and told, 'no more will you be free', within seconds of the dam gates closing. Moreover, further east in the Amazon, rivers such as the Marañón and Ucayali face a disastrous future too, with at least 70 dams billed for construction within the next 40 years on these two life-giving, life-sustaining waterways and their tributaries. It is depressing to think what price will be paid by the world's largest tropical rainforest for the eradication of biodiversity inevitably caused by the blocking of one of its key sources of nutrients.

In a part of Peru so long devoid of villages and settlements, camps have now been built to service the hydropower workers. In Quichuas, 60 km from the next town of Huanta, and a place distinguished by a few restaurants, two guesthouses and some shops, the tiny square was buzzing with men and women in bright orange and yellow jumpsuits, retiring after a day's work. Hundreds must be housed here, I thought, in what was just a small dot of civilization, existing for a singular purpose. Above, the sky was wide open, with a brushstroke of the Milky Way running across it and not a hint of light pollution to dull the splendour. The vastness of Peru's expanses and the wild nature of its mountains cannot hinder humans, who will get anywhere if they have a purpose or gain to extract. Once again, I found myself wondering what price 'progress' here will do to the natural bounty all around.

I was just two days from Ayacucho, and would spend them permanently hot and dusty. Cacti along the edge of the highway, and the grittiness of the surface, gave it an 'Old West' quality. Parched creeks frequently crossed under bridges and a dry wind blustered in from the north, stirring up the powdery earth. I was only able to sense changing climatic zones so subtly because I moved so slowly. In the north it was wet and misty, before turning to desert on the coast. The Cordillera Blanca brought ice and snow, thin air and cold. The central provinces meanwhile were characterised by green fields and agriculture, and bathed in a warm sun. And now, here, another type of terrain, steeped in aridity, fought for its place too.

Ayacucho, located at 2,760 metres above sea level, is known for its 33 churches – one for each year of Jesus' life. On the night I arrived, I took a shower, put on some clean clothes and walked downhill from my hotel to the main square, refreshed and ready to investigate this faith-inspiring architecture. I entered the square to have a look around, when suddenly I heard, behind me, the shrill screams of some local women. I turned around, to see a bull, its muscles bulging from its skin, charging at me from the cobbled road. As I hurled myself towards a park bench and the bushes beside it, the bull struck a dustbin and took off towards the market close by, petrifying old couples out for an evening stroll and children with ice creams in hand, walking beside their parents. As the animal barged through historical buildings and into courtyards, a cacophony of noise reverberated back and forth between the walls and stone. I later learned from a waiter the bull had escaped from its pen a few blocks away and had spent another hour harassing residents and visitors around the colonial centre before finally being subdued.

The next day, whilst reading in the park, I also made a new friend. Ali was a smartly-dressed, 22-year-old university student from Ayacucho, and he introduced himself with a strong handshake and a lengthy family history. I was, at this point, comfortably conversational in past, present, and future tense basic Spanish, and had the good fortune of being able to understand the clear accent and pronunciation of the Peruvians. On this occasion I also had a good idea of what was about to happen, since it was now a common occurrence in Latin America. Ali wanted to improve his English and so very gradually he slipped into a familiar tongue by substituting words here and there; eventually he was pushing to arrange a meeting, 'where we could talk about ourselves, our likes and dislikes, things we like to eat, our favourite bands and hopes for the future', as he put it. Ali was determined to practice, and in my book, anyone willing to ask a complete stranger in the park deserved some time. With that, we planned some food and beers in a café overlooking the square for the following afternoon.

When we met the next day as arranged, before I could remove my jacket, Ali had produced a Dictaphone. By the time I sat down, he had ordered two Cusqueña beers.

'Do you like the taste?' he asked me, as I poured mine into a glass.

'Yes, I do. It's tasty and cheap and that's the most important thing for me,' I said, fully aware this wasn't an organic conversation, but more a recording of the correct way to pronounce English words and structure sentences. I assumed a formal tone until the recording stopped, as I knew he would want to listen back. Once he switched the recorder off, we had a chance for a bit more spontaneity. I wanted to learn more about life here and his background, as a means of making it an equitable afternoon.

'I think it is also tasty and for the price, a very good flavour,' he responded to my original answer.

We moved through all the textbook topics and I told him about my family, friends, favourite music, and places I had travelled. He nodded eagerly at the end of every sentence but usually preferred to ask a new and unrelated question, instead of pursuing a line of dialogue about any particular subject.

'Do you think Michelangelo's "David" is a beautiful statue?' was a question I didn't anticipate just after an explanation of agriculture in Ireland. So too was the next: 'Do you think paragliding is a dangerous activity?' The more questions Ali asked, the more bizarre they came, forcing me to about think things I never would normally bother mustering the brain cells to consider.

'Is it a good job to work as an airline pilot?' Ali now asked, staring right into my eyes with entrenched eagerness and honesty. I admired the effort he made, and was aware that people like Ali saw opportunity in education and language. When I quizzed him about his own life, I learned that he was studying engineering and that, once he had finished his exams, he wanted to work in the United States – a destiny he will no doubt fulfil.

Ali wanted to wave me off in the morning, but I explained that I was a bad timekeeper and so should say goodbye now. He thanked me again and I him. He put his Dictaphone safely away and gave me directions to some of the churches I had yet to see, before walking off across the plaza and into the maze of streets.

Ayacucho has a distinguished history in the independence struggle of South America, as it was here in 1825 that the final battle between the Spanish and the Peruvian Army of Independence took place. Victory for the Peruvian patriots sealed the nation's independence, and consequently, freedom for South America. Of course, Ayacucho's most notable feature is its 33 churches. It would take far more than two days to visit them all, never mind have time to appreciate them, but those I saw in the centre were quite unassuming buildings, painted yellow, red, and grey. So I went to the market, selling *pan con queso* (cheese bread), *pan con aceituna* (bread with tuna) and *mate* (tea) for breakfast – a fortress of noise within which to spend the mornings, gawking at the fruit and vegetables coming in and out, observing animal carcasses being skinned and carved with prodigious precision, and talking with indigenous families, here to sell woven textiles and clothes made from alpaca wool. The further south and the higher I travelled in Peru, the more distinctively indigenous the faces of those I met became.

Between Ayacucho and Cusco, there are five of the toughest and reviled climbs on the road from Alaska to Argentina. The route is 583 km long and comprises over 12,000 vertical metres in ascent – equivalent to one-and-a-half times the height of Mount Everest. There are also 11,500 metres to be descended, meaning a total elevation gain of just 500 metres on the other side. Of these five climbs, the second – from Río Pampas to a peak after the mountain town of Uripa – is the stoutest test, rising 2,220 metres over 60 km and without a single downhill section. The fourth serves up 2,180 metres of elevation gain over 44 km, almost as cruel in terms of height, but far steeper due to the shorter distance. Some reprieve is granted to the cyclist due to the fact that about on 70 per cent of the route, there is a sealed surface, albeit a mediocre one; the remaining 30 per cent is comprised of a scattering of coarse stone and dirt. This is by far the most demanding and draining few days of the entire journey, but it is unavoidable, unless you wish to take a 1,000 km detour to the south; even then, you are only putting off an inevitable climb on another road, charging up the frontline of the Andes from the coast. It had been an almost impenetrable terrain for the Spanish Conquistadors, and now I fell into their footsteps, headed east on a bicycle, with the venerated Inca city of Machu Picchu as my destination.

Leaving Ayacucho for the initial leg-burning, heart-pumping pleasures of climbing, I met a gently graded road and soon after crossed a level area of grassland, where the sandy road zigzagged away into the distance. Past a distant hilltop, this road tumbled downhill to a little community marked as Ocros on my map – about 800 metres below the top, in a hollowed-out crevice of a valley that looked like an open-pit mine. The Andes were stunning in the evening sun and from a height, so I stood for 10 minutes, eating a jam sandwich and simply watching the shadows creeping along the mountains, far out to the west.

Ocros, which I now saw as a bundle of bright lights, was about 3 km away as the crow flies, although much longer when following the road. According to a woman holding a Stop/Go sign just before the drop, the village had a police station and if I could reach that evening, they might allow me to stay inside. I set off, in the hope that I could beat the dwindling light, but darkness soon welled inside the space between two mountains, and within 20 minutes I was riding by the light of my dim headlamp. On two occasions, I fell from the bike, after slipping on loose gravel that my 1.5-inch tyres weren't capable of handling. I knew I'd cut my right tendon on the big chain ring on the second occasion, but the light from my lamp was so weak I couldn't see the laceration. However, I did notice a spatter of blood on the ring, discoloured and collecting dust. Two hundred metres below me, as I crawled from side to side along the mountainside, I could hear the flapping of a car's blown-out tyre – another person was struggling in the enveloping dark. I had no choice but to walk the bicycle 6 km to Ocros, but could hear a stream by the road's edge and felt unenthusiastic about skidding off it into the water.

It was a good thing Ocros was so sleepy. The police officer on duty in the town's three-room station told me that they hadn't received a call in five days, and that my arrival was the only thing of note to happen.

'Nothing happens here, so we just drive around and inspect the roads.

Sometimes we go away on training to Ayacucho, which is the most exciting thing we do,' he said, leading me to the meeting room I'd stay in.

Indeed, the next morning I could understand how bored he must get. The town square was empty and calm, apart from a mild din coming out of a café. I ate an omelette and fried potatoes, silently amazed by the scale of the mountain walls around the town, washed in morning light.

'The only people staying here are the road crews, and they're gone at 5 a.m. When the surface is finished, there'll be nobody around again until the rains wash part of it away,' the woman serving food told me.

I bemoaned my poor choice in tyres, as I took the continuing descent from Ocros like a child on their first bicycle lesson. The Schwalbe Marathon tyres were quick and as puncture-resistant as you'd hope for, but a trifle inappropriate on a surface where you had to dodge potholes, large rocks, and pockets of sand. I needed fatter tyres with knobby edges, and thankfully I had some waiting in Cusco. By the time I reached the bottom of the valley I was exhausted from the effort of concentration and my face was covered with a thin layer of dust, which stuck to my sweaty brow and cheeks.

The Río Pampas was the sole resident of the valley bottom, and wove its way through the middle in a 'S' shape, wide beaches of sand surrounding it. Riding beside the river, I felt a twinge in my left knee, followed moments later by a sharp pain running down the inside of my leg. The last time I experienced that exact sensation was a couple of months before the trip, when the recurrence of an old injury had required physiotherapy. I stopped for a moment, laid my bicycle down in the middle of the road and stretched my legs, in the hope this would alleviate the pain. Of course, if eight weeks of physiotherapy had just about put it to bed the last time, then some roadside pulling and bending wasn't going to cure it now. An hour later, just 2 km further along and at the beginning of a 2,220-metre climb, my knee buckled. The pain shot under my kneecap and I toppled off the bicycle, staggering along the ground. A Dutch cyclist called Gerard, who I had met in Ocros the night before, turned up on the road behind me, but very soon moved on again, sympathetic yet unable to do anything to help me. I waved down the next passing truck and loaded my bicycle into the back. The driver, who was carrying sacks of grain, said he'd stop in Uripa and I could get off there, where I might find a pharmacy or a hotel for the night if I was inclined to stay.

Diary: 12 July 2012, Uripa, Peru

The pain isn't noticeable, walking now, just when I pedal with force. It was probably caused by pushing too bloody hard on the flat by the river today. I'm going to put a compress on it, and hope by tomorrow it's better. I still have 1,000 metres more uphill, before dropping into Andahuaylas on the far side. Such a shame, as it's pretty Peruvian countryside here and the people are friendly. Another meal of pollo y papas fritas (chicken and fries), seemingly the only thing Peruvians and I eat.

My knee was pain-free in the morning, but did feel incredibly stiff around the bone. I left at 6 a.m., wrapped in two base layers, a soft shell top, and my insulated jacket. Frost coated the grass and farmers walked the shoulder, hoes and axes in hand. As I continued at a gentle pace upwards, the views were splendid, with villages appearing on the horizon many kilometres and metres below, the smoke from the chimneys of dwellings gathering in a thin cloud in the air above. I could see another road threading a path through them, vanishing for a while and then re-emerging until it met the next settlement.

At 3,500 metres, I heard once more the most aggravating sound I had experienced on my tour. I didn't need to examine the source – I knew the rear rim had split again, possibly from weeks riding on a bone-shaking surface. When I did pull over, I saw a deep, three-inch tear. For the third time, the rim had broken under a combination of weight, poor surface, and perhaps too much tyre pressure. It may also have been a substandard part, so I decided to change manufacturer this time around. With 280 km remaining to Cusco, I was left with the choice of riding on and damaging the bicycle further, or catching a bus and reassessing the situation from there. I was fuming, and cursed the wheel, the weight, and the rotten roads I'd been on that had played as big a part as anything else. Yet there was nothing to do but stick my thumb out, wait for a bus, and go to Cusco.

On account of my premature arrival in Cusco, I decided to take one week's break and reboot my system before moving onto Bolivia, the thirteenth country of the trip. Continuous movement has a tendency to overwhelm the mind and cause sensory overload, which in my experience can only be righted by a temporarily sedentary life again. Peru had so far been a test of resolve and patience, but all challenges were short-lived, and generally made up for at night with a conversation and new acquaintance. Although more reserved than the effervescent Colombians and Ecuadorians, the Peruvians were just as welcoming and inquisitive – it just a little longer for them to open up. A friend of mine told me it could be on account of their history of civil war, which has perhaps encouraged the habit of keeping some distance from outsiders until they're better known.

Undeniably, Peru is a country of natural magnificence, but the gem in the colonial crown is Cusco, the historic capital of the Inca Empire and long-time centre of Spanish colonisation in South America. On the immediate face of it, evidence of the latter influence stands out in greater abundance. Cusco's architectural heritage has birthed churches, convents, plazas and important buildings of immaculate presence. The Plaza de Armas shines brightly in the centre of it all, holding the city's cathedral and the red brick *Iglesia de la Compañía* (Church of the Society of Jesus). The nearby *barrios* (neighbourhoods) are picturesque and pleasant, with arts and crafts continuing as they have for centuries. In the Barrio de San Blas, artisans turn out paintings and sculpture on the steep streets leading onto the plaza at the district's centre; it's a hub of intellectual and creative activity today, as it has been in the past. The whole city is an open history lesson, allowing you to visit the sites of colonial occupation as well as those of Inca rule, and to immerse yourself in a convergence of living history.

In El Molino market, contemporary life carries on with all the racket of consumer bustle. I visited with Gerard, who had caught me up after taking a bus, to make the most of his two-month stay in Peru. Electronics, cheap handbags, home accessories, light industrial equipment, from grass strimmers to cement mixers, shoes, cheap clothes, fruit and vegetables – all are sold under one steaming roof, where clatter and people seem impossible to escape. The market also sprawled onto the streets, where passers-by pulled in to buy milkshakes and pick up the daily newspaper. Everything away from these kinds of markets seems quite sanitised, especially in tourist cities like Cusco, so visiting them was, I found, a reminder as to the real pulse and temper of life.

Of course, Cusco's most famous local attraction, or at least near-local attraction, is Machu Picchu. The Incan city, whose image is identifiable the world over, is a unique example of an Incan settlement, which remained undiscovered by the Spanish during their conquest of South America. The hilltop estate of Emperor Pachacuti – as archaeologists believe it to be – is, without doubt, one the world's most remarkable cultural phenomena. Built on a slender ridge, 450 metres above the Urubamba River, the city faces its sister peak of Huayna Picchu, amidst the taller mountains in seemingly uninhabitable terrain.

Walking onto one of the many precipices and looking down at Machu Picchu is an experience worth living a thousand times over. Green agricultural terraces sloping treacherously towards the sheer edges of the ridge; the ruins of houses, temples, irrigation channels and ceremonial squares; the presence of a complex astronomical observatory: all of these make the ancient city a visual, architectural, and scientific open-air masterpiece. Llamas still graze grounds of patchy grass, and drink from water flowing through centuries-old man-made waterways. Even the sound of the roaring Urubamba River below and the sight of birds gliding in the expanse of hundreds of metres between river and city give the site a sense of everlasting wildness.

I had reached Machu Picchu before sunrise on my visit, and was hoping for a bright day. I picked a spot by the Hut of the Caretaker of the Funerary Rock, and away from the majority of tourists who poured in. There was a glimmer of light to the east and, as the minutes passed, a corona building over the lush green mountains. Soon, I could see stones turn into the recognisable shapes of buildings surrounding plazas, occupying residential quarters, or clustering on the hillsides. Just after 7 a.m., the first beams of cool morning sunlight broke through the hilltops, illuminating the peaks of western ridges, some over 3,000 metres high. As a navy blue sky transformed to pastel, the light fell upon the Urubamba's valley, then the terraces at a great height above it, before striking the drywall stonework, the vast green spaces, and the heart of the Inca's sacred city.

I sat in silence, as did many others, lost in wonder and imagination. How many sunrises ago did the last Inca leave this place? How many had watched day break on a winter's morning, as I just had, and gone on to their day's work? With the entire site basking in a now warmer sun, tourists began to occupy the empty spaces, and the flash of cameras began. It had been a wise decision, I thought, to get to the apex early on, and see it, without interruption, as it had been for centuries after the Inca departed. After all, I reflected, it had just been 101 years previously, in 1911, that archaeologist Hiram Bingham had discovered local farmers tending the very terraces the Inca had built, under the thick vines and brambles. Witnessing the original, post-Inca space in this way is something I'm glad to have seen – an experience as close to authentic as anyone can now get.

As soon as I felt like moving on, I left the perch near the Hut of the Caretaker and wandered downhill, to join the mass of camera-wielding visitors. It had been a special morning for me – not just for the tranquillity, the sunrise, or the sight of the remarkable setting in which the Inca *magnum opus* resides – but also because I had witnessed it all, exactly one year to the day since leaving southbound tyre tracks in Deadhorse, Alaska. Now I was 20,855 km further along the way, and that journey was an experience I felt rather privileged to have had. There was now just 7,000 km to go until Ushuaia, and, as I readied myself to enter Bolivia and continue towards the final straits to Patagonia, I knew this was the beginning of one of the last and perhaps most unpredictable chapters of the entire journey.

11
Salt and Sand

Cusco, Peru to La Quiaca, Argentina – 1,552 km

SHELTERED BETWEEN TWO ARMS OF the Andes, in a broad and blustery plain, lies Lake Titicaca. At 3,812 metres above sea level, it is the highest navigable lake in the world. Largely devoid of merchant vessels or liners, almost two-thirds of the lake is within Peruvian territory, while the remainder lies in Bolivia. Local fishermen trawling its waters in reed boats pay no heed, however, to the imaginary borderlines that separate its two parts.

My first glimpse of Lake Titicaca came the morning after a night camping under the stars. I had pitched my tent within the clay walls of an unroofed farmhouse, at the edge of a railway track. The temperature had plummeted as soon as the sun disappeared, and when I woke, I found ice replacing the water in my bottles. Even my tent had a film of frozen dew across its exterior and crunched as I folded it up. But as dawn broke, the sun tiptoed above the horizon and into a clear and empty sky, and the ice at last began to thaw. Lake Titicaca appeared as a pale blue line 10 km away, fringed by a foreground of golden wheat fields and potato farms.

I pedalled briskly into the day on the well-sealed surface – I knew that ambling along would only allow the bitter cold to return to my limbs. Since departing Sicuani the previous day, I had seen only desolate terrain, but now, there was a loveliness to my surroundings. Every now and again, I'd come across some Quechua women carrying sacks of vegetables or rounding up animals, somehow maintaining amidst their labour an elegance, in their traditional, kaleidoscopic woven clothes and distinctive, bowler-style hats. Often, I was gifted with a simple nod of recognition, but sometimes, a wave and a smile too. The men generally had more to say, but I never understood what it was, so I just shouted '*Hola*' back, and pedalled on by.

The Quechua – a term used to cover several ethnic Andean groups mainly occupying Peru and Bolivia – have many different languages and associated dialects, so I wasn't sure if it was their accents or the vernacular itself that confused me. Compared to the mixed indigenous and European populations in the cities and on the coast, the Quechua were more reserved and conservative in their interactions, perhaps the upshot of decades of historical oppression. As I proceeded towards Bolivia and the centre of their community and culture, I inevitably began to see them in greater numbers.

Along the western shoreline of Lake Titicaca are Juliaca and Puno, two boisterous cities built high up enough to see their own reflections in the water. They are dusty and discordant and do little for the visitor except raise some tentative sense of excitement that the prettier lake edges are just a few hours further to the south. I didn't grasp the true level of unattractiveness of Juliaca until I rode first into its smoggy centre, and I made sure to ride right back out after a lunch of deep-fried cheeses. I knew Puno would be similar, but felt that if I arrived there later that evening, I'd have a shot at reaching the backpacker haven of Copacabana in Bolivia the following day.

My plan turned out well, and Puno came and went as quickly as I could have hoped. The heavy traffic on the western edge of the lake calmed considerably and the road moved snugly beside the water, which had some remarkable views over its glossy surface and into Bolivia. The snowy peaks of Ancohuma and Qalsata materialised as ghostly apparitions 100 km away, and I could also see the crumbling remains of mud-built farmhouses with collapsing reed roofs, scattered throughout the countryside and by the lake's shore.

I cycled 135 km to reach the Bolivian border post, just as the temperature was cooling once more. I pulled on my thermal leggings – threadbare from a year of use – and fished my synthetic down jacket from the bottom of the pannier bags, and braced for a chilly finish to the day.

At the border, a number of teenagers were performing a dance act in the middle of a small square, beating drums and clashing cymbals. Tourists getting in and out of buses snapped photographs, and put the last of their Peruvian currency into little tin cans that were dotted around the square, clapping in appreciation as they walked away. At the border office, a queue of travellers had formed to wait for their entry stamps, and after 15 minutes, I was given my turn.

'What is your purpose in Bolivia?' asked a young official, scanning the pages of my passport.

'Travel, just passing through on my way south,' I answered.

'Where will you go here?' he grunted back. I tried to picture the map in my mind and bring some names forward.

'La Paz, Salar de Uyuni, Tupiza maybe,' I said, listing the only places I could think of.

'You must be tired? I think from your face and that bicycle outside, you've cycled a long way,' he said, this time leaning back, folding his arms and looking as if he was settling in for conversation. He grinned, as if about to deliver the punch line to a joke.

'Yes, I've come a distance. And I want to get to Copacabana tonight before it's too late,' I said, cracking a smile in the hope of hurrying him up.

Then it came.

'So, you *are* tired? I can tell you, the girls of Bolivia are the best to be around then. They can help you. So very beautiful, I can get you some, you know!' he bellowed, trying to get the attention of his colleagues.

It was a repetition of countless conversations I had already had, and I was honestly tired of them now. Just like with the police officer in Valladolid in Ecuador, I had no interest in playing along. 'It's getting dark, so is everything ok with my entry visa?'

'Of course my friend, enjoy my country,' he answered, handing my passport over. 'And enjoy the beautiful women. Don't forget to try.'

To my embarrassment, although it should have been his, three girls stood immediately behind me, unimpressed with his sleazy blathering. I wondered about this machismo, as I drifted downhill and into a dilapidated town with more doors boarded up than open. Even in the line of civic duty, it apparently knew no bounds, and with it came this possessive attitude to women that went unhindered, even in public.

Copacabana is known for its Basilica of Our Lady of Copacabana, a sixteenth-century shrine to the patron saint of Bolivia, and a popular pilgrimage destination for the Catholic population of the country. It wasn't until the next morning that I saw the shining white building, nestled at the bottom of a hill in the soft curve of a hillside. Inside the basilica is a carving of the Virgen de Copacabana, which is laminated in gold and adorned with jewels and silver, and is greatly revered by Bolivians. Indeed, Bolivia's independence in 1825 has been attributed by staunch believers to the people's untiring faith in this icon, which at that point had, according to popular belief, already been performing miracles for 250 years, making it one of the oldest shrines to the Virgin Mary in the Americas. Accordingly, the town sees a regular influx of nationals and tourists coming to pray at the foot of the Virgen's image. I was in Christian country now, and could feel it.

It was a crisp morning as I ascended the hills overlooking the Basilica and took the road that curves around the peninsula where Copacabana sits. At 4,251 metres – the highest point on the climb – it's possible to gaze west onto Lake Titicaca's sparkling surface, and then look east to see its sister lake, Winyamarca. Some believe that Lake Titicaca's name translates as 'Rock Puma', as locals believe the shape of it resembles a puma hunting a rabbit – the rabbit being Lake Winyamarca. In this case I was standing between both animals where a slim, 500-metre stretch of water joins the two lakes. The only way across is by taking a small wooden car ferry; I boarded it, refreshed from three coffees and a toasted cheese and tomato sandwich from the ferry dock's market.

On the far side, a quick and painless climb up the side of a scree field brought me onto a sealed road beside Lake Winyamarca. It was deceptively flat, avoiding all the knolls and perforations on the landscape. I sensed I had crossed another social and cultural border, but couldn't pinpoint why and how until later in the afternoon. I noticed how much poorer the people here seemed to be – if it's possible to deduce that from the greater number of clay brick houses in a reduced condition, the smaller and drier tracts of land attached to them, and the considerably lower cost of food and other commodities. My first lunch of rice, meat, potatoes, salad and a coke cost just $2 – half of what I would have paid in Peru. Yet, life seemed somehow amplified here. The women's dresses had more glitter and were brighter, and the bowler hats quite a bit bigger; I also passed two town festivals in full progress before I cleared the southern limit of the lake. At both of these, men, women and children of all ages played trumpets, horns, drums and guitars with pride and precision. Elderly people sat contentedly on the roadside, clapping as these musicians, in exquisitely sewn uniforms, marched by them, on their way to the town's square or church. And despite the run-down houses, bare land, and subsistence level of living, there was a palpable sense of cheer all around. Not for the first time, I found myself questioning the true measure of poverty, and whether it can be solely defined in economic terms – because if the colour of life was taken in account, then these might well be some of the richest people on earth.

I felt a real pang of emotion when I reached El Alto, the final town before La Paz. Since Copacabana, it had been another long and tiresome day, but I could see a huge fissure in the distant landscape, and I knew that La Paz was at the bottom.

Diary: 23 July 2012, La Paz, Bolivia

Arrival at 3,300 metres! It was a brilliant few hours on the ride to La Paz. All day, I was on an open, moor-like landscape, with lots of cars and buses hurtling by. I was always chasing that furthest curve in the distance where I knew La Paz would be, and once I saw that gaping hole in the ground, maybe 20 km away, I could sense the city's presence. Above it is all just flat, for tens of miles around, but the city itself sits in a deep valley. It's like edging towards the Grand Canyon and seeing the other side, but with the gap in the middle. In Alaska, the idea of getting here always seemed far-fetched, I think, but now it's real. And every now and again, I get a real sense of satisfaction, privilege and joy from comprehending the time and kilometres in between.

They say if you get lost in La Paz, just walk downhill until you find the Choqueyapu River and you will get your bearings again. The entire city is built in an oblong bowl that cuts deep into the Altiplano – a wide and high Andean plateau – giving some truly dramatic perspectives on the scale of human architecture and construction. From a height, terraces of brown-brick houses sweep down from 4,100 metres to 3,200 metres, until they converge in the valley narrows. The city's administrative buildings, main commercial zone and affluent neighbourhoods occupy the lowest elevations, while the economically disadvantaged areas cling to the valley sides, hundreds of metres further up. It is the most staggering example of economic disparity you will see, and an ironic stroke of circumstance that those who are less affluent must look down from a height at those who are wealthier.

Despite being perhaps the most well-known city in Bolivia, La Paz is only the third largest in the country, and neither is it the capital; Sucre holds that honour. The government may not be in La Paz, but the President lives and works here, as do the majority of civil servants. To Bolivians and South Americans, the city is also an important icon of independence, and was the focal point in the fight for the continent's freedom from Spanish rule. It was here in 1809 that Pedro Domingo Murillo, Bolivia's revered patriot, famously declared: 'Compatriots, I die, but tyrants won't be able to extinguish the torch I ignited. Long live freedom!' Sixteen years later, the final battle in that war was fought in Ayacucho, Peru, where I had been just two weeks previously. To mark this, the name of La Paz changed to 'La Paz de Ayacucho' ('The Peace of Ayacucho').

Today, Bolivia and La Paz are still inextricably linked to the fervour and passion associated with revolution, but in a modern context, the drive for change and reform manifests itself in very different ways. Since the election in 2005 of Evo Morales as President, the country has been on a crusade to achieve indigenous inclusion, and the nationalisation of industry. Morales, the son of Ayamaran farmers, acceded to the Presidency on the basis of an agenda which promised agrarian reform, the taxation of big corporations, literacy campaigns and anti-poverty projects. As the country's first democratically elected indigenous President, he is a symbol and a leader all in one, and is a strong voice for the indigenous 50 per cent of Bolivia's population. While Morales' supporters believe that equality and human rights are finally being championed, others see his rule as dictatorial. As far as I could discern however, from my superficial impressions on the streets, the country's future is still rooted firmly in the past, with the great majority of people making their living from running small family shops, manning call centres, receiving remittances from family abroad, and selling fruits, vegetables and food.

I had three days to spend in La Paz. On one of these, I decided to visit a place which had past associations for Áine. As an 18-year old, she had come to Bolivia for one year to work with Fundación Arco Iris, a charity focusing on helping young people on the streets out of extreme poverty, as well as tackling the problem of domestic abuse. Although I didn't know Áine at the time, I remembered her fundraising efforts for the trip, which got good coverage in the local newspapers and on the radio. It seemed like such a brave and bold step to take at that age – and now I was about to meet her Bolivian 'family' and revisit some of her memories.

Boris Borzinho, Áine's supervisor at the time, was still working with the Fundación, and he agreed to meet me on a sunny Thursday, with the intention of giving me a quick tour. Boris showed me around the dorms where children stayed, as well as the kitchens – where one boy had learned to bake and was now in professional vocational training to be a chef – and the basketball courts, where the kids hung out during the day.

'Be careful,' he told me. 'They might be in a shelter, but they still think of stealing.'

In the courts, there were over 20 boys, aged from seven to 16 years, throwing balls back and forth; others sat on the walls, talking. Their faces, although smiling, were dirty. Many had no shoes and others' T-shirts were torn and worn through. Some were the opposite – hair gelled and slicked back, with clean pants and shiny shoes.

'Many have families and return to them at night. Their parents work on the streets as vendors or washing cars, so this is like day care for their children, who can learn some computer skills or just get a good meal,' Boris told me, as we walked around.

Fundación Arco Iris works with almost 5,000 street children, offering boys' and girls' shelters, 'pass through', drop-in and day care facilities – like Casa Esperanza, where Boris had shown me around – as well as vocational training such as carpentry and handicraft courses.

'You've seen all those kids on the street, right? The ones begging at the feet of visitors like you, and others selling gum or cigarettes?' he asked me.

I'd seen them in every quarter of the city.

'They can work their lives at that, and worse still, get into circles with very bad people,' Boris said. 'The government allows them to, and it's legal for teenagers to be out of school, from just ten years of age. So many of them never see a meaningful education.'

Áine's memories of the experience were still fresh, six years on, but from what I was able to tell her, it seemed that the facilities and care offered had become better with the passing of time. As an 18-year-old, her other concerns at the time, naturally enough, involved exploring a new city, country and continent, and I had heard as much about her travels and exploits such as dancing in street festivals as I had about the nature of severe urban poverty.

'Oh yes, Áine was one of our best. She was always full of energy, ready to help and enthusiastic,' Boris told me. I was surprised he remembered her so well, considering the scores of volunteers which must have passed through in the intervening time.

'Unfortunately, none of the children that were here in 2005 are in the centre now. The last one left just four months ago; he's a trained baker now. It would have been nice for you to hear stories first-hand from the kids.'

Although my afternoon with Boris shone a light for me on Áine's life here, it was in the city itself and on its streets that I could sense her presence and connect with her stories most readily. La Paz was alive and spirited, each street corner crowded with vendors selling *salteñas* (savoury meat pastries), and every size and shape of bread. The markets, often hidden in a warren of underground passageways, were awash with spices and sacks of fruit and vegetables from the countryside. The smell was intoxicating and unfamiliar. As I walked around the Basilica of San Francisco and Plaza de Murillo, I could imagine Áine on the weekends, walking by with friends, racing through hordes of visitors and locals and venturing to some interesting quarter of the city she'd heard about. I hadn't seen her in three months, so I found myself shamelessly imagining and romanticising a series of scenes, which might have born no resemblance to reality, but which at least gave an extra dimension of meaning to my presence here.

It didn't feel as if much time had passed before I was leaving La Paz, taking the same serpentine, sky-bound route on which I had arrived. Four days off after five days on the bicycle was quite generous, considering my mind was habitually consumed by self-imposed time constraints; rest days had their duties too, however. Two of these were taken up with laundry, food shopping, stocking up on stove fuel, phoning home, sending emails, updating the blogs, editing a video, and washing and lubricating the bike, which was in need of some TLC. This had left just two days to visit the Fundación Arco Iris, and enjoy the city's attractions. But, as Robert Louis Stevenson once said, 'The great affair is to move' – and so, an inevitable itch to feel the road beneath me again surfaced again, reminding me of another obligation at hand.

From atop the voluminous Altiplano that extends westward, above and away from La Paz, Volcán Illimani – the city's great 'sentinel', according to local song – watches over northern Bolivia. At sunset, when the light is at its most forgiving, snow can be seen streaming off the Volcán's summit like the white contrails of a passing jet plane, as the mountain turns from brilliant white to soft pink and then fades into the night. As I cycle past them, I had a habit of anthropomorphising landscapes and their features – such as the wide-open wilderness or the giant mountains. I find these things as living as we are, subject also to the changing seasons and patterns of life at play in their surroundings. To my thinking, Illimani had welcomed – or during its periods of eruption, chased away – the area's first settlers, followed by the conquistadors and then their sackers, the brave and independent patriots of South America. Today the volcano stares upon a city desperately trying to succeed, caught in that transitional space where poverty and affluence, the traditional and the modern, continually brush against each other on its sloping streets, every minute of every day.

It was 220 km to Oruro, a mining town of 250,000 people in west-central Bolivia, and I intended to make it in two days. I was meeting two other cyclists there – Tauru Chaw and Christi Bruchock, a couple riding the opposite direction, from Ushuaia to Deadhorse. They were attempting the trip, despite having both been diagnosed legally blind, something I learned from emails we had exchanged many months before any of us set out on our respective journeys.

I hadn't cycled a truly dangerous road in a long time, but as it turned out, my seventeen hours in the saddle between La Paz and Oruro would be a perilous lesson in concentration. As a result of the ramping up of infrastructure improvement projects by the government (though I was soon to see just how far they still have to go in this respect), the first 50 km out of La Paz was nothing more than an open construction zone, with a dearth of red flags, warning lights and men in high-visibility jackets. It was a free-for-all, whereby trucks, vans, cars and motorbikes vied fiercely with each other for space to launch their next overtaking manoeuvre. On the right-hand side, heavy machinery dredged up soil, while, between the white posts marking the road extension, steamrollers flattened fresh patches of highway. The shoulder was cracked, as if an earthquake had shattered it, and I often momentarily lost my front tyre in a surface fissure, before it would reappear with a thud and a wobble. The road ran unobstructed into the horizon, and the view ahead was an ugly sea of moving yellow machinery, coughing black smoke into the atmosphere, while trucks and cars bolted forward at full pelt.

According to Lonely Planet, Oruro has an abundance of 'clean and comfortable' hostels, so I checked into the first one listed in the guidebook, and then went to meet Tauru and Christi, who were more comfortable meeting at their hotel, as Tauru couldn't see very well at night. When I arrived, Tauru gave me a hearty handshake and Christi a big hug. We shared a six-pack of Paceña Black, the closest drink to stout they could find.

'We figured you must miss Guinness,' Tauru said, as we raised our glasses for a toast.

The couple had decided to ride from Argentina to Alaska to raise awareness of the blind, but also to show others that, despite the physical impediments they may face, there's still hope in terms of achieving one's dreams and aspirations. Tauru suffers from *retinitis pigmentosa*, a condition that has caused his peripheral vision to deteriorate to the extent seeing for him is a bit like looking through toilet paper tubes. Christi has severe myopia and has lost all vision in her right eye. On their own, it would be impossible for each to individually ride over 17,000 miles, but as a team on a tandem, they can share the burden of navigating, watching for changing surface conditions, listening for cars and searching for campsites.

'I'm the stoker,' said Christi. 'It means I sit at the back and watch out for anything dangerous. Tauru looks right ahead, where his vision's best.'

'It's not easy,' Tauru admitted, while sipping his beer. 'You depend totally on each other, but we know each other's limitations and strengths. It's the only way we've gotten this far.'

As we chatted, the strength of their conviction for their cause became subtly apparent. They weren't interested in raising money, but instead, wanted above all to share their story with the blind, with children, or with anyone who would listen. On the trip, they were visiting schools and centres for the blind in South America, doing just that: talking about a simple vision of one kilometre after another, about each having a responsibility to the other, and about moving patiently from town to town, and country to country.

'You tell these kids about Alaska, and they don't have a clue where it is,' said Tauru. 'You can show them a map and some will get it, but others don't. But almost everyone knows how to ride a bicycle – maybe not all kids with blindness, perhaps, but most people have a fundamental understanding of what it takes. Then tell them you do that all day, every day for a year-and-a-half on the very roads they travel, and they see what it means to confront your limitations and achieve something.'

As I thought about the road to La Paz they were about to face, and how difficult I had found it, without any physical limitations, I had an immediate jolt of perspective.

'The blindness is just one part of it. We've had it for long enough that you don't think, "I'm blind" – but it's just there, and you enjoy life as everyone else does,' said Christi.

As cyclists on the same route are information-hungry for sights to see, roads to avoid, *casa di ciclistas* to stay in, and other titbits of knowledge that will the journey more interesting, it wasn't surprising that we spent most of our time talking about everything north and south of Oruro. I gave them my map of Peru: the first map they had had on the trip.

'Believe me, you'll need this one! It's tough up there and not a bad idea to know how far the next hot meal is away,' I said, thinking specifically of the back roads around the Cordillera Blanca.

I thought about Tauru and Christi a lot over the following days, as the last paved surface for hundreds of miles ended, and a single-track washboard road of crumbly white gravel and sand began. How must they have fared here, I found myself wondering. This was the great expanse of nothingness expected after Challapata, the final outpost of civilisation on my map before I would reach Uyuni. Over the next 400 km, there were just two towns – perhaps not even towns, really – marked in an otherwise blank patch on my map. East and west of the line through it, there were 10, perhaps 15 inches of bare green marked, a lack of text and contour I could relate proportionally to the landscape ahead of me. An inch on paper was further than I would be able to see on a clear day over flat terrain, and so the map told me that where I was about to enter was open and empty enough to disappear within.

Southwest Bolivia is one of the most remote and inhospitable regions of South America. Suspended in time at an altitude of 3,700 metres above sea level, there is little but cool, clean air, wind-sculpted mesas and grey scrub as far as the eye can see. In between run dried-up creek beds and decades-old jeep tracks; it is a land of stillness and timelessness, where nothing seems to change but the shifting dunes. In Challapata, I bought 6 litres of water and three days' worth of food — mostly energy bars, bread, some fruit, pasta and cheese that was likely to last. I had enough stove fuel to make four breakfasts and dinners. Although I had very much enjoyed the recent opportunities for the companionship of other cyclists, it had been a while since I had been completely on my own, and so I was happy to welcome the prospect of isolation again, after months of knowing where I would sleep at night.

Silence had a sound, out there in the wild. I noticed this again after veering onto Route 30, and taking a direct path through the desert. In the mountains, the closeness of rock and summits, gorges and running rivers is familiar and friendly. So too by the woods or in a forest — there's a sense of life and biology around, even if people are distant. But in the open wilderness, in a vast space, with only short scrub and sandy plains, where you are the only human presence moving for miles and miles around, the silence brings a sense of vulnerability and a self-consciousness which the other types of environment don't. In this desert, I could hear my mind outside of my head, my thoughts somehow externalised — an improbable percussion of hyper-awareness and the pure-cut breeze.

As I moved further into the desert, the colour of the road and its surroundings became less distinct from each other. Near the end of the first day, I came to a break in the track and was unable to tell which path was the natural extension of the road I had just been on. One path ran in a giant arc, going first to the west before curving back upon itself perhaps four kilometres ahead and eventually wilting out of view. The other snaked erratically east and then turned south, before hopping over the lip of a faraway ridgeline.

I examined the road for fresh tracks, hoping to find deeper ruts that would indicate the main highway (in itself, a generous appellation of the track on which I'd been travelling). The edge of the first path looked more cleanly hewn, as if there had been a deliberate attempt to delineate the road and its banks. There were a few screws scattered along it too, so I took this as a meagre sign it was more frequently used.

An hour later – almost an eternity riding if you think you've gone the wrong way – I spotted a cloud of dust in the distance, and then the soundless approach of a pick-up. The driver barely stopped to crawl for me to ask him if this was the way to Uyuni. He gave me a curt nod of the head in confirmation and took off again at speed, churning up pebbles and sand which blasted my bicycle as I stood there.

I had covered 89 km when the timer on my bike signalled 10 hours of riding, and so I resolved to find a campsite. I didn't have to look far, as the entirety of the wilderness was mine – riverbeds, sandy hovels, lifeless shrub and all. This was the best part, bedding down for the night in a spot unseen from the road, but in earshot of passing vehicles. It had been severely cold since I had met the Altiplano in Peru, and temperatures were hitting – 5 °C by 11 p.m., so I knew I needed to have the tent set up, the sleeping mat and sleeping bag rolled out, and my dinner boiling in the pot by 6.30 p.m. at the very latest, just before the moon appeared in the clouds and its background turned from navy to depthless black.

Diary: 30 July 2012, 10 km north of Río Mulatos, Bolivia

It was all about the washboard today! How it has never stopped since I entered the sand past Huari. The road had split there, the other branch going to Quillacas and entering the Salar from the north. It's a disheartening road if you like moving unrestricted, but I got used to the slow movement early and am anticipating two more days to Uyuni. As I write, the wind is lapping over the tent sheet, but I'm camped behind a strangely-shaped mass of rock and in an alcove. I feel good and enjoy this empty space and nights to read myself to sleep before the cold snap arrives, although my fingers are numbing a bit now.

The next day was more of the same, mind- and bike-shuddering washboard surface that constantly dislodged the spare tyre and water bottles strapped to my panniers. The breeze was biting until mid-afternoon, and a dehydrating sun and rough, ochre surface made for tiresome companions, to the point where I napped on the verge, half in the prickly sand and half on the road. Not a soul had passed all morning, so I wasn't surprised to find ten toes and two feet still intact when I woke up at 2 p.m., fresh from an hour's uninterrupted dozing and dreaming.

That night, I slept in an unfinished, roofless redbrick town house in the minute settlement of Chita, and boiled noodles on my sputtering stove as inquisitive llamas poked their furry heads over the wall to see what was on the menu. Chita was as much of a living ghost town as I had seen, just about holding on to its last reams of life. Long wooden poles, steel cord, and sheet metal held most of the main street's ramshackle buildings together, and under one of them, two men, both with sooty faces and an unfortunate lack of teeth, fixed motorcycles and acknowledged my presence with lengthy, dim stares, before going back to cleaning carburettors and realigning wheels. I felt quite out of time and place. I wanted to ask them about Chita and what people survived on here, but the standoffishness in their gazes discouraged me from pursuing my quest for information any further. Living, let alone prospering here, was a mystery as far as I could see, and I couldn't fathom how its economy could possibly work. There were few people around, and those that were seemed to be wandering the streets in a directionless and forlorn manner, as if going nowhere in particular. I surmised that Chita must have been an old mining town, since I had come across a railway track nearby, and I remembered Bolivia's long history of tin extraction in the south. The hills did have a colour of mineral wealth, after all.

I escaped Chita at sunrise — without being subsumed into the semi-hypnotic state of its few residents — and rode frustratingly slowly towards the Salar de Uyuni, the world's largest salt flat. At about 9.15 a.m., I crunched my way over the gritty shingle to the brow of a hill and before me, in the far right-hand corner of my field of vision lay South America's great white desert, with the blue sky shimmering in a thin line above the land.

At almost 11,000 km^2, the Salar de Uyuni is a staggeringly enormous salt flat. The area was originally part of the giant, prehistoric Lake Minchin, which dominated the southern Altiplano almost 40,000 years ago. However, when it dried up thousands of years later it left behind two lakes and two salt deserts, of which the Salar de Uyuni is one. In the rainy season, between January and April, the flat is covered in a layer of water and is the world's biggest mirror, reflecting the sky and clouds overhead. In the dry season, when I visited, it produces a master show in albedo, returning sunlight so intensely it can be seen from space. Visual displays notwithstanding, the area is also an important mining ground, as the brine-infused subsurface holds over half of the world's lithium reserves.

When I reached Colchani, a frightfully dead village right on the very edge of the Salar, I enquired what the best way onto the flat would be.

'That way, over there,' an elderly woman said, pointing directly into the whiteness.

I planned on cycling onto the Salar and playing about for a while, before coming back and making the popular tourist town of Uyuni by nightfall. Some cyclists navigate their way to Incahuasi Island in the middle and set up camp for night, revelling in the novelty of sleeping on salt and under the stars. However, I felt that a much more unusual pursuit was in order – a naked cycle across the salt. Inspired by a picture of Fearghal O'Nuaillain and Simon Evans, two Irish long-distance tourers who circumnavigated the world years before and had indulged in a similar activity here, I felt it apt to exercise my nudist calling, in the one place I was guaranteed the grace of privacy. Far in the distance, there were some tour jeeps careening across the salt with backpackers, but I made sure to cycle to my own secluded corner of the expanse. I then removed shoes, socks, cycling shorts, T-shirt and helmet, leaving only sunglasses on my face and a cold beer bought from Colchani in my hand. I cycled way out into the white until Colchani disappeared from sight, sipping my beer and taking in the untenanted flatness all around me. The salt was cracked in polygonal shapes, the product of water evaporating through clefts in the surface. To the north, Volcán Tunupa was in view, dormant in the wavy ether rising from the desert. I stopped for my first and only high-altitude nude photo-shoot, and then recorded a short video diary (clothed), extolling the virtues of disrobed cycling at 3,700 metres. At this point, both the thin air and beer may had gone to my head; I began taking photographs in which, by positioning my bicycle in the foreground and walking 20 metres or so into the distance behind it, I would look as if I was standing on the saddle, or holding the bike in my hand. By messing in this way with the perspective the vast salt plain provided, I had an afternoon of fun shrinking myself to the size of a beer can, and creating a number of other strange visual effects.

At this juncture, I had already decided to skip the famed Ruta des Lagunas, a track made up primarily of sand and dirt, which runs through the copper-coloured lakes and pink flamingo breeding grounds of south-west Bolivia. My decision was based largely on an assessment of the difficulty I knew this route would involve – I just didn't feel like five days pushing my bicycle out of deep sand catches and wrestling with the ever-unpredictable wind in the region. The route would also have taken me into north-eastern Chile at San Pedro de Atacama, which I wasn't interested in, since my intended path was to go through Argentina as far as Mendoza, before crossing the border into Chile, the final country of the trip.

Uyuni is small but a good base from which to explore the Salar; it also has a certain wild appeal. The town could very well have succumbed to the same fate as decrepit Chita, but for the steady influx of tourists seeking to hire four-wheel drives and guides for an exploration of the salt flats. As it's so far from anywhere else – La Paz being a two-day drive and Salta, Argentina three days away – it has evolved a sustainable pub and party scene of its own, propped up by a year-long cavalcade of transitory backpackers. I didn't stay long myself – just enough time to enjoy the leathery Bolivian version of 'authentic Italian pizza' – before I departed again in a cloud of dust, rattling over washboard at 7 km/h.

Diary: 5 August 2012, Atocha, Bolivia

Didn't I just find a pumping little town in the middle of nowhere? I'm sitting in The Alamo restaurant in Atocha, eating a lomo salteado (stir-fried beef), with a huge egg on top. Outside, music is blaring and the square is packed, occupying a notch under a barren mountain. I covered 101 km on a poor road that dropped and rose through these artistic rock formations, clearly sculpted by the wind over millennia. I'm pretty sure I saw the exact point where the Altiplano ended today – it was like approaching the drop off a cliff. I could sense coming to an edge of land and then, before me, there was a graded drop into a huge brown valley that dropped again in the distance, until I could see no further.

It was in this brown-, soon to turn red-rock landscape, that two of America's most notorious icons of the Wild West have been immortalised. At some time just after sunset on 6 November 1908, two bank robbers named Butch Cassidy and 'the Sundance Kid' rode into San Vicente, a little pueblo just outside of Tupiza, Bolivia, looking for shelter after hitting the Aramayo Mining Company. Locals, aware of the thieves' identity, alerted the authorities, and the ensuing gunfight ended the lives of both Cassidy and his sidekick. Of course, some researchers say that Cassidy actually died years later, after a stabbing in Paris and that the Sundance Kid was killed numerous times between 1920 and 1940 in Argentina, Chile, and Venezuela. What *is* true is that, in 1901, both men fled the United States to evade the Pinkerton Detective Agency, later to become the FBI, following a spate of bank robberies on the Union Pacific railroad. They made their way to Patagonia, as detailed excellently in Bruce Chatwin's book, *In Patagonia*, and worked as cattle ranchers before riding to Bolivia in search of one last job, before retiring to an Amazonian retreat to live out their days. The other certainty is that in San Vicente, close to where I was now heading, a humble grave marks Butch Cassidy's supposed final resting place – whether it actually is or not just serves to intensify the mystery that surrounds him.

It was easy to see similarities between this pocket of Bolivia and the American West. The rock was clay-red, the kind that glows deep in a burning sunset, and plant life was restricted to stubby and bristly grey-green bushes, which seemed to me to peak nosily from the rocky cracks in which they were embedded. Since I had dropped down from the Altiplano, it had become noticeably drier and warmer, which seemed to explain the hardiness of the vegetation and the people I encountered, who wore their personal histories in the creases of their faces.

I arrived in Tupiza on 6 August, Bolivia's National Day. That evening, I followed the crowds of people to a triangular plaza, where a stage had been erected; musicians were nervously pacing up and down in front of it. To begin, a group of five young girls, perhaps aged between 14 and

18, played three songs of mixed European and indigenous origins. They sang, drummed, strummed guitars and played some wind instruments I didn't recognise, with an innocence and earnestness the crowd at once warmed to. It was as if they were everyone's daughters, dressed neatly and appropriately for this important day, and now presenting their musical skills to an adoring community audience. In the crowd, elderly men and women held grandchildren's hands, friends giggled in groups, and families shared sweet-smelling street food with other. It was the first community get-together I had been to in quite some time, and it made me feel entirely at home whilst occupying a space amongst a town of strangers.

The festivities of the previous night bred a positivity which I carried with me the next day, as I left Tupiza for La Quiaca, Argentina, on a beautiful August morning. Of course, it was always exciting crossing the border into a new country. I knew to expect a continuing descent through the red canyon walls before a customary climb to a lower-level area of flatland, which would extend all the way to Salta. Within four hours, and with the help of a fully charged iPod, I had climbed an 800-metre hill, pausing only to catch my breath, drink some water, and snap some final shots looking back at Bolivia. The wind wisped dust devils across the road as I cycled 40 km to La Villazon, the Bolivian border town. I spent my last *bolivianos* on three colourful packets of biscuits and 2 litres of water, which I emptied into the plastic bottles in the bike holders that had now accrued sentimental value.

The buzz, life and noise of La Villazon dissipated into orderliness and cleanliness as I was stamped out of Bolivia and was then welcomed into La Quiaca and Argentina by an official with an immaculately trimmed moustache. Everything felt more modern – the streets had signposts, the roads were marked, cars were shiny and the green spaces were tended. I felt that I had crossed from one world to another. Once I received my passport and a thumbs-up from the officer, I placed everything neatly in my handlebar bag and set off to find a place for the night. On my way out, just as I left the row of immigration and customs buildings, I spotted a big green rectangular sign, which bore the words: 'Ushuaia – 5121 km'. Not long now, I thought, and rode into the newness of Argentina.

12

Crossing the Spine

La Quiaca, Argentina to Puerto Montt, Chile – 1,970 km

PASSING THE SIGNPOST FOR USHUAIA brought home just how close to finishing I was. Although 5,000 km is no small distance, it felt insignificant compared to the 22,000 km I had already travelled. My bicycle bore the scars of over one year of continuous travel: the frame was sand-stained and a mix of gravel and mud collected in Peru was still under the seat post and on the spokes; the stickers which adorned any spare space on the frame – from Deadhorse, Banff National Park in Canada, the Redwood forests in California, the Panama Canal and Cartagena, Colombia – had been discoloured by the sun, creased by the rain and were generally as weathered as the bike itself. Physically, I too wore the hallmarks of a life on the road, and my face sported a three-month old beard – slightly tangled, distinctly uncivilized, and definitely in need of a trim. It was strange to think that in just two months, as I calculated it, all I had would be tidily packed in one cardboard box and two suitcases, ready for a flight home.

I pressed out of La Quiaca on a sumptuous road, one so slick I didn't feel a semblance of drag from the surface. I found it calming every so often to remind myself how much freedom daily life on the bicycle afforded me. Everything I needed was right here within arm's reach, inside four pannier bags and a large dry holdall strapped to the rear rack. Stove fuel, water, food and basic bike repair equipment were the only essentials I needed from my immediate environment from time to time; any other engagement with the outside world, such as using the Internet or staying in a hotel, was made by choice rather than necessity. It was exhilarating to know I could take this road or that, and head east, west, north or south at any given moment, and, although I rarely strayed far from a southern course, it was nice knowing that I *could*. Riding 30 km uphill to the top of a mountain pass was a struggle, but it was a liberating one because of the knowledge that you had done it under your own steam. And, as every bicycle tourer will agree, enjoying the rewards of a spectacular view over the Andes or eating lunch by a glacial blue river is made far more special because of the very effort that goes into getting there.

It was easy to muse like this on roads as open as those in north-west Argentina. They were exquisitely paved, and, although such a description might seem misplaced, after my experiences in Peru and Bolivia, this was a cyclist's heaven. The roads here had clear markings, shoulders, and cat's eyes – three elements of highway design I had seen together only intermittently since the United States. The best thing, however, was that nobody else was on them. It seemed that people didn't travel big distances here unless they had to, and in this part of South America, it could take several hours to drive between the biggest towns and cities. For instance, from La Quiaca to San Salvador de Jujuy – a city of 230,000 – it was 320 km, with just a few mid-size settlements between.

I stopped for the night in Tres Cruces, a tiny village with just three dusty streets, a bus station, and a church. In the square, I asked a man if there was a guesthouse and he told me the closest was 60 km away, in Humahuaca. As the sun was setting, he grudgingly offered the spare room he kept for his son, who only returned from Buenos Aires when, 'it was absolutely necessary, or someone passed away'. He then led me to a house on the other side of the square, opened a side gate and made disgruntled motions towards a door at the end of the building. I couldn't figure out whether he was generally put out by my presence or angry at the thought of his son – on the brisk walk to the house, he seemed to be cursing him, from what I could tell.

He informed me I could keep my bicycle inside the room and if I wanted to use the toilet, I'd be welcome to the outhouse around the corner. 'There's no electricity,' he said, wagging his finger at the only socket in the room. 'I hope you don't mind the dark.' As he brushed ancient cobwebs from the windows and beat thick dust from the mattress standing in the corner, he continued to mumble irritably to himself, and I heard his son's name being muttered more than once. From the swirling dust and sense of annoyance which pervaded the room, I surmised that there hadn't been a death to force the son home in quite some time.

In the far northwest of Argentina, and especially in Jujuy Province, which I was now riding through, two very distinct ecosystems and landscapes overlap. In the very north, the temperate Altiplano at 3,500 metres slowly gives way to a semi-arid region, fed by a few lazy rivers which flow on a seasonal basis only. One of these rivers, the Río Grande, flows through the Quebrada de Humahuaca, a 155 km-long ravine vividly coloured by otherworldly red rock formations on its sides. The valley here is the most important link between the Altiplano and the temperate plains of South America, and has been used for centuries as a major trade route. It has such historical and present-day significance that it has been listed as a UNESCO World Heritage Site, and is therefore the main tourist draw to this otherwise unvisited part of Argentina. Fortunately, I had the pleasure of coasting along the valley's ever-so-gentle incline, past the town of Humahuaca and onto Tilcara, a place famous for its pre-Inca fortifications and archaeological remains, which date back over 10,000 years.

As I descended the rugged Quebrada de Humahuaca, I was on a high, as Ireland's Katie Taylor had won an Olympic gold medal in a boxing event that day. I had become more than a little emotional, watching the match in Humahuaca. The speedy downhill into Tilcara had sustained these feelings of exhilaration – as all downhills tend to do – and by late afternoon, I crossed the Tropic of Capricorn, the last major latitudinal landmark until Patagonia began near Puerto Montt, Chile.

As I then descended from 2,300 metres to 1,200 metres between Tilcara and San Salvador de Jujuy, my surroundings changed theatrically once more. Within half an hour, at a point where the highway drops suddenly before San Salvador, the red rock disappeared and the return of fertile soil was evident in the tall trees and leafy shrubs which began to populate my fleeting glimpses of the landscape as I sped by. The temperature had risen into the high teens, and even the noise of birdsong returned, something which had been notably absent during my high-altitude cycling. The Río Grande, now free of the valley, shifted east, away from its regular north to south bearing and entered the city, which I intended to avoid by using the bypass.

By noon, I had covered a pleasing 89 km and stopped at a gleaming service station for a BLT sandwich and chips: the kind of Western meal you will only find in a more developed country's gas stations. While chatting with two truck drivers and some petrol attendants outside, I observed that the Argentines seemed to be more confident in conversation than their northern neighbours. Whereas in Peru and Bolivia, the response to an inquiry about the distance to the next town or the location of the nearest place to camp, would on many occasions have been a blank stare, or a simple 'I don't know', here in Argentina they were more informed, and aware of what I was asking from a traveller's point of view. One of the drivers even went as far as to provide some insider advice on the weather and the roads through southern Chile, which I was very grateful for, conscious that many routes would be obstructed by fjords and seasonally swollen rivers at this time of the year. In short, the exchanges I had had since crossing to La Quiaca went beyond the basic 'I need' and 'You have' formula, which I had come to expect in interactions over the past few months.

Not content with such good progress in terms of distance travelled, I decided to ride the remaining 100 km to Salta that day. This decision, to push further rather than play it safe, was thoroughly vindicated by a completely unexpected section of rare beauty, which I encountered along Route 9. Cutting into the rural sun-dappled countryside away from San Salvador, this road narrowed into a single lane; as I skirted the Las Maderas reservoir, it then tapered into a path no more than three metres wide – just big enough to allow a car pass a cyclist. This was still the main highway, but astonishingly free of traffic.

In the village of El Carmen, I stopped and bought a huge bag of penny sweets, which drove my sugar and excitement levels through the roof. I took off like a giddy child around the southern edge of the reservoir, picking wine gums, cola bottles and sugary jellies from the bag I had tied to the handlebars. In fields along the road, apple and lemon trees were basking in a golden evening sun, and joggers were running the bike path on the lakeshore. Chocolate-box houses, painted in pastel colours, and with pink-and-yellow window boxes faced onto the road. Everything around me was alive and active, and it was hard to believe that I had just left the arid confines of the Quebrada de Humahuaca earlier that day.

I was pumping energy as I settled into a 600-metre climb before Salta, which wound its way into perfectly cambered and forested hills. At the top, the road levelled out for 3 km and I passed a lake and noticed that its waters were beginning to churn up in advance of an approaching storm. As the odometer clocked 170 km and I entered my ninth hour in the saddle, a few men mooring their sailboats on the lake shouted over at me, pointing at the blackening and thunderous sky. After such a long day, the last thing I wanted to face was the wind and rain, but by the time I reached the city limits of Salta, the storm had drifted eastwards and threatened little more than a light drizzle. With 186 km of riding behind me, this was the longest day of the trip so far.

While I imagine most visitors to Salta might regale the listener with descriptions of its grand and unspoiled colonial architecture, I found out almost immediately that another feature of aesthetic appeal, not often found in such high concentrations, was very much in evidence in the city. From the moment I arrived, as I pushed my bicycle down the pedestrianised Peatonal Florida Street, I was actually startled by the sheer number of beautiful women I saw walking around. I was used to men arguing vociferously in favour of the women of their city or province, often at the same time disparaging those from the other end of the country, or the next town over. From a national perspective too, I'd seen how patriotically-minded people in South American countries were always ready to argue that Nicaraguans were better-looking than Costa Ricans, or that Colombians were more attractive than Ecuadorians, and so on. Yet, I have never felt like such a blatant voyeur as when I wheeled my bicycle and few possessions down that crowded walkway in central Salta, unabashedly gawking at the youthful, golden skin and remarkably shapely figures of the *Salteño* women. Later that night, as I wrote a diary entry in a bar facing onto Plaza 9 Julio, I was regularly distracted by the striking women ambling by, and eventually had to abandon my writing in favour of street side admiration.

I rose at dawn the next day to walk the well-preserved heart of Salta which I had heard so much about. The best aspect to this time of the day was that it was before people left their homes on their commute to work and before the streets became awash with vendors and hawkers. Sunrise was at 7.30 a.m. each morning, and when on the road, I had conditioned myself to leave close to that time, which meant that on my days off too, I was generally wide-awake before the first light streamed through the window or tent. There was a certain peace and quiet that I found only existed in the very early morning – a calm made more gratifying by the fact my mind wasn't yet filled with the clutter of a day's thinking and planning.

I returned to Plaza 9 Julio and bought a coffee there to take away. The plaza had been stirred by the commotion of music, families, and groups of teenagers the previous night, but had now a much more tranquil air, and was pretty to look at. The majority of buildings flanking the square, including the brilliant white two-storey porticos, date from the 1800s and have seen the dedicated care of city authorities, such is their excellent state of repair. Salta retains an ambience of colonial timelessness which is often missing in other similarly founded cities. In San Cristobal de Las Casas in Mexico, or Antigua, Guatemala, for example, indigenous influence has permeated the cityscape much more, to the extent that Spanish-style architecture lives on only in patchwork. Salta, on the other hand, is like an open-air gallery, whose classic European design and structure hasn't changed very much at all over the centuries.

Diary: 11 August 2012, Salta, Argentina

I've rested quite a lot in Salta, and taken just a day to see the city. I've been catching up on calls to home and writing, more than anything else. Áine is leaving Tajikistan in two days and will be home in Ireland by the time I cycle from here. I've spoke to her and she's over the moon – but I'm a little down or, I don't know . . . just wishing I could be there when she got back. I'm also about to enter a very isolated and barren stretch of Argentina, with at least nine days on the road until San Juan and a few more to Mendoza, before crossing to Chile. Tourer blogs have said this stretch is demotivating for the wind and bleakness of the landscape after Cafayate, but I'm keeping my fingers crossed, hoping this has been exaggerated!

It would have been easy to spend a week in Salta, but with Áine leaving for Ireland, I was acutely aware of my mid-way position in South America and my desire not to ride into November, which would extend our time apart more than I wanted. We had been making tentative plans about where to move next, and she had already applied for a United Nations job in Laos, where I would be happy to follow her considering 13 months of absence. Conversely, it also made sense not to rush my arrival to Tierra del Fuego, or even northern Patagonia for that matter, as winter was still blowing across the tip of the continent. It was snowing heavily in the south, so I would probably ride into freezing temperatures and blizzards on the gravel roads of Chile's Carretera Austral and the famed Ruta 40 in Argentina. This would be inevitable, should I arrive in Ushuaia in October as planned, but something I had decided to regard as intrepid and resilient, rather than worrying and foolish. I liked colder climates and the snap of frosted mornings, as they always gave me the motivation to move and keep warm, with my survival instincts at the fore at the start of a day's travelling. Other cyclists had remarked that it would be crazy to push for October, when I could instead be guaranteed sunshine and warmth in December – the month most of those who set out from Alaska would generally plan to arrive in Ushuaia.

As I made my way from Salta, hawks circled stony hillsides and mud-green rivers until I found the red, wind-hewn gorge of Quebrada de las Conchas. Along the way, I crossed paths with several families who gave me water, biscuits, glazed croissants and offered well wishes for my journey. At a lay-by at Tres Cruces, one couple insisted that I take a detour to San Miguel de Tucumán, where they would offer me a true Argentine welcome and homestay. The principle seemed to be, the further I was from settlements, the kinder the reception I was given by passers-by. Some just said they had respect for the length of time I had spent on the road, my practice of wild camping, and the fact I would end my journey in Argentina: if then they could help a little, they would.

I rode towards Cafayate, the wine capital of northern Argentina. I didn't intend on a day off, but the owner of my hotel insisted it would ill-mannered of me to leave without taking a tour of a Torrontés vineyard.

'In the future, someone will tell you this is the world's best wine – and you'll be sorry you didn't try it in its home,' she scolded me, as I attempted to pay for one night instead of two.

The speciality Torrontés grape, as I discovered on a tour of Bodega Nanni vineyard, grows particularly well in Cafayate because of the area's low rainfall, lack of humidity and the productive soils of the Calchaquíes Valley. As you approach the town, instead of signposts to the places after Cafayate, you will find that the road is marked in terms of kilometres' distance to local wineries; these churn out, in a rather improbable-looking landscape, some of Argentina's most prized wine. I listened intently to the science and technique, but I had not advanced my Spanish much in recent months, so the more intricate details of the production processes eluded me. I was also a little conscious of my oil-stained pants, generally weatherworn clothes and haggard appearance in an atmosphere that I presumed required refinement and class, so I opted out of the question-and-answer session at the end, heading expediently towards the antiquated cask room and wine-tasting – the real objective of the afternoon, as far as I was concerned.

With enough wine consumed to make the ride back into town a wobbly one, I found a café on the main square where I could get on Skype. I knew Áine had arrived home from Tajikistan that day, and I was delighted to see the little green bubble on-screen, showing she was online. During the call, I could hear her sister making tea in the background, her nephews running around the kitchen, opening unusual Tajik presents, and a joy in Áine's voice that had been missing in previous months. Suddenly, I was missing home to an extent I hadn't before; my motivation to press on to the end of the road was stronger than ever.

I left Cafayate and my next target was Santa María, 95 km away, the only dot in this immediate area on my otherwise bare map. Throughout the day, I felt progressively wearier; my average speed reflected my lacklustre effort and irregular pedalling pattern.

> *Diary: 16 August 2012, Santa María, Argentina*
>
> *Very, very tired this evening and, well . . . lonely. Not in the sense where I need companionship, although that would be welcomed, but more because I've been missing home since yesterday afternoon. Coupled to this is the lack of 'food for thought' on the bike. Sometimes I drift into these stretches where I can't remember what passed in the previous five or 10 km. I left*

HALF THE WORLD AWAY

Lee almost 10 months ago, and from then, have travelled perhaps just two full weeks with others, such has been the scarcity of cyclists. Keeping the mind stimulated is often a tough job.

Ruta 40 (Ruta Cuarenta) extends from La Quiaca in northern Argentina to Río Gallegos in the very south of Patagonia, and it is one of the world's longest and most legendary roads. At over 5,000 km in length, it runs through a preposterously diverse range of ecosystems bordering the eastern Andes; it is known for its inimitable wildness and the untrammelled nature of the land it crosses, particularly in the provinces of Neuquén, Río Negro, Chubut and Santa Cruz. In these areas, which comprise the majority of Argentine Patagonia, Ruta 40 is unpaved, but other sections, such as that running out of Santa María, are yet to be sealed and as such highlight the faraway nature of the country's northwest. I eventually encountered this famous road in Cafayate where it intersects with Ruta 9 and which I had been following since the border. I now intended to ride Ruta 40 all the way to Río Gallegos, except for a detour into Chile to meet the Carretera Austral.

The wind, which is notoriously vicious in the far south of Argentina, isn't as powerful or soul-destroying in the north of the country, but it still defies one's expectations. Ten kilometres beyond Santa María, I noticed the sand begin to stream lightly over the road beneath me, as if I was watching a desert storm in miniature from above. Soon thereafter, I saw that the few hardy trees in the valley had taken on a distinctive lean. However, it was after I passed Pie de Medano, a freestanding hill that required an hour's climbing, that the wind liberated its full force. Now that the protection of Calchaquíes Valley was gone, I found myself being pushed from side to side and bullied into adopting my own lean into the gale, just to be able to remain upright. I pedalled at 6 km/h, a pace that felt like I was riding thorough a layer of thick mud. As I rankled in the moment, managing only slow-motion revolutions of the pedals, the wind roared mercilessly across the plain. I bent my neck down, head facing directly over the handlebars. I could hardly maintain my balance on the bicycle each time I glanced backwards, expecting to see a hurtling truck just seconds from me. All the while, stretching out in front of me, was a space so wide and grey that the distant hills seemed to blend indiscernibly into the atmosphere around them, with the highway continuing so straight ahead that it disappeared into a bleak distance-less dot.

I stopped to rest and sat on a bed of rocks that made up the buffer between the road and scrub. As the wind screamed past my ears and toyed with my hair, I looked towards a bulbous, flat-topped mountain far off to the west. I felt alone; I was physically exhausted, and I just wanted out of the wind. It was no fun, and I knew it wouldn't stop for days. Perhaps if I hadn't had the extra mental angst from Cafayate still hanging over me, I wouldn't have put my hand out for a passing car, having seen its two beams of white light approaching patiently from 2 km away. Eventually the vehicle – a pick-up as it turned out – stopped in front of me, and the driver rolled down his window.

'Can you take me to the next town?' I asked him.

Kindly, he agreed, and I squeezed into the back with his two young children. He said he would drive me 25 km to his hometown, a village that wasn't marked on the map. I wanted a respite and thought if I could remove myself from the wind and featureless terrain for even a short time, I'd find some drive to get back on the bicycle. This time, unlike Panama when I missed a day's cycling or Peru where I hailed down a passing taxi, I didn't feel guilty at taking what I had been telling myself was an easy way out. A part of me did feel like I was cheating again, robbing myself of a memory I could look back on as a testing time – one I could say I had got through because of endurance, fight, stubbornness and ambition. The hard days are the ones I look on now with more fondness than most of the others – but of course I didn't truly realise this at the time.

Thirty minutes later, I was repacking my bicycle on a dirt section of Ruta 40. It turned out that half an hour wasn't long enough for me to forget the wind or my dejection, so I admitted to myself that there was no point cycling this region of Argentina if I couldn't enjoy getting on the saddle each morning. Although I had suffered slumps in energy and had gone through periods of feeling low since Alaska, I knew that this was the worst I had felt in a long time. Even though I had ridden for 13 months and had just two more left, I needed to do something to alter my immediate mood into one more conducive to achieving productive days. I was tired of worrying about getting home on a schedule, and feeling anxious about my relationship. I was tired of being tired and complaining about it.

With this in mind, I cycled 12 km to the small town of Hualfín and enquired if there was a bus to Mendoza, 750 km away. If I was going to get space to think, it would be easier to do without having to cycle eight hours and 100-plus kilometres every day. A local shop owner said that if I removed the 80 empty gas canisters sitting in his truck and replaced them with full ones, he would, in return, give me a lift to Belén, 45 minutes away. In Belén, he told me, an overnight bus left nightly for Mendoza via Catamarca, and I'd be there by dawn.

> ***Diary: 20 August 2012, Mendoza, Argentina***
>
> *Arrived at 8 a.m. yesterday in Mendoza and it was still dark as I navigated the city. I'm glad I took a bus, despite missing one week of riding, as my head feels clearer and I've made some decisions. First of all, I'm booking my flights home from Ushuaia. That way, I have a set date for return and can stop agonising over the 'when'. I've spoken to Áine about all this too, which I hadn't before, and she has been amazing, putting my mind at ease and telling me to stop worrying, as it's a family trait! She says she can't wait to see me, but I am to enjoy the last few months. I also realise that, as much as I've felt down many times, I haven't spoiled the journey with the negative moments – I've just had to surmount them. Things, I definitely feel, are looking up.*

I took two days' rest in Mendoza, just long enough to reassess my priorities for the remainder of the trip. I set my return date home as 16 October, just under two months away. With 4,000 km left to go, completion was achievable within this timeframe and I would also have the room to take additional days off or explore any of the myriad routes into southern Chile and Argentina. Just knowing when I would be going home set my mind at ease, and also gave Áine an answer to a question she had been asking me sporadically since Mexico. My thought processes over the previous months had not, I realised, always been conducive to fully appreciating every step of the journey. But I also realised that a trip like this is in many ways, as much a mental as a physical challenge and that, just as I could not expect myself to be physically at my peak 100 per cent of the time, it was equally unrealistic – and unfair on myself – to assume that I would be positive and upbeat at all times for the entire duration of the trip.

Talk of Mendoza, and you talk of wine. As Argentina's wine-producing capital, the city's reputation precedes it, and that is perhaps why I was quite astounded at just how small the place actually is. The downtown area feels like little more than a large town, with quiet and spacious boulevards and tree-lined squares, and is one of the country's greenest urban centres. It is western Argentina's most celebrated city and now also the continent's principal centre of enotourism – a growing travel trend concerned with the tasting and purchasing of wine.

At altitudes of between 700 and 1,200 metres, Mendoza Province's vineyards are amongst the highest in the world. They may also be amongst the prettiest, framed against a backdrop of the Andes' white and jagged mountain pinnacles, their summits the dividing line between Argentina and Chile. With year-round stable temperatures, rich alluvial soils and enough rainfall to complement a maze of irrigation channels, the region maintains just the right equilibrium of conditions to produce its famous Malbec and Chardonnay varieties. As two-thirds of the country's wine is produced here, it's a major tourism hub. Taking advantage of this are the city's upscale restaurants and gastro-pubs, whose table staff will happily relate intricate histories of the grape, vineyard and region as they pour another glass of *Mendel Unus* or *Andeluna 1300* into your bell-bottomed glass. Of course, on a cyclist's budget, I had to forego a tour of the vineyards, opting instead for a more unassuming glass of a local vintage in a stylish bar overlooking General San Martín Park, which was pulsing with the noise of families out for picnics and children splashing in the central fountain.

The city, I came to realise quickly, was easy-going, airy, and architecturally dissimilar to any other of its size in Argentina. This latter feature is the result of an immense rebuilding scheme that took place after the 1861 earthquake, which killed 5,000 people and destroyed much of the city. From this scheme came the avenues and a plethora of quaint squares that give the city the gracious and modestly opulent appeal it has today.

Eager now to get back on the bicycle, I rode out of Mendoza in high spirits. The Andes were a soul-stirring sight to the west, emerging barefaced and grey from the earth to culminate in their tops of ice below a cloudless blue sky. In front of them were vineyards and fields left fallow for a season. I was on a path for Chile, but first would need to cross the Andes over the Cristo Redentor Pass, which separates the two countries. Other than perhaps a ride over the Karakoram or Himalayas, I can't imagine a border crossing as spectacular as this one, with the Pass at the top of a twisting, snow-lined road under the shadow of Mt Aconcagua – South America's highest peak, at 6,960 metres. It is no easy feat to trundle slowly along the side of an everlasting mountain, gaining a pittance in altitude as you go, and bearing the burn of the climb in your muscles, but it is a gratifying adventure the same. On the Chilean side, I found a series of dizzying switchbacks plummeting downhill amidst a monochrome blur of the white of the snow and the grey of the road and the black of the smoke being churned out by old, shabby trucks descending at a crawl.

It took only a short time to leave bitter mountain temperatures behind and return to a temperate climate once more. Thermals could come off, extra layers were stuffed into the panniers and it was warm enough to pedal in sandals again. Santiago would be an opportunity for me to rethink my clothing arrangements, as for the first time since Canada, I would be entering a wet and cold oceanic climate where sunshine, rain and snow were all possible in a single day. I'd need long-sleeved wool layers to insulate against the cold, waterproof socks to fend off the rain when I rode in sandals, and waterproof pants to keep my trousers from soaking up drizzle or heavy showers. For now, though, it was my last chance to savour temperatures in the mid-teens and the final big city of the trip. After that, it would be just 1,000 km to Patagonia.

Santiago is Chile's capital and its largest city. It's a youthful metropolis sprawling out into a circular basin and along a slender valley that runs south for 30 km. Its geography looks like a corrie (a deep hollow cut out of a hillside) at a glacier's head: the main city occupies the deep bowl-shaped area and suburban neighbourhoods spring up in any available space beyond it. To the east, the 6,000-metre peaks of the southern Andes vie for attention, while to the west, the crests of the gentler Chilean Coastal Range are hardly noticeable behind the city's downtown skyscrapers and tall office buildings – aspects of the city which represent the progressive nature of Chile's economy. Global financial corporations with regional interests and upscale retail brands with an eye on a proliferating consumer affluence jostle for space in the shadows of Mt Aconcagua, striking an odd harmony between the futuristic landscape of the city and the backdrop of its outlying natural topography.

Chile is ranked as a 'developed country' by the World Bank, and hence is a so-called 'high-income economy'. As I walked the streets of Santiago, the reality of this was evidenced in the 'Pay by MasterCard' stickers in most shop windows, the proliferation of chic restaurants in all quarters of the city, and the efficiency and excellent state of repair of the different public transport options on offer. The city was clean and orderly, safe and pleasant. It didn't have any particularly exemplary characteristics, but it wasn't uninteresting to visit either.

I had organised to meet my old college friend, Kieran Hennigan, who was living in the capital at the time. Kieran and I shared an apartment together along with two other friends during our studies in Dublin, and since then, he had lived in London and Tanzania, and was now teaching English and Philosophy to university students in Santiago. We shared a night out and I met some of Santiago's expatriate Irish community in an Irish bar, a few miles out of the city centre. It was a novelty to see a familiar face after a few years apart, and, after months of sputtering out broken Spanish in a pedestrian manner, I welcomed the return to the furious pace of conversation only Irish people can engage in.

Poring over maps, I was able to calculate that there was exactly 1016 km between Santiago and Puerto Montt, where Patagonia begins as it means to go on, with roads interrupted by fjords and protected areas. The busy and unflinchingly straight Highway 5 connects both cities, maintaining a course for its entire length within Chile's flat Central Valley, home to some of the world's most renowned vineyards. On such a road, one is tempted to test the limits of speed and planning, so I gave in to this urge, and set out to ride it in eight days, looking to complete an average of 125 km per day. I reckoned that my newfound motivation since Mendoza would act as a mental tailwind and a huge boost to getting there on schedule. The reason, of course, for creating such a timeline at all was that I knew there was little to see on this route, except for a noisy four-lane highway, some reputedly unimpressive large towns, and a very slowly changing and somewhat unexceptional landscape. Travelling at 15 km/h, I knew wouldn't miss much of it in any case.

I reached Rancagua on the first day, a mere 86 km from Santiago. The next morning, I rose early and found my way back onto the highway. By 2 p.m. I had covered 80 km – a feat to put a smile on any long-distance tourer's face – and then I set out again for a further push into twilight before finding a camping spot. It was after some conversation with a tollbooth operator that I was pointed to a rest area, where truck drivers take naps and bathroom breaks. Many of these areas have attendants that do everything from helping with simple mechanical repairs on vehicles to acting as night guards. They also apparently guide passing cyclists to comfortable and free places to camp, and my particular aide assured me that I wouldn't be disturbed under an open shed normally reserved for emergency vehicles.

Cooking on the gritty tarmac outside my tent had never felt as good. The sense of pure satisfaction after a day's cycle and an evening's accommodation in another unusual setting, made possible by the kindness of others, was a tonic. It was refreshing to feel chilly again too, wearing my thermal jacket, a woolly hat and leggings under my greasy trousers as I bedded down for the night. Despite what might be termed uninspiring or ordinary scenery and a rumbling highway for company, I was discovering contentment again.

The third day followed in the same vein as the second. I passed more towns of anonymous character, where a line of cars exited the road via multiple turn-offs and overpasses, as another one entered it. I was now in the Maipo Valley, a sub-section of the greater Central Valley – illustrious wine country, I'd been told. Indeed, hundreds, if not thousands, of acres of lush grape vines bordered the asphalt in fenced-off enclosures as I continued past the towns of Talca, San Javier, and Linares. Along the road a string of townships, vineyards, farms and service stations appeared and disappeared in quick succession. However, it was the service stations that would become the unlikely, yet standout memory of that 1,016 km trek.

Terpel and Copec are the two brands of service station that regularly punctuate Highway 5, and, as I set about maintaining a 125 km daily average distance, they turned out to be a guilty pleasure for me. In fact, I soon started targeting them as the only places to eat and sleep, and making sure I ended the day at either a Terpel or Copec quickly became a minor obsession. Both had hot food counters, coffee machines, seating areas, and a small mini-mart. They were ultra-modern in appearance and facilities, with some of the bigger ones even boasting showers and a Wi-Fi connection. They soon became the focal point for all of my childish fascination and glee, and every time I saw one approaching, I would find myself brimming with happiness and pedalling that little bit faster.

Terpel became my favourite as they generally sold freshly made sandwiches and burgers with French fries, almost always had an Internet connection, and offered expansive grassy grounds on which I could pitch my tent at night. A Copec was always a welcome sight too, but these were smaller, less common and were a bit down-at-heel, compared to Terpel's vibrant red paintwork. They did serve potato wedges, however, and were always a little more generous with their helpings. Safe camping space was always to be found at all these stations, and not once was I denied a place to stake my tent. In fact, it would have been difficult to find empty and suitable sites anywhere else in this region, as the land on either side of Highway 5 was fenced off with barbed wire to protect its most celebrated export – Cabernet Sauvignon grapes. And in any case, Terpel's Wi-Fi was strong enough to reach my sleeping bag – and that in itself was reason enough for me to seek out its grounds. My attitude towards service stations during this stretch of the journey never felt at so much at odds with my normal inclination, which would be to seek out wild camping space – yet now they had become something I actively looked forward to each night.

Diary: 29 August 2012, 39 km south of Loncoche, Chile

Rushed to a Terpel after Loncoche, having clocked 174 km. What a day to finish in the dark – but seeing that fluorescent red-and-white logo was like an apparition!

There were a few noteworthy sights on the final approach to Puerto Montt, ending a dearth of places of interest in the 700 km stretch since Santiago. Salto de Laja was a thunderous waterfall just off the highway near Los Ángeles, and such was the power of the river flowing over the rock that I could hear it half a kilometre away from a closed forest campground I had snuck into at dusk. And 40 km from Puerto Montt was the town of Frutillar, a former German colony, still hanging onto age-old Germanic culinary traditions. The mid-nineteenth century German settlers' choice to inhabit this particular place had apparently been determined by the presence of Lake Llanquihue, which was said to have reminded them of Lake Geneva in Switzerland, adding an extra attraction and sense of familiarity to a land so much further away from Europe for such travellers than it seems today.

At 5 p.m. on my eighth day riding from Santiago, I arrived in Puerto Montt, with a blustery wind at my back and a lazy drizzle falling from the sky. It was overcast and temperate, with some of the port city's tin-roofed dwellings rattling frenetically in the wind. Seagulls squawked overhead as I rode to the seafront, which is technically on the Reloncaví Sound, but the hint of salt in the air convinced me I was close to the ocean proper. The place reminded me of an under-populated Nova Scotian fishing village – probably always cold, damp and eternally hopeful of being fully bathed in sunlight, always to be disappointed. I found it fascinating: the red, blue and yellow wooden-framed houses and rusty fishing vessels docked in the harbour seemed to suggest a particular harshness to life often found in such weather-beaten settlements facing the elements. I imagined that every building and person was a potential repository of stories and intertwined histories – and yet, Puerto Montt is relatively new in terms of its foundation, with its first settlers clearing swathes of forest in 1853 to set the town up as a gateway for state-sponsored German immigration to Lake Llanquihue.

My room at Hostel Rico was a microcosm of the conditions outside. After a two-night stay there, most of my clothes were still soggy even though they had been hung on radiators. Also in Puerto Montt, I discovered, was André, who I had last seen in La Paz; we had been keeping a remarkably similar pace. Since I had first met him in San Cristobal, Mexico, over 11,000 km of road had passed under our respective tyres, and with just 2,500 km remaining, I wondered if we might end up completing it together.

André was in his usual upbeat form and he was buzzing at the thought of riding the Carretera Austral into the core of Chilean Patagonia. His biggest concern, as mine, was to prepare his bicycle for two or three weeks of unknowns on the Austral. At lunch in a little café set back from a grey sandy beach he showed me his wheel rims, which were thinning and showing three dots just underneath the surface, meaning that they were almost worn through. It would take a few days to get new wheels built up, but, since Puerto Montt wasn't known for well-stocked bike shops, he was worried about the quality of any work he could get done there. I, on the other hand, just bought some extra tyre tubes and a new chain, along with some tent stakes to provide extra strength against the wind, and a water filter, since towns would be few and very far between.

I decided to wait for André's wheel to be built so that we could set off together, which gave me another day to practice some aimless photography. By mid-morning, Puerto Montt was looking like an entirely different place, with a vigorous sun breaking up the earlier, rather moody sky, to reveal a maze of active streets. I visited the fish market a few kilometres from the town centre after a brisk walk along Angelmó Road. There a group of female vendors, practicing both coercion and encouragement by alternating scowls with friendly hand gestures, convinced me to try their salmon empanadas. These were so good and so fresh I bought four more for the walk home. I thought how very different it was, tasting hot food like this in a cold climate rather than a warm one – the experience being somehow far more enjoyable and comforting when the raw elements are against you. On my way back, just outside the market, I saw men loading clams and mussels into white plastic baskets, and weighing out large bags for waiting customers. The smell from their stalls was intense, and only for the bracing breeze, would have been enough to deter anyone from stopping there at all. Happy with the afternoon's bounty, I strolled back to town and wrote my diary for the day, trying to remember all the smells, sounds and now mental images of life here. Later, André called by to say his wheels couldn't be finished on time, and that I should go ahead. So we shook hands and agreed on Coyhaique, 600 km away, as a potential location to rendezvous.

Excited and full of anticipation, I went back to the hostel and packed my things. The Carretera Austral – all 1,240 km of it – was the leg of the journey I had been looking forward to perhaps more than all the rest. From what I'd heard, it offered everything I loved about bicycle touring – wildness, history, and the opportunity to be relatively self-sufficient. It would be a return, I imagined, to a similar way of cycling and living as we had had on the Dalton Highway in Alaska, and the ALCAN in Canada. In that sense, I felt that I was about to complete the circle, not only in terms of travelling style, but also in a return to a comparable climate and landscape. I knew that this next stage of the journey was going to be one to inspire more than any other.

13
Carretera Austral

Puerto Montt, Chile to Villa O'Higgins, Chile – 1,201 km

IN 1976 AUGUSTO PINOCHET – THE then President of Chile – ordered the construction of one of South America's most ambitious infrastructure projects; in doing so, his aim was to unite the nation and assert full territorial control in southern Chile. The Carretera Austral – literally meaning 'Southern Road' – would link Puerto Montt, and therefore the rest of the country, to the hitherto detached communities of Chilean Patagonia, thereby creating and enhancing a sense of nationalism and pride across the territory. Of course, these communities had been so isolated for so long for a very good reason – a landscape characterised by thick forests, fjords, glaciers, undiscovered rivers and not least, the impassable Andes.

The Austral was only finally finished in 2000, 24 full years after construction began. For a road that is still 70 per cent hard-packed gravel, it only amplifies the ferocity of Pinochet's determination to connect the rest of his territory with a mere 100,000 people living in an area roughly the size of Ireland and of whom half live in its biggest town, Coyhaique. Of course, the loss of life cannot go unmentioned either – many of the 10,000 or so Army engineers who worked on the project perished over the years in the effort to realise the grand vision of Chile's most infamous dictator. Even now that it is completed, the road is still punctuated in places by deep fjords, meaning the government has had to install jetties and seasonal small ferry services to carry vehicles, and the occasional cyclist, across these waters.

Breezing out of Puerto Montt, I noticed the number of houses and people decrease with every hour that went by. At lunchtime I descended into

Caleta La Arena, the first break in the Austral, and waited 45 minutes for the ferry to return before being able to board. It would be a short half-hour trip across the mouth of an inlet, in the company of five other vehicles. On deck, exposed to a fortifying wind, I watched as a pod of dolphins shadowed the stern, leaping out of the water with that special animation only they have. I disembarked on the other side, and rode carefully over the compacted soil surface, passing elderly farmers and white clapboard houses. The sky had been accumulating darkness all day and before long, the heavens opened as I crunched up brambly hills that were to be typical of the northern Austral.

In the space of a few hours, the fields had disappeared and I was able to stare into dense, deep green forest that had probably never seen human interference. The rain dripped quickly from the hood of my rain jacket onto my nose and dribbled down along my face to my chin, landing on the handlebars with flawless execution. My waterproof pants acted as a funnel for water to run into my shoes, in which I could feel a spongy, cold squelch with every rotation of the pedals. As I searched for openings in which to set up my tent, I eventually came across a sign that read 'Residencial Yohanna'. Turning down a country road, I came to a clearing with a few houses and fences, behind which sheep were sitting, patiently chewing grass in the rain. The fog was so thick that the road vanished 15 metres ahead, but after a few minutes, I came across a purple homestead, which I presumed to be the Residencial.

I knocked hard on the door but there was no answer. I knocked again and waited for about five minutes, wiping rain from my forehead and checking that water hadn't made it into my pannier bags. Eventually, I heard a door clatter open across the yard and looked over to see an old man in a blue woollen jumper approaching. I hadn't noticed until now the thin line of smoke coming from the chimney of the pre-fabricated structure he had emerged from.

'This is Resedencial Yohanna?' I asked him.

'Yes,' he replied and fumbled around with a set of keys before trying the lock of the purple house.

He said no more, but invited me in by waving his hand towards the open door, and pointed to a shed in which to store my bicycle. The house was cold but neatly decorated with light brown panelling; there a wood-burning stove in the corner with a stack of kindling beside it. Two sofas faced each other in the living area and, bundled in the corner, were some high chairs. On the walls, about a dozen photos of somebody's children – presumably the old man's – hung in clusters. In the adjoining kitchen, a row of pots and pans were suspended from hooks over a large cooking stove, and a simple table with a lino cloth was empty except for some salt and pepper containers.

'Do you mind if I change my clothes somewhere?' I asked, and again I was directed to a room across from the front door. When I appeared, dirty but dry, a cup of tea and some buttered brown bread were sitting on the table of the living area.

'Take, please,' my host said to me, lounging back meekly into an armchair. 'There's also a room for you tonight in the back. It used to be my son's but he's not here, so it's yours.'

Vicente, as I learned was his name, was leading an odd and, at that moment, rather a sad life, it seemed to me. This had been his house for over 40 years, but he had been relegated to the small pre-fabricated structure in the yard five years before, when his wife left him for another man. His wife decided to stay in the house, and brought her new boyfriend to live with her in the home in which she and Vicente had built a family and life together. Too old and attached to leave, Vicente had agreed to settle just 20 metres across the way and said that he would take care of the farm. As he told me the story, he didn't appear angry or openly upset, just tired and apathetic, as if it had been recounted countless times before. I never asked his age, but I guessed he was close to 65 or 70. The wrinkles on his face and pace of his walk certainly hinted at it.

Later in the evening, Vicente's wife (they never legally separated) came through the door and introduced herself as Maria, and her boyfriend as Renato. She was clearly more youthful than Vicente, while Renato was a tall and burly man with a refined black moustache. I was unsure whether to expect hostility from Vicente, but all Maria received was a helping hand to unpack the shopping.

'We go to Puerto Montt once a month to get all the things we need for the next one, things we can't buy in Hornopirén,' she told me. 'Have you eaten yet, or had some tea?'

'Yes, I have. Bread and tea from Vicente, it was needed after this rain,' I answered.

She was the very opposite of the old man who had creaked across the yard to let me in. Bubbly and bright, she barely took a breath between sentences. In the kitchen I could see Renato, leaning up against the stove with his arms crossed, chatting with Vicente about the trip to Puerto Montt. In an almost dejected manner, Vicente nodded and asked questions in a languid but dutiful manner, now and then however breaking a smile or putting his hand to his forehead, as if aghast at some news from Puerto Montt.

By a roaring fire later in the evening, Vicente, Maria and Renato told me about what the Austral road has meant to them. 'Just a few decades ago, we had to travel by *lancha* (small fishing boat) to Puerto Montt. There were no real roads, just tracks between farms and small villages,' Maria said, biting into a jam and honey sandwich.

I had been wondering whether the road had achieved Pinochet's ideal of uniting the country from north to south. Had a simple, six-metre wide gravel and sometimes-paved strip of ground brought Chileans closer together? After all, Chile was a sinuous country – 4,300 km from top to bottom – and, if geography had taught me anything on this journey, it was that, even within much smaller nations, culture and identity could swiftly change from town to town, or province to province.

'We were always Chileans,' Renato explained. 'The road has merely made life easier. Now we can get to a hospital if we are sick, or shop in a big supermarket like we did today. But it's also made it harder, too – it's easier for our sons and daughters to leave.'

'Do they ever come back?'

'Of course, but not for long,' he responded. 'But we're lucky here in Gualihue, we're just hours from a big town. Think of those in Cochrane, hundreds of miles further south, or those in some places with just a handful of people. They aren't as fortunate.'

Throughout the evening, Vicente idly stared at the television with the sound turned down. Every now and again, he'd add a sentence or two to the conversation, but otherwise appeared to have settled into a kind of lacklustre passivity.

Maria sent me to bed, making sure I had taken enough food and tea for the ride to Hornopirén in the morning. When I woke, the rain was still coming down, but without the power of the previous day. Somewhere between a damp haze and drizzle, it was still enough to steadily saturate my clothes as I dug deep to find from somewhere the energy to climb 22 km of steep and heavily forested hills all the way to town.

Hornopirén marked the second ferry crossing of the Austral, and in the 30 minutes I waited for boarding to take place, the sun split the low-lying clouds far enough apart to reveal teal mountains rising from the narrow inlets, with distant waterfalls cascading from their sparingly forested faces. Before the ferry left, I had time for two coffees and a television interview, having been approached by a film crew producing a documentary on southern Chile for the national tourism board, who had asked me what I thought of Patagonia and its people.

During the sailing – which took an hour, and brought us through achingly beautiful fjords of all shades of green – an intense silence reigned, broken only by the dull rumble of the engine. It was obvious I was entering a locked away, mysterious part of the planet. The waters were a deep marine blue and, except for several small fishing boats and a flock of seagulls gliding overhead, we were all alone.

I did however get chatting to two researchers from a Santiago university – Nick and Juan – who were about to begin an assessment of eco-tourism opportunities as far south as Coyhaique, the mid-point of the Austral.

'My hope is, if they ever connected all of these road sections, that it would be like Norway. I want the infrastructure to fit in as naturally with the environment as possible,' Nick said. 'But I can see problems.'

Nick explained that Douglas Tompkins, founder of The North Face clothing company, had bought the area we now sailed through. A conservationist and environmental activist, Tompkins had apparently been purchasing vast areas of land in Chile and Argentina and joining them together, in the hope of creating well-managed national parks that would inspire a conservation ethic amongst their visitors. Pumalín Park was his first major conservation project and I had been planning to camp somewhere within it that night. According to Nick, however, public opinion about these private philanthropy efforts had been divided from the outset.

'People are always protective of what they see as "their" land, and when

Tompkins came in and snapped it up, they worried about access. However, you can't deny that this work has been immense. And his idea is that, once these areas are designated national parks and have the government's blessing, he will give them right back to the people of Chile,' Nick explained. 'The only thing is that this very area is potentially an obstruction on the Austral, as he owns the land left and right of it, meaning he'd need to give the go-ahead if the roads were to be connected.'

I could see the benefit, and the hope, in such private philanthropy. Since this was an initiative of Tompkins', such a staunch defender of our natural world, I held faith that it might become a replicable model for other such special places. Unfortunately, however, Doug Tompkins died of hypothermia after a Patagonian kayaking accident in late 2015, and with his death, the world lost one of the greatest conservationists of our modern times, as well as a personal hero of mine ever since I learned about his work, in that setting of the sun-struck vales, free-flowing rivers, and unpopulated mountains of the northern Austral and Pumalín.

The ferry anchored at Leptepu, an empty mooring on an uninhabited strip of land, which we needed to get across under our own steam within 20 minutes. On the other side, a second boat would be waiting to take us to Caleta Gonzalo, the entrance to Pumalín Park. Knowing I'd be unable to cross 6 km in under 20 minutes, I loaded my bicycle into the back of a pickup and our convoy of eight cars hurried along the gravel surface, kicking up dust that was now split by the rays of a beaming sun.

One more short ferry journey, and I was repacking my bicycle at Caleta Gonzalo. By the time I hooked my panniers to the bicycle, every car had departed and I was left staring at a long, stony road shaded by laurel trees. It was close to 3 p.m. and I knew daylight would soon fade, so I moved on, knowing there was a system of campgrounds in the park whereby I could find a clear place to camp. The road wound around rocky intrusions and through stands of huge, unusually shaped flora with great big leaves. I cycled by trailheads leading to hidden waterfalls and sites showcasing the park's great biodiversity. As the road flattened a little, I caught glimpses of glaciated mountaintops through the trees, their slopes home to temperate evergreen forests. I passed through Lago Blanco campground, but decided to stop at Lago Negro instead, where several pitch sites were available with a small toilet block and picnic tables where you could cook and eat dinner. The light faded rapidly and within half an hour I was peering into darkness, with just the sound of a bubbling stream for company, wondering on which side of me the lake was.

In the morning, I woke to a slowly warming tent and partial sunlight on my green plastic walls. The sunshine peeked through the forest as I ate breakfast, drank some coffee and waited for the heat to lift the dew from my tent. A little further along the road, as I moved on, the trees began to thin, and suddenly, and as if desperate to impress, Lago Negro broke into view with the twin snow-covered peaks of a mountain looming protectively in the background. The lake water was so still it caught a pristine reflection of the glistening peaks on its clear surface. It was a moment of such instant pleasure. Noise, people, cars, modernity and normality were gone; in their place was an untouched vision in my mind of Patagonia as it had always been.

Just hours later, another moment of visual wonderment further enhanced the experience of what was already a majestic morning cycle. As I left Pumalín Park, a pyramidal volcano with a pointed and wholly snow-covered peak emerged to the southwest, apparently right out of the ocean. At first, I just noted how distinctive it looked. Then, after a minute or two, it dawned on me that I'd seen it somewhere before; it was burned into my recent memory. I recognised the strict conical shape, the lack of contours on its slopes and that oddly shaped pinnacle.

'Is it? Is that really Corcovado?' I said to myself, knowing it surely must be.

One of my favourite adventure documentaries, called *180° South*, follows the ascent of Volcán Corcovado by a team of climbers, including Jeff Thomas, the narrator, Yvon Chouinard, the founder of Patagonia clothing chain, and supported by none other than Douglas Tompkins. It was the first documentary I watched after deciding to undertake the bicycle journey, and it had galvanised me to reach this very part of the world. However, in the many months since leaving Alaska, I had forgotten about the film and the people in it. But now, catching this glimpse of Corcovado's distant, hazy summit upon rounding a corner, revived not just the magic of that original expedition, but also the feelings I had nurtured towards my own adventure.

On top of all this was the realisation that Corcovado was perhaps one of the most rugged and spellbinding mountains I had ever seen, most notably its northern face, which resembles a jagged tooth in this peaceful landscape.

In Chaitén, a fishing town of 3,000 people below Corcovado, I stopped for lunch and tasted the most delectable red salmon since the Brosnan's home in Fairbanks. On the walls of the restaurant, photos depicted the destruction Chaitén had faced in 2008. That year, Volcán Chaitén, 10 km to the northeast, erupted for the first time in over 9,000 years, blanketing in ash the entire area and significant portions of Chile's part of northern Patagonia. Just days later, a mudflow from the eruption caused water levels in the Río Blanco to rise, and in its haste to escape to the ocean, the river cut a new course straight through the town, destroying a large part of it. After months of deliberation, the government made the decision to relocate Chaitén 10 km further north, but when I arrived now, in September 2012, the surviving sections of town were standing as they always had, and it appears that no relocation will actually take place.

I hit asphalt out of Chaitén and continued on it for 45 km, after which the gravel returned, just beyond the village of Puerto Cardenas. There, road crews were busy surveying the land, compacting soil and sand, and fencing off the forest on either side of the Austral. To the east and 20 km away was the blisteringly white Amutui Quinei Icefield, tucked just inside Argentina's Chubut Province. Considering I could smell and oftentimes see the ocean to my west, Chile's trim figure was never as apparent.

Diary: 5 September 2012, 8 km south of Puerto Cardenas

Talk about having the outdoors to myself! I've set up tent beside a river, after spotting a broken-down wooden entrance to somewhere off the road, but when I got here there was nothing but a 10-metre wide river and a view into the mountains of Argentina. In my head I keep wondering what has me feeling so alive being out here? I guess it's the big, sudden change from superhighways to tracks, and from humans to purely nature. Part of me thinks, how important, and how great it would be, to have a fully paved road here, but the other part reckons that by doing that – by being completely accessible – this place might lose its special quality. But I'm just a visitor here, and not a resident, so I get to romanticise it forever in my head, while locals might not see it that way. Yet everyone I've spoken to says it's the most beautiful part of Chile – 'their' part of Chile.

The bite of a wintery cold woke me from a deep sleep at 5 a.m. and I was unable to drift off again for the last hour of darkness. My nose and ears were sore with cold, even though my woollen hat had become essential when sleeping. What I most looked forward to on waking, however, was tea or coffee. But, as had happened on several occasions throughout the trip, my multi-fuel stove flickered to life for 10 to 15 seconds, thought better of getting to work, and simply choked out with a small puff of black smoke. At the best of times, I'm not a particularly joyful riser, but when breakfast isn't accompanied by caffeine I'm best avoided until mid-morning. I had no choice but to finish off a solitary bowl of cornflakes mixed in powdered milk and eat a banana while watching my fingertips turn red. As remedy for my early grumpiness, I thought it prudent to get going quickly, and packed away the tent and sleeping bag, both wet from all the condensation absorbed during the night.

I followed an 8 km twisting climb to the snowline where conifer trees balanced slender drifts of snow upon their branches. The further south you travel in Patagonia, the lower the snowline gets, and in an ascent of 300 metres I had gone from thick, shrubby bushes and leafy trees to alpine conditions. In the hamlet of Santa Lucia, I was fortunate to find a shop selling coffee as well as some jam-filled baked goods and pastries. Since leaving Puerto Montt over three days before, I had come across just three towns; in between there was little but patchy pastureland, forest and some ongoing construction work. Silence was the dominant characteristic of the ride; when not in close proximity to those few towns, I might meet just one or two cars per hour. Today I had been quite lucky however, with the sound of egrets splashing in small ponds filling the air as I came upon Santa Lucia.

On account of some overly cautious planning, I had decided to carry at least three days' worth of food. I knew I could take water from streams and, if in doubt about safety, could purify it with iodine tablets. There was never a need to do this if I hadn't seen animals in the vicinity, and for the most part I was able to refill my 5-litre capacity of carriers in small shops. Lunch was proving the most enjoyable meal of the day, when I would pick an open grassy verge or rock by a stream as a base to eat heavily into my supplies – most importantly, reducing their weight on the bike – while my tent had a chance to dry in the afternoon sun.

I cycled 92 km from my riverside campsite to La Junta, the fourth town in four days, and which had the advantage of several restaurant-cum-guesthouses. However, about 20 km before my arrival, a turbulent mass of grey clouds hastily rolled in, darkening a sun that had so recently illuminated bright green meadows and fields of pink and white wildflowers. A heavy downpour followed, accompanied by swirling winds that made navigating the Austral to La Junta a taxing effort where the visibility and my resilience was fading fast. So, when I burst through the doors of a busy restaurant just after 6 p.m., all heads turned and conversations stopped mid-sentence. The owner – a plump lady wearing a stained white apron – was quick off the mark and, in response to the puddle of water that had collected at my feet, promptly scampered away to fetch a mop. When I had the wherewithal to return outside and remove my rain gear, she followed me, and invited me back inside for tea. She assured me of the three things I wanted most – a comfortable bed, a warm shower, and clear skies for my ride tomorrow. However, the weather in this part of the world being anything but predictable, I wasn't surprised to wake the following morning to the blustery clang of rain on the window.

I viewed every single settlement encountered on the Austral with fascination. They were so far removed from each other, not to mention the rest of Chile, and those living there practiced subsistence fishing and agriculture perhaps to a greater extent than the rest of the country. As much as I tried to research their histories online, I quickly realised that the best source of information was always the people themselves. Take Puyuhuapi, for example; it's a small fishing village of around 500 people located at the head of a fjord of the same name. It's 400 km from Puerto Montt and 220 km from Coyhaique, the Austral's biggest town. In between those are a few villages such as La Junta, but no other services. Over a hearty lunch of salmon, salad and potatoes in Puyuhuapi itself, I was interested to learn from a chatty lady that many of Chilean Patagonia's hamlets and towns were founded by foreign immigrants who had been promised free land by the government as long as they worked it. The area in which Puyuhuapi exists was first settled in the 1930s by Germans, who came on this very promise, but with the beginning of World War II, only some of them made it the entire way. Initially, fishing the fjord was the mainstay of a subsistence economy, before woodworking and textile production – skills brought from Europe – took hold as more reliable income generators.

'The land was good, but not great,' this lady told me, adding, 'It's an earth that you can take much from in some places, but in others, nothing.'

This was easy to see, as I had been cycling by fields of stony soil, where agriculture must be a tough and tedious industry. However, I'd also pedalled past green fields and valleys with ample space to keep cattle and other livestock.

'You see what we are like here,' she said. 'We're at the end of a valley, faced by steep mountains on one side, and a way to the ocean on the other. And when the snows come, well, you can do little with the land for four months of the year.'

Today, Puyuhuapi lives a calm existence. It's four streets wide and two streets across, and in the couple of hours I stayed there, I found one general store and a handful of restaurants, all of which were set up in family homes. After 7 p.m. these establishments closed their doors and were turned back to dining rooms, as husbands got home from work and wives began dinner for the family.

Leaving Puyuhuapi I made a sharp turn to the east, meeting the mountains of Queulet National Park. Hard-packed, potholed gravel disintegrated into a softer mix of sand and stone. As the rain fell once again, I kicked up mud until the chain and gears were clogged, so, half-hourly, I had to set about the task of clearing them with any stick I could find by the roadside. In amongst all the rain and bitter cold, my surroundings didn't fail to impress. Tiny streams gushed from indentations in the hillside, striving for the ambition of waterfalls. The Austral made no attempt to deviate from any available watercourse, and so the climbs were gradual and tempered to its incline. As twilight closed in, I rode on in the hope of finding the summit of a long climb that hugged a forested ridgeline, but finally, with corner after corner leading to further ascent, I decided to camp on a bend in the road that had some extra space alongside. It was one of the more senseless places to pitch a tent, but in the previous 10 km of continuous uphill there hadn't been one single area to safely stop for the night. Although perhaps 10 cars had passed me since I left Puyuhuapi at 3 p.m., I was still afraid of some tired driver pulling over in the middle of the night, only to feel the bump under his wheel of a comatose cyclist in his flysheet. To that end, I built what I saw as a protective line of large stones, covering these with any reflective clothing I had with me. If I was to survive the night, just a few rocks, a high-visibility jacket and a yellow rain mac I'd never used would have to be my guardians.

I woke to the sound of rain, and thankfully nothing more dangerous. I didn't hear any cars in the night, but I did fall asleep to some whistling noises emanating from the woods that began just metres from the tent. As had been the case each morning so far, my clothes were damp and it took 20 to 30 minutes to get acclimatised to the feeling on my skin. By this time, I'd successfully replaced the rubber rings and filter in my stove pump, so it hummed nicely and drew a great blue flame to ready hot water for coffee and oatmeal. As the fog attempted to lift, I checked the map and saw a thick red line, which indicated a paved surface not too far ahead from where I assumed I was. This looked to carry on for about 180 km or so, to Coyhaique, and at this, my mood became notably more positive. Normally I would cover 100 km of flat compact gravel surface in about nine hours, but with a paved surface, I could cycle this distance in about six. Considering I didn't anticipate any high mountain passes or overly difficult terrain, I knew the Austral to Coyhaique would be a relaxing and carefree ride, which wouldn't require me to keep my eyes assiduously trained on the road on the look-out for potholes.

By the time I reached the summit, the rain had turned to sleet, and then, in the space of 15 minutes, the high-mountain countryside was covered in a thin layer of crisp snow. The pine trees stood, wrapped top to bottom in soft white, with only the breeze to shake the thicker drifts from their branches into a flitter of windblown powder. The Austral had incredibly fresh air too, a feature of its environment I had been aware of since Hornopirén. Perhaps it was the dearth of towns, cars and industry, or just because every day I travelled was another step towards the cooler southern temperatures – but then again, I knew that such purity of air was a rarity in many countries.

Diary: 8 September 2012, Mañihuales, Chile

Never been in better form! I completely enjoyed the ride . . . again! Although I set out damp, my body heat eventually cast away the severe cold, as I reached the snowline at just 500 metres. I followed the Palena and Cisne rivers today, and they became my travel partners for a short while, each of us headed for a different destination. When they branched off, I crossed a pass and met a new gulch or stream in its infancy. 20 km or 30 km later, I'd be riding alongside a strong, dominant water flow. It's like witnessing a lifecycle in miniature, seeing the birth and being there into adolescence and maturity.

Mañihuales, the next town along, provided a good bed and a cheap dinner of *chuleta de cerdo* (pork) and French fries. Like Puyuhuapi, it too was hanging on by the thread of a singular industry, with the majority of its male residents working at a copper mine in the distant hills. The lady managing the charming wooden frame *alojamiento* where I stayed told me that every morning at 5 a.m. a fleet of buses leaves with dozens of men destined for a day's work in the mine before returning at nightfall. They must have been back, I thought, as the main street had more people on it than I'd seen in either Santa Lucia, La Junta or Puyuhuapi combined. For the first time too, I noticed the nocturnal attractiveness of Chilean Patagonia, as a full moon silhouetted the mountain ridges that spanned the western edge of the settlement.

Considering I had cycled for seven days straight, I planned a few days off in Coyhaique. I had two options for getting there, the first being a deviation from the Austral along the paved X-50 road. Or, if I wanted a return to gravel, I could continue on an unpaved section of the Austral that had an indeterminate length on my map. Unwilling to give up the pavement however, I chose the X-50 and set off from Mañihuales on a clear morning.

The X-50 wooed from the beginning. It ran through two softly sloping hillsides, where trim pale green grass and a scattering of wiry bushes were the land's only vegetation. This would have felt claustrophobic, had the hills been mountains, but once the road broke into an open valley, a huge swathe of pastureland foraged by cattle and goats came forth. It was here I met the Simpson River, which I followed into a set of interlocking canyons with sheer, vertical cliffs. This silt-choked waterway ambled its way amongst the walls of rock until it deserted the road for an easier course to Coyhaique. As it swung south, I faced a grinding climb onto a plateau with spectacular views into an icy Argentina. My legs were painfully sore from the unexpected ascent, which exacerbated the ache already in my muscles from a week's worth of cycling. Cars and lorries were passing more frequently, and houses started appearing on the hillsides and in the valley that I peered down upon. An hour later, I reached the top of the plateau, and paused breathless for a few minutes before pushing on for the final 8 km to Coyhaique, which soon came into view far off in the distance, sitting in a big bowl with a perfect arc of mountains curling away to its west.

Coyhaique is the capital of the Aysén Region and the Austral's biggest commune. With a population of 50,000 people, it accommodates half of the region's inhabitants. Originally established by nineteenth-century loggers seeking to harvest the area's abundant timber resources, today its economy is propped up by tourism and agriculture. From the former, many guesthouses have sprung up, and I checked into one that had the furnishings and character of a 1970s American home, much like that of the *Brady Bunch's*. The ambience was ideal however, as the elderly couple that owned it kept it tidy and clean, and the rooms were immaculate, if a little dated.

After receiving the keys to my room, I took a walk to the town centre, which is pentagonal in shape and designed in honour of the *carabineros*, the national police force. At Café Ricer, where I would spend three or four hours of each of my three days there, I settled in to writing some blogs and calling home. It seemed to be a meeting place for everyone in the area, from local politicians to environmental activists, to farmers and expatriates.

On the afternoon of my second day, a middle-aged man with black teeth, a woven flat cap, and a shaggy coat sat down beside me with two children and a teenager. I could tell from his attempts to catch my gaze that he was eager to talk.

'I'm in to use the Internet,' he told me, as if needing to explain himself. 'We can't get it on the farm, you know how it is!'

Peter was originally from Germany but had relocated to the foothills of Coyhaique's nearby mountains the previous year after purchasing a 100-hectare farm.

'I can tell you this without naming the price, but I paid the same as a year's rental for a parking space in central Berlin,' he said.

'And you've a family here?' I asked him.

'Yes, we've seven children, and this one here is from Colorado. She came here to learn Spanish, but now she's learning German instead.'

I wondered if it was common for foreigners to come to Chilean Patagonia and buy up land, as the way Peter spoke seemed to suggest that a lot more people were doing it than I imagined. In the week since Puerto Montt, I had only seen two travellers, and not a single expatriate living here, until now.

'Some will come to get away from their crazy European or American lives. It's why we came. I couldn't stand the bureaucracy and madness of Germany any longer. Although we've got a farm here, there's no electricity. We do use the generator sometimes, but the rest of the power comes from solar. We collect rainwater for washing and cleaning, and grow organic vegetables to exchange for other foods or a service – like someone laying a new floor,' he explained with pride.

I found it pleasing to think this could all be done on the back of a simple desire for an easier, more attractive life. Peter said his wife home-schooled the children, while he tended to the cattle they kept.

'We did make a mistake, though. The soil here isn't good, so I have problems feeding my dairy cows. I should've bought a place further north,' he said.

I could see the appeal of living in Patagonia – the prettiness of the landscape, and the isolation from modern-day worries. Of course it was hard work, but I could associate with the greater reward in harvesting a crop of vegetables and exchanging them with a neighbour, than in the life of high taxes, city pollution and stress many of us muddle through.

On my second day in Coyhaique, André joined me. He too was revelling in the experience so far and he suggested finishing the trip together, to which I agreed. We had kept an extraordinarily similar pace since Mexico, and felt that sharing some beers in Ushuaia as we crossed the finish line would be the appropriate salute to our joint accomplishment. We estimated it would take

6 to 7 days to cover the remaining 600 km to Villa O'Higgins at the very end of the Austral; according to the blogs of other touring cyclists, this section was to be as stunning as the north.

When we left Coyhaique, André became concerned with a noise coming from an unidentifiable part of his bike.

'Fuck, fuck, fuck!' he said. 'It sounds like it's from here,' he continued, pointing at the drivetrain. 'And now it's from here, the Rohloff hub.'

We got just 25 km out of Coyhaique, when, at a restaurant in the middle of vacant countryside, André decided to turn back. The next suitably competent bicycle shop on the road ahead would be somewhere in Argentina, perhaps weeks away, given the unknown nature of the road and towns in between. If it were the hub – a specially designed internal gear – then he'd need a replacement sent from Europe, but anything else should be fixable in Coyhaique. So, with disappointment, we had to say goodbye again and I forced on through a headwind to the south, while André caught its favour on the route back north.

My target for the evening was the village of Villa Cerro Castillo, which is overlooked by Mt Castillo, right behind it. Its name translates as 'Castle Mountain', but I could see the shape of a crown, rather than a fortress, in its multi-pinnacle summit. The afternoon had seen an emergence of glacial lakes and areas of pine forest atop some passes, the trees once more blanketed heavily in snow. I had stopped at a lake for lunch, and watched as small birds searched in the undergrowth for seeds, their whistles echoing up along the rocky crevice we shared. As I had set off again, clouds scurried across the sky, catching mountaintops as they went, and a burgeoning wind spurred me downhill towards my night stop.

When I departed Villa Cerro Castillo the next morning, it was to a very different landscape and feel. The Austral changed direction and locked into a westerly heading, directly into the prevailing winds. The greenery that had characterised the first eight cycling days of the road disappeared from view, and a series of craggy, roughly shaped gorges with shallow streams took its place. I was back on gravel again and for each corner that shielded me from the wind, another forced me straight into it, moving at just 5 km/h. This wind was so formidable and unrelenting that I couldn't even hear myself curse and scream into it. Each turn of the pedals required maximum effort and the use of every muscle in my body. If I even paused for some water, I had to stand behind the bicycle, leaning into the gale, just to stay upright.

It was some hours before the Austral realigned itself on its more habitual north-south heading and the closer mountains began to provide some respite from the winds. I dropped from 600 to 200 metres to meet the Río Murta, and I followed as it guided me to a finger of Lago General Carrera, Chile's largest lake. The day bore a gloomy face as rainclouds appeared on the horizon, heralding an afternoon of heavy rains. Despite this, the lake was an interesting specimen to examine, given its shape and character. It is of glacial origin, and therefore fills the open space originally carved out by ancient walls of ice; the deep valley it occupies stretches across the border into Argentina, 40 km away. There, it is the country's fourth largest lake, and bears the name Lago Buenos Aires.

When I reached the end of the lake's finger, I could see the lights of Puerto Tranquillo, a settlement of just a few hundred people, beckoning me towards them. Once more, in complete darkness, I was fortunate to find a guesthouse; this time the owner showed me to the spare room in her house, before she left for the evening. There were very few official hotels or guesthouses on the Austral – most places were just the homes of families who had one room available for tourists or cyclists passing through. But in the humble nature of this kind of accommodation were the simple comforts of home – a stove to make dinner, a kettle to boil water for tea, and sofas on which to sit back with the family, to watch television or have a chat. On days of rain-soaked travel, the warmth of a home was always much more satisfying than the sanitised atmosphere of a hotel room.

The next morning, I woke to the creak of a yard door swinging open and closed and, with stiffness in my muscles, I pulled myself out of bed, with high expectations of sunshine and plenteous kilometres being covered in the day ahead. Once again, however, I would be left waiting and wanting after such false optimism.

'Would you like something to take with you?' the owner asked me kindly in a soft tone of voice.

'I think I'm ok,' I said. I was confident that my restocked panniers had sufficient food.

'You'll find it hard from here,' she added. 'The hills get bigger around the turn-off to Chile Chico, and then you'll move very slowly.'

Chile Chico is a border town on an east-running road that makes best use of the gentler topography shared by both Chile and Argentina. Although the Andes rise high in Patagonia, there are a handful of places where it's possible to cross between both countries without the kind of exertion associated with most of the range's mountain passes. I was keen to make it past the Chile Chico turn-off, as I knew that the uneven terrain of the area would make camping a grim prospect. However, I hoped it would be possible to catch a glimpse, to the west of the junction, of the enormous North Patagonian Icefield, which drapes itself over 4,200 km^2 of crumpled mountains and ocean inlets. The highest peak in Chilean Patagonia – Mt San Valentin, at 4,058 metres – rises from the icefield's northern end, and I was desperate to see its summit peak out of the glacial covering.

The weather was atrocious, however, and I was not to see San Valentin or the icefield. A low fog hung around the middle-section of the hills and only after 11 a.m., when I rounded the southern end of Lago General Carrera, did it lift – but just to uncover the choppy waters and distant shores of the lake itself. I then crossed a bridge that stems a short neck of water, which is the official boundary between Lago General Carrera and Lago Bertrand. Here, the difference in colour between the two lakes was extraordinary – General Carrera was an ocean blue and not unattractive, but somehow completely ordinary, compared to Bertrand's emerald-green waters, which were fed by glacial meltwater from the icefield's many tongues of ice.

By early morning the next day, I reached the southern end of Lago Bertrand, where the magnificent Baker River begins. This is Chile's largest volume waterway, and rampages 175 km to the ocean at Caleta Tortel; along its entire path, the Baker maintains its emerald colour, as its tributaries join in its quest for the sea. I walked through the woods and sat for 30 minutes at the river's head, at the very place where Lago Bertrand drains into a valley narrow enough to deem it a river itself. In Coyhaique, I had learned of the plans to dam the ancient Baker, as well as several other rivers in the region. It's hard to describe the feeling that came over me, having witnessed it at its source, when I now imagined the irreversible destruction to its biodiversity and character which would inevitably result, should the project go ahead. In that instant, sitting in the drizzling rain, watching that wild, fledgling rush of water set off on its journey through forested gorges where humans have rarely been, I was struck as never before by what Patagonia truly is, and should stay: a landscape wild and untamed, answerable to no one.

Unpredictably changing terrain accompanied the Baker, until the town of Cochrane, when the river took a sharp westward turn towards the Pacific. In a brief interlude to the commanding view I had had, the peaks now vanished and I was surrounded by moor-like grassland within a series of U-shaped valleys. Cycling was tiring now and with every hour, my legs hurt a little more, requiring longer stops and stretching against roadside boulders. When I eventually reached the 3,000-inhabitant town of Cochrane, I made my way to the central park and removed my rain gear and all of my clothes, down to my boxer shorts, hoping they'd dry in the sun, which had just come out. After a near brush with nudity – fortunately, nobody was around to notice – I felt immediately better, getting into dry clothes for the first time in days. As a rule, I didn't put on dry gear if it was already raining, as within an hour I'd be saturated anyway, with the condensation from my waterproofs wetting everything from the inside.

Cochrane was like a ghost town and that's why I'd allowed myself to strip in the park. Not a soul was walking the streets, peering out of windows or driving in their cars – so I presumed it to be a national holiday. In a coffee shop I eventually found open, I asked the owner, who spoke very good English, why it was so quiet.

'It's like this every day,' he said. This is 2 p.m. on a Saturday. Nothing much happens around here.'

I liked Cochrane and its lack of activity, in fact. It had a nice park, one well-stocked supermarket, and a cosy feel to it. As an added bonus, the sun's appearance revealed some of the more charming aspects of the town, such as a pretty white wooden church. I didn't want to stay the night, however, as that would mean a rushed 140 km day on Sunday to make Puerto Yungay, where I would take the next ferry crossing. Instead, I chose a playlist of songs on my iPod, and set off on an uncommonly flat section of the Austral, resolving to camp when it was almost dark. Just two hours later, I had covered 30 km and found a wonderfully secluded spot in a clearing beside the road, with an overhead canopy provided by a grove of conifers. On the opposite side of the road was the golden, shimmering Lago Chacabuco.

Diary: 15 September 2012, 30 km south of Cochrane, Chile

I can feel a real tiredness now, and I guess it's the extra strain of riding through the rain. The road is getting muddier and it's difficult to push through that, so I have longer days to contend with. With all this rain, I haven't felt the need to stop early, as I'd just be in my tent or guesthouse, so have tended to keep going until the latest hour . . . In terms of north versus south, I have to say I found the north a more handsome region. I did have two days of sunshine there, however, which may have made a difference. Tomorrow, I have 100 km to go and then I'll be within reach of Villa O'Higgins the day after.

A steady pace was required to make Puerto Yungay, and so I made an attempt to keep my speed above 10 km/h, which gave me 10 hours to reach the launch. I didn't know however whether the boats were on schedules, or if I could just arrive and ask to be taken across the fjord. In the end, I rode 98 km in just under 10 hours, through an array of changing scenery. First, there was a tunnel of Coihue trees – a species native to southern Chile, whose branches of coin-sized shiny leaves hung elegantly over the road. Then, I entered a valley of glacial lakes, each broken by huge heaps of moraine, left there after the glaciers melted thousands of years ago. Finally, I met with the Baker River one last time, and cycled along its bank for several kilometres before it made its final run to the ocean. The Austral was on a different course now, and rose to meet a stubborn mountain in its way, clinging to its sides before emerging at 600 metres in a fresh fall of snow, with dozens of pretty lakes visible behind rows of trees. The greatest treat of all was that I could drink directly out of small streams spilling off the hillsides. For the past three days, whenever I ran short of water, I'd been able to hop off my bicycle and walk into the forest until I heard a babbling brook, where I'd fill up my carriers with litres of the freshest, clearest and coldest water. In very few places of the world can you access such a necessity naturally, and with such ease.

Dusk was closing in and a hailstorm struck on the descent to Puerto Yungay. When I turned the final corner, the fjord leapt forth, less than 100 metres in front of me, extending for kilometres ahead into the darkness. There were three buildings in my immediate vicinity, so I went to the one with the military logo on its wall, to ask for information.

When the door opened, I was almost dragged inside by the lone military officer occupying the barracks.

'I'm looking to cross the fjord,' I said. 'Is there a ferry?'

He looked sombre and mumbled something. Then, he turned his back and walked into the kitchen, where I could hear an extractor fan buzzing.

'Do you know if there's a ferry?' I asked again, this time shouting it a little more.

'Yes, yes, there's a boat leaving,' he roared back. 'But it's not going until tomorrow. Wait there, I'll make you some sandwiches.'

I sat down on a brown couch in the centre of the room. It was torn in several places, revealing the yellow foam inside. I looked around me, for any sign this was actually a military post – the only indication seemed to be a photo, in a tacky gold frame, of what looked like a highly-decorated official, sitting over the fireplace. The room was dark and the lights were off, with the only illumination being the flicker of a television in the corner. There was a wooden table under a window with two walkie-talkies on it, and beside the couch a few bags lay open, with clothes falling out of them onto the carpeted floor.

'Here you go. Some sandwiches and coffee,' the officer said. I knew he was military as he had the turf green pants of a soldier, but his uniform was incomplete, in that he was otherwise just wearing had a white polo shirt with two thin blue stripes across the chest.

'My name is Martin. What's yours?' he asked and sat down beside me.

'I'm Ian,' I answered. 'Nice to meet you.'

I wanted to ask about the ferry, but felt it rude now that I had a tray of ham sandwiches balancing on my lap. Instead I ate them quickly and let Martin continue speaking, as he had been doing since sitting down.

'I'm here alone right now. Sometimes there's two of us, but at the moment I'm the only one.'

As he let out exasperated statements such as 'What am I to do all day?', and, 'I couldn't be more bored', I watched his brow furrow, as his eyes flickered from the flash of the television set. He had a kind face, with big rounded cheeks.

'Look, look,' he said at one point. 'This is my favourite show, it's called *Pobre y Rico* (*Rich and Poor*).'

I sensed he wanted silence while the show began its recap of the previous episode, and once it broke into that day's, or that week's, edition, he let out a lengthy, jolly laugh and slapped his thighs with his hands, leaning forward off the couch a little.

'Have you seen it?' he asked.

I told him I hadn't, because I rarely saw television shows. But I did say that, if I could watch more, it might help improve my Spanish.

'No, no, you speak fine,' he said, and I hoped he meant it.

For the next 10 minutes, in between laughing at jokes on the show I didn't understand, Martin explained what he was doing here. He was part of the Chilean military's southern patrol, officers who were stationed at various remote postings on the Austral and Tierra del Fuego. He would work for 20 days straight and then get 10 days off, when he could return to his wife and two children in Concepción, a few hundred kilometres south of Santiago. It wasn't by choice that Martin had ended up in perhaps the most isolated mainland Chilean military outpost.

'The government has put us here because of Argentina,' he said, this time with a grave expression coming over his face.

'Argentina?' I said, a little confused.

'Look at how long and thin Chile is. For years, Argentina has taken small pieces of our land, claiming it as their own,' Martin explained. 'They haven't done this in a long time, but if we are here, they will think twice about doing it again. We Chileans must be strong.'

He obviously took his duty seriously, and was a staunch defender of the national border.

Martin said I could stay for the night and wait for the noon crossing the following day, an offer which I gratefully accepted. However, no sooner had I agreed to this, than one of the walkie-talkies started crackling.

'Martin, Martin?' I heard a voice say on the other end. I couldn't understand their conversation, but Martin told me it was just a regular check in from the ferry operator to close operations for the evening. Five minutes later, a bald man wearing bright yellow rain gear came through the front door. He handed Martin some papers and turned to me, asking where I was going.

'Villa O'Higgins,' I said. 'I'll catch the boat at midday tomorrow and cycle from the other side.'

'No need, come with me now if you like? We've got an unscheduled sailing in a few minutes, if you'd like a ride?' he said.

I could see Martin's despondent face. I guessed that just minutes ago he had received a notification of the sailing but didn't want me to know as it would another night without company in the barracks. I felt bad leaving on the ferry, but if I stayed, it would be two more days before I would reach Villa O'Higgins. By going now, I could camp on the far side and reach the end of the Austral before the close of the next day. An added bonus was that I'd get to Villa O'Higgins for Chile's national day, on 18 September.

Martin wrapped up the remaining sandwiches and bid me a safe journey. I rolled my bicycle down to the pier and up onto the deck, tying it to some pipes running along the inside of the stern. The engines came to life and the ferry turned smoothly on the spot to face down the blackened fjord, before sluggishly picking up a speed fast enough to see the waters break and the shadows of mountains pass by. It took all of thirty minutes to dock at Río Bravo, where a car, a pick-up truck and I steered onto terra firma once more.

Apart from the moonlit woods, there was nothing visible at Río Bravo but a small building that acted as a waiting room for northbound passengers. Soon the aft lights of the ferry vanished into the night, and I set about constructing my tent inside the building. I slept as soon as my head touched my makeshift pillow of trousers and T-shirts.

The final day, my thirteenth on the Austral, was the most challenging of all on this part of the route. It began as I rode 10 km in search of help for a man whose car had broken down at the boat launch. After several unsuccessful attempts knocking on the doors of wooden shacks on and off the road, I came upon a farm where a family were having a celebration. Although it was just 9 a.m., some of the men had been drinking, but luckily the women present seemed sober and of sound enough mind to understand my request. No sooner had my message been subsequently conveyed to a table of inebriated men, than they all rose immediately, and with great urgency, set off on horseback towards Río Bravo. One elderly gentleman took a rusty red pick-up instead, and charged in front with chains, towrope and a set of tools in the back.

People and houses were rare occurrences along the Austral's more remote countryside sections, and so this had been a fortunate occasion indeed. This was odd and uninhabitable land too – a vast area of marshes and sodden ground, where dead trees thrust their trunks into the air amongst reeds and abundant birdlife. The Austral was not about to let me go without a test however, and once it broke away from flat marshland, it decided to follow a tortuous series of shallow river borders – by far the worst kind of watercourses to stick by since they haven't yet gathered the strength to carve out wide and gently inclined passages through the landscape.

However, it was a gorgeous spring day, and there was a pleasant coolness in the air that prevented me from overheating on the climbs. Now and then, men on horseback, with dogs following obediently behind them, would jump from the woods onto the road, before giving a welcoming wave as they crossed over and trotted in amongst the trees on the far side. Later too, I met an English couple, Catherine and Dave, who were on foot – running from the southernmost point of the continent to the northernmost, somewhere in the Venezuelan jungle. They were pulling a two-wheeled trailer behind with all their supplies, and expected to take another year to reach their destination.

With arrival in Villa O'Higgins just hours away, I found myself thinking about how much I loved this part of the world. This had been my favourite leg of the trip so far, in terms of the landscape, wildness and freedom. I felt so in touch with my initial expectations and what I had originally hoped for from the journey. I knew that a great deal of the positivity I was experiencing was down to the fact that I was in a place of mental peace and balance with regards to Áine and returning home. I felt free of the shackles that worry had imposed on me for so long, and this allowed for clarity of vision, a wiping away of the mist from the lens that many parts of my journey had been viewed through. The Austral really had signalled a rebirth of my enjoyment and appreciation of what my time in the saddle was offering me, and this, I maintained, was better late than never. Parque Pumalín, Volcán Corcovado, and the Baker River were all natural wonders that had genuinely stirred me emotionally as I passed them, and they were all a reflection of what I treasured most about the ride – being outside amongst special places that I had worked to be able to witness.

I pedalled around Lago Cisnes, and could now see Villa O'Higgins under the sheltered guard of some smooth mountains. The sun now fully out and bathing everything in the most glorious light, and it seemed fitting that I had reached the end of the Carretera Austral in such a golden hour, with a magical colour being taken on by the flowers, trees, lake water, rumpled terrain and even the frontier housing of the town.

> *Diary: 17 September 2012, Villa O'Higgins, Chile*
>
> *When I got here, I looked south through an avenue of wooden buildings with smoking chimney tops, and thought about how the road goes no further – the only way out is through Argentina. I can't wait to rest, so I've spent lavishly on a cabin for the next two nights. For $15 per night, I have a double bed, sitting room, kitchen, wood-burning stove and TV. It's a castle in comparison to my tent, and a space in which I intend to recover from some really tiring days. The satisfaction upon reaching here is amazing, more so for riding on dirt 70 per cent of the way.*

With a population of just 500 people, Villa O'Higgins is southern Chile's furthermost outpost. Only in the year 2000 was it joined to the Austral, ending its many years of isolation. The town was named after Bernardo O'Higgins, the hero of Chilean independence, and so it seemed fitting then that I should be there for Independence Day. I could imagine that in larger communities there would have been parades, traditional music, and dancing, but due to O'Higgins' small number of residents, there was little but a short concert in a school hall. Still, the national flag flapped in the wind from every building, and red, white and blue bunting stretched from lamppost to lamppost. Apart from this, people seemed to be going about their business as on any other day. Minimarts and bakeries were open, but with only a handful of customers walking through their doors. The dearth of activity didn't justify staying any longer, but I felt an overwhelming weariness that begged me for at least another 24 hours of repose, so I decided to do just that.

There was just one way out of Villa O'Higgins, and that was over Paso Mayer, a relatively unused border crossing between Chile and Argentina, 40 km east of town. Normally, from December to February, a ferry service runs across Lago O'Higgins to Candelario Mansilla on the opposite side, where one passes the O'Higgins glacier sliding from the Southern Patagonian Icefield into the lake. From there, a footpath leads into Argentina and soon after, travellers will find the town of El Chaltén. As I was a couple of months too early for the ferry, Paso Mayer was the sole route out, but I had heard little about it. Some vague information on other cyclists' blogs indicated that there wasn't a road, but that I'd need to find a bridge crossing the braided Río Mayer, which was the official border between both countries. It all seemed rather adventurous, and I figured I'd be in Argentina by lunchtime the following day, sipping maté and delighting in the fact I was in another nation's Patagonia. But as Salva, the six-year around-the-world cyclist I met in Baja California, had told me, 'Adventure only happens when things go wrong.' How true this would prove to be.

14
To the End of the World

Villa O'Higgins, Chile to Ushuaia, Tierra del Fuego, Argentina – 1,791 km

'You'll need to find Mauche,' the Chilean border guard said, pointing irritably out his office window towards a rocky countryside, criss-crossed by directionless rivers. 'He lives on a mountain. He'll tell you how to get into Argentina.'

I was taken aback by the official's ability to renege on perhaps his most important responsibility – sending travellers in the right direction as they left his jurisdiction. Although he had initially attempted to explain how I was to cross the roadless 16 km expanse between Chilean and Argentine border stations, the effort was poor. How could he not know the way? Had he never been there before?

'So, Mauche will know more? He'll have better instructions?' I asked politely.

'Yes, yes. His house isn't far away. You'll be there in twenty minutes,' he responded, and set about finishing his lunch.

The morning's 40 km ride from Villa O'Higgins to Paso Mayer had imbued in me a deeply false sense of security regarding the imminent crossing to Argentina. A muddy and intermittently stony road followed a single river high into the mountains, where I passed lakes resting in pockets of ancient glacial quarrying. Despite the surface's unpredictability and effortless capacity to send shudders through the entire frame of the bicycle, at least we were on a direct eastern heading towards Argentina. However, when I reached the partly pre-fabricated, partly concrete border post, which sat at the head of a broad grey plain, the road ended at the exact point where sand, rivers and their pebbly beaches began. About 20 km away, at the farthest end of the valley, two massifs closed in on each other to form a rocky saddle. I would need to find a way across the higher range directly to the east, and 'Mauche' was apparently the only person capable of helping me do it.

I pushed my bicycle from the border post along a dried dirt track to a farm gate, exactly 20 minutes away, as I had been told. Inside the gate, which was the only entry through a barbed wire fence that surrounded the property, I could see a small wooden cabin through a copse of leafless trees. This was by no means a mountain, as the Chilean guard had told me – just a little brown hill. The closer I got, the louder the sound of laughing became. When I reached the front door, I could hear a radio too, turned up as loud as it would go, and almost drowning out the sound of the laughter.

'*Hola?*' I shouted towards the cabin, and I saw some immediate movement through the only greasy window in the structure.

The door opened and out stumbled a tall, wiry, brown-skinned man with a slender moustache clinging close to his top lip. He was wearing a chequered blue-and-white flannel shirt and dirty khaki pants with the zip open.

'*Hola amigo*,' he said, standing there, barefoot and wobbling, trying with all his might to assume a sober posture.

'Are you Mauche?' I asked.

'Yes, I'm Mauche. Would you like some wine?' he said smiling, showing off an entire mouth of chipped yellow teeth.

I wondered whether a refusal would be rude, but considering Mauche's dire state of inebriation and my nervousness about finding Argentina, I decided to pass. I asked Mauche how I could get to Argentine immigration in the quickest, most straightforward manner. But despite all he said in reply, I could understand perhaps just 30 per cent of it. Mauche was so drunk, so inconceivably shaky and terse in his responses, that I was getting worried about ever making it across. The basics of what I understood were that I needed to find 'the dead forest', cross 'the wooden footbridge', follow 'the horse tracks' and then 'the copper-coloured streams', until I found the border post.

The futility of talking to Mauche much longer was not lost on me, so I thanked him and set out across his farm to a gate on the other side. In front of me lay one obvious road but upon inspection, I found that it petered out just 300 metres further ahead. When I returned to the gate, Mauche was standing there, pointing to a rough horse track that ran beside the fence around his land.

'Over there, over there,' he said and shook my hand, wishing me a safe journey.

The rutted track was one metre in width at most, and on either side of it were prickly brambles. I pushed the bike carefully through this patch, as aside from the threat of cuts from the bushes, it was impossible to cycle on anyway. For the following three hours, I dragged the bike through an extensive network of almost impassable horse trails, which would split every few hundred metres, taking off into vegetation about six feet in height, never to be seen again. It was the footbridge, or *passarella* as it was referred to, that was key to finding a better and more obvious surface. After all, crossing it over the Río Carrera also meant I finally would officially be in Argentina, even if still many kilometres from the immigration building.

I knew east was the right direction in which to travel, so I took out my compass and wove along the tracks that had that general bearing. It was 4 p.m. and I could already see drawn out shadows appearing on the land. After 30 minutes I emerged into an area of dead trees, whose contorted branches were curling towards the sky. I figured this was the 'dead forest' Mauche had spoken of. Close by, I could see a river, but, unsure whether it was Río Carrera or Río Mayer – the major watercourse marked on my map – I decided to follow it anyway, in the hope of finding the *passarella*.

Wandering alone alongside the river, without any sign of a trodden surface and in amidst silent mountain peaks, a great sense of insecurity came upon me. For the first time on the trip, I felt a shade vulnerable. Although I knew I could backtrack and probably find Mauche's house once more, the knowledge brought no sense of calm.

At 5 p.m. I was exhausted and tense, knowing sunset was about 7.30 pm. I had pushed the bicycle a total of 5 km, and had come no closer to locating the *passarella* or a sign of a previous vehicle or bicycle passage. Since I seemed to have been travelling in circles throughout the day, I thought I might just make it to Mauche's farm before dark.

Just after 7 p.m. I rolled back to the front door of the Chilean border station, having opted for the comfort of an onsite shed over a bumpy patch of land beside Mauche's cabin. The officials inside were astounded I hadn't found the *passarella*, or any indication of wheel tracks on the ground.

'How many people pass through here every day?' I asked them, feeling stupid, after their assurances I had taken the wrong path.

'Today, you are the only one. Maybe we get one per week, but sometimes we can go for two or three weeks – especially at this time of year – without anyone coming or going,' he answered.

I didn't feel as foolish anymore. I couldn't imagine how I was supposed to identify vehicle tracks with weeks between passages? On top of this, I maintained that they must be travelling another way, because I knew that even the smallest of cars couldn't have traversed some of the horse tracks or marshes that I had needed to get through during the day.

The next morning brought with it sun and an air of greater positivity. I implored the border officials to draw a rough map for me, which they agreed to do, no doubt sensing my determination not to have to return here once more. At Mauche's house I met a fresh-faced man, completely clad in denim. He sported a sleek ponytail and brimmed hat, his image the very definition of the rugged outdoorsman. He asked if I would like to go to the *passarella* on horseback, but I insisted that I find it myself especially after yesterday's travails. Instead, therefore, he settled for showing me off Mauche's land.

I did as I had done the previous day. It took one-and-half hours to reach the dead forest, since, even though it was just 1 km away, I had to carry the bike and pannier bags in four trips up and down steep ravines and across several deep streams to get there. It turned out that I had been correct in following the river, and so I continued onwards until I met a solitary white post stuck in the ground at a bend in the river's banks. Here, I was told to follow a 50 ft ridgeline – marked as a tiny plateau on the sketch – due east, until I found the *passarella*. The map, although crudely drawn and labelled, gave some subtle indications via minor landscape features as to where I should change bearing. I was even fortunate enough to come across a narrow section of short grass that allowed a brief spell of cycling again; however, before long, a glacial-coloured river ripped through this area and I was soon waist-high in water, carrying the bicycle over my head and doing my best to stay vertical despite the slippery rocks underfoot.

From time to time, I allowed my senses to simply become immersed in the immediate surroundings. After all, this was a unique break in the normality and routine of the journey, travelling in part by compass at high altitude, and away from any infrastructure that hinted at the presence of humanity. But, as the adrenaline began pumping at the effort of scrambling up hillsides, and I dragged my possessions behind me, with mud spattering my face and hands, I was quickly brought back to reality again, and to the thought that it would be great to finally find the path – and Argentina – once again.

At 11 a.m. I trundled over a bed of large rocks where the bones of some cattle lay. It was just moments later that I spotted the *passarella* – a thin line extending across a roaring river in the distance. It was obstructed by the plateau that abruptly came across my view, so I scaled its sides in zigzag fashion for half an hour before finally getting bags and bike to the top.

The 200-metre long passarella swung from left to right, as the wind whistled through its wood and wire body. The blue Río Carrera was a wide torrent 20 metres below, thundering violently over immense boulders lodged for eternity in its path. Tentatively, I carried one bag at a time to Argentina, as gusts of wind rocked the fragile footbridge from side to side. I kept one hand firmly on the thick steel wire, but as it only reached waist-height, I was unsteady for the whole crossing. An hour passed before everything was across, and I could at last officially count myself as being in the country. I remembered that André was due through here any day now, so I taped a note to the struts of the *passarella's* iron frame, in the hope it might offer some comic relief for the soon-to-be frustrated German.

There was an extremely faint path in the stones on the Argentine side. There was no difference in surface height or indication of wheel tracks, just a discolouration of the rocks, which I assumed to be the road. It took three more hours and countless unloading and reloading of the bike over rivers and sand, before I entered a forest with a deliberately made mud path running through it. By late afternoon I at last found myself on the far side of the mountains that had earlier appeared to block my way – the path took a sneaky shortcut through a gap in the range I had failed to notice before. Eventually, with 15 km on the odometer, I saw smoke lifting from a green-roofed building about 1 km ahead, on the opposite side of some green space with lots of shallow streams cutting through it.

All but spent, I finally arrived at the Argentine immigration building, where I was stamped into the country for a second time. I stayed a while to chat with the four men inside, and enjoyed the frosted biscuits and cake they offered. They seemed happy just to meet someone new, just as Martin had been in Puerto Yungay, several days previously. I gathered their existence was probably even lonelier than his, as they worked at the station 30 days on, 30 days off, with no electricity and just four TV channels from a satellite receiver, mounted under their nation's flag on a concrete platform outside. They really were incredibly remote, being 240 km from Gobernador Gregores, a little town in Santa Cruz Province, with nothing but scattered *estancias* (ranches) and howling fresh air in between.

Temporarily refreshed, I pedalled against a light wind along a raised gravel road, letting out a big sigh of relief at the joy of cycling unimpeded again. The landscape around me was so indescribably magnificent that I just gaped at it. The mountains had deep green fields scurrying right up to their snowline, and contented sheep chomped on the grass. Small oblong lakes glistened in the evening sun, in a way that is only possible at that hour. Standing in their windblown waters were pink flamingos, pecking at food below the surface and preening their feathers, after a day spent wading in groups.

An *estancia* came into view and I rode up the long driveway, to be greeted by a young man of about 18 years of age, who, after brief introductions, showed me to an empty outhouse where I could set up my tent for the night. He was apparently the only person taking care of the land while the owner was away for several months, this being the end of winter and a time to prepare for summer ranching season.

Estancias in South America, and Argentina in particular, are huge estates usually dedicated to cattle and sheep rearing. They're a remnant of Spanish colonial rule and act as bases from which landowners can keep an eye on their livestock and hold claim to the surrounding land. On the Patagonian

Pampas – an area consisting of prairie grasses and steppes – the *estancias* have historically been the region's biggest and most profitable source of income. As fertile flatland is in abundance, and human population is not, these estates can be tens of thousands of hectares in size. For me, their presence in this unoccupied and infamously wind-beaten landscape meant shelter and a place to rest, as I travelled east and then south into the heart of Patagonia.

> ***Diary: 21 September 2012, Estancia 17 km southeast of Ribero Norte border post, Argentina***
>
> *Nestled up nicely in a dusty room, with my tent taking up most of it. The wind is rattling some doors outside and I can sense its force; even on the final turn here, it met my back and jolted me forward with such power. I guess the famous Argentine Patagonian wind couldn't even wait a day before making its appearance. I feel this may be the most remote place I've been on the trip so far, because of the wildness out here and the huge distances between just small towns. Thrilled to be having this experience at the very end of the trip.*

The Patagonian wind is something that must be felt to truly understand. Calm in the morning, it gains strength in tandem with the sun's ascent into the sky. It is a brute, primal feature of southern Argentina's climate, and has made living in such a place an eternal hardship. It sweeps in from the Pacific as westerly to north-westerly gales, moisture-laden and broken by the Andes in Chile. But once these gales cross the rocky spine of South America, they dry out and pick up a furious pace across the southern tip of the continent. The trees have no choice but to align to their direction accordingly, adopting the distinctive tilt so often seen in photographs of the region. The ground vegetation remains small, shrubby and hardy; the best physical conformation to allow it to draw from the soil any remaining water the wind hasn't already carried away. This wind is one of the cyclist's most fearsome enemies. Should you face directly into it, you will feel the most severe of mental and physical debility – a complete lack of will to go on. Pitching a tent is almost impossible, unless one can find a building or hill to break its nightly onslaught. It is hopeless to expect normal thoughts when driving directly into it, with the mind just languishing in frustration.

I left the *estancia* heading in an easterly direction and because of that, I had the wind ripping past me from behind. It was so strong that I didn't even need to move the pedals and held a speed of 26 km/h from its force alone. It really was incredible. The only real danger was the road, which was covered with a layer of loose gravel. I rode east for one day and then gently curved northeast on the afternoon of the second, until I met Ruta 40 once more, rejoining it four weeks after separating from it in Mendoza. Out here, in the westernmost portion of Argentine Patagonia, there was just wind and flatness. It was a stark change from those all stunning vistas of mountains, green fields and flamingos, and I realised that that had just been Chile bidding me farewell with its best. I would now drive into the immense, grey, treeless steppe, nature's counterbalance to obvious beauty. It was to be a place bereft of colour, and from what I could visibly discern, life.

Since leaving Villa O'Higgins, I had met six cars in five days. I passed seven or eight *estancias*, only sure of their existence from seeing large farm buildings, kilometres away, behind fenced enclosures. I eventually realised I was actually riding *through* the *estancias*, as every 40 to 50 km, the road would be blocked by a closed farm gate that I would needed to unhook and close again, before proceeding onwards. On Ruta 40 I found a sealed road and even more of a tailwind, which had me breaking my speed record on the flat ground, clocking 45 km/h. If I were ever to ride a full day like that, I thought, I could complete my usual distance in just two-and-a-half hours. Of course, my good fortune had to come to an end at some point. When I met a headwind, a day from Tres Lagos, the next town en route, my speed dropped to 5 km/h, meaning conversely it would take two-and-a-half days to ride my typical daily distance.

The comforts of previous months – hotels, restaurants, and people to talk to – all but vanished the moment I crossed from Chile into Argentina again. I was now meeting people on average once per day, and only because I was asking them for water. Usually these were members of three- to four-man highway construction teams, and they were more than happy to oblige by filling my water bottles, often passing me chocolate bars and bread too. On one occasion, I camped under a barren brown bluff, the only obvious bump I could find in the landscape after I had left Ruta 40; I lost four tent pegs and a bag of spices, which were prematurely snatched by the wind, and whisked out of sight unto the sandy plains in under a minute. I was sure that at some point my tent would be ripped from the ground into the deafening wind, leaving me naked and exposed in the wilderness under a sky full of stars.

When I reached Tres Lagos, a village of just 150 people, I was ecstatic to find a guesthouse and a store. I was also beaming widely, as somewhere 20 km before this, I had lost my woollen hat but hadn't noticed, and a kind elderly couple I flagged down had driven back to find it, covering 40 km on rough dirt. It's strange to think how sentimental we can be – but this hat had kept me warm all the way from Arctic Alaska, and I had no shame in asking someone for the favour of helping to secure its safe return. When the couple arrived back with it, I had a box of biscuits and chocolate cakes waiting for them as thanks.

The next day, well before sunrise, I woke and left town under the cover of darkness after a full breakfast of bananas, muesli, yoghurt and coffee – a feast in comparison to my usually modest first meal of the day. I planned on cycling 140 km to El Chaltén, a village under the spectacular spires of Mt Fitz Roy and Cerro Torre, two of Patagonia's most iconic mountains. Fitz Roy in particular was the image my mind had always summoned up when trying to imagine this part of the world before I saw it for myself, and so I watched the western horizon closely all morning, looking out for it.

When Fitz Roy did come into view, it appeared as a diminutive crest of snow and ice, packed upon slate-grey rock, tens of kilometres away. On either side of it sat numerous jagged prominences of the Andes. Although El Chaltén was 40 km off my route, I cycled there to try to glimpse a better view of Fitz Roy. As I rode through the cool breeze towards El Chaltén, Lago Viedma was to my left, filled with floating icebergs calved from a glacier at its western limit. On the other side of the mountains was O'Higgins National Park; I was now just 100 km from Villa O'Higgins itself, which highlighted the extreme, week-long detour I had had to make on account of the seasonal ferry not operating.

Mt Fitz Roy was first spotted by European explorers in 1877, and named after Robert FitzRoy, captain of the HMS Beagle, whose ship charted much of the Patagonian coast on its second voyage with a young Charles Darwin on board. In the twenty-first century, climbing has become the major human obsession with the mountain. At 3,405 metres, it's not exactly a giant, but is regarded as one of the world's most technically difficult peaks to summit because of its shape and angles. Its peak is so sharp that snow cannot fix to it, and neither can it to the surrounding rock. There is a basin of ice beneath and a slender ramp along one of the wider rock walls on its southern edge. It is, by all accounts, a mountain carved abnormally by the earth but in its rough asymmetry is a fine beauty.

In El Chaltén, I met a 29-year-old Swede named Andreas Fransson, who told me of his plans to freestyle ski the Wilhelm Ramp – the snow-packed southern ridge of Fitz Roy – and in doing so, become the first person to accomplish this feat. Even on a mountain so revered by the climbing and outdoor community, there are still records left to break.

'Do you not find it incredibly dangerous?' I asked him over a beer in the evening. He looked like a man who had been asked this question a thousand times.

'It is dangerous. No doubt about it. But people like me don't think in terms of danger, we are here to do, to achieve and we take enough safety precautions to make sure we stay as safe as humanly possible.' There was an unshakable confidence in his voice.

'Doing it this way, it is only through nature's unpredictability that we can suffer. It's a risk worth taking, to get where we want to be,' he said.

Andreas did manage to freestyle ski the Wilhelm Ramp. Two years later, however – just weeks before I wrote this passage – I heard of his passing, after an avalanche took his life further north in the Chilean Andes. Our conversation had begun when I spoke of how his fellow countryman Göran Kropp had inspired me to undertake this bicycle journey. I told him that after reading *Ultimate High*, I was compelled to do something similar, and cycling the length of the Americas was to be as close as I got. In that, we had a connection, because Andreas too was an admirer of Kropp, who died in 2002 climbing in Washington State. The undisguised risk of death was an inherent part of his pursuits, as it was for Andreas.

After El Chaltén, I returned the way I had come, and met Ruta 40 again. The sun warmed the day enough that I could remove my insulated jacket by 10 a.m. and an hour later, my thermal wear. I could see the lights of El Calafate across Lago Argentino, the second pointed lake to extend west from the Andes, and I picked up speed to reach there by dusk.

Most people visit El Calafate for one reason. Just 70 km away to the west is Perito Moreno glacier, one of the world's most spectacular natural wonders. I knew that I had seen some unforgettable places since leaving Alaska but nothing, absolutely nothing, prepared me for this. With fury and fragility in equal measure, a wall of ice, 5 km wide and 80 metres high, stared back at me across the Brazo Rico arm of Lago Argentino. The glacier, which is an extension of the Southern Patagonian Icefield, is one of three Patagonian glaciers that are still growing. It extends up the valley and curls around the protective mass of rock to its side, before meeting the brunt of the icefield. Towers of pointed ice dominate its surface, each audibly creaking and groaning as the glacier shimmies forward and into a more comfortable position at the water's edge. Every loud crack of ice signals a potential tear-away chunk destined to crash into the waters. How lucky I was see a piece, perhaps the size of two houses, break away from the front of the ice wall and thunder into the waters below, generating fearsome waves and leaving a raw, centuries-old hidden skin of blue ice exposed.

Most amazing of all, Perito Moreno goes through a regular, cyclical action in extending so far into the water that it blocks the Brazo Rico inlet of the lake. With no outlet, the arm's water level can rise by as much as 30 metres, until the pressure becomes so great that it ruptures the ice barrier and rushes into Lago Argentino once more, with ice and water meeting in a cataclysmic explosion of immense noise and freedom. The glacier almost immediately begins its motion towards the opposite shoreline and within a few years, the pattern repeats itself once again.

El Calafate — as comfortable and sociable as its wood-framed coffee houses and bars were — couldn't hold me for long. I intended to take a break closer to Ushuaia, most likely in Punta Arenas, Chile, four days away. I was so close to the continent's extremity that I would cycle just 400 km to reach it, crossing first west to east to the Atlantic, before traversing in the opposite direction to the Straits of Magellan and the Pacific. Leaving El Calafate also signalled the end of my connection with the greatest Andean ranges until their reappearance in slighter form in Tierra del Fuego. I would be heading through a harsh and damp terrain directly southeast to Río Gallegos and by noon on the day I departed, I lost sight of these mountain tops, to be greeted instead by drab brown soil interspersed with pockets of short grass and the odd blustering bush.

Now the roads were straight and heeded not a single invitation to deviate from their course to Río Gallegos. The rains also came in their worst incarnation. They moved quietly in, soon followed by a stiff wind, and lingered all day. I sought shelter in a large road maintenance shelter at the junction of Ruta 40 and Ruta 5, where my mind fumbled with the possibility of taking a detour to Puerto Natales. The only reason to consider this would be to see Torres del Paine National Park, a gathering of dagger-like mountains similar to Mt Fitz Roy. I longed to see the Atlantic, however, and didn't look forward to facing into a Patagonian headwind again, so I maintained a south-easterly course with the brush of tailwind.

Diary: 1 October 2012, Río Gallegos, Argentina

Pain, pain, pain in my knee now, but I'm glad I took Ruta 5 to Río Gallegos. It's boring, but not as much as some routes I've travelled and had two lovely 1 km descents, on one of which I reached 64 km/h! I've discarded my arguments against the price of meals and hotels, as I want a few days to ease the growing pain in my knee – it's flaring up a lot. Next week, I'll aim to camp and cook outside again, as I want to end the trip in the same manner I began it. I've been doing this anyway, but often on people's property or around other people. I think it will make ending more special.

I skirted quickly through Río Gallegos, of which my only outstanding memory was munching on mini chocolate *tortas* (cakes) that were sold in supermarkets and gas stations. They had been my one and only vice, food-wise, since entering Argentina, and at every opportunity I'd buy five or six and gorge them throughout the day, giving my sugar levels a rush that eventually led to an unpleasant down. Riding out of Río Gallegos was a reminder as to why I didn't stick around – it was smoggy and unkempt. Since riding the Carretera Austral, I found myself unimpressed with many towns, as experiencing days upon days of emptiness made human settlements seem wholly unnatural and superfluous – an affront to what we have so little of.

I passed customs at Monte Aymond border station without any problems, except for a rather rudimentary search of my panniers for fruit and vegetables. No sooner had I descended 5 km to the Straits of Magellan than I sighted, over the deep and turbulent waters, the final frontier, known as the 'land of fire' – Tierra del Fuego. I let out a euphoric yell at the top of my voice, while a fox scurried away in the undergrowth.

Following the arc of mainland South America, I could faintly make out some steel towers and smokestacks after the maritime village of San Gregorio, a ghost town of russet-red wooden warehouses and closed stores with cobwebs and dust in their display windows. I pedalled on, bolstered by a quickening wind, over hills and past beached old boats, until I came to the entrance of an industrial facility. I was at Terminal Gregorio, a monstrous petrol refinery with heavy security – some of whom came out without delay to meet me.

'Can I help you?' a uniformed guard said, with another looking on.

I enquired about the likelihood of a camp spot, considering the lashing wind and number of buildings here to break it.

'This is a restricted area, but I'll call my manager and ask,' the guard said. 'Wait here.'

A minute later he returned with a refusal.

'Can I stay here at the security post? I don't want to go inside,' I said. He paused for a moment.

'Ok. But only for tonight.'

I thanked him and agreed I'd just stay until morning – but I couldn't imagine how he might think I'd like to remain another day at a polluted refinery! Later in the evening, I had trouble trying to keep my stove alight in the wind. I primed it inside the tent vestibule and then behind a stack of wooden palettes. Under the moonlight, overhead wispy clouds scurried by, and grumpily I retreated, beaten, to a meal of energy bars and my last can of tuna. After a 154 km day, it was the kind of dinner that would send most to bed in poor form. My rations were low for the next day too, so at sunrise I requested something from a new security guard, who was only delighted to help a friend in need.

'Yes, anything, take anything. Look, do you want a loaf of bread? We've got this cake in the fridge, strawberry flavour!' he said.

When I had packed the food into my panniers, filled water bottles from a tap outside and loaded the bicycle, I came in to say one last thank you. The guard, who was now writing in logbooks, told me I was welcome, and motioned towards the table in the kitchen, just as a call came in on the radio. He'd prepared a mug of coffee, some cereal and toast.

'Eat, eat,' he whispered, covering the phone briefly with his hand. 'For strength!'

And strength it gave me. Wrapped up snugly in a long-sleeved base layer, two T-shirts, an insulated jacket and my woollen hat, I shot along towards Punta Arenas in true contentment. Most long-distance cyclists will know the feeling – it comes from breaking the wave of rough days in the saddle, or through the unexpected hospitality of others, as had been the case for me. As Gustavo – the chatty photographer I met in the hilltop town of Santa Barbara, Colombia – told me, it's the '*calor d'humano*' of others, literally 'human warmth' that makes the difference.

A fresh salt-water smell wafted in from the straits as the highway began to slip inland, avoiding brackish ponds and lakes that were close to the sea. I noticed that, with each small incline I went up, my speed would drop a little in comparison to the last. It didn't take long to realise that my front tyre had a slow puncture – just the seventh of the trip, and not bad after 26,800 km. As the air being released didn't hinder my progression too much, I opted to leave the tube in and just pump it every hour until I reached Punta Arenas. There, I would give the brake and gear wires one last tune-up, clean the chain and cassette, and replace the punctured tube.

When I arrived to Punta Arenas, I was amazed to discover it such a modern city, the like of which you wouldn't expect to find near the end of the world. I had read much about its history beforehand, and felt I had absorbed enough to create an authentic picture in my mind of what it would be like. However, I found well-paved roads, busy stores and even a modest shopping mall. There were also restaurants boasting of the quality of their European and traditional Chilean dishes, with one indicating that it had 'the best burger in Patagonia'. As it was 3 p.m., school children were just leaving classes for the day and getting into brand new cars and pick-up trucks.

But within this veil of modernity, I could sense the past. The old industrial factories on the city limits, converted turn-of-the-century shop fronts and wind-beaten streets suggested a place just recently emerging from the history I had read about. Even the street names – Avenida Magallanes and Calle Menéndez – pointed to stories of exploration and discovery. There was something inherently intriguing about it.

The area now known as Punta Arenas was first settled as a penal colony in 1848, as the Chilean government sent defectors and those deemed 'problematic' to the southernmost shores of the continent. Of course, the real motive for moving prisoners and some immigrants to this remote post was to assert authority over the Straits of Magellan. Its positioning along this narrow band of sea was central to the growth of commerce during the remainder of the century, and until the Panama Canal was opened in 1914, the strait was the principal channel through which trade ships passed from Europe and the eastern seaboard of the Americas to the west. Sheep and cattle farming, however, were to be the economy's core here, as entrepreneurial businessmen sought to exploit vast tracts of unused southern lands while building their fortunes.

One of the greatest and most influential of these was José Menéndez Menéndez. Born in Spain in 1846, Menéndez had departed his homeland at a young age in search of opportunity, only to turn up in Buenos Aires, Argentina some years later, where he pursued a career in bookkeeping. Just eight years passed, until, at the age of 28, he moved to Punta Arenas, where he saw in livestock farming and the merchant trade the profitable venture he had long been on the look-out for. His first project was transporting sheep from the Islas Malvinas (Falkland Islands) to San Gregorio, the ghost town I passed earlier in the day. Little did I know that one of the beached ships I had seen on the shore was the steamship *Amadeus*, which had carried the first shipment of bricks to build the Menéndez family's home in the area. Over the next two decades, Menéndez would become one of Chilean Patagonia's largest landowners, with 430,000 hectares of Tierra del Fuego in his name. He was also one of the first shareholders in the Sociedad Explotadora de Tierra del Fuego, a cattle-farming empire that went on to own over 1 million hectares of Patagonian land on both sides of the border. Today, oil extraction, fisheries, tourism and the surviving sheep industry keep the economy afloat, in a much more diversified manner than the recent past.

In view of the fact that Ferdinand Magellan's name is associated with the strait that joins the Atlantic and Pacific oceans, I decided to take a trip to the Punta Arenas Naval Museum to educate myself somewhat on the area's maritime history. Although Magellan's 1520 voyage on his ship, the *Nao Victoria*, was represented by some colourful presentations in the museum, substantially more space was given to Chile's contemporary seafaring activities. There was also an incredible video, filmed in 1929, of the windjammer *Peking*'s voyage around the treacherous and often deadly Cape Horn, which left me stunned at the violent nature of the sailing in the seas just south of Tierra del Fuego. Listed on the walls were the names of decorated Chilean naval officers and their accomplishments, and some old navigation equipment and shipwreck remains sitting in the halls made for a fascinating afternoon.

My feeling was that Punta Arenas is a place where human paths cross. As with Shackleton, Magellan and other seafarers of times past, the new generation of discovery is alive and kicking here too today. I met Antarctic scientists and mechanics just off the boat from polar latitudes, as well as glaciologists in transit, destined for South Georgia and the Islas Malvinas. The howling wind, tormented sky, tinned roofs, ships in the dock and scattered islands on the horizon – all of this generates a sense of place which strongly connects with that part of the consciousness which craves adventure and discovery. It's amazing to think that this place still exudes a sense of its remarkable history, which manages to co-exist with the Italian coffee shops, department stores, and an international airport, where 'skyfaring' has all but replaced the original seafaring.

On 6 October, I cycled 4 km north out of Punta Arenas to the ferry dock, and said goodbye to the continental Americas, the territory whose length I had been cycling since Prudhoe Bay. As I boarded the indigo-blue *Crux Australis*, my feelings of that morning were mirrored in the shifting of the steel ramp and the swaying of this stout, seasoned transport ship. For I was as restless as the ocean beneath it, and acutely aware that four more days' travel would mean the end of this way of being. I had a sense of anxiety about the return to normality, and it scared me, as if I wouldn't know how to cope with it. Sleeping in the same bed every night, with the static air in my bedroom replacing the fresh and moving breeze I was accustomed to in the tent; anticipating the dearth of all the things I knew cycling offered – new places, exercise, 100 km-plus cycling days and fresh human encounters – this now fostered a sense of unease in my mind. I thought about meeting, greeting people, telling my story a hundred times – how would I articulate what it had all meant to me in fleeting, five-minute conversations? Would I begin to believe myself the words I put on my experiences, and could they embody the reality of what happened? Taxes would need to be paid, and insurance bought for the car. I'd sit in traffic jams again and not be able to squeeze through them, as I could on the bicycle. Would I be expected to give some sense of the freedom and choices I had out here, and then just return to work as normal? I became twitchy, shaky and before too long, realised that I had picked my nails to the quick, so I went upstairs to the seating deck and leaned over the edge of the boat. I watched as three streams of frothy white foam stretched backward towards the land – one from the propeller and one each from the stern's sides. Soon they faded back into the grey-green waters, as we crashed up and down in the brooding Straits of Magellan, destined for Tierra del Fuego.

Porvenir is Chile's southernmost town and the largest settlement on its half of Tierra del Fuego, with just over 4,000 inhabitants. It began to snow, just as I arrived in the main square, after a cold and rainy ride from the ferry terminal 3 km north. There was an atmosphere of desolation about Porvenir, just as there had been in most southern Patagonian towns of a similar size. There was a sense of basic sociability lacking in the place – even in the square, quietness prevailed over the noise of a few far-off cars and the sound of someone drilling nearby.

Deciding against grappling with rain or snow, wind and cold, I checked into a hotel. Hotel Rosa had high roofs and a spacious dining area, where every table was flawlessly set with polished knives, forks and china. Yet there was not a person around. Finally, a little old lady came to greet me. Wearing a pressed white dress with a pink floral pattern on one side, and some sparkling jewellery on her fingers, she looked like a 1960s Manhattan socialite, even with her raspy Chilean Spanish accent. She allowed me to bring my bicycle into the room for safekeeping and while I unloaded it, she turned on a storage heater and warned me against going outside without enough clothing.

'We've just said goodbye to winter.'

'You couldn't possibly tell,' I answered, and drew back a curtain, smiling at the snow falling softly outside.

'Believe me, we've finished winter,' she said. 'You should have been here one month ago.'

I found a pizzeria on a side street leading from the square. I ordered a margherita to go and walked back along the semi-bricked pavement in the sleet. On the steps of a municipal building, I scoffed the slices before the chill air could spoil them. I was looking forward to tomorrow's journey across the island, and hoped for those ferocious westerly winds, as I would spend the day heading for the Atlantic Ocean, which I had failed to see in Río Gallegos. With such winds, I thought it might be possible to make the border that splits the island roughly in two, between Chile and Argentina.

In my wildest imagination however, I could not have predicted the power of that wind. It arrived with all its anger and might, as if the gods had summoned it to carry out a task no other elemental force could accomplish. I was pushed, no, *rammed* along to Inútil Bay, where long reedy grasses held the sand together in its curve. I was hurried past chipped green-and-yellow fishing boats rocking in petite coves, secured for now by thickly knotted ropes to their anchors. I saw seagulls buffeted by the gales, and cattle losing their bellowing groans to them.

By 5 p.m. I reached the border and got stamped into Argentina once more, having done 167 km in seven hours. I was still fresh and felt I could ride on until sunset, such was the minimal pedalling effort I'd needed to do all day. Río Grande was 80 km away and I planned to go for it, knowing that when I turned southeast, the wind would be even stronger and I'd have the advantage of asphalt to play with too. With just over two hours of daylight remaining, I rocketed along the fringes of the Atlantic Ocean: the first time I had seen it since leaving Ireland. I felt a certain sense of connection with home in it, as I observed its surface reflect the fading light of day.

Yellow streetlights and the build-up of traffic signalled Río Grande, the penultimate city of the trip. It was a 247 km day, the longest of the trip thus far by a full 61 km. In Santiago, I had tentatively planned to reach Ushuaia on 10 October, and considering it was a two-day cycle away and I was a day ahead of schedule, I took a day off, slept in until 10 a.m. and made my last Skype calls home before Ushuaia. Mam and Dad were in high spirits, knowing I'd be home in just one week. Áine, too, spoke excitedly about the end of our separation, and seeing me again. I could hear some nervousness in her voice and understood the complexity of feeling within it. I felt it too. After 15 months apart, with just two short weeks together in the middle, how would we continue our relationship, now that it extended beyond phone calls and emails? When you become accustomed to an unnatural way of maintaining a connection, the challenge is then in reinstating the old one, hoping that it works out, and you can begin to live without worry.

> **Diary: 8 October 2012, Río Grande, Argentina**
>
> *In my mind, I think I'm already there. I can feel Ushuaia with a palpable intensity, just around the corner. I keep imagining that if I could soar above the ground high enough, I'd see it over the mountains and rivers and fields. Should I view this as a reward and a major high point? I think so: I've looked forward to it from day one, although now in a different way than before, however. Ushuaia is the physical goal and shows I've achieved my destination. The rest – from Alaska to Central America to the South – was the important part.*

The Atlantic was blinding as the sun reflected off its early morning waters. I sped by cattle ranches and over streams and through a sprawling marsh on the outskirts of Río Grande. I was destined for the mountains once more, and as the day progressed I could see their peaks split the light white clouds far away. After lunch, when I'd sparked the stove into action for some coffee to warm me on a particularly frosty day, I rode past a large green signpost which said: 'Ushuaia 72 km'. However, it wasn't the distance to El Fin del Mundo that forced me to pull hard on the brakes – it was my name written below it. I checked behind and saw a truck coming up fast, so I waited until it passed, before swinging around in the road and pedalling back. On the sign, in white marker, was written:

> IAN: *This is nearly the end, my friend! The end of the world and the end of a big cycling adventure. From Alaska to Tierra del Fuego! AMAZING! See you at the end of the world. I will order one or ten beers for us. Suerte [Good luck]*, André: 9/10/2012 and 24,500 km.

I burst into laughter, reading it over and over again. 'André, you legend!' I said to myself, realising he must have passed me somewhere and was now probably in, or close to, Ushuaia. I was glad that my normally well-behaved German friend was beginning to experiment with the art of creative disobedience, and in doing so, had left a note for not only me, but also for every passing motorist and cyclist. And as far as I'm aware, the graffiti is still there, four years later.

I continued to the village of Tolhuin, where there is a famous bakery called Panadería La Unión. It is every Pan-American cyclist's duty to stop there and feast on all manner of cream-filled, strawberry-infused, chocolate-glazed buns, cakes and biscuits. The bakery also serves as a *casa di ciclista*, but as I wanted one last night in the tent before Ushuaia, I left under the influence of sugar, which soon wore off and brought on an annoying headache I could have done without. This is because from Tolhuin, one must climb the hills by Lago Fagnano, a slender lake that incises almost the entirety of southern Tierra del Fuego.

As the high mountains stole the evening sun, I made my way off the road and into a ravine which cut below the line of traffic. It was grassy but damp, so I wheeled the bike to a patch covered in dark soil and pitched the tent. This was the last time light would fade out while I camped, so I made sure to boil a half litre of water for pasta, mixed with some broccoli and carrots I picked up in Tolhuin. I had also cleverly purchased two jam doughnuts for dessert and after finishing them, I slipped into a deep sleep, with the hue of a crescent moon just above the mountaintops shading the inside of my tent dome.

When I took off onto the road at 8 a.m. the following morning, my heart was beating a little faster than usual – I was just 60 km from Ushuaia.

The sky was broken with grey clouds, the kind that threaten rain but only ever muster a slight drizzle. After an hour I began the ascent of the 490-metre Paso Garibaldi, the last mountain pass I would need to endure. In a valley crevasse to my right-hand side was Lago Escondido, and from its forested shores the white covering of snow grew thicker with every rising metre, until it ended where the pass began and I lazily cycled across. In this brief moment, between riding to the top and dropping back down again, I acknowledged, with a breath of sadness, this final, parting climb of the Americas. The rapid descent brought with it the slightly warmer temperatures of the Larsiparsabk River Valley, and I followed the river's disorderly course around interlocking hills and through a wide open plain, which afforded a direct view onto a spectacular mountain range rolling out westwards.

As the road made its last turn south, it tumbled hastily in altitude, and I knew this was the end – the concluding descent to sea level, back to the same elevation Lee and I had begun from, 15 months before. I rounded dozens of icy corners, following the course of a raging river destined to end its much shorter journey to the ocean just kilometres away.

As the road twisted and turned, I expected every change in direction to reveal a city resting by the ocean shore. Then, as I leaned into a steeper section of this snaking, wintry downhill, two giant wooden markers appeared, varnished brown and shining: 'Ushuaia' was carved carefully in white paint into their frames. I took one last glance over my shoulder, by way of a nod of appreciation and remembrance to the entirety of all roads and territory I had cycled upon until this moment. When I looked forward, the enclosing mountains had broken their tight clasp on the valley and were now spreading forth in front of me. Ahead, in the middle-distance, laid out in the most orderly fashion, was the city of Ushuaia, motionless and waiting on the fringes of the Beagle Channel. I let out a sigh of exaltation and punched the air, not for an instant taking my eyes off the rows of buildings and ships nestled along the smooth curves of the bay.

I cycled to the waterfront and into a vacant shipyard, where I could finally touch the channel. I sat there on the pebble beach for almost an hour, elated about having reached this, the southernmost city in the world. It was a quiet euphoria, and one worth the taking time out to appreciate. I had cycled 27,369 km over 452 days, through 15 countries on two continents and felt incredibly privileged for having been able to do it. For so long I had tried not to think of Ushuaia as the ultimate goal for the journey, but freewheeling around that last corner brought such a rush of emotion, that this town and the mere utterance of its name will forever represent one the most important periods of my life. It was because of the pure effort of getting here on a bicycle, through my own physical power alone that I had been able to witness and interact with the great wonder the Americas have to offer. The sheer work needed to achieve every metre of mountain ascent, the combined effort of challenging my mental strength and physical resolve, and the generosity of strangers in giving of their time, telling their stories and sharing their homes – all these together had become a simple and effective formula for happiness. Perhaps it was easy to wax philosophically about it all, now that it was over, but then again, after such a journey and so much time on the move, it was worth taking the time to consider.

As my final valedictory act on the journey, before it became consigned to memory alone, I cycled to the listing ship, the *San Christopher*, in Ushuaia's deep harbour. The most recognisable symbol of the town, it was the place from which I chose to take my first unobstructed look out over the Beagle Channel, a strait steeped in history and lore. It had seen the natives settle and explorers pursue their claim to new territory, naval skirmishes play out and modern trade bourgeon and wane. As I gazed seawards, wondering what lay beyond it, I found that my mind and body were already missing places I didn't even know about. So I set my eyes upon the familiar comfort and immortal splendour of faraway snow-capped mountains, and the forever motion of the restless sky above.

Epilogue

THREE YEARS AND NINE MONTHS have passed since I cycled into Ushuaia, at the end of what began as *350South*, but concluded as something entirely different. Some days it feels like yesterday that I was on the road, but on others, it could have been another life. The one constant that remains as strong within me as it did on the final day is the surge of emotion I get when remembering a person who offered to share a part of their day or week with me, or a hidden campsite in a beautiful valley or by a lake, or when the curve of a city or country road in Ireland reminds me of another, somewhere in the Americas. Thankfully these feelings have never faded and this is perhaps the greatest gift riding all those kilometres could impart.

I arrived back in Ireland on the night of 17 October 2012, and to partial fanfare at Dublin airport, where my family, representatives of The Carers Association of Ireland, and of course Áine, were all waiting.

As regards Áine and our relationship, I have only good news to report. Although it took some acclimatisation at the beginning – natural, after 15 months of communicating only via Skype calls, Facebook messages and texts – we were as before in a short time. It was odd for us initially, to realign to doing things as a pair; we had both been immersed in independent living for so long that even semi-interdependence felt unfamiliar. Yet, the core of everything we loved about one another was still there, and as soon as we recognised this, in spending time together, all the old habits and routines fell into place once more. To this day, I couldn't imagine a life without Áine in it.

Lee eventually made it to Ushuaia, one year after I did. His decision to stop in Guatemala to teach English appeared to have been a wise one, as I think he managed to capture the essence of what he always wanted from travelling – a pace and timeframe defined in a more spontaneous way, by his inclinations and circumstances at any given time. We maintained contact only sporadically on the road, but since his finish we've just been in touch once, when he looked over the manuscript. I guess time, distance, and the experiences we had together have all played their part in that, but I wouldn't change any of it. I learned a lot from that time, and assume that he did too.

Fortunately, I've been able to meet some of the other cyclists from the road again; I now just call them my good friends. Rob Fletcher moved back to Oxford, and Buff3y followed soon after, settling nearby in Stratford-upon-Avon and enrolling at Oxford University to study Shakespearean drama. Both came to visit me in late 2012, and since then, we are always hatching plans for our next reunion – but this could be tougher than expected, with Rob now spending much time abroad and Buff3y back in development work in Papua New Guinea. However, we hold out hope it will happen one day, and somewhere far enough away from ferries and motorised transport for Rob to be able to declare that he'll 'catch us up'.

Markus, Urs, Jorge and André all made it to Ushuaia. For Markus, it held perhaps greater meaning than for the rest of us, this having been his third attempt to ride there from Alaska. Urs moved back to Switzerland, Jorge to Spain and André to Germany. Just two months ago, when Jorge visited, I made sure to introduce him to the best Guinness in Dublin; it's my turn to pay a visit to Madrid next. André has perhaps stayed the most active of us all, and can often be found touring in mainland Europe, and as far afield as Iceland. In 2017 he plans to climb Mt Aconcagua in Chile.

In February 2013, just three-and-a-half months after I returned from Argentina, Áine and I moved to Laos, Southeast Asia, where she had a job lined up with UNICEF. We stayed for three years, with Áine continuing to work for the organisation, while I set about writing as a means to live. I've since worked as a sub-editor for Laos' largest English language newspaper, as the editor of a travel magazine, and in communications for the World Wide Fund for Nature. In December 2015, we returned to Ireland to be closer to family, after almost five years of absence.

I am still of the belief that the bicycle is perhaps the best way to see the world – as long as you don't mind a workout while you're at it. I was reminded of this in April 2015, when I took a two-week tour in Taiwan, and found the same wholehearted compassion was forthcoming from those I encountered on the road, as had been the case in North, Central and South America. For me, there is nothing comparable – a child's wave, a family not taking 'no' for an answer when offering you a place to stay, or just the general sense of concern expressed in questions as to whether you're enjoying their country from the saddle. I can also unreservedly say that I never felt as good, as sharp and as in focus as I did while cycling. It doesn't have to be for months on end, of course, but in my opinion that certainly does help.

The next challenge is in deciding where to cycle next, and when. Áine has indicated she'll come with me this time, which is wonderful news, after years of lobbying my case. Although one-, two-, and three-month tours would suffice, there is still something I'm drawn to when I look at a map of the world, as I did that time in Denver. Then, I decided to head south and down the world, so maybe next time, I'll go around.

Ian Lacey
Dublin, Ireland
June 2016

Acknowledgements

There is no doubt that, without the help and support of so many people, I wouldn't have started this journey, let alone finished it. I am forever indebted to those that donated money to The Carers Association of Ireland, offered a helping hand at fundraising events, sent emails with encouraging words and gave freely of their time to get this cycle off the ground, amongst other acts. I can't name everybody, but I do hope your kindness is acknowledged in the words below. If I have omitted any names, I do apologise.

First and foremost, I must thank my parents, John and Emilie. When I told them in 2010, while they were visiting me in Denver, of my plan to cycle from Alaska to Tierra del Fuego, they didn't seek to extinguish the idea in any way. It could have been so easy for them to convince their only son that riding the length of the Americas wasn't the wisest idea, and, knowing just how much they can worry, I am so thankful they didn't try to do so. Instead, they just committed to helping me achieve it by any means. While I was away, they were both tireless in organising the charity fundraising events, through which the majority of donations were raised, and they sent out spare bicycle parts I couldn't source to locations weeks ahead of my own arrival. I will never be able to thank them enough for their boundless energy and their will to see me achieve my goal.

I must also thank my sister, Alice. She doesn't appear much in the book but I should let you know she is a wonderful person and, without a doubt, the funniest I know. Behind the scenes she was always making me laugh on tough days, sending photos of everything I missed at home, and helping Mam and Dad coordinate events.

To Áine – I have said it countless times before, and I will once more here: thank you for putting up with me, for supporting me every inch of the way, and for the patience you had while we were apart. It is not easy to hear that your boyfriend is planning to take off on a bicycle for a year, only to be able to return as fast as he can pedal, but you never once felt the need to tell me I shouldn't go. Although being away from you was by far the most difficult aspect of the journey, knowing you were there at the end was also the sweetest. You are an amazing person and I love you.

My extended family shook buckets at fundraisers, and were constantly in touch to see how I was doing. To Mary and Pat, Paul and Joan, Annette and Charlie, Michael, Matty, and Lee, I want to say thank you again. The others, further afield, kept the positive words coming, for which I was and am very grateful.

My friends – 'the lads' (girls included!) – were incredible. There are too many names to list them all, but you really are a special lot. I do have to give some individual mentions, however: Kevin Curry and friends, who jumped out of an airplane to show their support; Kevin James and Conor Hogan, who gave feedback on the first three chapters of this book; everyone at Frenchs for my leaving party, who contributed to a specially designed *350South* Irish football jersey; and Kevin Roche, who designed the fantastic *350South* logo. All of you, equal in support, made the preparation stages of the trip more bearable with your humour and constant offers of help. Everyone did something unique and, again, I want to say thank you for that.

Michael Considine deserves a special mention. Preparing for a long-distance tour, with my only cycling experience having been a commute to work, was daunting to say the least; Michael, a seasoned cyclist, not only gave me advice on the physical aspects of what to expect, but also the on psychological side too. As a poet, writer and storyteller, Michael also appraised the manuscript and came back with invaluable input. Most of all though, Michael, I think your perspectives on life and your kind spirit influenced me the most. I'm lucky to count you as a friend.

I would like to say thank you to everyone in Gorey for the support along the way. I could never have shared my journey so directly with people, were it not for Fintan Lambe at the *Gorey Guardian* newspaper, who published my accounts every three months. So too, Dan Walsh at South East Radio, who invited me to speak on his weekly show. Peter Thompson at the *Arklow and Gorey Messenger* also featured trip updates. I must say thank you to the Bass Family Band and Full Moon Fever, who played at fundraisers. Students and staff of local schools gave so much of their time to raise funds for charity. Gorey Community School (Brendan O'Sullivan and Michael Finn), the Gaelscoil, Coláiste Bhríde Carnew, and Riverchapel and Kilanerin national schools deserve to be acknowledged. Gorey Lion's Club held a tea dance, Pettit's, Tesco and Dunnes Stores offered bag packing, while the Ashdown Park Hotel and Seán Óg's gave in-kind support. Gorey, Arklow (Bridgewater) and Dundrum shopping centres also provided space for fundraising. The magnificent staff at Hickey's Pharmacy in Gorey held a 'head shave' night and a skydive to raise money. So many other small businesses and individuals – many of whom I know, and others that I don't – donated money and time. To all of you, once again, thank you from the bottom of my heart.

Over the course of 15 months, approximately €30,000 was raised for The Carers Association of Ireland. It was my absolute privilege to support a charity that assists and advocates on behalf of thousands of Irish family carers, and my hope is that the journey shed a little more awareness on the critical work they do. In particular, I want to thank Emma Murphy and Annette McCaul, who worked directly with me on fundraising and communications.

I have to thank the team on the *Tom Dunne Show* on Newstalk FM, who invited me on regularly to talk about trip happenings. From a random phone box in the vast spruce forest of British Columbia, from the beach in Mexico and from high up in the soaring Andes, we somehow managed to make it work.

Before I even left for Alaska, the South East Road Club made me an honorary life member, which I was humbled to become. I have to thank Derek Webb and the rest of the club for the training spins before I departed, and for the invitations to come back out for a ride. Some members also participated in an on-the-spot cycle, and I very much appreciate all the kilometres pedalled during this.

A special *gracias* must go out to Cynthia McDonald at the Embassy of Mexico in Dublin, who sent medication for my ulcerative colitis to her charming grandmother, Roberta in Oaxaca. Without this, I would surely have worried more than normal about the road ahead.

I spent countless hours writing to businesses, bicycle component manufacturers, outdoor equipment specialists and a host of others to provide support for the ride. Out of hundreds of emails, there were a certain few, who replied with not just good news, but also with an enthusiasm to become a part of *350South*. Ken at EComGoLive built the original website; Rock Fitness gave a year's free gym membership; APT Signs produced pop-up banners; Bikebuddy supplied extra-large bottle racks; the Great Outdoors in Dublin discounted all my purchases far beyond what they should have; the Rudy Project supplied Lee and myself with state-of-the-art sunglasses and helmets; SPOT sent out a fantastic GPS device that transmitted our coordinates each day and was crucial in case of emergency; Tubus supplied the best bicycle racks in the business; and Ortlieb shipped us, without doubt, the gold standard of panniers. Thank you all so, so much.

I must also mention the team at Hollingsworth Cycles in Templeogue, Dublin, who built up my Surly Long Haul Trucker. Andy Bent listened to exactly what I wanted and put together something far better. Then, he took a sizeable amount off the cost to make life that little bit easier. Thank you very much, Hollingsworth.

Although filming for TV and the documentary officially ended in Costa Rica, I have to thank BeActive Media in Dublin and Portugal, for the faith they put in the *350South* trip. In particular, Triona Campbell and Nuno Bernardo, who led the production from the beginning and were instrumental in directing us on what and how to shoot, while Catherine O'Mahony organised all the logistics. Thank you for everything you put into *350South*. I also want to thank Anna Rodgers and Ros Bartley, who came to Gorey and to the Canadian Rockies to film us. You made us feel a little like film stars, and also provided some terrific company for nights in the outdoors.

The book that you have just read was not a single-person job, but required the keen eye and perspectives of an experienced editor. I must therefore thank Susan Feldstein of the Feldstein Agency for her meticulous edits, insights into the story development, and care throughout the process of polishing what is an incredibly important and personal work for me.

I also want to thank Chenile Keogh at Kazoo Independent Publishing Services who guided me so clearly and patiently through the design and layout process. Claire McVeigh at Red Rattle Design designed the cover and maps and understood my concept for them straight away. Thank you for your great attention to detail.

To Lee, I have to say thank you for taking the plunge with me. Every effort to get the cycle going involved us working as a team. We read a million gear reviews together, shipped essentials back and forth across the Atlantic to be tested out before we left, and then set off into the tundra, expectant and a shade nervous. You taught me how to identify every imaginable berry, made me laugh as loud as I've ever done, and were my closest companion in the formative months of our journey together.

To everyone who followed the cycle online through the website and social media, and especially to those who got in touch to pass on a thoughtful message, I want to say thank you. It meant the world to switch on the computer and see many others invested in what we were doing. I hope that you enjoy the book as much as I enjoyed communicating with you from the road.

Finally, I must say the biggest thanks to everyone we met on the road, and who made the trip into such a remarkable period of my life. So many people took us into their family homes, others showed us around their cities, some were cyclists heading in the same and opposite directions, and an innumerable number more bought me a meal or just gave a welcoming wave. I have mentioned just a fraction of the people that affected me, and I only wish that one day we will cross paths again, and that I can repay your generosity of spirit.

Bicycle Specifications and Equipment List

Bicycle   Surly 'Long Haul Trucker'
Drivetrain   Shimano XT; Front: 44-34-22, Rear: 11-34
Brakes   Avid cantilever
Wheels   Mavic A-719 rims, Phil Wood Touring hub, DT spokes
Tyres   Schwalbe Marathon Plus
Seatpost   Thomson Elite
Saddle   Brooks Standard B-17
Racks   Tubus Tara (Front) and Logo (Rear)
Panniers   Ortlieb Front and Rear Roller Plus
Handlebar bag   Ortlieb Ultimate 5
Dry Bag   80-litre Ortlieb dry bag

Camping

MSR Hubba Hubba 2-man tent
Groundsheet
Therm-a-rest Pro Lite Plus sleeping mattress
Mountain Equipment Titan 450 sleeping bag
Petzl head torch
Trowel

Cooking

Cooking pot
Frying pan
Bowl
Titanium cutlery x 2
Flask
MSR Dragonfly stove
MSR stove repair kit
MSR fuel bottle
MSR Miniworks water filter
Ortlieb 10-litre water bladder
Iodine water purification tablets
Lighter

Clothes

Altura waterproof trousers
North Face Gore-Tex rain jacket
North Face Momentum fleece
Ibex merino duo bicycle shorts x 2
Ibex ¾ El Fito cycling shorts
Cycling jersey x 2
T-shirt x 3
Icebreaker short-sleeved base layer
Icebreaker long-sleeved base layer
Icebreaker thermal leggings
Specialized waterproof gloves
Gore Bike Wear underglove
Haglöfs pants
Haglöfs shorts
North Face Hedgehog trail shoes
Columbia sandals
Underwear

Buff
Thermal socks
Rudy Project Impact X Genetyx sunglasses
Rudy Project Sterling helmet

Bicycle-related Equipment

Bikebuddy water cage and regular cage
Front and rear lights
Bicycle pump
Bicycle lock
Multi-tool
Spare tyre
Cycle computer
Extra gear and brake cables, spanners and zip-ties
Lubricant
Straps and bungee cords

Others

Travel towel
First Aid kit
Toiletries
Maps
Journal
Laptop computer and charger
Spot GPS device
Mobile phone
Canon 350D camera and tripod
External hard drive
Insect repellent
Sunscreen

HALF THE WORLD AWAY

Rucksack
Masking tape
Toilet paper
Bear spray
Medication
Compass
Wallet